Recent Developments in International Banking and Finance

Volumes IV and V

Recent Developments in International Banking and Finance

Volumes IV and V

edited by

Sarkis J. Khoury

Foundation for Research in
International Banking and Finance
Graduate School of Management
University of California
Riverside, California
U.S.A.

1991

NORTH-HOLLAND
AMSTERDAM • NEW YORK • OXFORD • TOKYO

ELSEVIER SCIENCE PUBLISHERS B.V.
Sara Burgerhartstraat 25
P.O. Box 211, 1000 AE Amsterdam, The Netherlands

Distributors for the United States and Canada:
ELSEVIER SCIENCE PUBLISHING COMPANY, INC.
655 Avenue of the Americas
New York, N.Y. 10010, U.S.A.

ISBN: 0 444 88626 5

Printed in The Netherlands

To Joyce Khoury

PREFACE

The fifth symposium on International Banking and Finance sponsored by the Foundation for Research in International Banking and Finance was held in Baden Baden, Germany at the fabulous Brenner's Park hotel during April 19-21, 1990. It followed a very successful symposium in April, 1989 at the Maxim's de Paris in Palm Springs, California.

The Baden Baden Symposium represented a balance between academic and nonacademic presentations. The focus was decidedly on Eastern Europe, and Western Europe after 1992. The speakers included some of the most prominent people in the field. They were:

Mr. Curt G. Olsson	Chairman,Skandinaviska Enskilda Banken
Mr. Daniel Passent	Editor, The World Paper
Mr. Joseph Rizello	President, Philadelphia Board of Trade
Mr. Stephen Ross	Professor, Yale University
Mr. Nicholas Giordano	President, The Philadelphia Stock Exchange
Mr. Hans Peter Peters	Member - Managing Board of Directors,Westdeutsche Landesbank
Mr. Peter Schmidhuber	Member, Commission of the European Communities
Minister Alexis Lautenberg	Switzerland
Mr. Wayne P.Luthringhausen	Chairman & CEO, The Options Clearing Corp.
Mr. Silvie Brucan	Romania
Dr. Michael Granito	Managing Director, J.P. Morgan Investment Management, Inc.
Dr. Robert Haugen	Professor, University of California, Irvine
Sir John Browne	Member of the British Parliament
Dr. E. Han Kim	Professor, University of Michigan

The organization of the symposium could not have been achieved without the superb effort put forth by Joseph Rizzello, Alexis Lautenberg, Crocker Snow, Clas Wihlborg, Lars Oxelheim and Michael Granito. I owe them the success of the symposium -- our best ever.

The quality of the articles contained in these volumes was assured by an outstanding editorial board who worked diligently and conscientiously to insure that the Foundation's high standards are strictly adhered to. I owe them a great deal and I shall continue to depend on their excellence and dedication.

The work required to produce a book of this quality is enormous. No one can do it without a firm belief in the objectives, and without a lot of sustenance from friends and family. The friendship, the understanding, and the support of three key individuals: Joseph Rizzello, Michael Granito, and Michael Adler, have been indispensable, especially when the task seemed all too overwhelming. Joyce Khoury helped relieve me of many of the details in an efficient and cheerful fashion. I owe her a great deal, as I do the rest of my family for their patience and tolerance. Kirsten Weiss deserves warm thanks for typing and for helping in the research of this volume.

The experience of 1990 has been overwhelmingly positive. It provided for further solidification of the premises and goals of FRIBF so that its message may be transmitted farther and wider than ever before. There can be no doubt that FRIBF will continue to play its critical role in the collection and dissemination of information about international finance and banking issues. The continued support of the business and academic communities is crucial to this process. We have been most fortunate to receive it in the past and we anticipate continued, even expanded support
in the future. There can be no substitute if the search for excellence and the truth is to remain a permanent feature of our foundation.

CONTENTS

ABOUT FRIBF

The Foundation for Research in International Banking and Finance (FRIBF) is a not-for-profit California Corporation headquartered in Santa Ana, California.

The objectives of the Foundation are to hold seminars and symposia in International Banking and Finance (IBF) anywhere in the world, to undertake research in IBF; to publish books, monographs and articles in the IBF area; to support University students studying IBF; and to provide financial and other support for research in IBF.

The foundation relies for its funding on the revenue from its various activities, on financial support from sponsoring institutions, and on contributions from organizations committed to the expansion and dissemination of knowledge in IBF.

The Foundation is run by its Board of Directors with daily activities and policy implementation supervised and executed by the Executive Director and his staff.

BOARD OF DIRECTORS

THE EDITORIAL BOARD

INTRODUCTION

This book is the equivalent of a research journal with emphasis on theory and application, and is published once a year. The contents are papers submitted and reviewed by at least two members of the editorial board. The level of rigor of the review is commensurate with that of the best journals in finance.

This book contains two sets of papers: submitted and invited. All of the invited papers were presented at the symposium held in Baden Baden, Germany at the Brenner's Park hotel during April 19-21, 1990. They are papers by leading scholars whose research topics were deemed well suited for the symposium.

This book contains theoretical and applied papers dealing with issues at the cutting edge of international banking and finance. We believe it constitutes excellent material for academic or advanced training courses with similar titles. This volume is a combination of two series of calls for papers: 1989 and 1990. We have grouped the papers as follows: invited papers, conceptual/policy oriented and applied papers and technical (theoretical) papers.

This book is a joint production by Sarkis J. Khoury and the Foundation for Research in International Banking and Finance. No effort has been spared to bring the reader the highest quality and the most relevant of papers.

The Foundation for Research in International Banking and Finance is sponsored by:

The Philadelphia Stock Exchange
Asian Finance
University of Gothenburg – Sweden
The Koblenz School of Corporate Management – West Germnay

CONTRIBUTORS

J.P. Morgan Investment Management Inc.
and
Michael Granito.

ABOUT THE AUTHORS

Michael Adler

Professor Adler has served as a consultant for the U.S. Treasury, U.S. State Department, Board of Governors of the Federal Reserve System, IBM, and other entities on a wide range of international financial issues. He has published and lectured extensively in the areas of corporate finance for the international firm, international finance, forward exchange, and futures markets. He is the author of a book on U.S. direct investment overseas and of over 40 major articles on international finance and trade issues. He is an associate editor of the *Journal of Banking* and the *Journal of International Financial Management and Accounting*.

Dr. Adler is currently a Professor at Columbia University and holds a D.B.A. from Harvard University. He has been a Visiting Professor at Wharton, Stanford, the European Institute for Advanced Studies in Management (Brussels), Koblenz School of Corporate Management, Stockholm School of Economics, the London School of Business Studies, and other major universities.

James B. Burnham

James B. Burnham is an Adjunct Fellow at the Center for the Study of American Business, Washington University (St. Louis). He received his AB from Princeton in 1961, studied in Brazil as a Fulbright Scholar, and received a Ph.D. in Economics from Washington University in 1970.

His background includes government service with the Federal Reserve Board, staff director at the President's Council of Economic Advisers (1981-1982), and U.S. Executive Director at the World Bank (1982-1985). He was also an officer with the Mellon Bank, Pittsburgh, serving as Vice President and Financial Economist, Head of the Office of Government Affairs, Chairman of the Country Review Committee, and Senior Vice President and Manager, International Treasury. From 1989-1990 he was John M. Olin Visiting Professor at the Center for the Study of American Business at Washington University, St. Louis. He has also taught and lectured at the University of Pittsburgh in the Department of Economics and the Joseph M. Katz School of Business.

Aswath Damodaran

Assistant Professor of Finance, Stern School of Business, New York University. B.Com. Accounting (1977) Madras University, M.S. Management (1979) Indian Institute of Management, M.B.A. (1981) and Ph.D. (1985) University of California, Los Angeles. His research interests include the examination of market efficiency, the effects of information and market structure characteristics and issues in international finance. He has published in the *Journal of Financial and Quantitative Analysis* and the *Review of Financial Studies*. He was a visiting lecturer at the University of California, Berkeley, from 1984 to 1986, where he received the Earl Cheit Outstanding Teaching Award in 1985. He has been at NYU since 1986, received the NYU Schools of Business Excellence in Teaching Award in 1988 and the University-wide Distinguished Teaching Award in 1990.

Ronald Giammarino

Professor Ronald Giammarino is an Associate Professor of Finance at UBC, Canada. He received his Ph.D. in Management in 1984 from Queen's University, Kingston, Ontario. He is the author of several papers appearing in leading finance journals and is an active referee for several journals.

Michael Granito

Dr. Michael Granito is managing Director of J.P. Morgan Investment Management, Inc. He holds a Ph.D. from the Wharton School - University of Pennsylvania and is the author of numerous articles on Portfolio Management and Strategy. His book on immunization laid the grounds for significant developments in the field. Dr. Granito taught part-time at New York University and Yale University.

Hossein B. Kazemi

Hossein B. Kazemi is Assistant Professor of Finance at the School of Management, University of Massachusetts at Amherst. He received his Ph.D. in International Finance from the University of Michigan in 1986. His recent papers appear in *Journal of Finance*. His current research interests are in the areas of models of foreign exchange rate determination, noisy rational expectations models, and multiperiod asset pricing models.

Sarkis J. Khoury

Dr. Khoury has been an active consultant on financial matters for the last six years. He has trained bankers all over the world in portfolio management, foreign exchange management and international financial strategy. He is currently professor of finance at the University of California, Riverside. He serves as Executive Director of the Foundation for Research in International Banking and Finance and editor in chief of its publication: **Recent Developments in International Banking and Finance.**

Dr. Khoury has authored or edited thirteen books and monographs dealing with international banking and a wide range of finance and international finance issues. His numerous articles, many appearing in leading journals, also deal with international banking/finance issues.

Dr. Khoury earned his Ph.D. from the Wharton School, University of Pennsylvania in December, 1978 and his MBA from Boston University, 1971.

E. Han Kim

Professor E. Han Kim is the Fred M. Taylor Professor of Business Administration at the University of Michigan. He is the author of numerous articles published in the leading Finance/Economics journals. He is the second highest contributor (in number of articles) to the *Journal of Financial Economics*. His work places him as one of the world's preeminent experts in the field of mergers and acquisitions. Professor Kim received his Ph.D. in Finance from SUNY at Buffalo with minors in economics and industrial engineering. Professor Kim serves as Associate Editor for *The Journal of Finance, Financial Review, International Journal of Finance, International Review of Financial Analysis,Review of Economics and Finance, Review of Economics and Finance, Review of Quantitative Finance and Accounting*, and a member of the editorial board of several other journals. Professor Kim is a member of the Board of Directors of FRIBF.

Johan A. Lybeck

Johan A. Lybeck, b. 1944, has been a Chaired Professor of Economics and Finance at the Gothenburg School of Economics since 1978. Before that, he was Associate Professor of Econometrics at the Swedish Social Science Research Council. He holds a Ph.D. in Economics from the University of Michigan and a Ph.D. in Political Science from the University of Gothenburg.

During 1985-87 he was on leave to serve as Senior Vice President in charge of Treasury operations at SwedBank. He is also President and CEO of "Finanskonsult AB", Stockholm, and its subsidiary, "Economic and Political Risk Analysis Consultants S.A.", Brussels.

Among his latest publications are *The Growth of Government in Developed Economies* (Gower Press 1986), *Explaining the Growth of Government* (Elsevier North Holland, 1987; with Magnus Henrekson), *Financial Strategy* (Raben & Sjögren 1987), *Instruments on the Money Market* (Raben & Sjögren 1988) and *The European Monetary System* (SNS 1989); the last three are in Swedish.

A.G. Malliaris

Dr. A.G. Malliaris is The Walter F. Mullady, Sr. Professor of Business Administration at Loyola University of Chicago. His primary area of interest is the use of mathematical methods in economic analysis and he has co-authored with Professor W.A. Brock two books on **Stochastic Methods in Economics and Finance**, published in 1982 and **Differential Equations, Stability and Chaos in Dynamic Economics**, published in 1989. He has also authored numerous papers in leading journals.

Dr. Jorge L. Urrutia is Assistant Professor Finance at Loyola University of Chicago. He specializes in the areas of investments, insurance economics and futures markets where he has authored numerous papers which appeared in *The Journal of Risk and Insurance, The Geneva Papers, CPCU Journal* and elsewhere.

Richard D. Marcus

Richard D. Marcus is an Associate Professor in the School of Business Administration, University of Wisconsin-Milwaukee. His doctorate is in economics from the University of Chicago and his masters is in finance from the University of Wisconsin-Madison. Professor Marcus teaches international financial management, corporate finance, and economics, for which he has won a teaching award. His recent research publications concerns international financial markets and event studies surrounding significant informational announcements.

Ed Nosal

Ed Nosal is currently an Assistant Professor of Finance at University of Waterloo, Waterloo, Ontario, Canada. He received his Ph.D. from Queen's University, Canada. His research interests are focused on the application of game theory to the solution of financial problems, and on contract theory. Professor Nosal is the author of several papers published in Canadian and U.S. journals.

Stephen A. Ross

Dr. Stephen A. Ross is the Sterling Professor of Economics & Finance at Yale University. Prior to this he taught at the University of Pennsylvania from 1970 to 1977. Professor Ross earned his Ph.D. in Economics from Harvard University in 1969 and has earned since then numerous prestigious awards and honors to include: Fellow of the American Academy of Arts & Sciences, and Fellow of the Econometric Society. During 1988, Professor Ross served as President of the American Finance Association. Professor Ross is the author of numerous pioneering articles published in the leading journals of economics and finance. His textbook with Professor W. Westerfield titled, **Corporate Finance** is a recognized leader in the market. Dr. Ross serves on many editorial boards and is a very active referee for leading journals.

Donald Solberg

Donald Solberg is an Assistant Professor in the School of Business Administration, University of Wisconsin-Milwaukee. He is currently on leave researching fixed income securities at the Federal National Mortgage Corporation in Washington, D.C. His doctorate is in finance from the University of Nebraska. His research publications includes asset pricing models, international investments, agency theory, futures markets, and option pricing.

Anant K. Sundaram

Anant K. Sundaram is Assistant Professor of Business Administration at the Amos Tuck School of Business Administration, Dartmouth College. He holds a Ph.D. from Yale University. His areas of research and teaching include finance, international business and strategic management. He has published in journals such as *Journal of International Money and Finance* and *International Environmental Affairs.* His current research interests include economic exposure to exchange rates, sovereign debt, the impact of limited liability for corporate governance in domestic and multinational settings, and the consequences of market power for the systematic risk of firms.

Suresh M. Sundaresan

Professor Sundaresan has consulted extensively in the fields of capital markets, financial economics, investment management, and corporate finance. He has priced equity notes for an investment banking firm, priced debt options for a government securities firm, and designed hedging programs for security portfolios. He has an ongoing consultancy with Shearson Lehmann Hutton in the area of fixed income securities research, options, and futures including risk management and capital adequacy systems. Dr. Sundaresan has also designed an in-house Management Training Program in the area of options, futures, and investment management for American Express.

Dr. Sundaresan has published numerous papers in refereed journals and will soon publish a book on futures markets. He is an associate editor of the *Journal of Financial and Quantitative Analysis, Review of Financial Studies, Journal of Futures Markets,* and *Management Science.*

Professor Sundaresan is currently a Professor in Finance at Columbia University. He earned a Ph.D. in Industrial Administration and an M.S. in finance from Carnegie-Mellon University.

Richard J. Sweeney

Dr. Richard J. Sweeney is the Sullivan/Dean Professor of International Business and Finance in the School of Business Administration at Georgetown University. Previously, he was the Stone Professor of Money and Finance at Claremont McKenna College and The Claremont Graduate School. He has served on the faculty at UCLA and Texas A&M, and has visited at the University of Virginia and the Tuck School at Dartmouth College. He served at the United States Department of the Treasury as Deputy Director of the Office of International Monetary Research.

Sweeney has more than 75 published scientific papers, included in the *Journal of Finance, the Journal of Financial and Quantitative Analysis, Economic Inquiry*, and the *American Economic Review* and other journals and collections. He has been involved as an author or editor of nine books. The latest are **Wealth Effects and Monetary Theory** (Basil Blackwell, 1988) and **Speculation in Foreign Exchange Markets**, written with Patchara Surajaras (Westview Press, forthcoming). He has been an editor of *Economic Inquiry* since 1984, and serves on the boards of a number of other journals.

Alan L. Tucker

Alan L. Tucker is currently an Assistant Professor of Finance at the School of Business and Management, Temple University, Philadelphia, PA, USA. He also is the Associate Editor for *The Journal of*

Economics and Business (North Holland Publishers). Prior to his recent appointment at Temple University, Dr. Tucker was on faculty at the University of Tennessee. Dr. Tucker holds a B.A. (Economics) from LaSalle University , an M.B.A. (Finance) and a Ph.D. (Finance, 1986) from The Florida State University. Among his research interests are the distributional theory of exchange rates and the valuation of currency options and futures. His recent research includes "The Probability Distribution of Foreign Exchange Price Changes: Tests of Candidate Processes", *Review of Economics and Statistics* Vol. 70 (November 1988), and "The Relative Valuation of American Currency Spot and Futures Options: Theory and Empirical Tests", *Journal of Financial and Quantitative Analysis* Vol. 23 (December 1988).

Terry L. Zivney

Terry L. Zivney is an Associate Professor of Finance. He holds the Clarence E. Harris Chair of Excellence in Business, School of Business Administration, University of Tennessee at Chattanooga. His doctorate is in finance from Georgia State University. Professor Zivney has won competitive awards for best research papers in investments at several recent finance association meetings. His publications include research in global investments, asset pricing, and the futures and options markets.

Recent Developments in International Banking
and Finance, S.J. Khoury (editor)

OVERVIEW

Sarkis J. Khoury

Graduate School of Management
University of California
Riverside, California

The developments of 1989 and 1990 in the international financial markets, in the geopolitical arena, in Eastern Europe, in Western Europe (1992), in the Soviet Union (perestroika), and in the rest of the world have been breathtaking indeed. What is dramatic about the developments is their unpredictability, their speed, their reach, their impact, and most interestingly, their domino-like nature. Almost no country in the world has been spared the effects and the bewilderment of these events which constitute very fertile grounds for analysis and action by policy makers, business leaders, and academicians.

The revolution in the financial markets continued at a quicker pace and at a broader level. The big surprises continued to flow. We know of not one single person, not even the head of the CIA or the KGB who, even in early 1989, predicted that the Berlin Wall would become a relic in the Reagan library, or that practically all E. European countries would discard communism and openly exhibit and criticize its failings. Further, no one ever thought that one man could singlehandedly break the Russian mold of subversion, autocracy, political and economic expansionism by force and even by terrorism, gross mismanagement of the natural resources of Russia, and widespread corruption. As the mold was broken, a new face of Russia emerged, and alongside it a whole new set of problems. Those who were breaking ground for the construction of a new Russia discovered that in fact the soil was heavily contaminated by intrigue, complacency, and massive mismanagement. The evidence also suggests that the skills of those on whose shoulders the new Russia is to be built are suspect indeed. There seems to be little hope that the other foot can be pulled out of Lenin's Russia. Russia remains a communist country and all moves on the democratic and capitalist fronts are minuscule indeed.

The drama of Eastern Europe varies from the Russian drama. It is multidimensional and multicolored and does not necessarily have a unique plot. It varies from the Greek to the modern version of a human drama being played on the world stage where the real heroes and the villains are unidentifiable and the end is unpredictable. It may yet end up a real tragedy. Some developments were easily comprehendible, others were surreptitious. No one is quite certain as to how much of the old good was preserved and how much of the evil has been dissipated. The world audience continues to watch the drama unfold, and has in effect joined the cast of actors, with all the proclamations of positive intentions and the appropriate slogans of support for democracy and capitalism.

These seemingly impossible sequences of events produced new risks and, simultaneously, great opportunities. The nature and level of the risks and opportunities are not homogeneous across countries or across regions. The exact models for measuring and managing these diverse risks and for capitalizing on the varied opportunities have yet to be devised. The techniques of analysis employed by banks have not been sufficiently adjusted and fine tuned to allow for the sorting out of the quality of the opportunities which range from mild optimism to euphoria. Mr. Percy Barnevik, the head of Asca Brown Boveri, the world's largest heavy engineering company, was quoted in the Dec. 18, 1989 issue of Fortune as saying: "The opening of Eastern Europe could prove even more important than the drive for a single market." There are many skeptics, however.

The "lumping" of the various E. European countries in a single model of analysis and policy recommendation is decidedly the wrong methodology for understanding the problem. Each country's infrastructure, political aspirations and flexibility, wealth in raw materials, level of experimentation with the free market , ethnic mix and geographical configuration, is different from the other. This is clearly reflected in the ranking of the economic potential of E. European countries provided by Fortune magazine (Exhibit 1). We believe the synthesis is correct, provided the political reforms are not halted or set back, responsible and noninflationary economic policies are pursued, and the necessary legal framework for property rights, investments, and capital flows is adopted. The West provides the basic expertise and the capital needed for transition from communism to capitalism. The first is history on this scale, and that the world economy does not slump into a recession. How much of these projections are Gorbachev dependent is anyone's guess. Many argue that events have carried reality well past the reversal point and thus events in E. Europe are currently Gorbachev independent and becoming increasingly more so.

EXHIBIT 1
ECONOMIC PROSPECTS FOR EASTERN EUROPE

	Population	Gross National Product			Fortune Ratings		
	(in millions)	Total in billions	Per capita	Eight-year average annual growth rate	Economic potential	Receptivity to foreign	Speed of reform
MOST PROMISING							
East Germany	16.6	$155.38	$9,360	1.8%	A	C–	C
Csechoslovakia	15.6	$118.56	$7,600	1.3%	B+	B	C–
Hungary	10.6	$68.90	$6,500	1.0% a	B	A	A
PROMISING							
Poland	38.0	$210.52	$5,540	0.7%	C+	A	A
LEAST PROMISING							
Bulgaria	9.0	$50.67	$5,630	1.2%	C	B	C+
Yugoslavia	23.6	$115.64	$4,900	1.2%	C	B–	B–
Rumania	23.0	$94.76	$4,120	0.0%	D+	C–	F
Albania	3.1	N.A.	N.A.	N.A.	D–	F	F

Source: Fortune, December 18, 1989, p. 84.

It is unlikely however, that political democracy can achieve permanency unless actualized and constantly nurtured by economic democracy. Deprivation and infighting cannot serve as pillars of a new democratic and progressive state. The ballot, if it cannot fill empty stomachs, may have to yield to the bullet. A return to a Stalin type era is still favored by some Russians with strong political orthodoxy. It may be the only choice left if food riots, large unemployment, western type problems like illicit drugs, and continuing revolts in the Baltic states and other republics continue to ship away at the Russian state. A poll conducted by the Guardian Ltd. and the BBC's Newsnight TV show reported in Paradie Magazine showed that:

-nearly half (49.5%) of the respondents believe conditions in the Soviet Union are worse than they were five years ago.

-Only 20% said they believe that life for them has improved under Gorbachev's leadership.

-29% declined to say how long the communist party would remain the nation's leading party.

Furthermore, economic "liberalism" in the Soviet Union, as in many E. European countries, is kept on a very short leash. The right to own business and personal property, although expanded, is still woefully short of western standards. For example, in March of 1989 the Soviets forbade joint ventures to engage in countertrade, one of only a few mechanisms by which joint ventures can generate hard currency. The draft law (proposed new law on joint ventures) would reinforce this prohibition.

An unpublished portion of the current joint venture legislation established an exception to hard currency self-sufficiency requirements. But the draft law would revoke this exception, requiring joint ventures to generate sufficient hard currency to cover their expenditures.

The draft law also gives short shrift to small entrepreneurial ventures. It would require the Western partner to contribute a minimum of

$120,000, 25% of which the Western partner must deposit in cash in a Soviet bank before the Soviets will register the joint venture.

These and many other laws in Russia and many other Eastern European countries suggest that the process of transformation is slow and may be too weak to produce western style open economies with competitive products on a world scale.

Instability (uncertainty) remains, despite all the reassurances and the promises, the key word in the 1990s. This concern is not the exclusive domain of E. Europe, yet it acquires a particular intensity when it deals with that region. The March 12, 1990 issue of Fortune considered the political outlook for Eastern Europe and found it to be mixed and, at best, not very reassuring (Exhibit 2). Bulgaria and especially Yugoslavia and Romania are walking a very thin political tightrope. They seem to be unable or unwilling to shake off completely the bankrupt ideologies of the nineteenth century.

The political pessimism about some European countries reflects itself in the economic expectations for those countries. In this regard, the "action" is largely in Central Europe. There is reason to be mildly optimistic about this region. The infrastructure, although deficient by Western standards in certain areas, seems to be able to sustain a steady economic growth.

The Federal Reserve Bank of Chicago looked at the Eastern European economic data in its publication: Chicago Federal Letter (May, 1990, Number 33). The geographic area covered by the Central European countries is about 45% of that of the 12 countries making up the European Community. This is equivalent to the land mass of Texas, Oklahoma, and Louisiana. The population is 113 million, with a labor force of the six countries estimated at about 49% of the population, a substantially higher proportion than in the EC where the labor force accounts for 43% of the population. On the education front the figures are very reassuring indeed: "The basic education level of the population in Central Europe is comparatively high. Its literacy rate averages 98%. This is slightly higher than the average reported for the E.C.... The number of scientists per thousand population [Exhibit 3] supports the idea that the educational infrastructure in (S&E)/1,000, excluding Luxembourg, stood at 1.3 and technicians at 1.3."

Looking at another key measure of the quality of the infrastructure: rails and roads, one finds them lacking (Exhibit 4). The cost of building the road infrastructure "could range as high as $100 billion to more than $130 billion," and no one knows where all this money will come from.

In the area of communications, a wanton deficiency is observed:

> "Communication facilities are another form of infrastructure in which Central Europe lags well behind the EC. Telephones per capita, as of the mid-1980s, ranged from 12 to 24 phones per 100 persons. These figures compare with those of the least developed of the EC members--Portugal--and are less than 40% of the telephone density in West Germany, the Netherlands, or France. Reliable and extensive communication facilities are vital to the development of an advanced commercial system. Here again the amount of investment in lines, switching gear, and the like needed to bring up the communications system to a level comparable to Western Europe is more than trivial."

These data indicate clearly that the task of building Eastern Europe is enormous. Who will finance this revolution in E. Europe? West Germany appears to be the most likely country to finance this revolution because it benefits the most from its success. W. German exports to the Soviet Union and its satellites were "ten times larger than America's, and more than 11 times larger than Japan's" (Fortune Dec. 18, 1989, p.85). Furthermore, Germany cannot ignore the huge consumer market developing at its borders. The GNP of the Central European countries: East Germany, Hungary, and Czechoslovakia already exceeds that of mainland China.

The interest of West Germany has yet to be fully translated into loans, factories, construction sites, training programs, etc. In these areas the banks play a major role.

Mr. Hans Peter Peters, member, Managing Board of Directors, Westdeutsche Landesbank, in a study "Financing the Economic Revolution in Eastern Europe" prepared exclusively for the symposium, "Recent Developments in International Banking and Finance" held in Baden-Baden, Germany, during April 19-21, 1990, reflected on the

EXHIBIT 2

Eastern Europe's Unsteady March Toward Democracy

COUNTRY Population GNP	HOW EVENTS UNFOLDED, MONTH BY MONTH	OUTLOOK
EAST GERMANY **16.6 million** **$155.4 billion**	**November** - Berlin Wall opens; thousands of East Germans daily flee to the West. - Reformist Politburo member Hans Modrow becomes Premier. **December** - Communist Party loses constitutional monopoly on power, changes its name. **January**- Six opposition groups unit to challenge Communists in March elections. Opposition joins Communist-led coalition. **February** - Modrow proposes German unification.	Rapid economic union with West Germany should produce strong growth after a bumpy transition.
CZECHOSLOVAKIA 15.6 million $118.6 billion	**November** - More than 200,000 demonstrate for free elections; millions of workers strike in support. **December** - Hard-liners resign; new government pledges elections. Deposed leader Alexander Dubcek and dissident playwright Vaclav Havel join government. Border with West Germany opens. **January**- Prime Minister Marian Calfa quits the Communist Party.	Making big strides toward a market economy.

HUNGARY 10.6 million $68.8 billion	**November** - In a referendum, Hungarians vote on how to choose a President in 1990. **December** - Premier Miklos Nemeth steps down as party leader. January - Government calls for withdrawal of Soviet troops in 1991.	Quickening reform has attracted U.S. investors, including GE and GM.
POLAND 38 million $207.2 billion	**January** New non-Communist government begins market-oriented economic reforms. Lech Walesa says Soviet troops must leave by the end of 1990. Communists say the party is too weak to run in the next local elections.	Great potential- if 40%-a-month inflation can be tamed.
BULGARIA 9 million $50.7 billion	**November** - After 35 years, hard-liner Todor Zhivkov is replaced by moderate Petar Mladenov as President. **December** - Amid massive protest rallies, Mladenov promises elections by June. Government talks about sharing power with opposition groups. **January**- Communist Party loses constitutionally protected dominant role. **February** Reformer Andrei Lukanov becomes Premier.	New leaders are encouraging investment, but progress will be modest at best.
YUGOSLAVIA 23.6 million $115.6 billion	**December** -Communists support recommendation to relinquish monopoly of power. **January**- Communist Party gives up dominant position; permits new multiparyt system.	Looks grim. Reforms are running into ethnic disintegration.
RUMANIA 23 million $94.7 billion	**November** - Nicolae Ceausescu unanimously reelected. **December**-Government opens fire on demonstrators Army joins demonstrators to bring down government. Ceausescu Executed. **January**- Communist Party outlawed. Provision government schedules elections for April.	Chaos still looms after the East bloc's bloodiest change of direction.

EXHIBIT 3

SOURCE: The World Factbook. Central Intelligence Agency

EXHIBIT 4

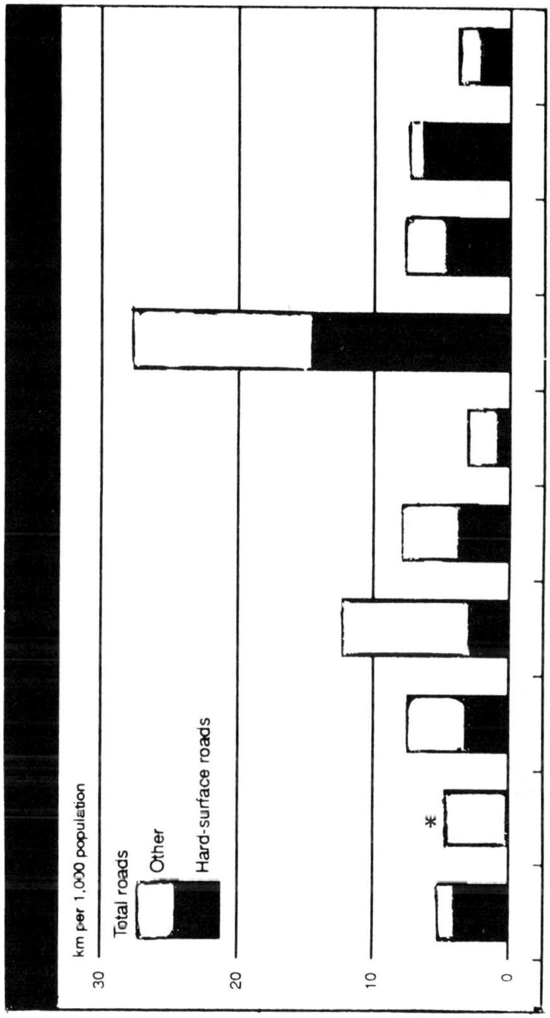

* Breakdown not available.
SOURCE: The World Factbook. Central Intelligenge Agency

Source: Chicago Federal Letter, May, 1990, Number 33

requisites, the approach, the role, and the outlook of W. German banking institutions with regard to Eastern Europe.

> Three elements go together if the reform process in Eastern Europe is to be successful and Western financial help to be spent in a worth-while way:
>
> - The first element is the market mechanism as the central means of resource allocation. At the core of this economic system stands the freedom of setting prices. This doesn't just mean the abolition of subsidies, but of all bureaucratic interference in the pricing process. It includes contract freedom in production and investment decisions as well as freedom of trade. To establish a competitive environment, it will be necessary not only to facilitate the establishment of new small and medium-sized firms, but to break up national monopolies and to abolish the external trade monopoly. The opening up of the internal market will be the only way to secure real competition in large parts of the economy.
>
> - The second element of reform is a change in the ownership structure. It is essential that ownership and the right to decide on a company's future are placed in one hand. Furthermore, to secure competition a widely dispersed ownership structure is necessary. There is no alternative to private ownership on a large scale.
>
> - The third element is a working monetary system. In the past, this aspect usually gained only minor consideration. But this neglect totally underestimates the importance of money and a functioning financial sector in a modern economy. First of all, people only have an incentive to work if the money they earn is of reasonable and stable value. By the way, this is the basic reasoning why the West Germany government has offered the D-mark to East Germans.

Furthermore, a financial system worth its name will be able to generate internal savings, savings that are necessary to finance the reform process from within.

These three elements - market mechanism, ownership reforms and monetary reforms - form the ingredients of the recipe for the economic reconstruction of Eastern Europe. Therefore, they should be used as a yardstick for the general credit worthiness of the region. If one classifies the Comecon countries according to these criteria, some distinctions can be made. Hungary has the longest record on economic reform of any Comecon country. Started in 1968 and reanimated in 1979, the economy was liberalized step by step. Since 1982, the maneuvering room for private business has been expanded, in 1989 the conversion of state-owned companies into private, even foreign-owned ones was made possible. Since 1987, a two-tier banking system, in which business and central banking functions are divided, has been in operation. Furthermore, up to 60 per cent of imports from hard-currency countries are free of state control.

Poland is the most radical convert to market-oriented economics in the East. The price reform started in autumn 1989 has led to free price-setting in 9 out of 10 cases. Import restrictions are being abolished, foreign direct investment of any kind is welcomed, state enterprises are going to be sold. Within a time span of two to three years the Polish government wants the ownership structure of the Polish economy to be the same as in Western economies, which seems to me too optimistic. The declining inflation rate during the last few months has generally been interpreted as an initial sign of hope that the programme may work.

At the moment, the USSR is still way behind in its economic reform process. The preconditions for joint ventures have been laid down by the Supreme Soviet, something coming very near to private property has been introduced in some sectors of the economy. If the new laws do come up to what Mr. Gorbachev has proposed in the Presidential Council, the Soviet Union seems to be on the way Poland chose a short time ago. But one has to read what the fine print in the law actually says.

In the cases of the other four countries, the situation is still unclear, due to those countries being latecomers to the political reform process. Certainly, the GDR is a special case because it will be absorbed rather quickly through a united economic and monetary zone with the Federal Republic and, subsequently, the EC. Czechoslovakia up to now has expressed itself as a radical reformer, but this verbal break with the past has not found its way into actual laws yet. In Bulgaria and Romania, the political process is still too much in a state of flux for the situation to be judged in detail. Both countries' governments - at least those continuing in power up to the elections late this spring - still seem to be in search of the third way. I have already commented on that.

All in all, the most reform-oriented countries are Hungary and Poland, followed by the USSR, Czechoslovakia and, in the last places, Romania and Bulgaria. This sequence of names can change very fast, especially in consideration of the free elections in several countries over the next few months. As I outlined at the outset: the more market oriented the reform approach, the more reasonable it is to finance the process from external sources, be it for short-term stabilization measures or for long-term structural adjustments. In both cases, Western money will be needed to finance imports. Whether the Comecon countries will get the money from private or public institutions - and to what extent - depends on the risk structure of the individual cases. At least as far as credits are concerned, this depends to a large degree on the indebtedness of the different countries.

According to the latest OECD statistics, the total gross debt of Eastern European countries, the Soviet Union included, increased from some $94 bill in 1981 to some $148 bill in 1989. In net terms, the rise isn't that dramatic, but still impressive. Net debt rose by about 40 per cent to $114 bill. These figures have to be interpreted prudently. We have witnessed in the past that some Comecon countries haven't published all the debt incurred. I'd just like to mention Hungary, which announced the - hopefully - true figures just last year. Another case of incorrect statistics is the GDR. In the OECD statistics, the figure for GDR net debt is $11 bill, the same as mentioned by official sources in East Berlin for months. But in the first annual report published by the East German central bank just three weeks ago, the figure given was $18.5 bill. So, the amount of $114 bill net debt for the whole of Eastern Europe has to be interpreted as the minimum, but not necessarily the correct figure.

Besides the mere size of the figures, what also gives reason for concern is the speed with which debt was incurred over the last few years. After the debt crisis in Poland at the beginning of the 1980s, the ensuing rescheduling of the country's debt in 1981, and the rescheduling agreement with Romania in 1982, Eastern European countries tried successfully to consolidate their debt situation. The main increases started again in the mid-1980s - in some cases from an even lower level of indebtedness than in 1981. Therefore, the figures just mentioned are an even more dramatic sign of the increasing decay of economic competitiveness and therefore vulnerability of Eastern Europe.

So much for the general trend. What is more important from the financial point of view is the situation in the individual countries. One important indicator for the relative indebtedness has proved to be the net debt/exports ratio. Since 1984, this indicator has increased for the entire region nearly all the time. Taking a value for the indicator of less than 1 as a light debt burden and a ratio of more than 2 as heavily indebted, Poland, Hungary, and Bulgaria have to be classified as highly problematic cases.

Poland is in the poorest condition. It can be compared with the heavily-indebted countries of Latin America. Its position hasn't changed since the beginning of the 1980s. Hungary and Bulgaria experienced a steep decline in their assessment during the last decade. Particularly in the case of Bulgaria, this wasn't to be expected because, according to this indicator, the country was one of the least-indebted of all Comecon countries at the beginning of the 1980s - roughly at the same level as the USSR - and therefore considered a no-problem case. As we learned three weeks ago, the country has ceased to honor its repayment obligations. It goes without saying that private banks will be very reluctant to broaden their commitments in these countries without guarantees by Western official institutions.

Just two countries remain in the low debt category. Czechoslovakia - ever since the crackdown after the Prague Spring very conservative and careful in its contacts of the West - and Romania, which started to pay back its debt after the aforementioned rescheduling in 1982 under immense losses for the home economy. The country has even turned into a net creditor to Western countries. The GDR and the USSR can be qualified as medium cases. Leaving the GDR aside because of the special German solution to the transfer problem, at least the other three seem to be in a position for a further increase in lending also from Western banks as part of their medium-term reform strategy. But how fast such an assessment can change could best be seen in the debt history of Bulgaria.

Western private banks are heavily involved in the process of financing Eastern Europe already today. In 1988, unguaranteed bank credits added up to more than half of total debt, while the officially guaranteed share of total debt of all seven Comecon countries was just 27 per cent. Banks are especially involved in Bulgaria, the USSR and the GDR. Private institutions are involved disproportionately low in Romania and Poland, giving only some 20 per cent of all credits outstanding. In the case of Romania, this is due to a political decision of the country's former government, in the case of Poland the risk of a further commitment was reckoned to be too high. Nevertheless, in absolute figures Poland is still at the top of the list.

In the past, banks viewed Eastern Europe as an interesting market for several reasons. Our industrial clients saw the Comecon countries as a stable market for export goods. It was only natural for Western banks to follow their clients on this way. Trade is also the reason for the high degree of involvement of West German banks in this business. The Federal Republic is strongly involved in trade with Eastern Europe, accounting for approximately 45 per cent of the European Community's total foreign trade with that group of countries. The special inter-German relationship, West Germany's geographical situation as well as the country's strong position in the investment goods sector are the primary determining factors here. Today, West Germany is the most important Western creditor nation for Czechoslovakia, Bulgaria and Poland. It is in second place in the cases of the Soviet Union, the GDR and Hungary.

All in all, trade-related business offered the opportunity to engage in inter-bank business with Foreign Trade Banks and State Banks of Eastern European countries which were in a position - due to the external trade monopoly of the state - to secure the foreign exchange needed to repay the credits. The only risk involved was sovereign risk, which for a long time was considered small due to the stable political and economic environment in those countries. This relative stability outweighed some features Western banks usually consider essential for a credit, but which none of these countries was willing to provide, namely detailed information about the economic and foreign exchange situation. In spite of the Polish and Romanian debt crises at the beginning of the last decade, the whole region was considered interesting enough by ever more banks, which decided to enter the market during the last ten years.

The strongest position Eastern Europe probably ever attained on Western capital markets was in late 1987. Since then the risk assessment by Western banks has changed. Besides the difficult situations in Poland and Romania, Bulgaria was evaluated as more and more critical. In addition to that, the general economic and political problems of the whole region became more and more obvious. On the one hand, this resulted in a firming of terms for these countries on capital markets, on the other hand, a change in business transactions took place. Unguaranteed export financing became less important while project finance and leasing arrangements increased. These transactions secured some claim on property, on equipment or on identifiable project earnings and therefore were considered less risky.

The higher risk rating of the Comecon countries was also due to the uncertainties resulting from the reform process. The old system started to collapse, but the new structures were not in place. In several countries, the state monopoly over foreign exchange has been loosened, central control rolled back. Today, many Eastern banks and companies are trying to deal directly with Western financial institutions - with or without the approval of the traditional foreign banks. A practical example of the problems arising from this situation can be witnessed with companies from the Soviet Union. Outstanding debts of Western firms from trade transactions with Russian partners have increased rapidly over the last twelve months, because the external trade organizations have ordered in the West without securing enough foreign exchange at the Bank for External Economic Relations in Moscow. Leaving the legal aspects of this procedure aside, this new way of doing business demands new methods of risk assessment for these clients. This is easier said than done, because banks are entering a new field, even if they are used to credit ratings of Western companies. For one thing, the future of East European companies once they have to compete on the world market is unsure. Furthermore, the assessment of the actual value of companies is extremely difficult due to inadequate accounting systems and totally distorted valuation systems. Just three weeks ago, the publication of debt data of companies by the East German central bank came as an unpleasant surprise to Western experts. Internal debt of these companies was a lot higher than everyone had expected and - which caused real concern - more than double the Western level.

Traditional finance instruments will also decline in relative importance due to increasing demand for equity capital. This way of securing the inflow of Western capital has several advantages for Eastern countries. First of all, they don't just import capital, but in addition to that, Western know-how in many fields of company management, organization, marketing and strategic business planning, in short: how to survive in a competitive environment. Maybe this kind of human capital is lacking even more than capital in a physical sense. In addition to that, the economies acquire a diversification of the ownership structure which they desperately need in order to achieve a functioning market mechanism. Under the aspect of external financing, a direct investment strategy offers two important advantages: first of all, Western investors don't expect profits on the first day of their investment. Especially in the transitional period lying ahead, this may ease the transfer problems of the region. Secondly, profit transfers will only take place when profits are made - therefore, there is a certain correlation between the economic situation of the country and the amount of transfers. An impressive example for the success of such a strategy at the moment is Spain. The country lives with a high current account deficit, but is still able to increase its currency reserves due to foreign investments.

It is not surprising, therefore, that all Comecon countries have introduced some form of joint venture law. All now accept joint ventures, although some countries still limit foreign equity participation to 49 per cent as a general rule. The number of contracts between Western companies and their Eastern counterparts is estimated to have increased more than 15 fold since the beginning of 1988. The highest number of joint ventures has been recorded in the USSR. During the last three years, some 1,500 cooperation agreements have been publicized with a total Western capital share of $2.1 bill. The number of active joint ventures is probably a lot lower. Experts estimate the share at roughly 10 per cent.

Most of the joint ventures intend to be active in consulting and trade business, only to a small degree are they interested in industrial joint ventures - quite contrary to what Soviet reformers originally expected. To intensify industrial cooperation, the introduction of special economic zones is planned. A general problem is the fact that most cooperations form a sort of island in the socialist sea due to the non-convertability of the rouble, thereby minimizing positive side effects for the Soviet economy. This is perhaps also one reason why the convertability issue has become a top priority in the new economic reform programme announced by Mr. Gorbachev.

Hungary has one of the most liberal joint venture laws of Eastern Europe. Today, 600 to 700 joint ventures exist with a total capital of some $400 to 500 mill. Last year, several bigger projects were announced, as Hungary also allowed the foreign acquisition of privatized firms. As the country is probably in the best position to introduce convertability, transfer problems could lose significance rather soon, removing another obstacle for Western companies.

As fast as it has introduced economic reforms, Poland has gained in importance in East-West joint ventures. During 1989, the number of such transactions increased ten-fold, with West German companies making up 50 per cent. Total foreign direct investment should add up to $200 mill. A major problem has proven to be the chaotic situation in the financial sector, with hyper-inflation and the Dollar as second currency, but this problem seems to be moving nearer to a solution.

Leaving the GDR aside, the other Comecon countries up to now are of no great importance in direct investment business. But this will probably change in the near future, when the reform process gets into full swing in those countries too.

The increased activity by investors creates some new opportunities for Western banks. Not so much in the traditional fields of banking activity, but in assisting direct investments - many Western investors especially in the Soviet Union, finance their participation not by their own capital, but by bank
credits-- in project finance and technical service contracts. Merchant banking activities such as looking for suitable partners for East European firms will become more important.

All in all, up to now the direct investment strategy hasn't helped the Eastern European countries to the extent they had expected it to. But one should always bear in mind that such projects demand time. It is therefore too early to come up with a final judgement, particularly as nearly all Eastern countries introduced or liberalized their joint venture laws just a short time ago. In addition to that, the Comecon states find themselves in a worldwide contest of locations. As long as their economic reforms cannot compete with the kind of liberal and market-oriented economies such as Spain, Portugal or South-East-Asia, the effect will certainly be modest. In this sense, economic reforms can well be self-financing.

The ability of East European countries to attract foreign investments depends also on the trade concessions granted by Western countries, especially by the European Community, the economic gravity center of Europe. On the one hand, easy access to these markets will make locations in the region more interesting for Western investors wanting to produce at low cost for the EC market and therefore eager to invest in Eastern European countries. On the other hand, open Western markets offer new export and therefore hard currency opportunities to traditional Eastern companies. The aid-by-trade slogan usually proposed for North-South relations is also true in East-West relations. After the general agreement between the EC and Comecon in the summer of 1988, wide-ranging trade and cooperation agreements between the Community and Poland, Hungary, the USSR, the GDR and Czechoslovakia were signed, opening up the Community to most products from these countries over the next few years. For the first two countries mentioned, many of the trade relief measures were brought forward to January 1, 1990.

All in all, access to Western markets has improved markedly over the last few months. But this will provide relief only in the medium term. This is so, because the export opportunities of the Comecon countries usually have not been constrained by trade barriers erected by the West, but by their own inability to produce competitive goods. The total share of Eastern Europe in OECD trade today is smaller than in 1965. And a look at the export structure of the region points rather to a 25-year stagnation period than to progress. Even today, these countries' exports are made up of resource-intensive products by more than 50 per cent. Another 15 per cent are labor-intensive. In all these product ranges, competitors especially from South-East Asia and from Latin America often find themselves in a better competitive position than the East Europeans. Therefore, trade concessions are no short-term solutions to financing problems, but will become more important when the reform efforts have led to first results in the form of a higher competitiveness of the region's products.

All in all, the Western private sector stands ready to finance at least part of the economic reform process in the East. Banks will be ready to offer credits, if there is a reasonable chance that those credits can be paid back. Private companies will engage in direct investments, if the regulatory framework comes up to their expectations. Export opportunities can be used if East European products are competitive. In every case, the precondition for these financial flows is a market-oriented reform programme along the lines I outlined at the beginning. Nevertheless, I expect capital transfers guaranteed by official agencies to increase over the next few years. This is so, because several countries have already reached their risk limit in the view of private banks and are not yet attractive enough for private direct investment. At least for the transitional period, official credits seem indispensable in my view.

There are two main sorts of official creditors: multilateral agencies and nation states. In the first group there are the traditional international financing institutions such as the IMF and the World Bank. Hungary, Poland and Romania are already member countries of the International Monetary Fund, Czechoslovakia and Bulgaria have applied for membership. In the past, only Hungary and Romania received credits from the IMF for temporary stabilization measures. This will change in the future. Both the IMF and the World Bank are ready to become involved in Eastern Europe. The IMF is going to approve a $710 mill standby credit for Poland. In the second half of this year, the Fund will begin talks on a larger three-year programme, possibly totalling $2 bill, provided Poland sticks to the conditions the IMF sets. Such an agreement will also be the precondition for a rescheduling programme of the country's huge debt burden. Conditionality was the key for the Ecu 1 bill loan by the European Community - by the way, the first EC loan ever to a non-member country - to Hungary. In this case, the signing of a letter of intent for a $210 mill one-year standby arrangement with the IMF was the necessary precondition set by the Community.

The World Bank will also be active in Eastern Europe. As Mr. Conable announced in Warsaw, the Bank will provide up to $5 bill for its member countries in Eastern Europe, of which 50 per cent will be reserved for Poland. If other countries from the region were to join the World Bank, they would be eligible for additional credits of up to $2.5 bill. The World Bank, too, is using IMF conditionality for its programme.

I mentioned already the five-year Ecu 1 bill loan by the EC. In addition to that, the European Investment Bank has initiated an Ecu 1 bill lending programme over three years for infrastructure and industrial projects in Poland and Hungary. These funds are supposed to be spent in cooperation with the World Bank. Another project under the leadership of the Community is the planned European Bank for Reconstruction and Development, designed along the EIB or Asian Development Bank lines and open to non-EC members. Talks are well under way, even if there are still some disagreements about the Soviet role in the Bank, but a basic capital of Ecu 10 bill can be taken for granted.

Another international forum for financial aid to Eastern

Europe is the Group of 24, which first met in September of last year and is coordinated by the EC commission. This group of countries is trying to coordinate aid given on a national level in order to secure an efficient resource allocation. A first common step was the introduction of a $1 bill stabilization fund in addition to emergency programmes of food aid for Poland.

> In addition to these coordinated efforts, there have been several national measures such as a special debt relief agreement between the Federal Republic and Poland and indirect help through higher ceilings on official export credit insurance, whose importance will probably increase over the next few years in order to guarantee imports of reform-oriented countries.
>
> All in all, a lot has been done during the last few months in order to facilitate the external financing of East European reforms. The success of the operation will depend on the implementation of drastic reforms. That will force some harsh decisions on governments, governments that in most countries will have to act in a democratic environment. What might lie ahead for some countries can be witnessed at the moment in Poland. Political pressure will surely increase to drop some of the unpopular measures. We can only hope that East and West European leaders stand firm in their agreement for the necessity of reform. As Mr. Giersch put it, "Well-meant policy is often contrary to sound policy". If the sound way is chosen, I believe the financing part of the operation can be managed."

Europe 1992

The linkages between economics and the political evolution in a country or a region are evident in Eastern Europe as well as in Western Europe.

Speaking at the Baden Baden conference, Sir John Browne, a member of the British Parliament, talked about:

"This chicken and egg question... politics drives economics or economics drives politics... The key to integration in the end... is politics, and unfortunately, politics sometimes hinders and holds back an otherwise natural economic integration process. Politicians tend to think of domestic jobs, domestic prices, and domestic monopolies and home companies being threatened. There is also sometimes a wish to exercise strategic control over some industry...

The trouble with political integration is that it is basically about sovereignty. That is the real issue when you come to political integration, you are talking about sovereignty and sovereignty is a subject of great emotion. It is not a subject dealt with in the head like finance and economics. It is a subject dealt with from the heart and people often act economically irrational for reasons of sovereignty... Politicians when faced with survival start to yield sovereignty and so when we look for the very roots, the birth of the European Economic Community, we see that it was basically founded out of fear, the fear of two major threats. First, the threat of military aggression from the Soviet Union, and secondly the threat of economic aggression from the United States. Now of course, times have changed, and maybe the motivation for the European Community has changed with it. Economic and political survival dominate the move toward integration. Just as rats want to leave the sinking ship and every single bit of the Soviet Union's trying to get away, everyone who has got an excuse to be a member wants to be a member. If it is the fact that you're a German, or a Germanic speaking person, I believe you'll tend to want to be with the German ship or on board the German ship.

So the challenge for all of us, and I didn't mean just Europeans, but for Americans, Japanese, and all the real people of influence in the world, economic and political, is what really and ideally is in the interest of the world. What should Europe be, where should its barriers, or boundaries be and what sort of Europe should it be? An economic association of soft sovereign powers, or a federal state? What should its outside relationships be with Eastern Europe. What should its relationships be with the remains of the Soviet Empire and the Soviet Union?

> I believe in summary, that the headlines of the 21st century will record this coming decade as a time of great change, of unprecedented opportunity for peace --strategic peace, for prosperity and for the restoration of the environment on a big scale. I believe it will be recorded as a time of legend -- our legend, and I think that each one of us in this room and many more besides will be very, very proud to tell their grandchildren, 'I was there,' and even more proud to say, 'I played a part.'"

Sir John Browne's optimism about the prospects for a United Europe, despite his reservations about the exchange rate mechanisms being proposed, has a solid basis indeed. This is despite the underlying instability in the Soviet Union as Gorbachev continues to struggle to prevent the "abysmal" state of the Soviet economy from suffocating the drive for political reform.

Steps continue to be taken to further unification of Europe militarily, economically, and eventually politically. The May 5, 1990 issue of The Economist reports that,

> "An immense amount of the law governing the average EC citizen is now being shaped in Brussels. Add to that the prospects of a European central bank, of some central refereeing of government finances, of mounting de facto constraints on indirect taxation, and of steps towards a common foreign policy: all show that it is right to worry about a 'democratic deficit' in the Community's affairs. Much of the old power of national veto in the EC is gone, so voters and their representatives in national parliaments are today bound to accept deals hatched by ministers behind closed doors.

> To deal with both these needs, governments have to be clear how much European politics the average European is ready to accept. At the moment, the European Community is not peopled by 'Europeans'. Frenchmen are French first, European a distant second. The Germans have just reacquired more German-ness. Scotsmen are still Scots first, British second and European third (though don't count on the order of two and three much longer). National sovereignty is intact because, backed by their own armed forces, members can still walk away from an EC that has no military power to stop them. But on a growing number of issues they are ready to put that sovereignty aside and submit themselves to Euro-laws passed by a majority of other governments.
>
> Any durable moves towards "political union" must not run ahead of the shifting mix of pragmatic European-ness and visceral nationalism. A joint foreign-policy device that told France what to do about New Caledonia, or Britain about the Falklands, would get short shrift. So would a call for a European army that was more than an alliance of national forces. Here is the weakness in the most popular remedy for the democratic deficit--more clout for the European Parliament. The parliament does not build upon the different political traditions of the EC's democracies, it hopes to transcend them. It is an assembly for a Europe of People that does not yet exist."

One of the essential ingredients in economic unification and in preparing the grounds for political unification is the simplification and the streamlining of the tax codes so that the overlap is eliminated and overall tax liability is minimized so as not to suffocate economic growth.

This issue was comprehensively addressed by a paper prepared for the Baden Baden conference by Mr. Peter M. Schmidhuber, member of the European Commission. The paper was presented by Dr. Jurgen

Schuler.

The paper begins with the traditional economic analysis of the effects of taxation (among many variables) on the cost of capital, on investment and ultimately on economic growth.

> "Since the publication of the Whitebook on the completion of the internal market, an investment boom has occurred in the Community despite substantial differences between the Member States in the area of taxation. The basic corporate tax rate varies from 50% in Germany (for retained profits), 35% in the UK, to 34% in Luxembourg. The average corporate tax rate - that is corporate tax payments as percentage of corporate gross operating surplus, is thought to be about 20% in Italy and even less in Germany. In the UK the introduction of 35% corporate tax had a strong incentive on the attraction of foreign capital although depreciation and other allowances are less developed than for instance in the Federal Republic. In certain countries accelerated depreciation schemes do not exist at all, but they exist for example for small enterprises in other Member States. Investment tax credits are used particularly in the less advanced economies of the Community but less in the more developed industrialized Member States.
>
> Which of these differences do really matter? A growing number of EC-countries depreciation allowances and investment tax credits are being phased out. Heavy concentration of government incentives on capital costs has not proven to be as effective as was previously believed. Special investment incentives certainly affect investment decisions. But they are also a source of distortion of sectoral allocation of capital. Empirical evidence shows that in nearly all EC-countries - and Western industrialized countries in general - the influence of relative capital cost variations on private investment seems to be much less significant than the impact of demand and profits. The consequences of this observation I would state in the following way: Efficient

investment promotion policy by the Community and its Member States has less to do with subsidies for capital formation than with a good climate for economic activity in general.

A major issue of internal market policy is tax harmonization. From the point of view of the Commission this is a particular challenge because the Single European Act requires unanimity in the Council for this category of decisions (i.e. in contrast to decisions on technical norms and similar areas based on article 100a for which qualified majority is required).

As far as direct taxes are concerned, initiatives in favor of a uniform system seem unrealistic and even economically ineffective to me. Within a context of increasing profitability of investment, each Member State should know best what kind of 'motivation' for entrepreneurs it believes to be efficient - provided of course that it is in accordance with the basic rules of free competition and non-discrimination. Finally, in the internal market it will be market forces and no 'grand design' from the top that will determine investment promotion policies.

Tax policy, however, is something to which the European Commission is giving enormous thought because certain differences between national tax systems will become more apparent after the elimination of physical and technical barriers in the European market.

The Commission has adopted an internal report on company taxation a few days ago that implies a new approach. The 1975 Commission proposals to harmonize the national systems of corporate tax and withholding tax on dividend are outdated and not in line with the principle of subsidiarity. Instead, the European Community should now concentrate on the following aspects, which are already the subject of various Commission initiatives:

- Tax rules for companies with branches in different Member countries should be harmonized.

- Common rules for mergers of companies located in different Member countries should be set up.

- An arbitration procedure tending to eliminate double tax burdens caused by transfers of undistributed profits between associated companies is the subject of a third initiative.

- The Commission is currently preparing proposals on the abolition of withholding taxes on interests and licence fees inside a conglomerate.

- The Commission will examine as well if the transparency of tax allowances and of pricing schemes inside conglomerates can be improved.

- A group of experts should study the question if further harmonization of direct taxes is necessary in the long run.

- National tax policy should be discussed in annual meetings of national policymakers with the Commission.

The free movement of capital flows will be an essential pillar of the European internal market. As from 1st July, 1990, investors shall cross Intra-Community borders as easily as businessmen and tourists. For Spain, Portugal, Greece and Ireland full capital liberalization shall be achieved by 1st January 1993. Portugal and Greece might obtain, conditioned by an additional Council decision, a prolongation of existing restrictions until the beginning of 1995.

Across the board capital liberalization has raised the fear of large-scale tax evasion within some Member countries. The Council decision on the liberalization of capital transactions suggested that the Commission should take an initiative to counter tax evasion and tax fraud resulting from different national taxation of capital revenues. In February 1989, the Commission made a proposal for a directive which would introduce a minimum withholding tax of 15% on interest revenues (but not on dividends) all over the EC. However, already in May 1989 strong opposition to this idea was voiced not only by Luxembourg, the FRG and the UK but also by the Netherlands, Denmark and Greece. On the other hand, France and Italy insisted on EC-wide regulations. Subsequently a solution was sought for by means of clear reporting obligations and closer administrative cooperation concerning capital exports instead of a withholding tax. These new elements were discussed at the informal meeting of the finance ministers in September 1989. So far, the EC partners have only come to an agreement on the principle of intensified cooperation between different national tax authorities. The Commission proposed a directive to introduce some sort of obligation to provide information at the request of another Member State. But so far the concrete proposals made to achieve this objective have been opposed by Luxembourg and, remember, unanimity in the Council is necessary. Personally I am convinced that this issue needs to be handled with extreme caution by the Community. We are not alone in the world, too strict a regulation could drive European capital 'off-shore'. Adam Smith described the capital owner as a 'citizen of the world'. Nevertheless, a closer cooperation of tax authorities against tax fraud is a legitimate and, with some experience, likely to be an efficient instrument. In particular, the more efficient the method of collection a tax system is, the more transparent and growth-oriented it can be.

As far as indirect taxes are concerned, interests are focusing in particular on the value added tax. In view of the objective of a complete abolition of border controls inside the Community, including those in place for fiscal reasons, the Commission has suggested a harmonized band of tax rates - between 14 and 20% for the normal rates and between 4 and 9% for reduced rates. In addition, the Commission has - since 1987 - put forward and supported the principle of levying VAT in the country of origin instead of the existing destination. The system in operation throughout the Community today is not only complicated but also expensive for all parties concerned, both for the tax authorities as well as for private companies, and especially for small and medium sized enterprises.

The buyer in the country of destination of a good pays the VAT of the country of origin together with the sales price to the seller who passes the tax to his home tax authorities, After the certification of the export (at the border), the seller receives the tax back and sends the sum to the buyer. After importation the buyer has to pay the VAT in accordance with the conditions applying in the country into which he is importing. The approach followed in the original Commission proposal would modify this procedure:

The first step would not change : The buyer pays the tax perceived in the country of origin. But there would be no border controls, export certification nor repayment between seller and buyer. Free circulation of goods and less bureaucracy would be the consequences.

For the redistribution of tax revenues between the buyer's and the seller's countries, the Commission has suggested a clearing system that if necessary could even function on simple macro-basis of trade statistics instead of tax declarations.

The compromise designed after lengthy negotiations between the EC Member States and intended to be applied as a temporary solution is a mixture between the status quo and the Commission proposals. Company sales shall be taxed in the country of destination. The goods, at first, will be sold net of taxation. After importation the buyer is taxed in accordance with conditions of his home country. Border controls would be abolished, but the clearing system of tax revenues between the Member States would be based on comprehensive sales records submitted by the individual buyers and sellers. This means that about 50 million bills per annum would have to be listed by the companies and verified by tax authorities.

As far as the Commission is concerned this compromise solution is reminiscent of the traditional definition of a camel - namely a horse designed by a committee. In particular the prospect of the additional bureaucratic and administrative burden of examining and verifying 50 million different transactions is, to say the least, unappealing. Moreover it is to be feared that these transitional arrangements will offer greater scope for fraud. The Commission is not unnaturally keen that public opinion should be aware that it was the famed 'Brussels bureaucracy' which proposed a lighter deregulated system for the collection of VAT and that it was the Member States which decided to adopt a more costly, cumbersome and bureaucratic method.

Finally some words on <u>excise duties</u>. In 1988 the Commission had submitted proposals for the harmonization of five taxes: alcohol, wine, beer, tobacco and petroleum products. Other excises have been considered as being either irrelevant for internal trade or being incompatible with the internal market and bound to be abolished (e.g. taxes on tea or coffee). An internal clearing system was not provided for. Excises were to be charged when excisable goods were released in the country of final consumption. The excise duty rates were to be harmonized at an average level as compared with national rates. In general the aim was to achieve single rates.

This approach did not meet the agreement of the Council. Substantial critics were raised in particular that the proposals of the Commission were by far too rigid.

In May (17th May, 1989) and October (25th October, 1989) the Commission modified its proposals with a view to achieving a higher degree of flexibility. In general single rates were replaced by minimum rates or bands of rates. For 1993 the proposal defined in addition some target rates which national policies should commit themselves to achieve in the long run. Agreement has not yet been reached.

You might, of course, raise the question, to which extent these areas may have a bearing on investment. Well, as long as there will be border controls - and be it only for alcohol or petroleum products - investors cannot rely on the existence of a real internal market. Hence, there is a risk that some special national interests in the area of indirect taxation might deprive the Community of the great advantages of the single market.
While we are progressing towards the internal market, in some fields faster than in others, the businessmen and women in Europe have already the next stage in mind: European Economic and Monetary Union. In a survey among industrialists conducted by the Commission a few weeks ago, more than 80% expected Economic and Monetary Union to have a positive or even very positive impact on the business climate. However, it is also clear that the effects of EMU on businesses will extend beyond the obvious immediate impact of the reduction and ultimately the elimination of exchange rate fluctuations. As we move towards closer coordination of fiscal policy between Member States, so a new context will evolve for the relationship

> between taxation and investment. The further and the faster that EMU progresses, the more that present differences in taxation and investment will be noticeable and play a decisive role in influencing business decisions. It will be this pressure of market forces, and not some power-hungry urge from Brussels, which will provide the driving force for closer approximation of national systems in the future."

The transformations in the European tax codes and in every other aspect of European economies, and the massive drive towards the integration and the streamlining of European corporations through mergers and acquisitions and de novo setups intended to capitalize on new opportunities and to position one's entity competitively, create specific and very significant new sets of strategic considerations for the corporate manager. How does one compete in the New European market? What are the essential ingredients for success?

Mr. Curt G. Olsson, chairman of the Board of Skandinaviska Enskilda Banken, the most profitable bank in Europe, in a keynote opening address at the Baden Baden conference offered very important insights into those factors critical for "Maintaining High Profitability in an Integrated Europe."

> The critical success factors may be grouped under the following headings:
>
> * Strategy
> * Leadership and management
> * Size and structure
> * Product range
> * Distribution and delivery
> * Technology
> * Cost control
> * Risk management
> * Human resources
>
> a. Strategy
>
> As the financial markets tend to be oversupplied - not only

by providers of services but also by products - there will have to be a certain weeding-out process in the years to come. The tendency in Europe will probably be towards a kind of two-tier banking system, where tier one will consist of fairly large universal banks, dominant in their domestic markets, but also operating internationally and with global networks. Tier two will contain niche banks with a high degree of specialization, and banks operating in local geographic areas. To be able to operate on the right track a clear strategy as to which of the two tiers your institution wants to aim for will be necessary. Besides, in the case of tier two it will be necessary to decide in which niches to operate. These will have to be chosen carefully, be well-defined and be given the resources they need to be competitive. It is important to have a good assessment of the profit potential before entering the business and the courage to stick to the project through the initial unprofitable phase. When assessing the profitability of a certain niche or business line a certain degree of patience will be required. Long-term trends will have to be distinguished from short-term trends and the profit potential be estimated for different time-frames. Many players have pulled out of business too early because they did not know the profitability profile. It is no good being over-cautious or too impatient.

b. Leadership and management

In the increasingly competitive climate which the banks and other financial institutions will have to face during the 90s the quality of leadership and management will be of the utmost importance. Managing a bank is no longer an administrative task, which it often was a number of years ago, due to the protective shelter of regulations. Even after the recent years' deregulation, banking has, in many countries, been fairly troublefree, with rapidly growing lending volumes and loan losses lagging comfortably behind. In the profit-driven, fiercely competitive market of tomorrow, strong leadership as well as qualified management at all levels of the organization will be needed to carry through the strategic plans and their implementation. To grasp the business opportunities of tomorrow, the leaders will require vision, and to form the organization for handling these businesses they will require both perseverance and flexibility, qualities which are not always easily combined in one single leader. Group leadership can be a solution, but the ultimate responsibility must be clearly defined.

c. Size and structure

Among the banks that have decided to play in tier one we shall see a great number of mergers and acquisitions in the years ahead. The objects acquired will be both high-priced niche banks - where the aim of the purchaser is to complement the product range - and lower-priced institutions with poor prospects of surviving on their own. Size is, of course, no end in itself, but there are still many reasons for growth.

Firstly, large corporate customers will increase their international operations as the Single European Market is fully opened up to them. That means growing financial needs, which, in turn, demands larger banks with extensive international networks. However, I still believe that even the largest banks will consider their domestic markets as the principal basis of their operations. Thus, truly pan-European banks are still years off. I think it is good advice to expand selectively in Europe.

Secondly, for the banks with the financial resources to grow, acquisition is often an efficient way to take advantage of economies of scale and to regain market shares which have been lost to new players in the field. This is true primarily in the retail market and in payment services.

An acquisition can also be the most cost-efficient way to enter new lines of business in order to diversify activities and thus spread risks. However, once again a warning: diversification has often proven disappointing and many financial services companies are at present refocusing on their core business after a period of detours into various new areas. Diversification must be done selectively. A prerequisite is that there are synergy effects to gain, which means that the sum of the whole must be larger than the sum of the parts. Questions that should be asked in this context is "Who is our customer, what needs do we try to meet and what profits do we expect to get out of it?" If there are obvious possibilities of cross-selling through diversified activities, the idea might be good.

The large universal banking groups will increasingly be formed into holding company structures, with subsidiaries not only in the traditional banking areas but also in such areas as insurance, sales finance, leasing, investment management, real estate sales, financial planning, information technology, etc. The niche banks and local banks have good chances to service as long as they can maintain their competitive advantages, i.e. high competence in a special field or local customer knowledge. Many of these players will, however, be purchased by larger entities.

d. Product range

The "tier one banks" will probably provide a fairly complete array of financial services and aim at cross-selling to a great extent. There is always pressure on the leading banks to be in customers' needs and the ability to grasp market opportunities. Good knowledge about the customer is, needless to say, very important. In the retail market it is also necessary to be aware of ongoing demographic changes which affect both your customers and your workforce. Baby booms, labor participation, double incomes, etc. are factors that might change your selling potential and product range. Customers' behavior also changes. With a rising living standard there is an increased tendency for customers to be investors instead of depositors, and with improved education in most countries customers will be more demanding and price-sensitive.

Even if it is necessary to grasp business opportunities, it is no good "shooting at everything that moves". The point is to select the areas or markets where you can add value and make profits and at the same time control risks. In the markets selected it is probably worth while to strive for dominant market shares. However, if the returns prove to be inadequate in certain markets it is necessary to exit, even if that requires a great amount of courage. Divestitures will probably be increasingly common in the 90s.

e. Distribution/Delivery

In the 80s it was primarily in corporate banking that customers grew more and more price-sensitive and banks' interest margins were rapidly squeezed as large corporations began to procure more and more of their financing directly in the markets. Certainly, competitive pressure has been fierce in the retail financial markets too, but I am afraid that the worst is still to come there. A new generation of customers with more sophisticated needs and far better knowledge of financial matters will pick and choose among the ample supply of services and will turn their back on the services that they don't find suitable. They will be more price-sensitive and less loyal to their bank than their predecessors.

For the banks it will be necessary to approach the customers or customer groups more individually. The customer's needs will have to be more focused and a better segmentation of customers will be necessary. With the help of modern technology and relatively cheap computer capacity we can build up customer databases with a lot of valuable information about our present and potential customers. In Sweden the information potential is huge because of our long-standing system of personal identification numbers, which makes it possible to cross-view various registers. In a wider perspective there are of course related integrity problems, but customer protection is taken care of through legislation and supervision. For the purpose of penetrating the bank's own database, the identification system is, however, very useful and opens many avenues to mapping the customers' needs. This will be even more important in the future when marketing will be increasingly targeted and product development more customer-oriented. When penetrating customers' needs and defining the markets, it is essential to keep in mind the 80/20 rule - that is 80 per cent of the transactions account for 20 per cent of the returns. This means that low-yielding transactions must be handled in a cost-efficient way through far-reaching automation, while high net wealth customers require personal service by competent staff. In our bank an important feature in recent years' strategy for retail operations has been to automate simple transactions and extend self-service wherever suitable. This has increased cost-effectiveness and freed resources for more advanced services.

The banks' distribution or delivery systems of today are often very cost-consuming and staff-intensive. Much can be done to rationalize the handling of routine transactions, for instance, through automation and by centralizing back-office functions. Many simple transactions can be handled with a minimum of human resources, whether it be in ATM's, through a PC, on the telephone, via telefax etc. On the other hand, new products and new customers may require aggressive selling through other channels than the traditional ones. Even if a well-located branch network continues to be of strategic importance for servicing private individuals, we shall certainly see a trend towards a more mobile sales force, paying visits to customers at home or at their offices and with a portable PC as their main working tool. Revenue goals must be established for the sales force and pay incentives related to these goals. More customer-friendly opening hours will also be demanded.

f. Technology

As in the recent two decades, technology will, of course, be a major driving force in all segments of the financial markets. A prerequisite for a bank's success will therefore be in the forefront of technology and rapidly respond to innovations in this area. Product development will to a great extent be technology-driven. Marketing and customer penetration will be highly dependent on information data bases. Top management will be provided with better decision support through computer-based information systems. Controllers and financial officers will get better tools for monitoring activities, control costs and make what-if-analyses, etc. The examples can be multiplied.

The problem with technology is that it sometimes requires large investments, the benefits of which are difficult to assess and quantify. Despite this, I think that it is sometimes necessary to make this decision without absolutely water-proof analytical support. It might be more expensive to refrain and be outstripped by competitors.

g. Cost Control

One of the undoubtedly most critical factors - not to say the most crucial one - for maintaining high profitability is to keep a close watch on cost development. In the fiercely competitive climate of the 90s great emphasis will be put on profitability and performance, and that requires continuous control of costs throughout the organization. We shall need to know exactly in what business lines and on what products we earn money in order to allocate our scarce capital to those areas. The information on costs and profitability in various areas will be more easily available than today thanks to more user-friendly technology, and it will be the responsibility of every manager at all levels to optimize the return of every cost unit.

The threatening cost pressures are many. Firstly, funding costs will be relatively higher in a more competitive market, In other words, margins will continue to be squeezed and banks will try to increase the portion of fee-based business to reduce the dependence on interest margins. They will also look for alternative funding sources where interest rates are lower. With liberalized currency regulations the funding possibilities have become global and it is often possible to find cheaper financing abroad than in domestic markets. This, however, increases the currency risks and requires well-functioning reporting and supervision routines in large decentralized organizations. Also, the funding costs can vary in different markets, and to minimize them it will be necessary to have a competent and alert treasury function.

A second cost threat is rising lending losses. As competition intensifies, it is very easy to be somewhat too benevolent or easygoing when offering credits and assessing credit worthiness. We have seen many examples of hangovers in the wake of rapid credit expansion in deregulated markets. As long as the economic climate is comfortable the risks might be well hidden, but when the downturn comes the risks are bound to rise up to the surface.

Another cost-driving factor is, of course, rising wage claims and social charges. In Sweden, as well as in Finland, there has recently been such an unusual event as a labor market conflict in the banking sector due to what we considered unreasonable wage demands. The outcome of the final agreement was well below demands but still costly for the banks.

I am convinced that cost-cutting measures will be necessary in many European banks in the next few years. Hopefully, this can be done less bluntly than previously if we try to improve our instruments for measuring profitability and thus more often take into account the revenue related to specific costs. Competent controllers and management-oriented information systems are necessary for better cost performance. Such systems will in the short run add to costs as they require certain investments, but, in the long run, they will most likely pay off.

Costs should also be kept down by trying to increase staff productivity in various ways. Automation, rationalization, reduction of staff, overhaul of management levels, etc, will probably be necessary to an increasing extent.

h. Risk Management

Many markets have in the last decade become much more risky than previously, and the demand for competent people and systems to handle the risks has increased. Many of the risks can be quantified and counterweighted by other transactions, while other types of risk are handled mainly by personal judgement. All types of risk management are important areas worth devoting time and resources to if profitability is to be maintained. Avoiding risks completely is not compatible with banking, as risk-taking is an essential part of the business. What should be avoided is excessive risk exposure in single areas, in other words, too much concentration in risk-taking. The risks taken must be well defined and controlled.

As regards credit risks it is also important with established routines for both the credit approval procedure and for the following-up of outstanding credits. Frequent contacts with the customer is the most personal way of following-up, but that is not sufficient. Systemized analyses of corporate accounts, budgeting, etc, are necessary and can be managed quite easily today with PC or mainframe support. Built-in early warning signals are just as valuable in these systems as they are in your own company. More of the credit risk should also be taken care of in pricing. The natural difference in interest rates between a riskfree and a risky credit has often been nonexistent, among other things, because capital adequacy requirements have not been differentiated on these grounds. Even if the new international requirements are not particularly fine-tuned in this respect, they will at least be more risk-oriented than our previous national rules have been. International harmonization will also make it easier to take the risk into account in pricing, as we are all playing on the same field.

i. Human Resources

The new competitive climate in the financial markets will have great impact on human resources activities, such as recruitment, training, compensation systems, etc. The requirements for staff qualities will not be the same as they were a number of years ago. Aggressive selling has not been the main activity of a banker of our generation, but it will have to be for many of our successors. In this respect we still have a lot to learn from other industries. As we have to compete with many other industries when recruiting talented people, it is important to appear in the market as an attractive employer offering good opportunities for a predictable job career including training, job rotation etc. Incentive pay programs linked to performance and profitability are one way of attracting the right kind of people. It is also important to create a corporate culture

> that nourishes staff commitment and creativity. A few years ago it was popular to try to define some sort of shared values within the organization. Even if this is not done in formalized statements I think it is of great value if the management can actualize the company's profile and draw up guidelines not only for the business strategies but also for the corporate culture in a broader and less tangible sense. Ethics and social behavior are factors that must not be neglected in a fiercer and increasingly inhuman business climate."

We now look at how all of the changes in the European landscape and indeed in the world have actually reflected themselves in the major financial markets.

Developments in the U.S. and the Euromarkets

The developments in the U.S. financial markets were overshadowed by four major problems (events) not altogether unrelated:

1. The failure of the S&Ls and the massive bailout expected from the Federal government estimated to cost as much as $500 billion.
2. Financial scandal and associated fines -- unprecedented in the financial history of the United States:
   - Mr. Ivan Boesky
   - Mr. Michael Milliken
   - The S&L related indictment and convictions and
   - The indictment in Chicago for floor practices on the futures exchanges resulting in abuses of the broker/client trust and in the reexamination of the premises of self-regulation.
3. The demise of Drexel-Burnham -- the creator and the major market maker for junk bonds.
4. The two October crashes: 1987 and 1989.

The failures of S&Ls and the junk bond market have yet to work themselves out of the financial system in a comprehensive fashion.

S&Ls remain big investors in junk bonds as are U.S. pension funds. Much of the junk bond assets on the S&L's books are recorded, however, at face value instead of the much lower market value. The difference is not adequately reserved for. Thus one of the reasons for the continuing concern about the health of the surviving institutions in that industry. The total size of the junk bond market as of the end of 1989 is $187 billion of which only 27.3 percent (contrary to publicly held beliefs) was used to finance leveraged buy outs. The bulk of this debt (35.2 percent) was raised as "development capital."

Despite the negatives, the U.S. financial markets continued to evolve and to grow. The extent of foreign participation in the stock and bond markets also grew markedly. Foreign purchases of U.S. stocks grew from $181,185 million in 1988 to $212,977 million in 1989 (Exhibit 5). Foreign purchases of U.S. bonds grew from $86,381 million in 1988 to $120,346 million in 1989. Net purchases of bonds grew by about $7 billion in one year. The involvement of Japan in the U.S. financial markets was extensive. Of $9,835 million in net stock purchases by foreign countries, Japan accounted for $3,348 million, or 32 percent of the total. On the bond side, the net purchases by Japan accounted for only 18.7 percent of the total net bond purchases, trailing European countries and even Middle Eastern countries.

The interest in foreign securities did not improve from 1988 to 1989. In fact net sales were experienced in both the stock and the bond markets.

The borrowing by U.S. corporations dropped significantly from 1988 to 1989 from $409,925 million to $232,307 million. The drop was experienced both in the stock and the bond markets (Exhibit 6).

Foreign net borrowing in the United States increased by only $8 billion in 1989 (Exhibit 7). Total net borrowing by the U.S. nonfinancial as well as the financial sectors slowed down in 1989 compared to 1988. The signal here is not necessarily negative for corporations in 1989 reporting record profits.

The Euromarkets

The Euromarkets continued to play a major role in the flow of capital across national borders. Total issues in the Eurobond markets

EXHIBIT 5

FOREIGN TRANSACTIONS IN SECURITIES
Millions of dollars

Transactions, and area or country	1988	1989	1990	1989						1990
			Jan.– Jan	July	Aug.	Sept.	Oct.	Nov.	Dec.	Jan.
	U.S. corporate securities									
Stocks										
1 Foreign purchases	181,185	212,977	13,741	17,122	22,112	19,595	22,350	13,830	15,410	13,741
2 Foreign sales	183,185	203,387	14,127	15,087	20,942	17,047	20,988	14,947	16,868	14,127
3 Net purchases, or sales (–)	–2,000	9,591	–385	2,035	1,171	2,548	1,363	–1,117	–1,458	–385
4 Foreign countries										
	–1,825	9,835	–354	2,052	1,154	2,599	1,340	–1,116	–1,411	–354
5 Europe										
6 France	–3,350	248	–183	779	–98	1,461	–107	–1,655	–281	–183
7 Germany	–281	–700	–155	75	–251	–5	–265	–296	–255	–155
8 Netherlands	218	–865	41	–79	–238	–65	–117	–119	–41	41
9 Switzerland	–535	168	–18	12	–63	37	226	–34	–9	–18
10 United Kingdom	–2,243	–3,470	–240	–23	–333	64	–244	–509	–442	–240
11 Canada	–954	3,727	–275	546	773	894	–34	–718	391	–275
12 Latin America and Caribbean	1,087	–864	–141	8	14	–265	–140	–137	–459	–141
13 Middle East	1,238	3,102	–111	109	250	602	149	–24	–478	–111
14 Other Asia	–2,474	3,530	– 27	456	554	110	112	303	69	–27
15 Japan	1,365	3,414	231	729	423	631	1,138	342	–124	231
16 Africa	1,922	3,348	166	626	424	611	975	310	–53	166
17 Other countries	188	131	2	2	22	24	–6	19	9	2
	121	274	–125	–30	–11	38	193	37	–147	–125
18 Nonmonetary international and regional organizations										
	–176	245	–31	–17	17	–52	23	–1	–48	–31
Bonds										
19 Foreign purchases	86,381	120,346	9,463	10,045	10,944	8,603	10,930	11,133	13,587	9,463
20 Foreign sales	58,417	86,264	7,404	7,552	9,361	6,857	6,772	6,656	9,310	7,404
21 Net purchases, or sales (–)	27,964	34,082	2,059	2,494	1,583	1,746	4,158	4,476	4,277	2,059
22 Foreign countries	28,506	33,737	2,054	2,516	1,607	1,740	4,106	4,464	4,224	2,054
23 Europe	17,239	19,780	1,135	1,976	–138	1,400	1,986	2,712	1,317	1,135
24 France	143	372	118	121	–35	78	–41	–14	6	118

25 Germany	1,344	-239	-114	-53	-121	-33	113	-117	-33	-114
26 Netherlands	1,514	850	-43	-22	95	28	30	143	41	-43
27 Switzerland	505	-165	157	81	-201	-27	74	54	-277	157
28 United Kingdom	13,084	18 395	1,132	1,937	-9	1,311	1,711	2,328	1,842	1,132
29 Canada	711	1 112	178	79	76	155	175	-86	204	178
30 Latin America and Caribbean	1,931	3 682	493	300	63	233	247	539	492	493
31 Middle East	-178	-171	87	19	44	20	140	-57	242	87
32 Other Asia	8,900	9 060	152	35	1,574	-108	1,553	1,343	1,954	152
33 Japan	7,686	6 331	170	-44	1,167	-179	1,263	1,045	1,728	170
34 Africa	-8	56	3	3	5	-3	0	8	27	3
35 Other countries	-89	218	5	103	-17	42	4	4	-11	5
36 Nonmonetary international and regional organizations	-542	345	5	-22	-24	6	53	12	52	5
					Foreign securities					
37 Stocks, net purchases, or sales (-)	-1,959	-13,690	345	-808	-1,706	-648	-1,341	-927	-2,008	345
38 Foreign purchases	75,356	103,068	12,438	7,640	9,489	8,473	10,309	9,426	9,643	12,438
39 Foreign sales	77,315	116,758	12,093	8,448	11,195	9,121	11,650	10,354	11,651	12,093
40 Bonds,net purchases,sales (-)	-7,434	-5,750	567	-1,406	1,005	-1,845	-615	478	-270	567
41 Foreign purchases	218,521	234,029	18,452	20,222	24,106	18,325	21,266	20,463	18,543	18,452
42 Foreign sales	225,955	239,779	17,885	21,628	23,101	20,170	21,881	19,986	18,812	17,885
43 Net purchases,sales(-),of stocks and bonds	-9,393	-19,440	913	-2,214	-701	-2,493	-1,956	-449	-2,278	913
44 Foreign countries	-9,873	-19,415	805	-2,366	-887	-1,926	-1,618	-527	-2,286	805
45 Europe	-7,864	-18,621	1,013	-2,534	-860	-2,099	-2,487	-193	-762	1,013
46 Canada	-3,747	-4,066	-58	-697	-250	-201	924	-325	-967	-58
47 Latin America and Caribbean	1,384	435	33	-75	314	-61	187	-102	-269	33
48 Asia	979	2,956	78	921	327	412	-232	-2	-512	78
49 Africa	-54	93	-14	12	-4	-3	12	13	56	-14
50 Other countries	-571	-212	-248	8	-414	26	-21	83	168	-248
51 Nonmonetary international and regional organizations	480	-25	108	152	186	-568	-338	77	8	108

1 Comprises oil-exporting countries as follows: Bahrain, Iran, Iraq, Kuwait, Oman, Qatar, Saudi Arabia, and United Arab Emirates Trucial States).

2 Includes state and local government securities, and securities of U.S. government agencies and corporations. Also includes issues of new debt securities sold abroad by U.S. corporations organized to finance direct investments abroad.

3 As a result of the merger of U.S. and U.K. comapny in July 1989, the former stockholders of the U.S. company received $5,453 million in shares of the new combined U.K. company. This transaction is not reflected in the data above.

Source: Federal Reserve Bulletin, May, 1990, p. A67

EXHIBIT 6

NEW SECURITY ISSUES U.S. Corporations

Millions of dollars

Type of issue or issuer, or use	1987	1988	1989	1989							1990
				June	July	Aug.	Sept.	Oct.	Nov.	Dec.	Jan.
All issues	392,339	409,925	232,307	24,770	18,094	14,950	14,629	24,654	20,697	21,537	14,278
Bonds	325,838	352,124	201,031	21,942	13,040	12,915	12,356	20,974	16,457	17,592	12000
Type of Offering											
Public,domestic	209,455	201,246	178,433	19,034	11,620	12,099	11,156	19,866	14,383	15,987	10,000
Private placement, domestic	92,070	127,700	n.a.	n.a.	n.a.	n.a.	n.a.	n.a.	n.a.	n.a.	n.a.
Sold abroad	24,308	23,178	22,598	2,908	1,420	816	1,200	1,108	2,074	1,605	2,000
Industry group											
Manufacturing	61,266	70,595	42,366	3,502	2,850	2,670	2,247	3,646	3,551	4,193	1,847
Commercial and miscellaneous	49,773	62,070	15,968	1,649	1,354	1,090	1,393	1,830	1,253	347	551
Transportation	11,974	10,076	3,586	480	0	423	30	906	312	1,083	35
Public utility	23,004	19,318	13,682	2,936	1,346	705	1,059	1,748	1,022	1,098	825
Communication	7,340	5,951	3,859	4	300	358	308	632	812	577	15
Real estate and financial	172,474	184,114	121,574	13,372	7,190	7,669	7,320	12,213	9,507	10,296	8,727
Stocks	66,508	57,802	32,225	2,828	5,054	2,035	2,273	3,680	4,240	3,945	2,278
Type											
Preferred	10,123	6,544	6,194	335	920	1,013	519	570	160	626	50
Common	43,225	35,911	26,030	2,493	4,134	1,023	1,754	3,110	4,080	3,319	2,228
Private Placement	13,157	15,346	n.a.	n.a.	n.a.	n.a.	n.a.	n.a.	n.a.	n.a.	n.a.

Industry Group											
Manufacturing	13,880	7,608	5,081	630	593	393	193	190	378	279	835
Commerical and miscellaneous	12,888	8,449	4,428	512	438	343	155	728	498	1,045	248
Transportation	2,439	1,535	532	0	0	0	0	50	0	0	0
Public utility	4,322	1,898	2,297	125	25	137	709	465	211	244	106
Communication	1,458	515	471	25	29	20	0	0	0	0	0
Real estate and financial	31,521	37,798	19,250	1,536	3,969	1,020	1,195	2,214	3,153	2,377	1,090

Figures which represent gross proceeds of issues maturing in more than one year, are principal amount or number of units multiplied by offering price. Excludes secondary offerings, employee stock plans, investment companies other than closed–end, intracorporate transactions, equities sold abroad, and Yankee bonds. Stock data include ownership securities issued by limited partnerships.
Monthly data include only public offerings.
Data are not available on a monthly basis. Before 1987, annual totals include underwritten issues only.
Sources: IDD INformation Services, Inc. the Board of Governors of the Federal Reserve System, and before 1989, the U.S. Securities and Exchange Commission.

Source: Federal Reserve Bulletin, May, 1990, p. A34.

Source: Federal Reserve Bulletin, May, 1990, p. A34.

EXHIBIT 7

FUNDS RAISED IN U.S. CREDIT MARKETS
Billions of dollars; quarterly data are at seasonally adjusted annual rates.

Transaction category, sector	1985	1986	1987	1988	1989	1988						
						Q2	Q3	Q4	Q1	Q2r	Q3r	Q4
						Nonfinancial sectors						
1 Total net borrowing by domestic nonfinancial sectors	846.3	831.1	693.2	754.5	695.2	817.5	749.3	734.2	770.6	641.7	693.6	675.1
By sector and instrument												
2 U.S. government	223.6	215.0	144.9	157.5	149.8	113.7	162.5	142.1	199.9	70.9	149.0	179.4
3 Treasury securities	223.7	214.7	143.4	140.0	150.0	106.0	141.6	100.5	201.1	65.8	149.1	184.0
4 Agency issues and mortgages	–.1	0.4	1.5	17.4	–.2	7.7	20.9	41.6	–1.2	5.1	–.2	–4.6
5 Private domestic nonfinanc'l sectors	622.7	616.1	548.3	597.1	545.4	703.8	586.8	592.2	570.6	570.8	544.7	495.7
6 Debt capital instruments	451.4	460.3	458.5	454.6	393.8	551.0	458.8	432.4	418.0	396.9	374.8	385.6
7 Tax-exempt obligations	135.4	22.7	34.1	34.0	24.2	37.9	34.8	34.3	29.3	23.0	32.2	12.4
8 Corporate bonds	73.8	121.3	99.9	114.1	114.2	135.2	110.9	98.4	100.0	127.9	102.4	126.4
9 Mortgages	242.2	316.3	324.5	306.5	255.5	377.9	313.1	299.7	288.7	246.1	240.2	246.9
Home mortgages	156.8	218.7	234.9	231.0	196.1	299.8	230.9	214.0	206.6	197.6	180.6	199.8
Multifamily residential	29.8	33.5	24.4	16.7	15.8	14.5	19.4	17.3	27.4	7.9	19.0	8.7
Commercial	62.2	73.6	71.6	60.8	43.9	65.2	65.4	67.7	59.1	38.5	40.6	37.3
Farm	–6.6	–9.5	–6.4	–2.1	–.3	–1.6	–2.6	0.7	–4.4	2.1	0.0	1.0
14 Other debt instruments	171.3	155.8	89.7	142.5	151.6	152.8	128.0	159.8	152.6	173.9	169.9	110.0
15 Consumer credit	82.5	58.0	32.9	51.1	46.1	51.9	35.5	73.1	34.8	46.0	34.5	69.2
16 Bank loans n.e.c.	38.6	66.7	10.8	38.4	33.0	58.8	2457.3	66.6	23.1	29.9	59.0	20.0
17 Open market paper	14.6	–9.3	2.3	11.6	20.8	6.8	17.1	20.0	41.4	39.2	16.7	–14.3
18 Other	35.6	40.5	43.8	41.5	51.7	35.2	68.0	0.1	53.3	58.7	59.7	35.1
19 By borrowing sector	622.7	616.1	548.3	597.1	545.4	703.8	586.8	592.2	570.6	570.8	544.7	495.7
20 State and local government	90.9	36.2	33.6	29.8	24.7	37.0	28.1	30.6	29.7	27.6	29.5	11.9
21 Households	284.6	289.2	271.9	289.8	258.5	346.2	291.4	283.5	264.5	239.4	258.4	271.9
22 Nonfinancial business	247.2	290.7	242.8	277.5	262.2	320.6	267.3	278.0	276.4	303.7	256.8	211.9
23 Farm	–14.5	–16.3	–10.6	–7.5	0.3	–3.3	–2.2	–11.8	–2.2	0.2	4.7	–1.5
24 Nonfarm noncorporate	129.3	103.2	107.9	87.4	65.9	83.6	100.5	80.4	85.9	65.8	67.2	44.7
25 Corporate	132.4	203.7	145.5	197.5	196.0	240.3	169.0	209.4	192.8	237.7	184.9	168.7

26	Foreign net borrowing in United States	[illegible].2	9.7	4.9	3.9	8.0	5.4	4.1	13.3	−1.1	−1.9	24.3	10.6
27	Bonds	3.8	3.1	7.4	3.9	5.1	2.6	5.9	5.1	3.2	10.7	8.4	−1.9
28	Bank loans n.e.c.	−2.8	−1.0	−3.6	−1.8	1.0	−3.3	0.0	−5.7	4.9	1.7	−1.2	−1.4
29	Open market paper	6.2	11.5	2.1	3.6	12.3	6.5	10.3	21.0	12.1	−8.1	20.4	24.9
30	U.S. government loans	−6.0	−3.9	−1.0	−7.8	−10.5	−.4	−12.1	−7.1	−21.4	−6.3	−3.3	−10.9
31	Total domestic plus foreign	847.5	840.9	698.1	761.4	703.2	822.9	753.3	747.6	769.5	639.8	718.0	685.7
								Financial sectors					
32	Total net borrowing by financial sectors	20[illegible].3	318.9	315.0	246.5	201.5	245.9	216.3	302.5	384.0	119.0	141.1	161.9
	By instrument												
33	U.S. government related	10[illegible].5	187.9	185.8	119.8	140.4	86.3	128.6	156.7	205.7	101.4	129.7	124.8
34	Sponsored credit agency securities	20.6	15.2	30.2	44.9	25.0	11.1	46.5	62.3	84.9	12.5	10.0	−7.4
35	Mortgage pool securities	79.9	173.1	156.4	74.9	115.4	75.1	82.1	94.4	120.8	88.9	119.6	132.2
36	Loans from U.S. government	[illegible].1	−.4	−.8	0.0	0.0	0.0	0.0	0.0	0.0	0.0	0.0	0.0
37	Private financial sectors	99.7	131.0	129.2	126.7	61.1	159.6	87.7	145.8	178.3	17.6	11.4	37.1
38	Corporate bonds	50.9	82.9	78.9	51.7	38.7	71.1	32.5	43.0	52.7	31.4	25.5	45.0
39	Mortgages	0.1	0.1	0.4	0.3	−.1	0.1	−.1	1.2	0.3	0.0	0.0	−.5
40	Bank loans n.e.c.	2.6	4.0	−3.3	1.4	1.3	5.7	−5.6	−.3	3.0	0.3	1.7	0.1
41	Open market paper	32.0	24.2	28.8	53.6	32.2	70.5	35.1	70.4	53.2	2.8	27.9	44.9
42	Loans from Fedreal Home Loan Banks	14.2	19.8	24.4	19.7	−11.0	12.3	25.8	31.4	69.1	−16.9	−43.7	−52.4
	By sector												
43	Total	201.3	318.9	315.0	246.5	201.5	245.9	216.3	302.5	384.0	119.0	141.1	161.9
44	Sponsored credit agencies	2[illegible].7	14.9	29.5	44.9	25.0	11.1	46.5	62.3	84.9	12.5	10.0	−7.4
45	Mortgage pools	79.9	173.1	156.4	74.9	115.4	75.1	82.1	94.4	120.8	88.9	119.6	132.2
46	Private financial sectors	99.7	131.0	129.2	126.7	61.1	159.6	87.7	145.8	178.3	17.6	11.4	37.1
47	Commercial banks	−4.9	−3.6	7.1	−3.9	0.7	−1.6	−.9	3.7	−13.4	−.9	12.3	4.7
48	Bank affiliates	16.6	15.2	14.3	5.2	7.5	22.4	6.1	0.8	6.4	6.5	16.5	0.8
49	Savings and loan associations	17.3	20.9	19.6	13.9	−14.6	19.1	24.1	26.3	71.3	−16.2	−48.3	−65.2
50	Mutual savings banks	[illegible].5	4.2	8.1	1.9	−1.6	1.1	0.5	3.8	−2.8	−1.1	−3.3	0.8
51	Finance companies	57.2	54.5	40.3	67.0	49.0	85.4	40.7	63.6	78.4	32.8	29.7	55.0
52	REITs	0.5	1.0	0.8	4.1	−1.2	1.7	−5.9	15.0	−.9	−2.2	−1.4	−.4
53	SCO Issuers	1[illegible].5	39.0	39.1	32.5	21.3	31.5	23.1	32.5	39.3	−1.4	5.9	41.5

Source: Federal Reserve Bulletin, May, 1990, p. A41.

amounted to $212.8 billion in 1989, up 20 percent from the 1988 total of $175.8 billion. This level of activity in the Eurobond markets represented 37.3 percent of the global debt markets in 1989, and 20.7 percent of the global debt markets including government securities (Exhibit 8a).

The most active countries in the Eurobond markets were Japan, with 35.1 percent of the 213,000 issues in 1989, European countries, with 21.2 percent of the total, the United States (6.7%) and Canada (5.7%) (Exhibit 8b).

The U.S. dollar continues to be the dominant currency of debt denomination, followed by the Sterling and the D.M. (Exhibit 9a). The largest group of borrowers were corporate and private individuals, followed by governments, private banks and supranational entities (Exhibit 9b).

The top four bookrunners of all Eurobond issues were Japanese, once again. These firms, led by Nomura Securities, (Exhibit 10) dominated the Eurobond markets for they accounted for 37.8 percent of all issues. The first American firm was in the seventh position in 1989, up from the 10th position in 1988. The same four firms also played a major role in the management of all international issues (Exhibit 11). Their major competitors were Credit Suisse/First Boston, Deutsche Bank, Merrill Lynch Capital Markets and J.P. Morgan.

The same four Japanese firms also dominated, interestingly, U.S. dollar Eurobond issues accounting for 60.5 percent of all issues in 1989 (Exhibit 12a).

U.S. companies, however, seem to deal typically with U.S. investment banks as Exhibit 12b shows. In the lead was Goldman Sachs International followed by Credit Suisse First Boston. The Japanese showed the same preference for their home country investment banks, giving 33 percent of all Japanese Eurobond issues to Nomura Securities alone (Exhibit 13a).

The syndicated international loan market was dominated, once again, by U.S. banks, led by Citicorp with 12.18 percent of the volume. Manufacturers Hanover improved its position substantially from 1988 by moving from the fifth to the second position (Exhibit 13b).

EXHIBIT 8a

The global debt markets, 1989

Total: $569.7bn

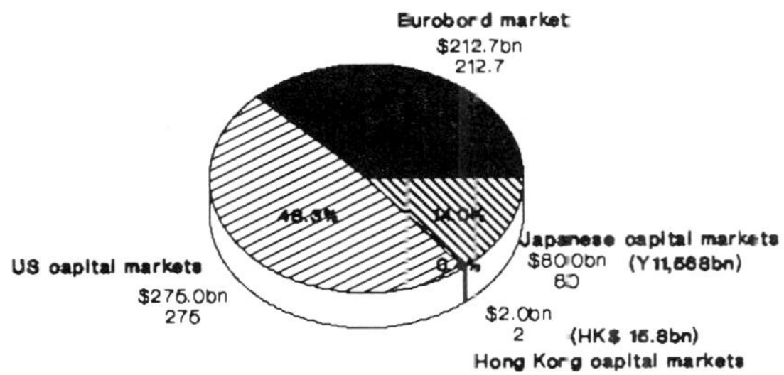

The global debt markets, 1989
(Including government securities)

Total: $1024.9bn

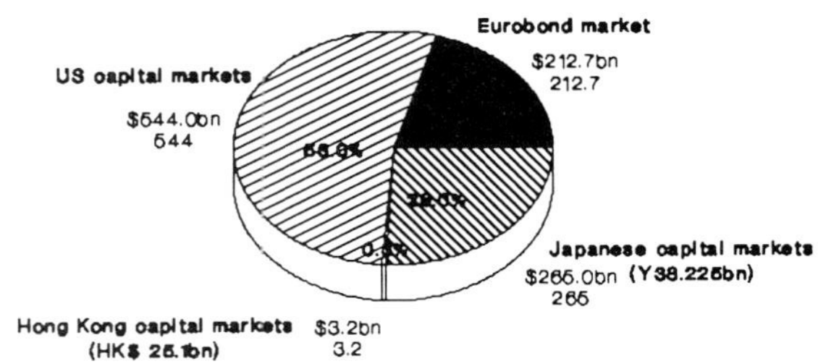

Source: Annual Financing Report, Euromoney, March, 1990, p.2.

EXHIBIT 8b

ISSUERS BY COUNTRY

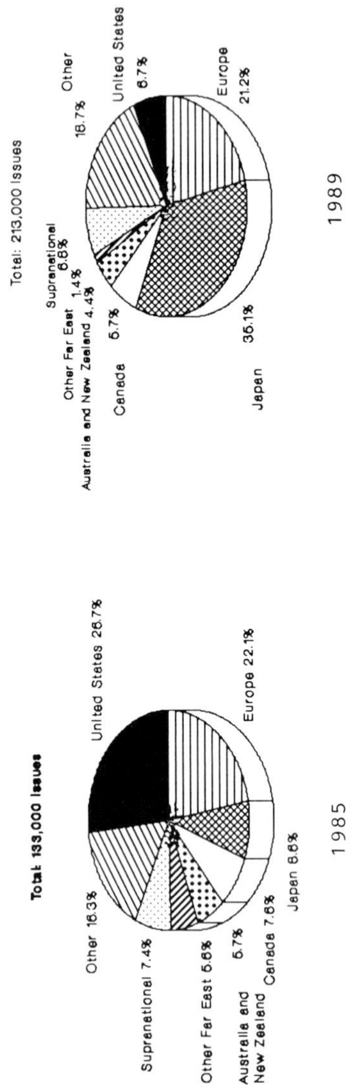

Source: Annual Financing Report, Euromoney, March, 1990, p.2.

EXHIBIT 9a

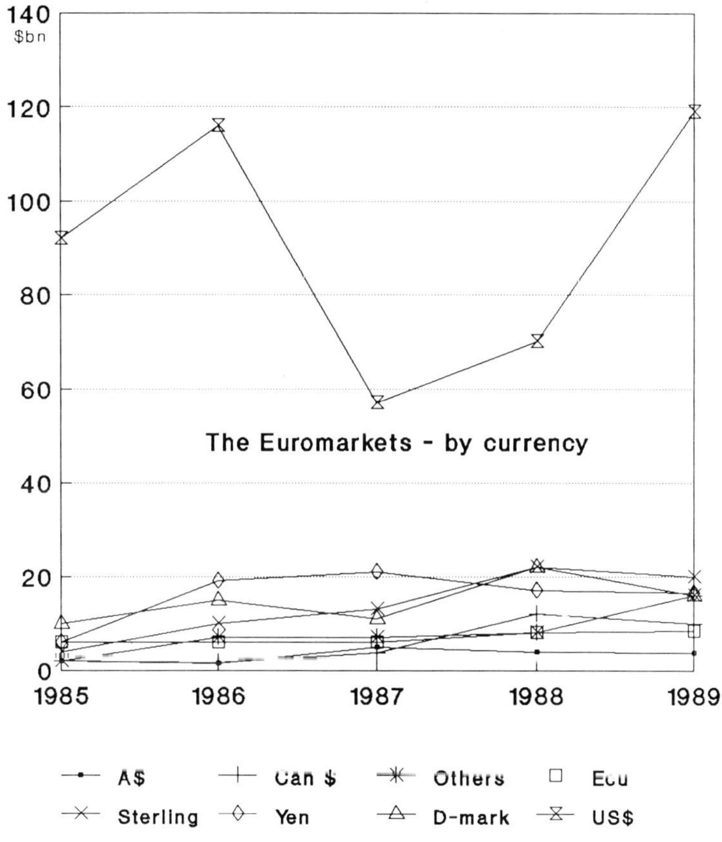

Source: Annual Financing Report, Euromoney, March, 1990, p.2.

EXHIBIT 9b

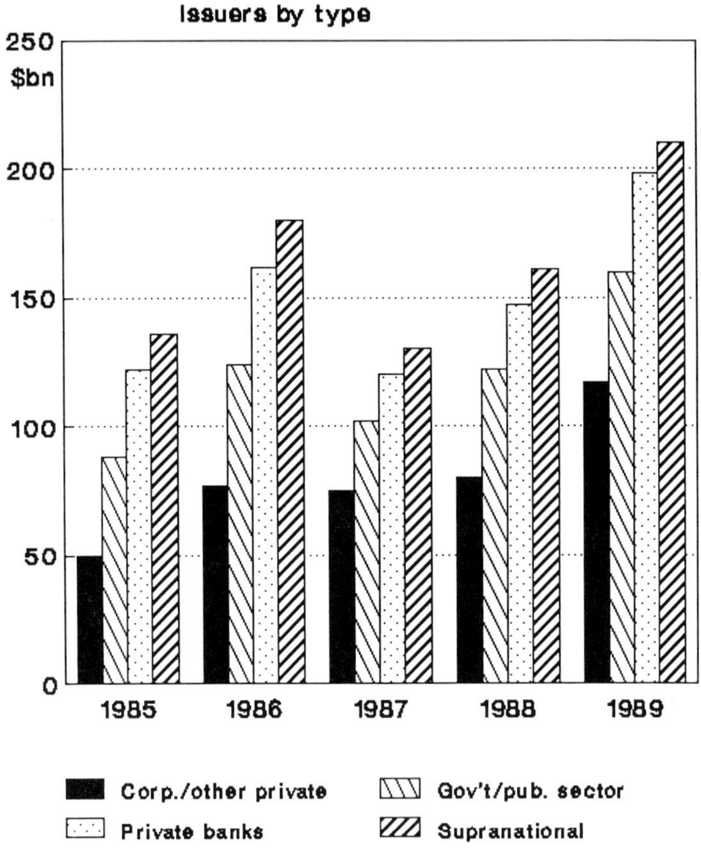

Source: Annual Financing Report, Euromoney, March, 1990, p.2.

EXHIBIT 10

Top 50 bookrunners – all Eurobond issues

Rank 89	Rank 88	Bank	1989 Amount $m	1989 # of iss.	1989 Share %	1988 Amount $m	1988 # of iss.	1988 Share %
1	1	NOMURA SECURITIES	31,892.2	148	15.0	17,637.40	134	10.00
2	4	DAIWA SECURITIES	16,862.0	92	7.9	9,454.70	85	5.40
3	5	YAMAICHI SECURITIES	16,329.1	78	7.7	7,268.55	61	4.13
4	6	NIKKO SECURITIES	15,286.4	52	7.2	6,858.90	61	3.90
5	3	DEUTSCHE BANK	10,677.0	62	5.0	12,118.42	84	6.89
6	2	CRDT SS 1ST BOST/CRDT SS	9398.5	57	4.4	14,403.52	85	8.20
7	10	JP MORGAN	7,615.3	39	3.6	5,603.76	34	3.19
8	7	MERRILL LYNCH CAP. MKTS.	7,437.7	50	3.5	6,178.39	35	3.51
9	17	MORGAN STANLEY INT'L	6,614.3	38	3.1	3,565.57	29	2.03
10	13	SALOMON BROTHERS	6,141.5	27	2.9	4,882.97	27	2.78
11	9	PARIBAS CAPITAL MKTS GRP	6,076.5	42	2.9	6,029.23	46	3.43
12	8	BANKERS TRUST INT'L	5,917.6	68	2.8	6,029.30	50	3.40
13	11	INDUSTRIAL BANK OF JAPAN	4,845.0	55	2.3	5,590.37	49	3.18
14	15	GOLDMAN SACHS INT'L	3,814.9	29	1.8	3,962.58	26	2.25
15	12	UNION BANK/ SWITZLND	3,416.9	29	1.6	4,882.97	47	3.11
16	33	CREDIT LYONNAIS	2,870.8	23	1.4	1,097.25	9	0.60

17	14	SG WARBURG	2,810.1	15	1.3	4,413.93	21	2.50
18	20	HAMBROS BANK	2,765.4	47	1.3	2,676.35	46	1.50
19	21	LONG–TRM CRDT B.OF JAPAN	2,729.4	30	1.3	2,345.19	25	1.30
20	16	DRESDNER BANK	2,612.7	17	1.2	3,810.96	24	2.25
21	25	W.DEUTSCHE LNDSB. GIROZ.	2,213.6	22	1.0	2,009.39	27	1.30
22	27	CREDIT COMRCL DE FRANCE	1,951.9	20	0.9	1,811.05	19	1.00
23	29	BARCLAYS BANK GROUP	1,828.4	9	0.9	1,331.77	9	0.80
24	48	BANQUE NATIONALE/PARIS	1,816.5	17	0.9	477.96	5	0.27
25	18	COMMERZBANK	1,747.6	17	0.8	3,565.57	29	2.00
26	35	MITSUBISHI FINANCE INT'L	1,731.0	34	0.8	957.72	12	0.60
27	23	WOOD GUNDY	1,705.8	18	0.8	2,107.70	28	1.20
28	34	SAMUEL MONTAGU	1,704.4	13	0.8	985.97	8	0.60
29	38	BANK OF TOKYO	1,622.6	14	0.8	886.89	9	0.50
30	28	SOCIETE GENERALE	1,588.6	21	0.8	1,331.77	9	0.76
31	22	BARING BROTHERS	1,563.3	9	0.7	2,118.09	18	1.20
32	59	KIDDER PEABODY INT'L	1,425.0	12	0.7	281.02	2	0.16
33	31	ALGEMENE BANK NEDERLAND	1,388.1	16	0.7	1,143.57	13	0.68
34	19	SWISS BANK CORPORATION	1,265.0	10	0.6	2,676.35	25	1.60
35	26	AMSTERDAM–ROTTERDAM BANK	1,226.8	13	0.6	1,945.71	21	1.10
36	43	NIPPON CREDIT BANK	1,214.3	37	0.6	627.10	11	0.40
37	51	BANCO DI ROMA	1,195.0	11	0.6	467.53	8	0.30
38	74	IST. BANC.S.PAOLO/TORINO	1,156.4	8	0.5	182.54	2	0.10

39	39	TRINKAUS & BURKHARDT	1,023.3	7	0.5	885.89	9	0.50
40	30	SHRSN LEHMAN HUTTON INT'L	1,005.1	10	0.5	1,297.40	11	0.70
41	***	SUMITOMO BANK	998.2	8	0.5	40.34	1	0.02
42	–	BANQUE INDOSUEZ	838.8	8	0.4	–	–	–
43	37	SCOTIA MCLEOD	736.2	8	0.4	886.91	12	0.50
44	32	CHASE MANHATTAN	674.7	6	0.3	1,143.57	9	0.65
45	76	SVENSKA HNDLSBANKEN GRP	661.6	11	0.3	174.29	2	0.10
46	72	KREDIETBANK	656.5	10	0.3	188.48	3	0.11
47	46	MITSUI FINANCE INT'L	655.5	12	0.3	519.00	5	0.30
48	24	KLEINWORT BENSON	606.1	4	0.3	2,065.58	13	1.17
49	41	NATWEST CAPITAL MARKETS	606.1	5	0.3	775.88	11	0.43
50	96	CREDITANSTALT–BANKVEREIN	605.8	3	0.3	91.43	2	0.05

Source: Annual Financing Report, Euromoney, March, 1990, p.6.

EXHIBIT 11

Top 50 lead managers – all international issues

Rank			1989			1988		
89	88	Bank	Amount $m	# of issue	Share %	Amount $m	# of issue	Share %
1	1	NOMURA SECURITIES	37,725.5	199	13.9	19,586.2	152	8.1
2	5	DAIWA SECURITIES	19,543.8	115	7.2	10,849.3	87	4.5
3	8	YAMAICHI SECURITIES	18,012.5	94	6.7	8,690.3	71	3.6
4	1	CRDT SUIS 1ST BOST/CDT SS	17,969.2	157	6.6	25,361.0	204	10.5
5	9	NIKKO SECURITIES	16,997.1	64	6.3	8,277.7	69	3.4
6	4	DEUTSCHE BANK	11210	72	4.1	12,401.2	88	5.1
7	6	MERRILL LYNCH CAP. MKTS	10,502.1	72	3.9	10,109.6	55	4.2
8	10	JP MORGAN	8,355.2	50	3.1	7,967.8	41	3.3
9	3	UNION BANK OF SWITZERLAN	8,201.6	85	3.0	13,180.4	136	5.4
10	17	MORGAN STANLEY INT'L	7,963.4	58	2.9	5,308.4	45	2.2
11	11	SALOMON BROTHERS	7,565.4	38	2.8	7,288.8	45	3.0
12	12	PARIBAS CAPITAL MKTS GRP	7,422.3	89	2.7	7,273:0	103	3.0
13	15	BANKERS TRUST INT'L	6,586.9	79	2.4	6,029.3	50	2.5
14	13	GOLDMAN SACHS	5,783.7	41	2.1	6,310.5	38	2.6
15	7	SWISS BANK CORPORATION	5,722.4	68	2.1	9,138.0	108	3.8
16	16	INDUSTRIAL BANK OF JAPAN	5,139.2	69	1.9	5,824.7	54	2.4
17	14	SG WARBURG	3,330.6	22	1.2	6,206.3	45	2.6
18	30	BARCLAYS BANK GROUP	2,941.1	15	1.1	1,515.5	10	0.6
19	32	CREDIT LYONNAIS	2,911.8	31	1.1	1,466.6	16	0.6
20	22	LONG-TERM CRDT B./JAPAN	2,799.2	33	1.0	2,487.5	28	1.0
21	20	HAMBROS BANK	2,765.4	47	1.0	2,676.4	46	1.1
22	18	DRESDNER BANK	2,704.4	18	1.0	3,811.0	24	1.6

23	25	WESTDEUTSCHE LNDSBK GIR	2,313.7	24	0.9	2,220.3	29	0.9
24	28	CREDIT COMMERCIAL DE FRA	1,951.9	20	0.7	1,823.3	20	0.8
25	22	COMMERZBANK	1,920.1	20	0.7	3,483.3	31	1.4
26	62	DREXEL BURNHAM LAMBERT	1,903.5	8	0.7	451.5	8	0.2
27	36	MITSUBISHI FINANCE INT'L	1,901.6	38	0.7	1,169.5	18	0.5
28	31	SOCIETE GENERALE	1,896.0	28	0.7	1,470.1	20	0.6
29	55	BANQUE NATIONALE DE PARIS	1,857.9	21	0.7	486.4	9	0.2
30	40	SAMUEL MONTAGU	1,744.9	14	0.6	996.9	6	0.4
31	27	WOOD GUNDY	1,705.8	18	0.6	2,107.7	28	0.9
32	37	BANK OF TOKYO	1,703.6	16	0.6	1,166.1	14	0.5
33	67	CITICORP GROUP	1,665.7	18	0.6	419.6	6	0.2
34	52	KIDDER PEABODY INT'L	1,625.0	13	0.6	681.0	5	0.3
35	23	BARING BROTHERS	1,563.3	9	0.6	2,412.4	20	1.0
36	33	ALGEMENE BANK NEDERLAND	1,557.3	19	0.6	1,379.4	15	0.6
37	50	NIPPON CREDIT BANK	1,363.8	41	0.5	642.8	12	0.3
38	21	SHEARSON LEHMAN HUTTON I	1,228.3	14	0.5	2,546.3	23	1.0
39	24	AMSTERDAM-ROTTERDAM BA	1,226.8	13	0.5	2,261.4	20	0.8
40	64	BANCO DI ROMA	1,195.0	11	0.4	443.4	5	0.2
41	60	IST BANC. S.PAULO/TORINO	1,156.4	8	0.4	459.1	4	0.2
42	76	SUMITOMO BANK	1,082.3	10	0.4	309.6	8	0.1
43	34	KREDIETBANK	1,071.8	49	0.4	1,369.9	52	0.6
44	42	TRINKAUS & BURKHARDT	1,023.3	7	0.4	885.9	8	0.4
45	29	NATWEST CAPITAL MARKETS	987.8	21	0.4	1,599.9	32	0.7
46	45	SANWA BANK	980.6	41	0.4	740.4	14	0.3
47	91	BANQUE INDOSUEZ	897.3	10	0.3	221.0	8	0.1
48	26	KLEINWORT BENSON	877.0	6	0.3	2,412.4	20	1.0
49	41	SCOTIA MCLEOD	736.2	8	0.3	886.9	12	0.4
50	130	CREDITANSTALT-BANKVEREIN	678.5	4	0.3	91.4	2	0.0

Source: Annual Financing Report, Euromoney, March, 1990. p.6.

EXHIBIT 12a

Top 20 lead managers – U.S. dollar Eurobond issues

Rank 89	Rank 88	Bank	1989 Amount $m	1989 # iss.	1989 Share %	1988 Amount $m	1988 # iss.	1988 Share %
1	1	NOMURA SECURITIES	28,728.3	99	23.8	13,990.0	98	13.2
2	4	YAMAICHI SECURITIES	15,250.0	63	12.6	6,146.0	53	8.0
3	5	NIKKO SECURITIES	14,726.6	45	12.2	5,620.0	42	7.3
4	3	DAIWA SECURITIES	14,340.0	60	11.9	6,965.0	52	9.1
5	12	MORGAN STANLEY INT'L	5,750.0	26	4.8	1,990.0	12	2.6
6	7	JP MORGAN	4700.3	19	3.9	4,328.1	12	5.6
7	2	CREDIT SS 1ST BOSTON/CRDT S	4,560.0	24	3.8	8,156.5	38	10.6
8	14	DEUTSCHE BANK	3,500.0	8	2.9	1,275.0	8	1.7
9	13	SALOMON BROTHERS	3,444.4	13	2.9	1,390.0	9	1.8
10	6	MERRILL LYNCH CAP. MKTS.	3,043.5	17	2.5	4,447.0	16	5.8
11	10	BANKERS TRUST INT'L	2,955.0	25	2.5	2,190.1	12	2.9
12	8	GOLDMAN SACHS INT'L	2,695.0	17	2.2	2,900.0	13	3.8
13	9	INDUSTRIAL BANK OF JAPAN	2,276.2	20	1.9	2,505.0	14	3.3
14	11	PARIBAS CAP. MKTS. GRP	1,675.1	9	1.4	2,084.7	9	2.7
15	35	KIDDER PEABODY INT'L	1,425.0	12	1.2	200.0	1	0.3
16	15	LONG–TRM CRDT BK OF JAP	1,379.0	10	1.1	1,240.3	8	1.6
17	22	BANK OF TOKYO	1,315.0	8	1.1	620.0	4	0.8
18	44	MITSUBISHI FINANCE INT'L	946.0	15	0.8	100.0	1	0.1
19	40	BANQUE NATIONALE/PARIS	925.0	6	0.8	150.0	1	0.2
20	–	SUMITOMO BANK LTD.	775.0	4	0.6	–	–	–

EXHIBIT 12b

Top 20 lead managers – U.S. corporate Eurobond issues

Rank 89	Rank 88	Bank	1989 Amount $m	1989 # iss	1989 Share %	1988 Amount $m	1988 # iss	1988 Share %
1	1	GOLDMAN SACHS INT'L	1,730.9	8	15.0	2,012.00	11	16.40
2	2	CRDT SS 1ST BOST/CRDT S	1,505.1	8	13.1	1,345.80	10	11.00
3	8	MERRILL LYNCH CAP. MKTS.	1,283.5	8	11.1	602.60	4	4.90
4	7	BANQUE PARIBAS	1,088.7	8	9.4	604.20	4	4.90
5	3	MORGAN STANLEY INT'L	923.0	9	8.0	1,130.30	7	9.20
6	–	KIDDER PEABODY INT'L	750	3	6.5	–	–	–
7	4	SALOMON BROTHERS	618.9	5	5.4	711.80	5	5.80
8	12	BANKERS TRUST INT'L	570.5	7	5.0	604.20	3	2.80
9	6	JP MORGAN	545.0	4	4.7	637.10	5	5.20
10	9	UNION BANK OF SWITZ.	437.5	4	3.8	601.30	7	4.90
11	–	SCOTIA MCLEOD	315.9	3	2.7	–	–	–
12	14	HAMBROS BANK	305.9	6	2.7	251.00	5	2.10
13	21	NOMURA SECURITIES	200.0	1	1.7	130.10	2	1.10
14	–	SG WARBURG	164.3	1	1.4	–	–	–
15	19	KLEINWORT BENSON	154.6	1	1.3	139.10	1	1.10
16	11	SWISS BANK CORPORATION	137.1	1	1.2	445.90	4	3.60
17	–	SAMUEL MONTAGU	125.2	1	1.1	–	–	–
18	28	WESPAC BANKING CORP.	103.4	2	0.9	79.90	2	0.70
19	–	YAMAICHI SECURITIES	91.9	1	0.8	–	–	–
20	10	DEUTSCHE BANK	82.8	2	0.7	461.30	5	3.80

Source: Annual Financing Report, Euromoney, March, 1990, ps.16 & 22

EXHIBIT 13a

Top 25 lead managers – Japanese Eurobond issuers

Rank 89	Rank 88	Bank	1989 Amount $m	1989 # iss	1989 Share %	1988 Amount $m	1988 # iss	1988 Share %
1	1	NOMURA SECURITIES	24,703.6	81	33.0	10,733.00	76	32.80
2	2	YAMAICHI SECURITIES	14,417.1	55	19.3	5,631.90	46	17.20
3	4	NIKKO SECURITIES	14,234.5	40	19.0	5,136.40	38	15.70
4	3	DAIWA SECURITIES	11,857.2	44	15.8	5,465.00	39	16.70
5	6	DEUTSCHE BANK	1,379.6	17	1.8	671.40	5	2.10
6	5	INDTRIAL BK OF JAP	1117.4	12	1.5	833.20	6	2.50
7	7	LONG–TRM CRDT BK/JAP	1,038.9	7	1.4	550.00	3	1.70
8	8	BANK OF TOKYO	983.4	7	1.3	520.00	3	1.60
9	11	PARIBAS CAP MKTS GRP.	932.3	5	1.3	250.00	1	0.80
10	14	W.DTSCHE LNDSBNK GIROZ.	562.9	5	0.8	220.90	3	0.70
11	–	DRESDNER BANK	477.1	6	0.6	–	–	–
12	23	AMSTERDAM–ROTTERDAM B	467.1	4	0.6	77.80	1	0.20
13=	–	SUMITOMO BANK	300.0	1	0.4	–	–	–
13=	–	NATWEST CAPITAL MKTS	300.0	1	0.4	–	–	–
13=	–	DAI–ICHI KANGYO GROUP	300.0	1	0.4	–	–	–
13=	20	MITSUBISHI FIN INT'L	300.0	1	0.4	100.00	1	0.30

17	–	COMMERZBANK	214.8	4	0.3	–	–	–
18	–	CREDIT LYONNAIS	211.8	1	0.3	–	–	–
19	–	NORINSHUKIN INT'L	200.0	1	0.3	–	–	–
20	15	JP MORGAN	169.2	1	0.2	200.00	1	0.60
21	–	WOOD GUNDY	128.5	1	0.2	–	–	–
22	–	BERLNR HNDLS-& FRKFTR B	108.9	1	0.2	–	–	–
23	25	DG BK DTSCHE GENOSSFTS	106.8	2	0.1	53.10	1	0.20
24=	10	NIPP. KNGYO KKUMRU (EUR)	100.0	1	0.1	320.50	3	1.00
24=		YAMATANE SECS. (EUR)	100.0	1	0.1	–	–	–

Source: Annual Financing Report, Euromoney, March, 1990, ps.16 & 22

EXHIBIT 13b

Top 50 arrangers – syndicated loans

Rank 89	Rank 88	Bank	1989 Amount $m	1989 # iss	1989 Share %	1988 Amount $m	1988 # iss	1988 Share %
1	1	CITICORP	64,959.80	200	12.18	63,171.50	222	12.14
2	5	MANUFACTURERS HANOV	56,873.80	139	10.67	29,659.10	132	5.70
3	3	BANKERS TRUST	45,381.70	126	8.51	30,494.50	147	5.92
4	4	CHASE INVESTMENT BAN	33,088.10	204	6.20	29,872.50	207	5.74
5	9	BANK OF AMERCA	26,797.90	84	6.03	15,606.70	86	3.00
6	2	JP MORGAN	20,183.70	60	3.78	45,230.60	116	8.69
7	6	CHEMICAL BANK	18,563.20	62	3.48	24,938.50	85	4.79
8	10	NAT'L WESTMINSTER BK	17,671.70	73	3.31	14,688.10	83	2.82
9	7	BARCLAYS BANK	17,066.00	81	3.20	16,017.20	86	3.08
10	11	1ST NAT'L BK/CHICAGO	15,402.90	64	2.89	12,504.80	52	2.40
11	15	SG WARBURG	14,991.90	36	2.81	6,368.60	48	1.22
12	12	CRDT SUISSE 1ST BOSTO	10,627.70	41	1.99	11,772.20	52	2.26
13	48	ROYAL BANK OF CANADA	9,950.42	35	1.87	1,937.44	12	0.37
14	8	MIDLAND MONTAGU	9,643.48	73	1.81	15,764.70	74	3.03
15	21	HONG KONG BANK GROU	7,378.07	30	1.38	5,079.93	49	0.98
16	17	SECURITY PACIFIC	6,874.09	79	1.29	6,308.54	50	1.21
17	18	CREDIT LYONNAIS	6,421.90	29	1.20	6,236.93	56	1.20
18	13	SWISS BANK CORP.	6,096.11	31	1.14	11,512.60	38	2.21
19	31	LLOYDS BK CAP.MKTS.GR	5,877.82	33	1.10	3,168.65	27	0.61
20	22	TORONTO-DOMINION BA	4,819.04	30	0.90	4,882.69	22	0.94

Source: Annual Financing Report, Euromoney, March, 1990, ps.16 & 22

It can therefore be said that the Eurocurrency markets had a good year in 1989. They continued to play a major role in the flow of capital from surplus to deficit units seemingly with considerable operational efficiency as spreads continued to narrow in the face of mounting competition.

We now look at some of the changes in the financial markets anticipated for the 1990s.

The Future of the Financial Markets

The future of the financial markets is hard to predict. There are some trends which a careful observer can discern, however. Also, there are some plans which are being implemented in order to cope with a set of expectations about the future of the financial markets. No one is more involved in these plans than Mr. Nicholas Giordano, president of the Philadelphia Stock Exchange. In his address to the Baden Baden conference he considered "the shape of the securities markets in the 1990's." His talk was intended to give insight into the thinking of his exchange and the planning for the 1990's as regards the markets as a whole. The issues were:

> Some of the issues that we are discussing, will give you insight into our thinking and planning for the 90's as respects the markets as a whole.
>
> 1. Technology
>
> - We are building a computer complex throughout the U.S. securities markets that will accommodate the trading, comparison, and clearance of one billion shares per day. The one billion total does not include derivative products such as options or trading in the over-the-counter markets. The accommodation of this level of activity assumes that all components of the U.S. markets will receive their proportionate share of this volume, such as the exchanges in Chicago, California, as well as Philadelphia and New York, and that other markets such as options, OTC trading, bonds,

etc., will be similarly affected. Another critical component is member firm or broker/dealer readiness and the ability of clearing corporations to process this volume efficiently. They must all be ready. The bad news is that their readiness must be financed with daily volume of 150 million share days. Perhaps if we stopped planning for the billion share day it might come sooner.

2. Preparing for Disaster

- What has also been on our minds these days is the readiness to react to a disaster at one of our Exchanges. We have retained outside experts to advise us on the most effective method to support a trading floor or a computer facility that has been eliminated by a fire, earthquake, or some other disaster. We experienced both a fire on Wall Street, and an earthquake in San Francisco in 1989. We were able to recover relatively quickly but it reminded us of our vulnerability and we hope that by the end of 1990 to know whether a proper backup facility, perhaps jointly owned, would be cost effective as well as practical.

3. Payment for Order Flow

- A relatively new and possibly dangerous trend developing in our listed marketplace is the payment by market makers and specialists for customer order flow. This trend is being particularly exacerbated by the third market. The questions being raised are:

a. Is the public customer receiving the benefit of this payment? and

b. Is the public customer's execution being compromised in any way?

There seems to be no practical way to prohibit this practice because hard dollar payments can be converted to soft dollar payments, and such soft dollar payments are limited only to the imagination of the soft dollar payer. In the case of hard dollar payments, the retail firm is required to disclose the practice to his customer on the trade confirmation.

4. Multiple Trading of Options

- The options exchanges in the U.S. have been told by the SEC (Securities and Exchange Commission) to adopt a linkage plan by June 30, 1990. This resulted from the SEC's May 1989 decision to abolish the lottery system used to list stock options exclusively by the five options exchanges.

The PHLX led an effort to propose a linkage system and was joined by the Pacific Stock Exchange and the NYSE. In September of 1989, a concept was advanced to the Commission that would enable the markets to be linked in an ITS type system at a cost of $3 -- $6 million. The CBOE and AMEX subsequently authorized their own study which suggested that an ITS type linkage is not sufficiently sophisticated. They have since proposed their own linkage system which deals only with ten contract orders. We have met several times since January and will be meeting again next week in Florida at which time the PHLX will be advancing a system with time priority. This will undoubtedly cause controversy but may in fact be the only system that will treat all market centers and customers on a fair basis. I hope the Options Exchanges can voluntarily come to some agreement on a linkage plan, because if we do not do so voluntarily, the SEC has indicated that they will impose their own brand of linkage. And I think we all know what will happen if the government decides to build the system.

In Philadelphia we have always believed that multiple trading has more risks than benefits. But, if in fact we have to be faced with multiple trading, then there must be an electronic integration of the markets.

5. Group of 30

Brokerage and banking executives from the major money centers have been meeting for the past few years and are now making recommendations for the clearance and settlement of securities transactions that strike at the fundamental principles of clearance. The Group of 30 is recommending the following proposals, among others, for implementation in 1992:

a. Stock transactions be settled in three days instead of the current five day settlement.

b. That the stock certificate be removed from the owner and placed in a depository. They call this dematerialization.

6. The SEC versus the CFTC

The stock market crash of 1987 taught us many things and has left many scars. In fact almost three years later we have still not recovered from that day -- but of particular note it taught us that the stock options and futures markets are in fact linked but regulated separately. And since that fateful day 30 months ago, several other incidents have taken place which make it quite clear that the regulation of stock related products in the U.S. is badly in need of reform. There have been a number of market experiences that brought us vivid reminders of the October 19, 1987 event and the fact that very little in the way of fundamental reform has taken place.

In August of 1989, the point was made ever so clear when the Federal Court of the Seventh Circuit, based in Chicago, rendered its now infamous decision that the CIP product was not a security but rather a future because it has elements of futurity in it. This was a product invented by the PHLX, copied by the AMEX, and now copied by exchanges around the world and is in fact trading successfully in Toronto, Canada. CIPS has interesting features:

a. S & P 500 index

b. Cash settled

c. Pays dividends

d. Perpetual -- looks like GM

e. Cash out

f. Appeals to the public investor

We seem to be the only country in the world with such split regulation, and as a consequence, this very worthwhile product which was invented in Philadelphia, and approved by our Securities Regulator, can only be witnessed from afar rather than traded by a U.S. Securities Exchange.

The Multi-Trillion Dollar Financial Pie

As we look toward the 90's and beyond, we see a growing financial marketplace -- I like to call it the multi-trillion dollar financial pie -- and each of us must determine how best to obtain our slice of that pie.

The clues to our future success may be best learned by reviewing the past decade or two and considering why certain financial products were successful:

- Treasury Bond Futures - the volatility of interest rates and the vast holdings by world wide bankers and financiers fueled this product.

- Currency Options - the many fold increase in international commerce, exposing so many more businessmen to the instability of the dollar to other currencies.

- Energy Futures - since the late 70's we came to realize our vulnerability to the rising and falling prices of energy. Result -- a very active contract on the New York Mercantile Exchange in fuel contracts.

Stock Market Volatility

The 80's certainly taught us that stock market volatility is here in a new dimension and likely to stay. It also taught us that the pools of managed money are growing at frightening paces, and the combination of the two guarantees the need to be able to hedge portfolios either with options, futures, or some other form of basket or index instrument.

Well, where are the products of the 90's and beyond? Tell me where the businessman will be exposed and I'll tell you which financial products will be successful. Certainly we can begin to see some shapes forming, such as:

1. Foreign Stock Portfolio Accumulation

   As Foreign stock markets become more viable due to increased technology, increased regulation, increased wealth of the citizens in these countries, and increased awareness of emerging companies in Europe and Asia, the public shares of these companies will be finding their way into more and more portfolios -- and consequently the need to protect against volatility. This protection will take the form of foreign stock market index hedging. That hedging may involve a transaction in a foreign currency derivative product. The successful Nikkei warrants trading in the U.S. are an example of this emerging trend.

2. Inflation

   Will it return? If so, how do we protect ourselves?

3. Medical Costs

   This is a seemingly insurmountable problem to the U.S. businessman -- how can we help?

4. Skilled Labor

   There is a shortage ahead. This will be a major problem for businesses in the U.S. as well as in Europe and Asia. Is there a way to serve this need?

5. Weather

   Sometimes a calamity like the weather should be hedged against. Is there not a way to shift the risk of weather to a willing speculator? Maybe the answer to this is yes.

I am sure you can identify many more risks to the businessman that are emerging. The challenge to the financial markets is to develop a financial product to meet these needs. Such a contract must be relatively simple and easy to understand by the businessman and the potential investor. The market place creator must then be prepared to educate both of these users.

Electronic Trading and 24 Hour Trading

The 90's will undoubtedly bring a clash between man and the machine -- it has been predicted for almost 20 years now -- and perhaps the 90's will finally witness the contest in earnest.

My personal opinion is that an auction market system with the ability to receive the maximum assistance from technology is the superior system of trading. It should have the following features:

- Auto-Ex - small orders
- Quote - automatically
- Audit Trail Technology
- Paperless as possible
- etc.

But the ability for humans to interact must never be lost.

We in Philadelphia have chosen the human approach to 24 hour trading. Today our trading hours are from 4:30 a.m. to 2:30 p.m. and 7:00 p.m. -- 11:00 p.m. Beginning in September, we will be extending our hours between the 11:00 p.m. close and the 4:30 a.m. opening so that our new hours will permit trading from 7:00 p.m. -- 2:30 p.m. the following day. These hours (20 1/2 in total) incorporate the business hours of the entire world. As long as we have the people prepared to commit to these hours, it should be an effective trading center for foreign currency options.

Now the competing approach to this is Globex -- a type of electronic trading system that operates off hours and is centered at the CME. Entry to the system occurs off the floor.

Perhaps both of these systems are compatible in the

90's, but certainly the likelihood of greater and greater uses of electronic trading will be a fact in the coming 10 years. We now offer a preview of the chapters to come.

Preview of Chapters

In chapter one, Professor Ross looks at the state of the discipline of Finance and the driving forces behind financial innovation.

The revolution in the financial markets reflected in new markets and products owes its origin to academic researchers. The design and the valuation of new instruments by financial engineers is the financial equivalent of the building of bridges and airplanes by engineers. The level of precision and the quality of the scientific inferences differ significantly, however.

Professor Ross then looks at the foundation of financial innovations. He finds that quantum leaps in financial theory combined with entrepreneurship and technology explain the dramatic changes in the financial markets. The rise of financial institutions and institutional trading also plays a major role.

Financial innovation, argues Professor Ross, arises as a "natural adjunct of the supply and demand of aging constrained participants, and transactions costs help to shape the form of the new institutional features."

Institutions, because of their size and opaqueness, generate demand for certain types of assets and have an incentive to undertake certain risks. Modern finance theory, unfortunately, does not incorporate the role of institutions and treats them as "big investors. Unless this changes, we will remain uninformed and uninformative on the wave of institutional innovation."

Chapter two deals with the nature and the consequences of mergers and acquisitions. Professor E. Han Kim argues that the evidence on the consequences of mergers and acquisitions does not provide in any way for a basis to change public policy in order to limit or to ban mergers and acquisitions.

Dr. Kim summarizes very ably the relevant literature on mergers and acquisitions and concludes that the weight of the evidence confirms:

1. Stockholders of target firms are clear winners in acquisition cases.
2. Stockholders of acquiring firms realize positive abnormal returns unless they are involved in cases with intense competition among multiple bidders.
3. There exists no wealth transfers between stockholders and bondholders. The gains to stockholders did not come at the expense of the bondholders.
4. The biggest losers in a bidding war are the stockholders of bidding firms making unsuccessful bids in a multiple bidder contest.
5. Successful corporate takeovers are wealth enhancing events: "The combined value of the target and acquiring firms increases substantially."

The remaining issues yet to be fully resolved in merger cases are the effects on competition and on employment.

Chapter three analyzes the present-day foreign exchange market from the perspective of its institutions and practices in the United States. Although the focus is on the U.S. market, the worldwide nature of foreign exchange trading makes most of the observations and analysis applicable to the global market. The emphasis is on the largely unregulated over-the-counter activity and its core, the interbank market.

Using data from the 1989 central bank surveys of activity in each key trading center, the paper reviews possible causes for the rapid expansion in trading activity in recent years. The author emphasizes the importance of the removal of short- and long-term capital controls in Europe and the Far East during the 1980s. He also points to the institutional structure of the market which leads in many instances to a multiplicative series of transactions when commercial customers which to enter into outright forward or cross currency contracts, or when marketmakers find themselves given an unwanted position by a counterparty. He suggests further research into the actual values of such multiplicative factors would be useful.

The author also stresses the importance of the swap forward market as a venue for speculation in interest rate differentials and the use of the spot market as the preferred venue for exchange rate speculation.

In addition to rapid increases in volume during the 1980s, the author discusses the reasons for the introduction of a viable foreign exchange options market, citing a better understanding of the dynamics of option pricing and the desire of investment banks, commodity brokers, and the Philadelphia and Chicago Mercantile exchanges to challenge the commercial banks' domination of the foreign exchange market.

A variety of other issues, including reasons for the slow introduction of screen-based trading and the likely impact of the recent BIS capital requirement on forward contracts, are also discussed. The intent throughout the paper is to emphasize important institutional details of the market that can provide insight into patterns of pricing, firm entry, and trading practices.

Chapter four provides an illustration of the new theories of "competition in regulation." Under the influence of benign authorities and deregulation, the Swedish money and bond markets, begun first in 1980, had by the spring of 1987 introduced all the major internationally traded instruments: a liquid short and long market in fixed-income instruments (including a large market in commercial paper), futures on several underlying bonds and Treasury bills, options on Treasury Notes, FRN's with both cap's and floor's, a deposit market with FRA's, interest-rate swaps, etc. Liquidity was high, not least because of the immense turnover. In the spring 1987, the average daily turnover on the money and bond market was over SEK 40 billion, corresponding to an annual total of ten times the Gross Domestic Product. Of the daily average amounts, about 20 billion was in futures and 5 billion in interest-rate options (in terms of underlying values).

In September, 1987, the head of the Trade Union Council (LO) unexpectedly proposed a tax on market turnover in order to "reduce the overly large and socially worthless activities on the money market." The government immediately agreed, believing that the new tax would mollify the unions into lower wage demands. A tax on money and bond market transactions was accordingly instituted from January 1, 1989.

As a result of the tax, turnover had by the end of 1989 fallen by 95 percent. Since a much larger part today of the total stock of bonds outstanding is liquid, perhaps it is more correct to say that efficiency in the market has fallen by 98-99 percent. The futures market is almost dead, being limited to one contract and a few hundred million in daily turnover. Interest-rate options have all but vanished.

The limited turnover has had the predictable consequence of increasing interest-rate volatility. This is bad in itself, not least because it severely impedes Central Bank monetary policy. It is, however, even more serious in the Swedish setting, where liquidity risk has always been highly priced. As a result, the spread between Government and housing mortgage bonds (having virtually no credit risk) has widened from less than 20 to over 60 basis points.

A further predictable effect of the lower turnover has also been to increase interest-rate volatility in times of market unrest. The growing economic crises in Sweden during the spring of 1990 has seen not only a rise in interest levels to some 15 percent but also a marked increase in daily volatility.

The market has reacted to the tax by resorting to untaxed instruments: FRA's on the short side and interest-rate swaps on the longer. After all currency regulations were lifted on July 1, 1989, the market is also gradually moving abroad.

Quite in line with the dialectics of the theory of "competition in regulation," the tax is now being scrapped. The turnover tax on the money market was abolished on April 15, 1990, and the corresponding tax on the share market will be halved (to 1 percent for a round trip) on January 1, 1991.

Chapter five presents an equilibrium model of the determinants of risk premiums in forward exchange rates. A continuous-time investment-consumption model under uncertainty is employed. This model is less restrictive than previous studies and it can therefore examine the interactions among many economic variables that affect the risk premium.

First, a synthesis of previous results regarding the determinants of risk premiums in forward rates is provided. It is shown that risk premiums are functions of the covariances of exchange rates with national price indices and with deviations from PPP. Moreover, risk premiums depend on net supplies of outside nominal assets and on net foreign investment positions of countries.

This paper shows that the covariance between a country's price index and the exchange rate determines whether the country's supply of outside nominal assets influences the size and the sign of the risk premium. That is, if changes in the country's price index are not a major contributing factor to variations in the exchange rate, then a change in the supply of its nominal outside assets will not affect the risk premium.

When two countries are of equal size and when they follow similar inflationary policies, the major determinants of the risk premium will be their net foreign investment positions and the covariance between changes in the exchange rate and deviations from PPP. It appears that a major source of time-variation in the risk premium is the nonstationarity of the covariance between deviations from PPP and exchange rate changes. Finally, these results, which are initially developed using a two-country framework, are extended to the case of many countries. This enables us to show how economic variables of one country can affect the risk premium in the forward rate between two other countries.

In chapter six the authors analyze the price and quantity responses of firms reacting to real currency movements in a dynamic setting with imperfect (quantity) competition, with a view to understand currency pass through behavior. The analysis examines dynamic economies (learning), with temporary and permanent currency changes, in the context of products which can be strategic substitutes or complements. Given a currency depreciation, strategic complements, no economies for either firm and/or economies for the foreign firm alone, will result in a no-pass-through ("skimming") pricing strategy by the home firm, while strategic substitutes and/or learning for the home firm alone will result in pass-through ("penetration") pricing strategies by the home firm. The chapter integrates a number of the previously derived results on currency pass-through, and suggests possibilities of extensions to consider features such as differentiated products, generalized conjectures, etc.

Chapter seven presents evidence that technical analysis in the foreign exchange markets could pay off handsomely. The author argues that there is substantial evidence that well-designed technical strategies can generate economically and statistically significant risk-adjusted measured profits in foreign exchange markets. These profits may not be economic profits either because of measurement errors of several types or because of time-varying risk premia. While there is much evidence that expected returns vary in foreign exchange markets, there is little evidence that these movements are due to changes in risk premia. The few tests examining whether trading profits are due to risk premia find little evidence this is so. The chapter should be of special interest to traders (speculators) in the foreign exchange markets and to scholars and regulators concerned with the efficiency of those markets.

Chapter eight deals with optimal global asset mix of stocks, bonds and futures currency contracts. The authors are able to show that a fully hedged portfolio is <u>not</u> optimal under all but the most extreme circumstances. These findings contradict those published by Perold and Schulman and make a major contribution to the literature on optimal hedging.

Chapter nine presents very interesting evidence that the payoffs from international diversification may not be as promising as historically believed. The dramatic cross-sectional reduction in risk found by Solnik and others were based on very short investment horizons. The risk-reducing benefits of international diversification are shown to be greatly attenuated once longer investment horizons are considered. The reason for the diminishing benefits to international diversification is the increasing correlation of returns across countries by length of holding period. If returns across international markets have important cross positive autocorrelations of various orders, longer holding periods will be more highly correlated than shorter holding periods. The authors demonstrate how this effect differs from the time diversification literature. Indeed, time diversification argues that longer holding periods act like greater diversification, whereas the authors find that longer holding periods reduces the risk-reducing benefits of diversification.

Chapter ten attempts to detect lead-lag relationships between four major equity market indexes: New York S&P 500, Tokyo Nikkei, London FT-30, and the Frankfurt DAX. The study covers the time period April 22, 1987, when the Wall Street Journal started reporting international stock market indexes, through December 31, 1988. For analytical purposes the information is divided in three data sets covering the time periods before, during and after the market crash. Unidirectional, feedback and contemporaneous causality are analyzed based on the Granger and the Modified Sims tests. The authors test two hypotheses: (i) the crash was initiated in the United States and (ii) the crash was initiated overseas.

The Granger's tests find little causality relationships between the four market indexes for the periods before, during and after the market crash of October, 1987. The exception is New York leading Tokyo, during the period of the crash. However, the additional tests designed to detect possible linkages indicate that contemporaneous causality was present during the period of the crash, September 23, 1987 through November 23, 1987. Moreover, these tests also show that during the period of the crash there was an increase in causality, with New York leading Tokyo and Frankfurt, and feedback between New York and London, London and Tokyo, and London and Frankfurt. The modified Sims tests indicate that New York led Tokyo and London during the period of the crash. However, the significant coefficients can be due to correlation rather than causation.

In summary, the tests suggest that New York appears to have played an important role during the October, 1987 market crash. Tokyo, on the other hand, appeared to lag the other markets. Nevertheless, contemporaneous causality was also present during the period of the crash. The authors' empirical results indicate, partially, that the United States played a leading role during the crash; but, at the same time, the authors observed strong simultaneous causality and even feedback between markets. There is statistical evidence to suggest that both mechanisms were at work during the crash: first, the international fundamental common factor suggested by Roll with its emphasis that the crash started outside the U.S. and, second, the belief of American and Japanese institutional investors that the crash started in the United States.

Chapter eleven looks at the information and price adjustment process in the U.S. and Japan.

Portfolio managers in the United States have increasingly turned to stocks listed on foreign markets in recent years both to augment returns and to reduce risk. In spite of the success of these international diversification efforts, many investors remain wary of foreign stocks because of the perception that the markets they trade on are not as efficient as the U.S. exchanges. While there is fairly widespread agreement among financial economists that an efficient market is one in which information is reflected quickly in prices, there is remarkably little evidence on whether the price adjustment process is indeed slower in foreign markets.

This chapter develops a simple measure for the price adjustment coefficient, from returns data and for various return intervals, and uses it to compare the speed of price adjustment on stocks in the S&P 500 with those in the Nikkei 500. The derivation of the measure draws on the description of the return process contained in Amihud and Mendelson as a combination of an intrinsic value adjustment factor and a noise term, and uses the information in various return intervals to arrive at the estimate of the adjustment coefficient.

The approach developed here is used to estimate price adjustment coefficients for the firms that comprise the S&P 500, trading on the New York Stock Exchange, and those firms that comprise the Nikkei 500, trading on the Tokyo Stock Exchange, using five years of daily returns data, from January 1983 to December 1987. The authors find strong evidence that price adjustment processes are very different for the two groups. There is some evidence of a lagged price adjustment for stocks in the S&P 500, with about 92% of new information being reflected in prices by the end of the day on which it is released. In contrast, there is evidence of market overreaction for the Japanese stocks, with one-day to three-day price adjustment coefficients significantly greater than one. To illustrate that these differences are not due to outliers, the authors report the same pattern in the median statistics for the price adjustment coefficients. Both the t statistics, testing the hypothesis that means of the two groups are equal, and chi-squared statistics, from a Wilcox on rank sum test, indicate that the differences across the two groups are significant at the 99% level. If we define speed of adjustment in terms of the speed with which the price adjustment coefficients converge to one, the median statistics seem to indicate that prices adjust slightly more quickly for Japanese stocks than for the S&P 500 stocks.

The reasons for the differences in price adjustment behavior are not clear. While one would have expected the stocks in the S&P 500, which have more private information generated and disseminated about them by analysts and institutions, to have much speedier price adjustment paths and be more likely to evidence market overreaction than stocks in the Nikkei 500, the reverse seems to be true in the data. One explanation may be that private information is impounded in prices through extensive insider trading in Japanese stocks. Since other investors can learn from these trades, albeit noisily, about the information, prices may reflect the information just as effectively. This explanation would also be consistent with the market overreaction observed on Japanese stocks, if one is willing to accept the arguments of some that trading sometimes results in prices overshooting true values. The fact that prices adjust much more quickly to new information for Japanese stocks may be viewed as evidence that Japanese markets are more efficient, though this has to be weighed against the higher volatility induced by market overreaction.

Chapter twelve provides a framework for the valuations of interest rate swaps in general with applications to foreign currency swaps and options on swaps. Many important features of swap contracts including discrete reset dates, lags between reset dates and payment dates, arbitrary index maturities, various averaging rules and option features are explicitly modeled and incorporated into the valuation procedure.

A simple stochastic term structure model is used to obtain closed form solutions to many swap contracts. Options on swaps ("swaptions") are also priced in this setting to examine the value of such options when the underlying swaps have different terms and contractual features.

The chapter also provides a brief treatment of default risk consequences on swap valuation. The swap spreads due to default are computed for different credit risks and interpreted. The differential effects of credit risk under different term structure scenarios are characterized.

Chapter thirteen looks at exchange rate jumps and currency options pricing.

The valuation of option contracts depends critically on the sample path of returns exhibited by the option's underlying asset. Thus the pricing of currency options depends largely on the distributional properties of exchange rate changes. Early models of currency option valuation assumed that exchange rate changes follow a standard diffusion process with constant mean and variance. However, such models exhibit systematic pricing biases. The patterns of these biases suggest that spot currency prices may possess random jumps. The purpose of Dr. Tucker's paper is to derive and test a model of currency options which incorporates the possibility of such jumps. Specifically, Dr. Tucker adapts a model, attributable to Professor Robert Marton, that entails the existence of lognormally distributed jumps, and demonstrates that such a model exhibits superior forecasting than a foreign exchange option model which ignores the jump structure.

After a brief literature survey and description of the sample data (transactions currency option prices provided by the Philadelphia Stock Exchange), Dr. Tucker tests for the presence of jumps in the historic sample paths of exchange rate changes for five major trading currencies: the British pound, Canadian dollar, Deutsche mark, Japanese yen, and the Swiss franc. Employing a maximum likelihood test procedure developed by Professors Clifford Ball and Walter Torous, Dr. Tucker documents that jumps indeed occur for daily currency returns (Table I). These jumps occur infrequently but are large, and may be associated with central bank intervention and realignment activities. Also, these jumps are found to be unsystematic, in the sense that they are not linearly correlated with U.S. stock market returns (Table II).

Following a description and comparison of the two currency option pricing models, the paper's principle empirical results are reported (Table III). The results demonstrate that the pricing model which incorporates jumps has significantly greater accuracy than the competing no-jumps model. Specifically, the inclusion of the jump component appears to reduce forecasting errors by 50 percent, on average. This improvement appears to be consistent across all option categories examined.

Thus, Dr. Tucker's research implies that much of the pricing bias exhibited in earlier studies may be accounted for by the recognition and inclusion of potential jumps in exchange rate changes. His work therefore has significance for the valuation of currency options and the hedging of exchange exposure.

Chapter fourteen offers a new theory of foreign direct investment. Domestic oligopolists may gain a purely strategic advantage by precommitting to foreign production when faced with exchange rate uncertainty.

The proposed model is a two-period model where a unique symmetric sequential equilibrium in mixed strategies is endogenously determined in the marketplace, and the probability of precommitment by firms depends on the implicit variance of the random exchange rate.

This is the first theoretical model of foreign direct investment which endogenizes the effects of exchange rate uncertainty and develops a rigorous model steeped in the game- theoretic literature. It goes well beyond the other FDI model for it adds the stability of an important financial variable to the existing market structure as an explanatory variable for FDI.

Chapter fifteen deals with the problem of debt overhang for sovereign nations. Sovereign lending takes place in the absence of a well defined body of bankruptcy law. This implies that: i) lenders may not have the means to seize assets in settlement of their claims, and ii) borrowers may be unable to obtain a 'fresh start' by having claims against them legally discharged by a third party. Most studies of sovereign lending focus on the former and its implications for debt repudiation. In this study we focus on the latter, the debt overhang problem, and its implication for the efficiency of rescheduling. In the model advocated by the authors, a country requires an injection of new funds which, in addition to increasing the welfare of the borrowing country, will also generate a state contingent improvement in the value of the reorganized loan. The authors find that, under some conditions, the efficiency of the reorganization is impeded by the existence of asymmetric information in that mutually beneficial projects are not funded.

Recent Developments in International Banking
and Finance, S.J. Khoury (editor)

CHAPTER I

Innovation in the Financial Markets

Stephen A. Ross

Yale Management School

I am grateful for helpful comments to Joel Demski, Phil Dybvig, Bengt Holmstrom, Jon Ingersoll, Offer Kella and Richard Roll. Any errors are my own. (See Stephen A. Ross (1989) for a more analytic exposition of some of the points in this talk.)

I. Introduction

I began my career in finance in the early 1970's with an idea for saving corporate taxes that a friend and I had thought up. We had observed that the U.S. tax code permitted corporations to amortize discount debt obligations on a straight line basis for tax purposes rather than requiring scientific amortization. This seemingly innocuous wrinkle in the code meant that by issuing a straight bond and calling all of its coupons and its balloon payment individual discount bonds the corporation could get tax writeoffs in the early years that were more than twice the actual coupon payments. In other words, with no change in tax flow, the corporation could more than double its tax offsets.

In the then world of 50% corporate taxes, the present value of issuing such a bond was so great that the company would actually be better off by giving them away. Armed with our new insight, we headed down to Wall Street and a well known but anonymous investment bank expecting a warm greeting and a great reward.

Unfortunately, early wealth was not to be our destiny. Not only were the bankers skeptical, they brought in a major accounting firm to examine our product. One of the senior tax partners of the firm pronounced that there were actually no such benefits and try as we would, we were unable to convince them otherwise. As a postscript, a few years later some companies actually followed our approach and reaped enormous benefits from it, and it took nearly a year for the IRS to close this loophole.

Now I am not sure that all of this activity devoted to slipping through loopholes in the tax code is of any social benefit, and I ask you to please excuse it as youthful excess, but I must say that I have often reflected on that incident and I have learned much from it. Not to mention the good relations that it has helped me to establish over the years with that same investment bank.

But, this is all of only historical significance and probably seems a bit other worldly to the academics and finance practitioners of today. For one thing, it just doesn't work that way now. The investment banks regularly call on academics and academics and former academics are visible and line members of these firms. When we write our academic papers on financial products, it is not uncommon for practitioners to call and ask when we expect them to be done, and often they send self addressed envelopes for us to send them out in 'hot off the press'. Nor is it a one way street; professors are as anxious to read about the latest wrinkle in the work of the traders as is the other way around.

All of this is a tribute to the profound changes that have occurred in the financial markets over the past two decades. Financial entrepreneurs have created markets and products which owe their very existence to the work of academic researchers. In their hands, a staid old business has been transformed into a field on the cutting edge of mathematics and economic science. Indeed, some would say that economics has at last arrived as a science. If the 'rocket scientists' have not yet taken over the world of finance, they dominate the trading floor and they have become indispensible. Is this a permanent change? Of course, however much we may long for a more comfortable and predictable world of simple underwritings, it is gone forever. The 'quants' are not even the first to go, although the recent Drexel Burnham bankruptcy threw a necessary splash of cold water on an overheated market.

The explosive changes in the financial markets are so varied as to defy analysis, but, broadly they seem to fall into two classes. First, there are the new securities and their markets. Beginning with puts and calls we have moved on to Euromarkets, mortgage pass throughs and CMO's, strips, straps and swaps, putable convertibles, primes and scores and S&P futures and all of the other instruments that inhabit the financial zoo. Second, there are the dynamic trading strategies that make heavy use of the new instruments. Basket and program trading, the asset pricing theories that now characterize different types of money management, and the various incarnations of portfolio insurance, have changed financial decision making as dramatically as the available array of instruments has changed.[1]

As financial engineers, we both design and value the new instruments

---

[1] See Miller (1986) for a more exhaustive list of financial innovations as well as an exciting analysis of the recent history of financial innovation. An interesting database of financial innovations is provided by Tufano (1988).

and strategies. Like engineers who use physics, financial engineers use the techniques of modern finance to build the financial equivalent of bridges and airplanes. Unfortunately, though, when asked to explain why all of this is happening and why it takes the forms that it does, our answers are much more timid.

II. Why Innovation

No phenomenon as complex as the changes that have occurred in financial markets can admit of a simple explanation. There are many forces at work. We have begun our story with the most obvious one, the change in technology. Whatever the forces of demand and supply for such innovations, it would not have come about without the incredible advances in our understanding of the dynamics of financial markets. The theories of option pricing developed in the 1970's along with their attendant asset pricing theories and models opened up the science of finance. However badly man might wish to go to the moon, it was not possible until the rocket was invented.

We now have the ability to design and price financial strategies and instruments to serve an enormous variety of purposes. From hedging out exchange rate risk for a multinational corporation, to designing investment strategies for retirement planning financial engineering provides the way. But, given the technology and the obvious interplay between the technology and those who use it, who demands it and why?

It seems to me that there are two major forces at work that have fueled the entrepreneurship that, in turn, has used the technology to generate the wave of financial innovation in the world markets. First, our financial markets have become institutional markets. Institutions are often the most significant traders and holders of active positions. In studying their role, I have found it useful to characterize financial institutions on a scale from transparent through translucent to opaque. Most mutual funds are transparent institutions. Insurance companies and savings and loan organizations are opaque. Pension funds are translucent institutions, and transparent institutions are pass throughs that trivially and rather directly reflect retail forces. Opaque institutions are clouded and veiled from the view of participants and, at best, are only weak reflections of those forces. The scale is an attempt to array the participants in the financial markets according to the extent to which they are controlled, constrained and regulated in their pursuit of the financial goals of the constituents they ostensibly serve.

The most unconstrained individual is the retail player. Only slightly less transparent, many open end mutual funds are really just efficient vehicles for individuals to hold securities. The control and agency problems are manageable and relatively innocuous. The participants in the fund are continuously informed about the assets of the fund, and the principal compensation for management is simply a percentage of the assets under management. Compared with more opaque institutions there is not a lot of scope for a divergence in interests between management and the participants.

By contrast, in opaque institutions the monitoring, bonding and control costs, i.e., agency problems, are most severe. Information is asymmetric between the participants and the institution, and the need for control and contractual structures to permit them to function is so critical that they essentially define these institutions. A depositor in an S&L has almost no knowledge of the particular loans the institution is making. Are they local or national, secured or not? Little of this is visible to the participant.

The situation is even more clouded for the insurance industry. How many insurance customers know the investment strategies of their insurance companies? The insurance company is paid a premium which it invests and out of which it must pay claims. The very integrity of the contract between the insured and the company depends on the company's investment strategy, yet this is generally invisible. Even more removed is the typical manufacturing companies whose financial activities are generally sidelines to their main businesses.

The monitoring and bonding requirements of institutions are often so well established that they become part of a regulatory environment through the workings of political economy. For our purposes it doesn't matter whether monitoring and agency restrictions arise from the natural needs of the market relations between institutions and participants or whether they are imposed exogenously by the government. Although, presumably in the latter case an argument can be made that regulation serves as an efficient device for establishing contracts that the private sector would have written anyway or of solving free rider problems in contract design and enforcement that would be too costly or incentive incompatible for the private sector to implement.

It is by no means clear that the demand and supply for financial assets by opaque institutions simply reflects retail forces. In the prevailing equilibrium models of securities markets, demand comes from individuals solving portfolio optimization problems. But, when we take account of the intervening contractual relations under which opaque institutions operate, it seems heroic to think that they mirror these forces. Furthermore, given the significance of opaque institutions in the market it seems unlikely that retail forces and individual portfolio optimization will be dominant in price formation. The only hope for this position is that somehow or other these institutions in aggregate will act like individuals.

Of course, to the extent that credit restrictions and the like prevent individuals from behaving as the unconstrained players of the simple optimization models, and to the extent that regulations restrict their actions they, too, can be a focus for a different description of supply and demand at even the retail level. In this case, though, it is often large institutions that force innovation. For example, the options markets began as retail markets. Institutions saw options trading as a way to develop retail interest where the alternative was to try to solve the agency (and regulatory) problems associated with extending credit to retail clients. Instead of having a client take a beta of 2 position in a beta 1 stock by leveraging, options provided a limited liability approach.[2]

To view the financial markets as institutional markets is not to say

---

2 Similarly, government intervention brings other constraints on activities that cause deviations from unconstrained maximization. Taxes, for example, as Miller (1986) has argued, are a source of much of the motivation for financial innovation. To the extent to which the government induces payment, taxes will introduce agency-like constraints. We will not deal explicitly with taxes and Miller is certainly correct that much financial innovation is the effort to deal with an ever changing tax code, but what we say will be consistent with such tax induced innovation.

that they are solely markets where institutions operate, but, rather, that institutions are major and significant forces. To summarize, institutions are financial market players whose activities are governed by agency relations. Institutional markets are markets where such players are important.

III. A Framework for Analysis

To understand how all of this works we combine some familiar themes agency theory and financial spanning, into a less familiar construct, but one within which financial innovation is natural. The demand and supply for financial products depends on players whose actions are constrained by agency type considerations and, explicitly, by contracts and regulations that reflect such considerations. Within this model, the marketing of new instruments is governed by the cost structure of the marketing networks and distribution channels.

The resulting analysis complements the work of both Miller (1986) and Merton (1988). Miller makes a compelling argument for the centrality of taxes and regulations in the recent wave of innovation. Merton provides a detailed examination of the production function underlying the creation of new derivative securities, paying careful attention to the role of transactions costs as the raison d'etre for the existence of financial intermediaries. By contrast with Miller, we consider taxes and regulations as part of a larger framework within which institutions are controlled and monitored. Since we ignore production costs, and focus instead on the role of marketing costs, the paper provides a converse to Merton's work.

In our analysis, financial innovation arises as a natural adjunct of the supply and demand of agency constrained participants, and marketing costs help to shape the form of the new institutional features. A major role of investment banks is to run the marketing networks. Below we will apply our analysis to two such divergent issues as the market for junk bonds and the invention of the CMO (Collateralized Mortgage Obligation) in which a pool of mortgages is formed and then stripped into bonds and a residual component.

Consider a stylized model of an opaque financial institution, perhaps an S&L or an insurance company. The institution is assumed to serve its stockholders who have contributed capital infusion and who wish to maximize the value of their holdings, i.e., the total wealth of the institution minus the amount that will be paid to the participants (depositors or claimants). We will ignore any possible divergence between the desires of the stockholders and those of the incumbent management.

If the firm can be perfectly monitored, then the clients of the firm, be they depositors in an S&L or the insured who are paying premiums to an insurance company can guarantee that their implicit investment in the firm will be protected and that the investment policy will work to maximize the value of their commitments. An opaque firm, however, generally has access to risky investments which the participants can neither observe nor analyze. We will refer to such investments as 'low grade'. Conversely, highly visible and relatively riskless 'high grade' securities are also available and traded in competitive securities markets.

Notice that nearly all securities can be decomposed into both high and low grade components. For example, a mortgage can be stripped of its 'kickers' and a tranche of subordinated debt can be constructed to insulate the bulk of the mortgage against default risk. This decomposition suggests several ways in which regulatory or contractual agreements could be enforced that would guarantee the safety of the institution with respect to its contracts with its clientele.

A natural approach would be a reserve requirement of a minimum holding of high grade securities. Equivalently, there could be an upper bound on the amount invested in low grade assets. Such constraints could arise endogenously within the private sector or they could be imposed externally by government regulation. In fact, government regulation is common for opaque financial institutions and the lack of incentive compatibility between the clientele and the institution is the most straightforward rationale for such regulation.

IV. Innovation

We can now see how innovations occur. In the ordinary course of business, institutions will find themselves moving into and out of their acceptable sets. A regulatory shift or a tax change or a shift in the competitive environment - a 'New Europe' - can do it. Merton Miller

(1986) calls such shifts the "grains of sand in the oyster". Although it is easy to see how such shifts can provide the impetus for financial innovation, we now have the framework for understanding how financial innovation can persist even beyond their initial rationale.

An innovation will survive because it permits the institution to achieve a better risk return tradeoff in the presence of the pervasive constraints that exist to deal with the agency problems of opaque firms. In the private sector a contractual structure - such as limitations on investment grades - has arisen to deal with agency problems and in the regulatory arena the tax code or government regulations can serve the same functions. It is the institutional structure of contracts and incentives that permits such innovations to continue, be it the Japanese tax rules for insurance companies, government regulations on S&L's, or the private placement lender's insistence on loan priority.

Whatever the initial shock, typically the institution will find itself in a situation where its holdings of assets that it acquires in the ordinary course of business, e.g., mortgages for an S&L, would put it in an unacceptable position. This provides a ready opportunity for the financial engineer. By stripping out the low grade portion of such assets and/or melding them with other low grade assets to form hedges, the institution can achieve the required mix of high grade assets. The ability to add assets to form high grade assets out of two inversely correlated low grade assets is extremely important. To the extent to which the low grade assets of a given institution are idiosyncratic and would only trade in very thin markets, this provides a vehicle for achieving an acceptable or desired risk return exposure for the institution without selling off difficult to market low grade assets. To a very great extent I believe that this ability to transform low grade assets into high grade assets and to strip out assets explains the great demand for the esoteric products that arose in the mortgage markets. The IO's, PO's and the like of these markets are surgical tools for raising and lowering the overall risk of a fixed income portfolio.

The above analysis could also be used to characterize the demand for junk bonds on the part of such institutions. Facing constraints that require them to maintain a certain proforma risk profile, perhaps by precluding any leveraging, the innate desire to achieve a greater risk exposure leads to the packaging of stand alone risky investments that implicitly contain the leverage and the risk in a prepackaged form.

This arises from the familiar conflict between stockholders and bondholders in corporate finance. Stockholders, all other things being equal, have an option on the assets of the firm with an exercise price equal to the amount of the debtholders' claim. By taking on riskier investments, the value of the stockholders' claim increases at the expense of that of the bondholders. This is the source of their inherent appetite for risk. For opaque institutions, the natural solution to the problem, as we have seen, is to impose credit conditions on its assets, and this, in turn, creates the demand for stand alone risky alternatives which - for example, as high yield debt - can masquerade as acceptable investments.

V. Summary and Conclusion

We have painted a theory of financial innovation with rather broad brush strokes. In no way can the above description serve as a substitute for a complete theory of all financial innovation. But, to a large extent, I do believe it captures much that is essential for such innovation.

Having said that, though, it must be admitted that the role of institutions and what I have called institutional markets is almost completely unexplored in modern finance and in industrial organization. To a large extent, financial theory and, more generally, economic theory is insensitive to such institutional features and with the sole exception of a 'central bank' (and even without that exception in hyper modern rational expectations macroeconomics) institutions are absent from our models. Until we recognize that institutions are not simply 'big investors' we will remain uninformed and uninformative on the wave of institutional innovation that is now occurring around the world and must offer a rather unscientific wisdom that serves neither the doctor nor the patient. This is an odd and dismaying situation at a time when the success of modern financial economics has caused so many countries to turn toward a restructuring of their capital markets. Nevertheless, finance is not exactly without its uses in such an environment and I believe that the basic intuitions of our subject, e.g., the tradeoff between return and risk and the pricing of options, will still be our best tools for these muddied questions of policy.

Bibliography

J. S. Demski, D. E. H. Sappington, and P. T. Spiller. "Incentive Schemes with Multiple Agents and Bankruptcy Constraints", Journal of Economic Theory, vol.44, no.1, February 1988, 156 - 167.

P. H. Dybvig and S. A. Ross. "Arbitrage", in Eatwell J., M. Milgate and P. Newman, eds. New Palgrave, A Dictionary of Economics. London: The MacMillan Press, Ltd. 1987, 1, 100-106.

P. H. Dybvig and C. Spatt. "Agency and the Market for Portfolio Managers: The Principle of Preference Similarity", Yale School of Management Working Paper #86, July, 1985.

B. Holmstrom. "Moral Hazard and Observability", The Bell Journal of Economics, Spring, 1979, vol.12, no.1, 74 - 91.

S. Karlin and H. M. Taylor. "A First Course in Stochastic Processes, Second Edition", Academic Press, New York, 1975.

R. C. Merton. "On the Application of the Continuous-Time Theory of Finance to Financial Intermediation and Insurance", Geneva Association Lecture, July 1988, Centre Hec-Isa, France.

M. Miller. "Financial Innovation: The Last Twenty Years and the Next", Journal of Financial and Quantitative Analysis, vol.21, no.14, December, 1986, 459 - 471.

S. A. Ross. "The Economic Theory of Agency: The Principal's Problem", American Economic Review, vol.63, 1973, 134 - 139.

S. A. Ross. "Institutional Markets, Financial Marketing, and Financial Innovation", Journal of Finance, vol.64, 1989, 541 - 556.

P. Tufano. "Financial Innovation and First-Mover Advantages: An Empirical Analysis", Unpublished manuscript, Harvard University, November, 1988.

Recent Developments in International Banking
and Finance, S.J. Khoury (editor)

CHAPTER II

Corporate Takeovers: Winners, Losers and Some Remaining Issues

E. Han Kim

*Fred M. Taylor Professor of Business Administration
and Finance Department Chairman
The University of Michigan
School of Business Administration*

I. Introduction

The 1980s will be remembered in the United States as a decade of intense corporate takeover activity--the number of announced mergers and acquisitions rose from under two thousand in 1980 to over thirty-three hundred in 1988. The intensity of takeover activity is even more pronounced when viewed in terms of the value of these transactions. For transactions reporting purchase prices, the average price rose from $50 million in 1980 to $215 million by 1988, up 330%. The number of transactions involving $100 million or more rose from 94 in 1980 to 369 by 1988; and the number involving $1 billion or more rose from 4 to 45.[1] During this period of intense takeover activity, no U.S. firm was safe, as demonstrated by the "Megadeal of the Century" in the RJR Nabisco acquisition for an unbelievable $24.6 billion price in 1988.

Critics of this trend argue that takeovers are bad for a number of reasons. First, they claim that takeover bids are often coercive and prevent target shareholders from making decisions that are in their own best interest. Second, they assert that shortsighted investors undervalue companies whose current earnings are temporarily depressed by high research and development expenditures or by other long-term investments. This underpricing, as the claim goes, makes well-run companies vulnerable to corporate takeovers, thereby discouraging corporate managers from taking a long-term perspective. Third, the critics argue that raiders are concerned only with short-term profits. Thus upon successful completion of takeovers, they sell off the most profitable parts of the acquired firms. The sell-offs reduce the productivity of the assets sold as well as that of the remaining assets; that is, the sell-offs create negative synergies and the stockholders suffer a wealth loss. Fourth, corporate takeovers reduce employment by closing plants, which in turn swells welfare rolls, erodes the tax base, forces cutbacks in municipal services, and diminishes the overall quality of life. Fifth, the recombination of large corporations may lead to the

---

[1] See Mergerstat Review (1988).

creation of market power with customers suffering from the resulting monopolistic inefficiencies.

More can be added to the above list of complaints about corporate takeovers. The crux of the criticisms is that everyone loses from corporate takeovers, except the raiders, whose only motive is a quick profit regardless of the long-term consequences.

The purpose of this paper is to describe the American experience with corporate takeovers. Our experience is unique, and studying it may help predict whether other countries will also witness similar levels of hostile takeover activity in the near future. To this end, I will analyze the evolution of interfirm tender offers in the U.S. Tender offers have been the most commonly utilized device in implementing hostile takeovers. Analyzing the evolution of tender offers will illustrate how changes in the ownership structure of publicly held U.S. corporations have made them vulnerable to hostile takeovers. Specifically, our experience suggests that when a nation's corporate ownership structure becomes diffuse, tender offers will emerge as a viable and efficacious mechanism by which to acquire corporate control.

The rest of the paper will be devoted to a reexamination of each of the criticisms regarding takeovers outlined earlier. I will summarize scientific evidence concerning the wealth effects of tender offers on the stockholders and bondholders of firms involved in both successful and unsuccessful takeover attempts. Based on this empirical evidence, the real winners and losers in takeovers will be identified.

II. Evolution of Tender Offers as a Takeover Device

A. Tender Offers vs. Merger Proposals

The two capital market transactions most commonly used to effect corporate acquisitions in the U.S. are negotiated mergers and interfirm tender offers. The distinguishing feature between these two devices is who has the first opportunity to accept or reject the acquisition offer, the target managers or the stockholders. Merger proposals are made by the managers of a bidding firm to the managers of a target firm. Only after the managements of the two firms have arrived at an agreement regarding the terms of the combination is the proposal presented to the stockholders of the two firms for ratification.[2] If the managements fail to reach an agreement, the negotiations are discontinued and the merger process ends. Thus, target managers have veto power over merger proposals, and many merger proposals never reach the stockholders because they are unacceptable to the target managers.

Tender offers are bids made by the management of the acquiring firm directly to the stockholders of the target firm. Specifically, the management of the bidding firm offers to purchase a certain fraction of the outstanding shares of the target firm for a specified price on a specified date. These bids are made directly to the stockholders of the target firm and hence do not require the acquiescence of the target management. Thus, if the target managers are not favorably disposed toward a merger proposal, the bidder can circumvent the target managers altogether. Consequently, many tender offers are made and successfully executed over the expressed objections of the management of the target firm.

The tender offer's use as a takeover device is a relatively recent phenomenon even in the U.S. Although negotiated mergers were frequently used to effect changes in corporate control even before the turn of the century, the tender offer did not become a popular mechanism for transferring corporate control until the of the 1960s[3] In fact, only 9 interfirm tender offers were reported between 1956 and 1960. By comparison, 238 tender offers were made over the following 8 years (1960-1967).[4]

B. Separation of Ownership and Control

The advent of the interfirm tender offer in the 50's and its popularity

---

[2] In some cases, the managements' proposal takes the form of a negotiated offer in lieu of a proposal for stockholder confirmation.

[3] Nelson(1959) reports that between 1895 and 1904 over 3,000 mergers were effected by U.S. corporations

[4] See Austin and Fishmann(1970).

since the 60's coincide with a period of significant change in the ownership structure of U.S. corporations. Many firms that were closely held by insiders before World War II emerged from the 50's and 60's with a majority of their shares being held by outside investors.

During the decades of the 50's and 60's, the annual growth rate in the number of securities listed on the New York Stock Exchange was 10%, compared with an average growth rate of 4% from 1935 to 1949. Furthermore, the annual growth rate in trading volume tripled from 3% to 9% for the same periods.[5] These data suggest that the 50's and 60's witnessed a veritable explosion in both the availability of and trading activity in U.S. equity securities. Moreover, the number of U.S. citizens holding common stock grew from 6.5 million in 1952 to 31 million in 1970.[6] Apparently, the separation of ownership and control in large corporations, discussed by Berle and Means (1932) in the 30's, became a reality for many U.S. corporations by the 60's.

C. Ownership Structure and The Choice of Takeover Device

I believe it was this increase in the degree of separation between ownership and control that led to the emergence of the interfirm tender offer as an important vehicle for transferring corporate control. In a 1984 paper that my colleague, Michael Bradley, and I wrote, we developed a model which showed that it is cost effective to negotiate a merger only if the target management holds controlling ownership interest; otherwise, a public tender offer is more cost effective. Consistent with this hypothesis, we found that the fraction of target shares held by insiders is significantly higher in those cases where targets were acquired through merger negotiations than in those transacted via tender offers. The mean percentage of target shares owned by the officers and directors in the merger sample was 19.8% as compared to 9.2% in the tender offer sample (the median values are 14.1% and

[5] See Fact Book 1984.

[6] See Shareownership 1983.

6.4%, respectively.)[7] Our data also showed that in none of the tender offers did the insiders hold a combined fraction greater than 38% whereas in the merger sample the maximum was 99%.

Based on this evidence and the American experience with changes in ownership structure during the 50's and 60's, I conclude that when a nation's corporate ownership structure becomes diffuse, interfirm tender offers emerge as a viable and efficacious mechanism by which to acquire corporate control.

III. The Evidence on Tender Offers

Ever since the interfirm tender offer became a popular takeover mechanism in the U.S., it has been alleged that bidding firms making use of this method have engaged in "unfair and coercive" tactics to acquire their targets. Critics frequently allege that, because of a lack of regulation of interfirm tender offers--cash tender offers were not regulated until 1968--corporate raiders were able to gain control of targets with swift, secretive tender offers, after which they bled the targets of their valuable resources. The most infamous of these tactics was the so-called Saturday Night Special: tender offers that were announced on Friday and executed the following Monday. These offers were usually effected on a first come, first served basis and often involved bids made on behalf of "unnamed parties". During testimony before the U.S. Senate hearings on the Williams Bill in 1968, many critics argued that such offers did not give target stockholders sufficient time or information with which to make a rational tendering decision, and as a result, many well-managed firms were taken over and subsequently pillaged by corporate "pirates disguised as honorable businessmen".

In July of 1968, the U.S. Congress enacted into law the Williams Bill, which restricted the alleged abuses of hostile tender offers. Congress

---

7

The sample consists of 192 targets acquired through merger negotiations and 112 targets of successful tender offers during the period 1969 through 1980. All target firms in the sample were listed on either the New York Stock Exchange or the American Stock Exchange at the time of acquisition.

subsequently amended the Act in 1970, and in doing so specifically brought interfirm cash tender offers within the purview of the Securities and Exchange Commission. Many states, beginning in 1969, also enacted "anti-takeover" statutes, which are even more restrictive than the federal code.

Provisions of the Williams Amendment require bidding firms to provide detailed information about how the tender offer will be financed and what changes in the operations of the target will be made if the offer is successful. The regulations also specify a minimum number of days over which a tender offer must remain open and a minimum number of days before the target shares can be purchased. The Amendment outlaws first come, first served offers, and requires that all oversubscribed offers be effected on a pro rata basis. It was reasoned that disclosure provisions, time for deliberation, and pro-rationing of tendered shares would allow target shareholders to make a more rational decision. In sum, the regulations were designed to protect target shareholders from corporate raiders.

Whether or not such protections were warranted can be determined by observing the stock market's reaction to announcements of takeover bids. The stock market's reaction is informative because the market is forward-looking in that the current market value of a firm is the present value of its expected future cash flows. Thus, the change in a firm's market value at the announcement of a tender offer reflects the unbiased estimate of the change that will take place in its future cash flows due to the tender offer.

Several studies have measured the announcemnt effects of tender offers on the stock prices of bidding and target firms. These studies measure any abnormal returns to stockholders by taking the difference between actual and expected normal stock returns. The abnormal returns around the offer date provide a measure of the wealth effects of tender offers. Let me summarize the evidence provided by these studies.

A. Target Stockholders

The early studies which examined the wealth effect of tender offers include Dodd and Ruback (1977), Kummer and Hoffmeister (1978), and

Bradley (1980). Dodd and Ruback show that during the month of and the month following a tender offer announcement, the stockholders of successful targets realized a 21% abnormal return while the stockholders of unsuccessful targets realized a 16% abnormal return. Kummer and Hoffmeister report abnormal returns of 17% for successful targets and 21% for unsuccessful targets. Bradley (1980) documents abnormal returns of 32% for successful targets and 47% for unsuccessful targets. These collective findings provide overwhelming evidence that the wealth of target shareholders increases substantially as a result of tender offers. The evidence is clearly inconsistent with the notion that takeovers are harmful to target shareholders.

Furthermore, Jarrell and Bradley (1980) report that target shareholders experienced an average abnormal return of 20% as a result of tender offers made prior to the enactment of Williams Amendment. This evidence does not support the claim that takeovers were harmful to the target shareholders prior to regulation. Clearly, there was little need to protect them through regulation.

The early studies also provide evidence suggesting that the positive revaluation of target shares does not depend on whether or not tender offers are successful. Specifically, Dodd-Ruback and Bradley report that stock prices of targets of unsuccessful tender offers remain substantially above their pre-offer level even after the offer fails. They conjecture that this phenomenon occurs because it is the announcement of a tender offer per se that precipitates the positive revaluation of the target shares, not necessarily the successful combination of the target resources with those of the acquiring firm. In other words, announcements of tender offers in and of themselves prompt the stock market to revalue previously "undervalued" target shares. This "underpricing" hypothesis is consistent with the notion that shortsighted investors undervalue companies with temporarily depressed current earnings due to long-term investments, and that the underpricing makes well-run companies vulnerable to corporate takeover attempts.

To provide a more direct test of the underpricing hypothesis, we reexamined the evidence concerning targets of unsuccessful tender offers in a 1983 paper in which I collaborated with Michael Bradley and Anand Desai. Our findings contradict the underpricing hypothesis. In that study, we divided a sample of 112 targets of unsuccessful tender offers into two groups: 86 targets that received a subsequent successful bid and 26 that did not. Consistent with the earlier findings, we found that target shareholders of both subsamples realized significantly positive abnormal returns during the announcement month: 42% and 29% for the first and the second subsample, respectively. However, these gains are entirely due to the emergence and/or the anticipation of another acquisition bid. That is, the positive revaluation of target shares is permanent only if the unsuccessful offer results in a subsequent successful bid which leads to the combination of the target resources with those of an acquiring firm. Furthermore, the target shareholders receive an additional abnormal return of 28% when they receive a subsequent successful bid.

If the target is not subsequently taken over, however, the entire initial gain experienced by the target shareholders disappears when the market realizes that there will be no subsequent bid. This evidence is not consistent with the hypothesis that target shares are "undervalued." If the firm were truly underpriced and the tender offer served to bring this underpricing to the market's attention, then the target firms should have retained at least part of the initial gain regardless of the eventual outcome of the offer.

This evidence also implies that when a target management successfully fends off a takeover bid and prevents any subsequent takeover bids from being successful, it does a serious disservice to its shareholders. Such actions by the target management will deprive shareholders of an opportunity to increase their wealth by anywhere from 29% to 70% (42% plus 28%).

B. Acquiring Stockholders

Turning now to the wealth effects on acquiring stockholders, the three earlier studies reported average abnormal returns ranging from only 3% to 5%. These returns are substantially smaller than the large upward revaluation in the shares of successfully acquired targets. However, a simple comparison between the mean abnormal returns could be misleading because of the size disparity between the target and acquiring firms. The average market value of acquiring firms is on average about eight times that of their targets.[8] Thus, even if the dollar gain from an acquisition were evenly split between the two stockholder groups, the percentage return to the acquiring firm's stockholders would be lower due to the larger capital base.

In an article that Michael Bradley, Anand Desai, and I published in 1988, we examined the dollar gains to the stockholders of the target and acquiring firms.

[9] Based on a sample of 236 successful tender offers during the period 1963 through 1984, we found that the average dollar gains were $17 million and $107 million for the acquiring and acquired firms, respectively. Thus, not only is the average rate of return to targets greater than the average rate of return to acquiring firms, but the dollar gain to the target is greater as well.

C. Effects of Regulation and Competition among Bidders

Although the evidence on acquiring firms suggests that their stockholders earn, on average, small positive returns from tender offers, there have been considerable variations in their realized returns over time. One of the important determinants of the returns to acquiring stockholders is the regulation of tender offers, which in the U.S. was first introduced by the enactment of the Williams Amendment in July 1968.

The three key words in the Williams Amendment are disclosure, delay, and withdrawal. The disclosure requirements force bidding firms to reveal valuable information about the target company and the planned use of its resources. This disclosure of information, together with the delay requirement, enables other potential acquirers to obtain valuable information about the target and permits further production of

---

[8] This observation is based on 186 successful tender offers during the period 1963 through 1980.

[9] The dollar gains are defined as the product of the market value of the firm eight days before the announcement of the first tender offer and the abnormal returns to the stockholders from one week before the announcement of the first bid through one week after the announcement of the last successful bid.

among bidders. The withdrawal privilege allows target stockholders to recontract and tender their shares to the firm that makes the highest valued offer, thereby enabling target shareholders to take full advantage of competition among bidders.

The evidence provided by our 1988 paper supports the premise that the Williams Amendment led to increased competition among bidders. The percentage of tender offers which involved more than one bidding firm, which we shall refer to as "multiple-bidder contests," increased from 18% before the July 1968 enactment of the Williams Amendment to 35% thereafter. Furthermore, this increased competition resulted in increased returns to target stockholders and decreased returns to acquiring stockholders. The average abnormal returns to target stockholders were 27% in tender offers which involved only one bidder versus 40% in multiple-bidder contests. For acquiring stockholders, the average abnormal returns are 2% in single-bidder offers but -1.33% in multiple-bidder contests.[10]

We also examined the simultaneous effects of both regulation and competition among bidders. The evidence shows that the marginal impact of competition among bidders is to increase returns to target shareholders by 13% and decrease returns to acquiring shareholders by 1.7%; the marginal impact of the regulation is to increase returns to target shareholders by 8% and decrease returns to acquiring shareholders by 2.5%.

The significant marginal impact of the regulation suggests that the federal and state regulations gave greater bargaining power to target shareholders in addition to providing them with the benefits of increased competition among bidders . Furthermore, our evidence shows that the regulation had no marginal impact on the total synergistic gains created by successful acquisitions implemented with tender offers. Apparently, the effect of increased regulation has been a zero sum game. That is, the greater gains to the stockholders of target firms have come entirely at the expense of the stockholders of acquiring firms.

---

[10] See Bradley, Desai, and Kim (1988).

D. Further Evidence on Bidders

To provide further evidence on the shareholders of acquiring firms, we divided the sample period into three subperiods: 1963-1968, 1969-1980, and 1981-1984. Although this division is somewhat arbitrary, these subperiods correspond roughly to the three distinct regimes that have existed in the legal and institutional environment surrounding tender offers since 1963. The distinguishing feature between first and second periods is, as mentiond earlier, the enactment of the Williams Bill. The third period (1981-1984) is distinguished by three factors that have drastically influenced the environment in which tender offers take place. First is the avowed laissez-faire attitude of the Reagan Administration toward corporate takeovers in general.[11] Second is the development of sophisticated tactics used to repel takeovers: poison pills, targeted share repurchases, lock-up provisions, and supermajority and fair-price amendments, to name a few. The third factor is the advent of investment banking firms that specialize in raising funds to finance corporate takeovers. Each of these factors has increased competition among bidders: the frequency of multiple-bidder contests in our sample increased from 27% during 1963-1980 to 46% during 1981-1984.

As might be expected, the increased competition when combined with existing regulations has had a significant negative impact on the shareholders of acquiring firms. The average abnormal return declined from 4.1% during 1963-1968 to 1.3% during 1969-1980 and to -2.9% during 1981-1984. Acquiring firms gained the most (4.6%) in single-bidder offers effected during the unregulated period of 1963-1968; they lost the most (-5.1%) in multiple-bidder contests effected in the 80's.

Perhaps the most surprising finding is that acquiring firms suffered a significant abnormal loss of -2.9% during 1981-1984. Although this period is associated with a significant increase in competition among bidding firms, competition per se cannot explain negative returns to

[11] See the Economic Report of the President, 1985, especially Chapter 6.

acquirers. Moreover, the loss of -5.1% to the winning bidders in multiple bidder contests during the 1981-1984 period raises the issue of why the acquirers would attempt to win a multiple bidder contest if making a winning bid only makes the acquiring firm's shareholders worse off.

There are two possible, though not mutually exclusive, explanations for these findings. The first is provided in our earlier Bradley, Desai, and Kim paper (1983). In that study we examined 67 firms which made unsuccessful bids in multiple bidder contests over the period 1963-1980. The results of that study indicated that the shareholders on average suffered an abnormal return of -8% as it became apparent that they were losing a multiple bidder contest. In contrast, the shareholders of winning firms in the same contests neither gained nor lost, experiencing an insignificant average abnormal return of 0.5%.[12] Thus, once a firm finds itself in a bidding war, it is better to win than to lose, even though in winning, the firm's stockholders may still suffer a capital loss.

The above result suggests that when a firm loses the competition for a target firm to a rival bidding firm, the market perceives it to have lost an opportunity to acquire a valuable resource. The transfer of control of the target resources to another firm places the losing firm at a competitive disadvantage vis-a-vis the successful bidding firm. In other words, the revelation that a rival bidding firm has sufficient specialized resources to effect a successful tender offer has a value-decreasing effect on the shares of an unsuccessful bidding firm. For example, an acquisition induced increase in efficiency may lead to a lower price and/or a higher quality of the acquiring firm's product, thereby reducing the quasi-rents available to the unsuccessful bidding firm. The reduction in quasi-rents would manifest itself in a decrease in the share price of the unsuccessful bidding firm.

E. Acquisitions that Hurt Acquiring Shareholders

The second explanation is that some acquisitions hurt shareholders because they are made by managers who deviate from their stated goal

---

[12] See Table 6 in Bradley, Desai, and Kim (1988).

of maximizing shareholder wealth in order to pursue their own self interest. These managers make acquisitions based on non-wealth maximizing motivations such as the desire to increase the size of the assets they manage beyond the optimal point, reduce the riskiness of the firm's activity albeit at the expense of profitability, or make it harder for shareholders to replace them with a superior management team.

Consistent with this alternative view of managerial behavior, Lang, Stulz, and Walkling (1989) found that poorly managed firms with poor investment opportunities tend to make acquisitions with negative synergies. The frequency of these bad acquisitions increases with the amount of excess cash available within the firm. Had the managers of these firms been maximizing shareholder wealth, they would have distributed the excess cash to the shareholders. Similarly, Morck, Shleifer, and Vishney (1988) found that acquisitions made to build a conglomerate tend, on average, to hurt the shareholders. We found in our 1988 paper that acquisitions made by White Knights on average hurt the acquiring shareholders. White Knights are the acquirers who make friendly acquisitions at the invitation of target management who are attempting to fend off hostile takeover bids.

If these acquisitions are indeed made to benefit managers at the expense of shareholders, they should be followed by poor earnings. As poor earnings depress stock prices, firms which make bad acquisitions will themselves become attractive targets for takeovers, because potential bidders see an opportunity to acquire the firm and increases its value by restructuring assets. Consistent with this prediction, Mitchell and Lehn (1989) found that firms which make bad acquisitions, as measured by negative returns at the announcement of a bid, are more likely to become the targets of later takeover bids themselves. In a related study, Bhide (1989) found that of 81 businesses that were sold off following hostile takeovers, 78 had previously been acquired by the target and only 3 had been developed internally. The overwhelming majority of the businesses served distinct markets with distinct products. Thus, it appears that the targets of "bust-up" takeovers are companies that had diversified through acquisitions of unrelated businesses.

The most extreme form of sell-offs in corporate restructuring is a sale of the entire firm. These "voluntary" liquidations--as opposed to involuntary liquidations in bankruptcy proceedings--are achieved through either a series of sell-offs or a sale of the entire firm. Thus, if the sell-offs in a corporate restructuring have any impact on the shareholder wealth, the effect should be most pronounced when a firm goes through voluntary liquidation. In a study (1987) that I conducted with John Schatzberg, we found that voluntary liquidations produced positive revaluations averaging 34%. This finding suggests that the liquidating firms' assets had been underutilized prior to liquidation. The gains from liquidation were generated by the redeployment of the liquidating firms' resources into higher valued uses.

As the "bust-up" takeovers and voluntary liquidations illustrate, there is a built-in mechanism in the market for corporate control that disciplines managers when they make acquisitions that hurt shareholders; namely, hostile takeovers. Hostile takeovers are beneficial to the economy because they prevent managers from deviating too far from the goal of shareholder wealth maximization. And when the managers do deviate, hostile takeovers correct their actions by forcing corporate restructuring which restores the efficiency of corporate resources and reestablishes shareholder wealth.

F. Bondholders

Some critics of takeovers argue that the premiums paid to target shareholders represent wealth transfers from bondholders. They note that mergers and takeovers often increase the financial leverage of the combined firm. Everything else being equal, an increase in leverage means an increase in default risk and hence a decrease in the value of outstanding bonds; as a consequence, the bondholders suffer a wealth loss.

In a study (1982) that Paul Asquith and I coauthored, we investigated the wealth effects of merger announcements on the bondholders of both acquiring and acquired firms. Our results showed that mergers on average had no significant effect on either bondholder group and generated no wealth transfers between stockholders and bondholders.[13] These results were confirmed in a later study involving

---

[13] See Kim and McConnell (1977) for the theoretical explanations for the result.

a large sample of mergers, as well as in a 1987 study of 108 leverage buyouts occurring from 1980 to 1984. None of these studies found evidence that the gains to stockholders came at the expense of bondholders.[14]

G. Synergistic Gains

Another potential source of gains to target shareholders is a wealth transfer from acquiring firms' shareholders. It is possible that the wealth loss to acquiring shareholders is greater than the wealth gain to target shareholders. If this were true, corporate takeovers would be counter-productive, resulting in negative synergies. In our 1988 paper we measure synergistic gains by using matched pairs of target and acquiring firms. The total synergistic gain is defined as the sum of the change in wealth of stockholders of the target and acquiring firms.

The results of that study showed that the combined value of the target and acquiring firms increased, on average, by 7.43%, with 75% of the combined revaluations being positive. This percentage synergistic gain was statistically greater than zero and translated into $117 million per transaction. In sum, corporate takeovers are wealth enhancing events, and there is no evidence that takeovers reduce the productivity of corporations.

IV. Winners and Losers

Based on the empirical evidence just described, it is clear who the real winners and losers in corporate takeovers are. Contrary to the claims made by the critics of takeovers, there are many beneficiaries. The biggest winners are the target shareholders of successful takeover bids, and their gains almost double when their firms become targets of bidding wars.

Target stockholders lose an important opportunity to make profits if their management successfully fends off a takeover bid and prevents

---

[14] See Denis and McConnell (1986) for the merger study and Lehn and Poulson (1987) for the leverage buyout study.

potential bidders from making subsequent bids. To target stockholders, remaining independent after a hostile takeover bid implies the loss of an opportunity to increase their wealth by anywhere from 29 to 70%.

The shareholders of acquiring firms also experienced significant wealth increases from corporate takeovers prior to the Williams Amendment. However, that regulation has both increased the bargaining power of target shareholders and increased the competition among bidders. Consequently, the average gains to the shareholders of acquiring firms have experienced a steady decline over time, becoming negative (-3%) in the 80's.

The biggest losers in takeovers are the shareholders of firms which make unsuccessful bids in multiple bidder contests. While shareholders of successful acquirers lose a little (-1%), losing bidders lose much more. The shareholders of losing bidders lose, on average, 8% of their pre-offer value. Thus, once a firm finds itself in a bidding war, it is better to win than to lose, even though in winning, the firm's stockholders may suffer a capital loss.

A plausible explanation for the large loss to the losing firm in a bidding war is that the transfer of the target resources to a rival bidding firm places the losing firm at a competitive disadvantage vis-a-vis the successful bidding firm. For example, an increase in efficiency achieved by the combination of the target with the rival bidding firm may lead to a lower product price and/or a higher product quality, which will reduce the quasi-rents available to the unsuccessful bidding firm. In this case, the real winner is the consumer.

The shareholders of acquiring firms also lose if managers make acquisitions to further their own self interest. Examples of such acquisitions are conglomeration/diversification driven mergers which increase the size of the firm beyond the optimal scale, reduce the exposure to risk at the expense of profitability, or make it more difficult for shareholders to replace the current management with a better management team. Acquisitions of this type create inefficiencies and decrease the value of the firm. This in turn makes the acquiring firm itself vulnerable to hostile takeover bids, which are usually followed by sell-offs of unrelated businesses in an effort to streamline the operation. In such cases, the hostile takeovers serve to restore the efficiency of corporate resources and enable the shareholders to regain the wealth they lost as the result of previous bad acquisitions. The only losers here are the managers who lose their jobs during the restructuring/downsizing. But this is precisely what is needed to discipline managers and restrain them from making decisions that hurt shareholders.

Finally, successful corporate takeovers are wealth enhancing events. The combined value of the target and acquiring firms increases substantially. The gains do not arise because raiders acquire targets that are undervalued by shortsighted investors. Nor do they represent wealth transfers from bondholders. Rather, the value created by the combination results from more efficient management, economies of scale, improved production techniques, the combination of complementary resources, the redeployment of assets to more profitable uses, the exploitation of market power, or any number of value-creating mechanisms that fall under the general rubric of corporate synergy.

V. Some Remaining Issues

Given the evidence that successful corporate takeovers generate substantial synergistic gains and lead to a more efficient allocation of corporate resources, it is tempting to conclude that everyone wins from takeovers. Such a conclusion, however, requires some caveats.

First, it is possible that the gains from corporate takeovers may stem from the creation of market power and not necessarily from increased allocative efficiency. If mergers decrease competition in the market place, consumers and/or suppliers will suffer from monopolistic inefficiencies. While existing studies provide some circumstantial evidence that corporate acquisitions have no measurable effect on the degree of market power in the economy,[15] I believe we need more in-depth research before we can safely conclude that mergers do not reduce competition.

Second, the effect of takeovers on employment has important

[15] See Eckbo (1983 and 1985) and Stillman (1983).

implications for public policy.[16] The fate of employees and communities following a corporate takeover is an emotion-laden issue which receives substantial public attention. In a recent study (1989) Bhide examined the immediate employment effects of 28 hostile takeover bids during 1985-1986. He reported that about two thirds of his sample firms had layoffs, plant closings, and withdrawal of pension plans. He argues, however, such actions would have taken place in about half of the cases even if there were no change in control, because the firms were either facing or anticipating financial difficulties. Further, employment had been shrinking in most of the targets before they came under attack. Thus, it appears that in most cases the reduction in employment would have occurred even if the firms had not been taken over.

Although Bhide's study is informative, it fails to measure the long-run effect of takeovers on employment. If takeovers indeed increase the efficiency with which corporate resources are utilized, they should increase the marginal productivity of capital, thereby inducing greater corporate investments. Thus, takeovers may have a favorable impact on the level of employment in the long-run. Providing scientific evidence on this takeover-induced change in employment is an important task for future research.

---

[16] Schleifer and Summer (1988) also argue that th eemployment issue is also related to the efficiency issue. They argue that the ability to enter into long-term implicit contracts between labor and target management is valuable to firms. If hostile takeovers make it easy to violate the implicit contracts, the market for implicit labor contracts will be ruined, thereby forcing the firm to use less efficient contracting devices.

References

Asquith, P. and E. H. Kim, "The Impact of Merger Bids on the Participating Firms' Security Holders," *Journal of Finance*, December 1982, pp. 1209-1228.

Austin, D. and J. Fishman, *Corporations in Conflict - The Tender Offer*, Ann Arbor: Masterco Press, 1970.

Berle, A. A. Jr. and G. C. Means, *The Modern Corporation and Private Property*, New York: Macmillan, 1932.

Bhide, A., "The Causes and Consequences of Hostile Takeovers," *Journal of Applied Corporate Finance*, Summer 1989, pp. 36-59.

Bradley, M., "Interfirm Tender Offers and the Market for Corporate Control," *Journal of Business* , October 1980, pp. 345-376.

Bradley, M., A. Desai and E. H. Kim, "The Rationale behind Interfirm Tender Offers: Information or Synergy?," *Journal of Financial Economics*, April 1983, pp. 183-206.

Bradley, M., A. Desai and E. H. Kim, "Synergistic Gains from Corporate Acquisitions and their Division between Stockholders of Target and Acquiring Firms," *Journal of Financial Economics*, June 1988, pp. 3-40.

Bradley, M. and E. H. Kim, "The Evolution of the Tender Offer as a Take Over Device: An Analysis of Ownership Structure, the Free Rider Problem, and the Prisoner's Dilemma," *Proceedings of Seminar on the Analysis of Security Prices by Center for Research in Security Prices*, Graduate School of Business, University of Chicago, November 1984, pp. 277-302.

Dodd, P. and R. S. Ruback, "Tender Offers and Stockholder Returns: An Empirical Analysis," *Journal of Financial Economics*, December

1977, pp. 351-374.

Eckbo, B. E., "Horizontal Mergers, Collusion and Stockholder Wealth," *Journal of Financial Economics*, April 1983, pp. 241-273.

Eckbo, B. E., "Mergers and the Market Concentration Doctrine: Evidence from the Capital Market," *Journal of Business*, July 1985, pp. 325-349.

Economic Report of the President, February 1985.

Fact Book 1984, New York: New York Stock Exchange, June 1984.

Jarrell, G. and M. Bradley, "The Economic Effects of Federal and State Regulations of Cash Tender Offers," *Journal of Law and Economics*, October 1980, pp. 371-407.

Kim, E. H. and J. J. McConnell, "Corporate Mergers and the Co-Insurance of Corporate Debt," *Journal of Finance*, May 1977, pp. 349-365.

Kim, E. H. and J. Schatzberg, "Voluntary Corporate Liquidations," *Journal of Financial Economics*, 1987, pp. 311-328.

Kummer, D. and J. Hoffmeister, "Valuation Consequences of Cash Tender Offers," *Journal of Finance*, May 1978, pp. 505-516.

Lang, L., R. Stulz and R. Walking, "Free Cash Flows, Tobin's q, and Bidder Gains in Successful Tender Offers," Ohio State University Working Paper, September 1989.

Mergerstat Review 1988, Schaumberg: Merrill Lynch Business Brokerage & Valuation, Inc., W.T. Grimm & Co., 1989.

Mitchell, M. and K. Lehn, "Do Bad Bidders Become Good targets," *Journal of Political Economy* (forthcoming).

Morck, R., A. Shleifer and R. W. Vishny, "Do Managerial Objectives Drive Bad Acquisitions?" University of Chicago Working Paper, 1989.

Nelson, R., *Merger Movements in American Industry 1895-1956*, Princeton: Princeton University Press, 1959.

Share Ownership 1983, New York: New York Stock Exchange, April 1984.

Shleifer, A. and L. H. Summers, "Breach of Trust in Hostile Takeovers," in A.J. Auerbach, ed., *Corporate Takeovers: Causes and Consequences*, Chicago: University of Chicago Press, 1988, pp. 33-56.

Stillman, R., "Examining Antitrust Policy Towards Horizontal Mergers," *Journal of Financial Economics*, April 1983, pp. 225-240.

The 1989 Yearbook on Corporate Mergers, Joint Ventures and Corporate Policy, Eleventh Edition, Boston: Cambridge Corporation, 1989.

Recent Developments in International Banking
and Finance, S.J. Khoury (editor)

CHAPTER III

Current Structure and Recent Developments in Foreign Exchange Markets

James B. Burnham*

* Visiting Professor, Thomas J. Murrin Chair in Global Competitiveness, Duquesne University, School of Business Administration. Adjunct Fellow, Center for the Study of American Business, Washington University, St. Louis.

This paper is a substantially revised version of a working paper prepared for the Center for the Study of American Business, while the author was the John M. Olin Visiting Professor. It has benefitted from suggestions by participants in the Money/Macro Workshop at Washington University, St. Louis in addition to stimulating questions by Steven Sheppard and the extensive comments of an anonymous referee.

Introduction

The purpose of this paper is to analyze the foreign exchange market from the perspective of its institutions and practices in the United States. The emphasis is on the over-the-counter (OTC) market and its core, the "interbank" market, where the bulk of foreign exchange activity takes place. Although the focus is on the U.S. market, most of the trading techniques and practices reviewed are common to all major foreign exchange centers, since substantial trading is conducted between the U.S. and off-shore centers. Consequently, with the exception of regulatory issues, most of the observations and analysis in the paper are applicable to the global market.

The paper starts with a short overview of the market. It then discusses the relationship between interest rates and exchange rates as it is worked out in the forward market, and describes the chief players -- marketmakers, customers, speculators, and brokers. The importance of credit and settlement issues is described and the linkages with the futures market are discussed. It concludes with a section on regulation of the U.S. market and a final note.

I. Overview

Although the technology of the marketplace has changed radically since the 19th century, and incorporated institutions have replaced private banks as the chief marketmakers, the OTC market remains remarkably close-knit, with an element of clubiness. Even in a highly competitive market, characterized by high volumes and operating on a global scale, personal contacts and reputations of individual traders and managers play important roles. Since only two words by a trader (for example, "mine 5," meaning "I buy 5 million") make a binding contract, mutual trust is a necessary element if the market is to function well. The high volume of repeat business between traders and institutions, and the mutual advantages of exchanging market information provide incentives for all parties to conform to generally accepted if informal rules of conduct.

Volume in the U.S. OTC market is on the order of $130 billion daily, according to data collected by the Federal Reserve Bank of New

York in 1989.[1] The U.S. market volume compares to daily turnovers in the two other key centers of $115 billion in Tokyo and $187 billion in London. As Table I demonstrates, activity in all three centers has grown rapidly in recent years.

Table I

The Leading Foreign Exchange Markets

(Daily Average Turnover, U.S. $ Billions)

	1986	1989
United States	$ 58	$129
United Kingdom	90	187
Japan	48	115

Notes: Transactions between each market by non-affiliated parties are counted twice. If exchange-traded turnover not covered in the Federal Reserve survey for the U.S. were included, total turnover would be $135 billion in 1989.

Sources: Federal Reserve Bank of New York release dated September 13, 1989; Bank of England Quarterly Bulletin, November 1989; Financial Times, September 14, 1989, p. 1; author's calculations (of exchange-traded activity).

A substantial portion of growth in the market is due to the removal of restrictions on short- and long-term capital account transactions in Europe and the Far East. This process received a major impetus in 1979 when the British government eliminated the last elements of long-standing restrictions on overseas transactions. The Australian and New Zealand governments followed with major market-opening measures. The Japanese government in 1985 greatly liberalized the rules under which corporations could enter into foreign exchange contracts, which immediately led to substantial volume increases in that market. During the 1980s, Continental Europe gradually reduced barriers to external borrowing activity in domestic markets as well as non-resident portfolio transactions. For reasons discussed in Section IV, the increase in the number of allowable commercial and financial transactions has contributed importantly to swelling volumes in the overall market through the normal multiplier effect. Growth in securities-related transactions has also been fueled by rapid increases in U.S. portfolio investment abroad and trading in foreign securities.

Also adding to increased volumes of trading is the use of the U.S. dollar in non-dollar ("cross currency") transactions. For example, the bank handling a transaction involving the purchase of German securities by a Japanese investor will normally first purchase dollars for yen and then sell dollars for marks, even though the rate quoted the investor will be the yen/mark rate. When added to the normal method of covering outright forwards, described in Section III, it will be seen that a single cross currency forward deal - and the offsetting hedge - can result in a minimum of five additional transactions of the same amount.

Some increase in direct cross currency transactions has taken place in recent years. In 1989, 4% of trading volume in the U.S. was in cross currencies, while volume in London rose from 3% in 1986 to 9% in 1989. In both New York and London, the deutschemark figures prominently in cross currency trading. Although such trading has increased measurably in recent years, it entails a variety of increased transactions costs such as the need for active management of non-dollar balances in relatively under-developed money markets and increased complexity in accounting and control systems.

Granted, there are apparent inefficiencies in using the dollar as an intermediary currency in moving between yen and sterling, for example. And the further growth of off-shore money markets is facilitating increased cross currency activity. But it remains to be seen if the offsetting efficiencies of having one dominant currency, the U.S. dollar, as the numeraire and transaction medium of the global system can be maintained.

The process of deregulation of currency and capital markets, combined with new technology and declining communications costs, has also spurred the growth of near 24-hour global trading. However, there are periods (on weekends and holidays in one of the three major trading centers) when the market is extremely thin, and only spot transactions in major currencies are possible in moderately large amounts. Some major foreign exchange banks have experimented with three-shift operations in a single trading center to gain 24-hour coverage, but this approach normally has proven not to be an effective substitute for trading teams in the other two key centers. The incentives to have dealing rooms worldwide include the face-to-face contacts and resulting information flows developed by traders in their own markets and the problems that can arise in supervising trading desk activities and back office operations in a 24-hour mode.

For the major participants in the market, access on a near 24-hour basis is a necessity given the substantial price movement that can occur in different time zones. Important commercial and speculative customers will either leave orders for execution at specific prices, or they want to have the ability to communicate directly with a trading desk outside normal trading hours in their own time zone. Although orders can be left with other banks (and sufficiently large orders are eagerly sought as attractive business), as a general rule customers are assured of better executions if a single dealing system retains the order.

The emergence of a functioning options market in the 1980s was one of the most striking developments in the foreign exchange market. Standard manuals for corporate foreign exchange managers in the early 1980s made little or no mention of the options market.[2]

Forward contracts with optional settlement dates ("option forwards") had long been available to meet normal commercial customer requirements. However, unlike true options, settlement eventually had to be made and pricing was based entirely on interest rate differentials. It appears that a better understanding of appropriate option pricing models and hedging strategies[3] and the emergence of an effective stock options market in the U.S. were important factors in the emergence of a true foreign exchange options market. In addition, the competitive energies of two exchanges - the Chicago Mercantile Exchange through its subsidiary, the International Monetary Mart and the Philadelphia Stock Exchange - were key developments. The exchanges sought to develop new products for their members and customers, including smaller speculators who were generally shunned by commercial banks.

Traditional commodity trading firms and brokers also began to identify opportunities with potential corporate customers in both exchange-traded and OTC options and futures. Commercial banks as a group were somewhat slow to respond to these developments, but most major institutions are now full participants in both the exchange-traded and OTC markets. Some corporate customers and securities firms now use standard options up to one year in maturity on a regular basis. However, options still account for only a small share of the overall U.S. market - about 6% in 1989.

Despite substantial investment by a number of banks in the design and marketing of complex options-based products, few appear to have gained general acceptance. The requirement for sophisticated risk management systems and knowledgeable managers to monitor a portfolio of such instruments may be a factor here. However, simpler instruments, such as foreign currency warrants issued in conjunction with securities issues, are one recent successful innovation.

II. The Forward Market

In the foreign exchange market, the forward rate is viewed as another way of expressing interest rate differentials between two currencies.[4] This approach is reflected in the view and daily operations of all major participants in the over-the-counter market.

Although speculative activity will be discussed more thoroughly in Section IV, it is important to point out here that nearly all purely speculative transactions in the OTC market are executed in spot contracts, even if the intended horizon for the speculative position is several weeks. (In the 1989 survey of the New York OTC market, only about 5% of total volume was accounted for by outright forward exchange contracts.) Professional traders strongly prefer to take positions in the spot market, where the ability to cover an open position quickly is far greater and bid-ask spreads are significantly less than on longer dated contracts. Liquidity in the forward market is highly variable, with distinct peaks in short-dated transactions of up to one week and in the 1-, 2-, 3-, and 6-month forward dates. If a speculator initially established his position with a six-week forward contract, but wishes to close it out after only one week has passed, he will normally incur extra costs compared to the spot/short-date approach.[5]

This approach means that major market participants with a speculative exchange position continually "roll over" their position by executing a short-dated "swap" (buying the shorted currency to meet the obligation under the initial contract and reselling it for deliv^_ery within a few days). The transactions costs are relatively trivial compared to the amounts involved, and will normally be less than those for using the forward market. It is precisely because of this method of taking positions that central banks are occasionally able to break speculative surges against their currencies by raising overnight interest rates to extremely high levels: the high interest rate is reflected in the "swap" rate for the speculator who is continually refunding his foreign currency account with a forward swap. (A previously established outright forward position, however, would not have to contend with the sharply higher financing cost.)

A. Covered Arbitrage

Although normally neglected in exchange rate speculation, the forward market is of considerable interest to traders for the opportunities it presents for arbitrage as well as outright speculation on interest rate differentials. The basis for this is the interest rate parity theorem, which dominates the workings of the international money and exchange markets. The theorem states that the premium or discount on forward delivery of a foreign currency (the price above or below the spot price) is equivalent to the difference between the two currencies' interest rates.[6] In practice, allowances must be made for processing, brokerage, and cost of capital considerations. It should be borne in mind that in addition to these transactions costs, credit facilities must also be available (see Section VI). To arbitrage $50 million equivalent will require $100 million in credit lines for both the initiating bank and the counterparties.

B. Interest Rate Speculation

Speculation on interest rate differentials via the forward foreign exchange market is a little understood but far more important activity than is generally realized.[7]

To establish a speculative position on interest rate differentials in the forward market, a swap is executed for, say, six months (transaction #1 in Table II, where a position in the Spanish/U.S. interest rate differential is being taken). The position is then "funded" with a second short-dated swap (transaction #2). At day 2, if the trader wishes to maintain his position, the projected outflow of dollars (and inflow of pesetas) will be covered by executing another short-dated swap forward (transaction #3). If he wishes to close out the position, the swap would have a terminal date identical with the original swap transaction.[8]

Table II

Establishing a Position in the Forward Market

Transaction	Future Settlement Date			
	3	4	5	180
#1 Swap	buy pesetas sell dollars			sell pesetas buy dollars
#2 Swap	sell pesetas buy dollars	buy pesetas sell dollars		
#3 Swap (executed on day 2)		sell pesetas buy dollars	buy pesetas sell dollars	

The significance of the above transactions is that a position on interest rate differential shifts has been established without the necessity, when each day is finished, of having any significant on-balance-sheet assets or liabilities (and the associated capital requirements and regulatory constraints), even though there may be substantial receipts and payments flowing through an account on a particular day. The forward trader's objective is to time cash flows to and from his accounts so that the only occasion any significant balance appears it will be, hopefully, a positive one representing the profit on a position. (In the example given in Table II, a small peseta balance representing the interest rate differential would be accumulating gradually.) Of course, if a currency is subject to exchange controls in the forward market, on-balance-sheet transactions (overdrafts, deposits, or the acquisition of liquid securities) will have to come into play, assuming they are not also controlled.

The potential volatility of a forward position of this sort arises out of the double jeopardy from interest rate movements in two different currencies. Although interest rates may move in the same direction, with little or no impact on the position, they may also move in opposite directions, with dramatic changes in the differential, and the profit or loss.

The lack of liquidity -- and consequent wide spreads -- in the forward market for "broken dates" between the normal 30-day intervals means that banks will frequently assume a speculative position on interest rate differentials as a result of customer business. This takes place when a bank fails to cover the corporate customer's transaction for the exact forward date and instead executes a swap for a standard date short or long of the corporate deal.

The trader is also at risk from movements in the spot exchange rate, even if there is no change in the interest rate differential. For example, assume a position has been established by a 10 million pounds sterling six-month swap forward. The six-month forward rate is $1.50. The position is then "funded" (as in transaction #2 in Table II) with another short-dated swap at a spot rate of $1.60 (equivalent to $16 million). Now assume that spot sterling strengthens to $1.80 when the time comes to roll over the short-dated swap transaction. The trader will now have to enter into an $18 million deal to maintain the 10 million sterling cover. In effect, an additional $2 million has to be borrowed to maintain zero foreign exchange exposure.

The above description of interest rate risk taking in the forward market suggests that the measurement of exposure is not a simple calculation, since both the levels and shapes of two different interest rate yield curves are involved. Furthermore, a trading room with a large forward "book" (set of contracts) may have substantial unrealized gains or losses on unmatured contracts. The accounting treatment of positions varies from one institution to another, with a tendency by banks with large portfolios in excess of one year in maturity to present value such contracts for quarterly income purposes.

Finally, mention should be made of the impact of the recently agreed-upon international capital adequacy standards for commercial banks. Foreign exchange contracts in excess of one year have been given a "credit equivalent" weight of 5%. If the contract is with a private counterparty, the risk weight has been set at 50%. The effect of these standards, given other reasonable assumptions, is to require an additional 2.5 basis points return to such a contract to maintain pre-agreement rates of return. This calculation should then be doubled, to reflect the capital charge for the offsetting contract which nearly all banks would have on their books to hedge the first exposure. Finally, if a contract on a mark-to-market basis is being carried at a loss, this will also raise the capital requirement. (The gain on the offsetting contract is not creditable against the loss.)

While five basis points is not a major increase in costs, the general sense in the market is that use of the traditional forward exchange contract for longer dates has already been hampered. This has substantially lessened the commercial bank appetite for an active long-dated currency swap book, and has facilitated interest by insurance companies in guaranteeing counterparty performance. Consequently, commercial banks' incentives have been further strengthened to develop foreign exchange instruments which call only for net settlement at maturity of any differences in rates prevailing between the initial and final dates of the contract. In this respect, the standard interest rate swap and forward rate agreements have demonstrated that this approach can be successful.

III. Marketmakers and Customers

In sharp contrast to the organization of most markets for equities, there are no designated marketmakers in the foreign exchange market. In the U.S., any creditworthy dealer may become a marketmaker without any regulatory requirements.

A. Marketmaker Techniques and Objectives

Marketmakers stand ready to quote two-way prices to customers and other market participants for whom they have credit facilities. One way of viewing the marketmaker is as a supplier of liquidity in a market where ultimate buyers and sellers do not place their orders simultaneously. The marketmaker holds an inventory that ensures orders can be executed as they arrive. The spread in the two-way price is compensation for providing this service.[9] Alternatively, the marketmaker can be treated as a writer of short-lived put and call options, with the difference in strike prices representing the spread.[10] Ideally, if the marketmaker consummates a transaction with a counterparty who wishes to buy U.S. dollars against deutschemarks, there will be a second counterparty who wishes to sell dollars in the same amount against deutschemarks at the same quoted spread. The marketmaker's revenue accrues entirely from the spread quoted to the two customers, and in this situation the function is little different from that of a broker. The marketmaker incurs no direct foreign exchange exposure.[11] Clearly, however, the success of a marketmaker is closely connected with the volume of requests on him to "make a two-way price."

The volume of requests to quote is heavily influenced by (1) the narrowness of the spread between the trader's bid and offered prices, (2) the time required to respond to a request for a quote, (3) the size of the transaction he is willing to quote on, (4) his reputation for quoting a price that reflects actual market conditions and levels -- that he is "on the market," (5) the willingness of the trader to quote in a wide variety of market conditions, and (6) the credit standing of his institution, which is reflective of his ability to deliver the currency as agreed.

Narrow spreads between bid and offered prices are encouraged by competition between dealers and uncertainty as to whether the counterparty is a buyer or seller of the currency in question. In addition, while the marketmaker is expected to consummate the transaction at the prices quoted, market convention means the prospective counterparty typically has a short period (2-3 seconds) to search for more attractive quotations from other counterparties or a broker. At the same time, the marketmaker has the right to withdraw his quote at any time. In practice, although quoted spreads on interbank transactions are normally quite narrow (amounting to about 3/100 of 1 percent or slightly over $500 on a $2 million dollar transaction in a major currency), personal observation suggests that it tolerates a fair degree of "price dispersion."[12] This is certainly likely in view of the global organization of the market, the lack of any central, immediately available record of actual prices paid (except those which are recorded on the futures exchanges when they are open -- and even then the record will lag actual transactions by a minute or more), and search costs that vary between customers.

Narrowness of the bid-ask spread (and the marketmaking approach by a trading desk) is also influenced by order processing costs and whether or not the price is being offered to the market via a broker or directly to counterparties.

To become a well-known marketmaker in a particular currency is the driving dream of many foreign exchange traders and managers, given an institution's willingness to provide sufficient capital for such activities. To be widely known as an institution or individual which is able to "make a price" on $100 million transactions without any delay in response to a request from a customer or recognized interbank counterparty is one of the pinnacles of professional recognition in the foreign exchange markets. The esteem arises out of the fact that the marketmaker is willing to "make a price" without necessarily having an offsetting counterparty (having "the cover in hand"), and thus be exposed to a loss in the event that the quoted price was "off the market" or the market price shifts before an offsetting counterparty has been found. In all of this activity, there is no necessary requirement that the trader/manager be speculating on a change in the market price. The speculative dimension is uncertainty surrounding the marketmaker's estimate of what the market price is, and the probability that the bid/offer spread will remain unchanged.[13]

Outside of institutions with sizable volumes of retail activity, the above ideal state of affairs occurs very infrequently in the marketplace. While currency traders and managers at major institutions strive to achieve the ideal in at least one currency, the commitment to "making a two way price" with few restrictions will often result in the trader acquiring a position in a currency without any offsetting cover. At this point, the trader must decide whether or not to speculate and hold the position, or to sell it into the market by seeking quotes from other marketmakers. (There may be no question as to having to sell the position: the trader may have limits which permitted him to quote on a transaction larger than he could hold as a speculative position.)

In more general terms, the marketmaker's equilibrium position has been disturbed by its receipt of a currency position occasioned by its willingness to quote two-way prices. It now seeks to restore its own equilibrium by going to another marketmaker or the broker market for a two-way price. A game of "hot potato" has begun. Eventually, another party willing to accept the position at the market price is found, or a new market price is established and at least one marketmaker accepts a loss on the position.

It is this search process for a counterparty who is willing to accept a new currency position that accounts for a good deal of the volume in the foreign exchange market. Some commentators observe that the bulk of foreign exchange activity (over 85 percent) is between banks and conclude that vast amounts of speculation are taking place. But rather than being speculative, part of this activity is actually the means by which speculative positions are avoided.

However, a student of the foreign exchange market might ask, "if the market is trading at a given bid-asked spread, won't the first marketmaker always incur a loss at least as large as the difference between buying and selling prices?" The answer is that in normal market conditions the usual degree of price dispersion encourages the marketmaker with an unbalanced position to seek a quotation at which he can sell out at a better price than is implied in his own bid-asked spread, assuming that the position was acquired in a transaction that did not change the dealer's view of market "fundamentals". Thus, the present structure of the market is marked by a substantial volume of transactions which can take place without disturbing the central tendency of an underlying market price. Consequently, to the extent that electronic, screen-based trading systems reduce price dispersion (see Section V, for further discussion of such systems), there should be a tendency for transaction volume to decrease.

One of the special features of the OTC foreign exchange market is the extent to which marketmaking competitors rely on each other for liquidity. If a marketmaker is sad^_dled with a position he wishes to get rid of immediately, he must ask another marketmaker for a quote. Thus, although a marketmaker wishes to receive a large number of requests for quotes, he will discourage them if they come from non-reciprocating marketmakers. The obligation among marketmakers to reciprocate can be explained in terms of Copeland's concept (Copeland, 1983) of the marketmaker as a supplier of put and call options: the cost of the option is the obligation to reciprocate in quoting.

Since the intention is that reciprocal quoting should mutually benefit the parties concerned, a trader's manager will discuss with potential marketmaking counterparties the terms under which they deal, such as normal transaction size, the time of day during which the understanding will hold, and the total amount of outstanding deals that might be permitted at any one time.

B. Customers

Customers are most easily defined as counterparties who are not expected to reciprocate in offering prices to the marketmaker (e.g., they will not supply liquidity when asked to do so). Consequently, they should expect to be offered slightly wider spreads when two-way prices are quoted for them, compared to interbank marketmakers. Even though the intentions of frequent corporate customers are frequently known as to whether they are buying or selling a particular currency (for example, dividends from a foreign subsidiary are known to be converted at a particular time every quarter), the customer with access to several banks may insist on a two-way price. The customer knows that if the first marketmaker is too far off the market price, he can unexpectedly take the other side of the quote and resell the position to a second marketmaker. Alternatively, if the corporate management does not permit such an arbitrage transaction, bids will be requested from two or more banks.

In order to distinguish between marketmaker counterparties and customers, banks with large trading operations typically establish separate dealing units. The customer unit obtains its price for major currencies from the marketmaking group and adjusts it for quoting to customers. It should be emphasized that the marketmaker's customer base will usually include many banks and nonbank financial institutions, as well as nonfinancial firms, nonprofit institutions, etc.

Sometimes, however, a customer may jeopardize its relationship with the marketmaking bank by repeatedly giving it positions under two-way quoting which are of substantial size, and result in significantly greater risk taking by the bank. Under such conditions, the bank is likely to ask the customer to either be prepared to reciprocate in giving quotes or to announce what side of the transaction it intends to be on if it wishes to continue to deal.

For example, the evolution of the foreign exchange relationship between many U.S. security firms and the marketmaking commercial banks in the 1980s was marked by much ambiguity and uneasiness. As the investment banks and brokerage firms became more and more global in their securities and customer trading operations, they ceased to behave as traditional commercial bank customers, recognizing that the size of their own transactions were of marketmaking significance. Some became marketmakers in certain currencies or new instruments, such as foreign exchange options, as noted earlier. They have now achieved sufficient market presence in their own right and account for a significant share of the market. The 1989 New York Federal Reserve Bank survey of the New York market showed that nonbank financial institutions accounted for 14 percent of the overall market and over 30 percent of the options market.

C. Volume Factors

In addition to the "hot potato" search process and cross currency transactions which increase trading volume, another factor is the frequent necessity to execute several contracts to achieve a single objective. Although the broadest and deepest of any global market, the foreign exchange market for major currencies cannot provide depth and liquidity in every currency pair for every date in the future. Consider the following example.

Table III
Covering an Outright Forward Position

Transaction	Future Settlement Date	
	3	45
#1 Corporate customer		sell pesetas buy dollars
#2 Spot interbank	buy pesetas sell dollars	
#3 Swap	sell pesetas buy dollars	buy pesetas sell dollars

A corporate customer wishes to buy Spanish pesetas against U.S. dollars for 45 days from now. The commercial bank's quote is accepted for an outright forward contract. The bank is now short pesetas and long U.S. dollars, for settlement 45 days from today, and wishes to cover its position. However, obtaining immediate cover in Spanish pesetas in the precise amount of the position for 45 days forward is unlikely, unless the bank is willing to bid very aggressively and incur an immediate loss on the customer transaction. A more common technique of covering the position involves entering into a series of three transactions in two contracts.

The outright foreign exchange exposure incurred in transaction #1 with the corporate customer is immediately covered with spot interbank deal #2 for settlement two business days in the future (day 3). However, the bank is still exposed to possible losses arising out of interest rate differential movements between the peseta and the U.S. dollar between today and 45 days in the future. One alternative might be to deposit the pesetas acquired in transaction #2 and use the balances at maturity to meet the obligation to the customer. However, this involves a series of on-balance-sheet transactions with heavier credit and capital requirements and, perhaps, tax consequences as well as administrative complications. The use of a foreign exchange swap, combining both a spot and forward transaction with the same counterparty in the same contract (transaction #3) provides the same degree of protection with fewer complications. Thus, by the time the original transaction is executed, 45 days in the future, three additional transactions for the same amount will also have been executed.[14]

IV. Speculators

The focus in this section is on what should be called "outright speculators" - those who buy or sell foreign exchange solely on the basis of intending to profit from a change in its price. (This definition tends to neglect the substantial number of participants, ranging from tourists to governments, that actively speculate when their underlying activities give rise to a foreign exchange exposure.) In the sense used here, marketmakers are always potential speculators since they normally do not accept positions given to them by counterparties with the expectation of a loss.

The vast bulk of banks' speculative positions are taken and closed within the course of a single trading day. Much of this position-taking activity arises during the course of marketmaking activities. However, a number of such banks frequently take substantial speculative positions either for their own account, or that of a substantial customer.

A second important group of outright speculative players are financial and nonfinancial firms that have no marketmaking functions, and view their foreign exchange speculation as simply another line of business. By one count, there may be 50-70 multinational firms with in-house banks, trading staffs, and well-defined profit centers.[15]

A third group are the full-time managers of speculative funds, many of whom view currency speculation as a subset of a more varied speculative portfolio. Such traders are frequently managing assets for others, either in an informal manner or in more formally organized speculative funds. The leverage that is available to such operations can be considerable.

In some cases, speculators with sufficient financial standing may be able to obtain an interbank-type foreign exchange line of credit from a bank willing to execute his contracts, which restricts him to a specified level of outstanding contracts in specified currencies. However, since the speculator may well be doing business with other parties as well, most banks require collateral (cash, securities, or a letter of credit), expressed as a fraction of the outstanding contract value or the net foreign exchange position. While minimum margins for trading futures on organized exchanges are set by the exchange, banks are free to set their own levels. Under certain conditions, these might be as low as 2% of the contract value, providing a speculator with $1 million an opportunity to take a $50 million position. Smaller speculators almost exclusively trade on the exchanges, since banks have been leery of the potential legal and public relations complications in developing such business.

In all these arrangements, the bank retains the right to close out customer positions when limits are reached. Given the thinness of the required margin in certain cases, 24-hour monitoring of such a speculator's position by the bank or broker is required, thus limiting this segment of the business to institutions with global capability.

Larger speculators, with access to two or more banks, are able to negotiate "give up" agreements which give them the right to initiate a position with one bank and close it out with a second, which transfers, in effect, the closeout contract to the first bank. This gives the speculator the ability to solicit a more competitive price when he wishes to close out a position.

As discussed in Section II, speculative positions are normally taken in the spot market, with the position "rolled over" on a day-to-day basis, so that actual currency balances are kept close to zero, with the exception of any realized gains or losses. The major exception to this technique has developed with the growth of the futures markets, particularly the Chicago Mercantile Exchange's currency trading adjunct, the International Monetary Market (IMM). Consequently, it is now not unusual to find marketmaking commercial banks prepared to quote IMM futures dates for the benefit of speculator customers. In addition, "give up" agreements which permit the speculator to initiate or close out an IMM position with a commercial or investment bank when the exchange is closed can also be negotiated.

V. The Brokers

Foreign exchange brokers play an extremely important role in the interbank OTC market, although remarkably little has been written about them. In the 1989 Federal Re^_serve survey of the New York market, the 13 recognized brokers surveyed were involved in 44 percent of the gross volume transacted for a daily average total of $57 billion. (Brokers in the London and Tokyo markets account for roughly comparable shares.) The larger brokerage firms have affiliates in all major trading centers, and are able to offer customers immediate access to counterparties throughout the world through open telephone and telex lines between each center.

The broker market provides a variety of advantages to banks transacting business through it: a bank can reach a large number of counterparties quickly, its name is not revealed to the counterparty unless a transaction is consummated, and there is no requirement for reciprocity in quoting, as there can be when a marketmaker is approached directly. Commissions are paid to the broker by both parties to a transaction.[16]

Although the practice of "blind trading" through brokers is a feature of most organized markets, it creates a special tension in the OTC foreign exchange market, since the settlement of a transaction is entirely a matter between the two parties, and not through a clearing house or settlement agent. Thus, conveying a quote from one party to another imposes an obligation on the broker to know in advance if the two parties are authorized by their managements to deal with each other. Not surprisingly, given the large number of participants in the market and the frequent turnover of broker personnel, mistakes are frequently made. Similar difficulties arise when transaction amounts do not match or a broker finds one party to a transaction cancelled his price at the same moment it was being accepted on the other side.

While brokers and their clients try to devise mutually acceptable procedures to deal with these difficulties, the necessarily close relationship between individual brokers and traders, both of whom are normally on incentive-based compensation schemes, can make implementation of such procedures difficult.

The OTC interbank market should be a logical candidate for screen-based trading, and over the past decade a number of efforts to introduce such systems have been made. The primary reason no such system has been successful to date is the necessity for an extremely high degree of reliability in its operation. The volume of foreign exchange trading and the speed with which substantial positions are taken or reversed means that even a momentary outage on a screen-based system can leave traders uncertain of their true position. If the operator of the system is unwilling to assume nearly unlimited liability for financial losses occasioned by such outages, trading rooms are reluctant to commit themselves to the system. (It should be noted that retail-oriented systems for corporate customers and correspondent banks have been introduced.)

The first dealer-oriented system with prospects for success is currently being marketed by Reuters. If successful, it is likely to provide substantial competition to the broker market, as well as generating pressures for narrower spreads and less price dispersion, as was the case when such a system was introduced in the U.S. government securities market.[17]

However, screen-based trading is unlikely to do away entirely with the more traditional broker market, since the advantages of dealing through an intermediary that can provide more qualitative information (such as the existence of major orders in the market) than will appear on any screen-based system will remain. In addition, even if such a system has a high degree of reliability, major marketmakers are unlikely to want to conduct all their broker-type transactions through a single proprietary system.

VI. Credit and Settlement

Reference has been made in previous sections to the credit and settlement risks inherent in the OTC foreign exchange market. In some respects, this aspect of the market has yet to advance to the standards of the 16th century northern Italian currency fairs (where multicurrency net settlement among traders was made at the end of each fair).[18] Among most interbank participants, on settlement day each party sends to an account designated by the other party the amounts agreed upon.

If a U.S. bank has sold yen to a German bank for dollars, the U.S. bank will instruct its branch or correspondent in Japan to send the agreed upon number of yen to the Japanese bank designated by the German counterparty; the German bank will instruct its U.S. branch or correspondent to make the required payment in dollars for the account of the U.S. counterparty at a U.S. office.

Since the U.S. dollar is a currency in the vast bulk of all foreign exchange transactions taking place throughout the world, it is not surprising that well over $100 billion a day involving foreign exchange contracts flows through the CHIPS system of the New York Clearing House.[19] However, the foreign currency payments on the other side of this $100 billion are taking place at different times of the day: marks will be delivered in Germany before dollars are received in New York, leading to what is called "daylight exposure" in the settlement process.

While the efficiencies and added security of a well-capitalized clearing house are obvious in the current environment, and much advertised by the IMM, the institutional rigidities in the OTC market have made any movement in this direction extremely difficult. Indeed, it took the failure of the Herstatt Bank in 1974, which was closed by the German authorities while payments were still outstanding in New York, to impress upon market participants that settlement risks were very real possibilities.

The institutional rigidities in the market have revolved around concerns as to how a trustee in bankruptcy would treat offsetting transactions between commercial banks. In general, the belief has been that separate contractual obligations in foreign exchange need not be consolidated, and that a trustee or receiver (including a government agency, such as the FDIC) would tend to "cherry pick" those contracts which favored the firm and dismiss the rest.

The initial step in rationalizing the payments process has been the development of bilateral interbank netting agreements, providing for net settlement when more than one contract for a given settlement date in the same currency pair is outstanding between two parties. Since the major marketmakers in each center frequently deal with each other directly or through brokers during the course of a trading day, the concept is a relatively simple one, and can lead to immediate operational efficiencies. The FXNET system, originally introduced in

London in the late 1980s is a good example of such a system.

However, until recently the legal status of such arrangements, and their implications for credit exposure, were cloudy. The Basle agreement by banking regulators on commercial bank capital standards has led to the acceptance of "novation" as a definitive form of netting for legally-recognized risk reduction purposes. In netting by novation, contracts are not offset, but are subsumed into a new contract each time an eligible deal is contracted between two parties.

In addition, some banks are attempting to develop forward contracts in which only net settlement is made, as is the case in interest rate swaps and forward rate agreements. Instead of exchanging the gross currency amounts in the contract, only the difference arising out of exchange rate movements between the original contract date and the settlement date would be remitted.

All of these efforts are being stimulated by the Basle requirements to recognize explicitly, for capital adequacy purposes, off balance sheet exposure such as forward foreign exchange contracts. Continuing efforts to develop new instruments that minimize capital requirements can be expected.

VII. Linkages with the Exchange-Traded Markets

There are two exchanges in the United States where foreign currency contracts are actively traded. The currency adjunct of the Chicago Mercantile Exchange, the IMM, has futures and options contracts on seven currencies; the Philadelphia Stock Exchange trades only options on the same seven currencies. IMM daily average trading volume in April 1989 was \$10.1 billion, while Philadelphia options trading was approximately \$2.1 billion.[20]

Users of exchange-traded contracts include corporations and small firms, as well as large and small speculators. Perhaps the greatest attraction for commercial customers is the price transparency offered by the publicly available record of transactions and the end-of-day settlement prices, which provide definitive valuation data for accounting and auditing purposes. This is especially useful in the case of options. Although recent investigations of trader practices on the IMM and elsewhere emphasize that exchange trading does not eliminate the possibility of abuses of customer confidence, the formal oversight of trader activity is in sharp contrast to the OTC market. An additional advantage in a period of concerns about bank creditworthiness is the relatively high degree of confidence in the standing of the exchange or clearing house as a party in the settlement of transactions.

Offsetting these advantages for commercial users is the use of standardized contracts with a limited number settlement dates. This means that any actual movement of currencies to a beneficiary nearly always take place through the OTC market. The inability to match dates and amounts exactly to underlying commercial transactions also poses accounting and operational issues which an infrequent user of foreign exchange may find excessively burdensome. This may account for the fact that larger corporate users tend to be the most frequent business users of the exchanges, despite the fact that bid-asked spreads tend to be wider and brokerage fees ($5-$10 a contract for larger users) are charged.

Small speculators are particularly drawn to the exchanges, since commercial banks have traditionally shown little interest in them, perhaps because of concern about regulatory issues, such as jurisdiction by the Commodities Future Trading Commission and consumer liability issues. However, the arbitrage possibilities that immediately became apparent between the futures and OTC markets rapidly increased bank interest on their own trading accounts. Most of the largest banks now have holding company subsidiaries that are active on the exchange floors.

For large speculators, the major drawback of the exchange market has been their limited trading hours. One technique to circumvent this problem is use of the "give up" technique, described earlier, that permits speculators to use OTC contracts to offset exchange-traded positions. The other response has been by the exchanges to extend their hours or enter into agreements with exchanges in different trading centers to enable customers to trade on a near-24 hours basis.

As with trading in most other types of financial instruments, there appears to be room for both the OTC and the exchanges. Large, sophisticated, and frequent transactors will continue to see advantages in working with the OTC market, even while they use the exchanges to monitor OTC marketmakers. Small speculators have limited alternatives to the exchanges, while large speculators will be prepared to use either market in response to initiatives by the various competitors.

VIII. Regulation

The OTC foreign exchange market, particularly in the U.S., is notable for its lack of regulation. As a general rule, trading practices, price movements, disclosure of positions, and instruments traded are not subject to any regulation. For certain regulated participants, such as commercial banks, the federal regulatory agencies require periodic (but not daily) disclosure of positions. In addition, the banking regulatory agencies concern themselves with the risk levels and internal management of foreign exchange trading by banks under their jurisdiction. The agencies normally are not concerned formally with market practices unless a transaction can be defined as a loan (as can be the case with certain types of forwards). Innovation in instruments is occasionally constrained by the desire to avoid possible Securities and Exchange Commission or CFTC jurisdiction. Investment banks and others are subject to minimal legislation in addition to what is related to their membership and trading activity on exchanges. There is no federal legislation of interbank brokers.

The banking agencies' overall supervision of commercial banks guarantees, in effect, that they will be able to fulfill their contracts (as was the case with Franklin National Bank in 1974) and, at the same time, imposes limits on the total amount of contracts they may have outstanding with a counterparty at any given time.

The primary window on the OTC foreign exchange market for the U.S. regulatory authorities is the Federal Reserve Bank of New York, through the conduct of its own operations and through the Foreign Exchange Committee. The Committee consists of a dozen representatives of various U.S. and foreign banks, brokers, and one observer from the foreign exchange dealers association. Two Federal Reserve Bank officials are ex officio members of the Committee. This group develops suggested guidelines for the conduct of business by marketmakers, other dealers and brokers, and addresses a variety of technical operational and accounting issues. For example, it appears to have been an important factor in convincing the Federal Reserve

Board in 1988 to reduce the proposed capital requirements on forward exchange contracts during the development of risk-based capital standards for commercial banks. It also supplements information which the Reserve Bank gains from its participation in the foreign exchange market as agent for the U.S. Treasury, other central banks, and various international agencies.

What is especially noteworthy is that the market in the United States -- at least the dominant OTC part of the market -- has developed with the total absence of direct government regulation. While indirect regulation through supervision of the commercial banking system does provide assurances of bank counterparties being able to fulfill contracts, the central disciplining factor is the need to maintain reputation (and reciprocity, for marketmakers), given the premium on constant involvement in the market. To maintain involvement in the market one must be viewed as a reputable counterparty by other participants. Individuals who fail to measure up (for example, by spreading false information or failing to honor their verbal commitments) are eventually weeded out by their managers; institutions that do not measure up find spreads quoted to them widening, and eventually fewer and fewer counterparties ready to do business with them.

The CFTC is responsible for regulation of exchange-traded foreign exchange, including approval of contract terms and trading practices. The agency initiated a major controversy in 1985, when it sought to expand its jurisdiction into OTC activity that did not involve transactions between "banks and other sophisticated informed investors."[21] While that proposal failed when it met with a hostile response by most commentators, it does suggest that any major scandal involving customers in the OTC market will stimulate efforts to regulate the OTC market more closely. This threat has provided an additional incentive for commercial banks to move cautiously in developing their own speculative customer base.[22]

IX. Summary

The global foreign exchange market expanded rapidly during the 1980s. While broad institutional factors, such as the liberalization of exchange controls in Japan and Australia, and the relaxation of restrictions on capital movements - particularly portfolio investment - were important factors, market practices and dynamics were also responsible for growth in the market.

The technique by which banks hedge outright forward contracts, the use of the U.S. dollar as an intermediary currency in "cross currency" contracts, and the dynamics by which marketmakers lay off unwanted currency positions received from counterparties are examples of important "multiplier" factors in the market. Further research will be needed to quantify their importance.

A significant market development during the 1980s was the introduction of viable options markets in both the OTC and exchange-traded settings. A better understanding of the dynamics of option pricing, as well as the search for new products by nonbank competitors were important elements in the establishment of the options market. The successful introduction of a futures market in foreign currencies similarly showed nonbank competitors gaining ground. Additional new products are likely to be stimulated by recently-introduced requirements for commercial bank capital against foreign exchange exposure and the continuing competition between established commercial banks and nonbank competitors.

Despite rapid advances in communications and computer technology, screen-based foreign exchange trading has yet to be successfully introduced, in contrast to its success in equity trading. Currently, systems for both exchange traders and OTC dealers have been designed and marketed. However, the requirements for systems with extremely high reliability and an operator willing to assume substantial financial liability in the case of equipment or system outages were still holding up a fully operational system in early 1990.

The OTC market continues to be notable for its lack of direct regulation. The market, over time, effectively qualifies buyers, sellers, dealers, and brokers on the basis of their perceived credit standing and past conduct in respecting market conventions. Nonetheless, the more active search by a number of OTC participants for business from outright speculative accounts could eventually lead to the imposition of more direct regulation over the market.

ENDNOTES

1. See details in Federal Reserve Bank of New York (1989).

2. Cf. Euromoney Publications (1982).

3. On this point, see Levich, (1988), pp. 233-234.

4. This is known as the Cambist approach: "banks act as brokers in the forward market and are always willing to provide forward exchange at the interest rate parity rate," Simon Brooks, et al., (1986), p. 55.

5. The futures exchanges with a limited number of contract dates have a superior potential for speculators in this respect.

6. More formally, if S is the spot rate and F the forward rate, with i the U.S. interest rate and i* the foreign currency interest rate, $(F - S)/S = (i^* - i)/(1 + i)$. Any deviation from this relationship, after allowance for transactions costs, signals a risk-free arbitrage opportunity. With interest-rate parity dominating the markets, "spot and forward speculation are equivalent investments in that they lead to the same time series of expected profits." (Levich, 1984, p. 1029.) Thus, the practice of traders to speculate almost entirely in the spot market provides further evidence that interest-rate parity does, in fact, prevail in the foreign exchange market.

7. For example, J. P. Morgan, parent of Morgan Guaranty Trust, reported that at year-end 1988 it had $82 billion equivalent in forward exchange contracts with a remaining maturity of between 10 days and one year, just slightly smaller than total balance sheet assets of $84 billion J. P. Morgan & Co. (1989), p. 55. It is reasonable to assume that a substantial portion of the foreign exchange contracts were associated with interest-rate arbitrage.

8. The actual calculations might run as follows: Assume that Spanish interest rates on 180 day deposits are at 12 percent and U.S. rates are at 9 percent and that the current spot rate is 120 pesetas per U.S. dollar. The 180 day forward rate will be 121.65 through the action of arbitragers following the interest-rate parity theorem, adjusted for the actual number of days involved: 121.65 = 120 x (180/360 x (.12 - .09)/(1 + .09) + 120 (from footnote #11). This implies that the difference between the spot and forward rates will be equivalent to slightly less than .01 peseta for each day forward.

If there is any change in the differential between U.S. and Spanish interest rates, the difference between the spot and forward rates will adjust to reflect the new differential. Now assume that at the end of 90 days, the interest differential suddenly closes to 1.5 percent per annum while the spot rate remains unchanged. The trader will now be earning only half of the previous fraction of a peseta per day, and at the end of the 180 period, he will have only 121.24 pesetas to meet his obligation to pay out 121.65. On a $10 million position this would result in being "short" 4.1 million pesetas after 180 days which would have to be purchased at the spot rate of 120 for a loss of $34,167.

9. See Garbade, (1982), p. 474.

10. See Copeland, (1983).

11. There is an indirect exposure: final settlement of the two transactions depends upon the counterparties delivering the agreed-upon sums at the agreed-upon dates. One party's failure to perform would expose the marketmaker, at a minimum, to the potential cost of acquiring the currency needed to satisfy his contract with the other party at an added cost due to changes in the exchange rate.

12. This would be consistent with the models suggested by Burdett and Judd (1983), pp. 955-969. See also Garbade, (1982), pp. 481-491.

13. It should also be noted that striving to obtain a high volume of transactions is another form of seeking information about the trading interests of buyers and sellers, and thus being in a better position to become aware of the true equilibrium price in the market.

14. Market volume data collected by the major central banks counts the two separate transactions under a "swap" contract only once.

15. See Euromoney, May 1989, p. 102.

16. In a spot trade in a major currency, both sides might be charged $10 per million by the broker.

17. Garbade, (1982), pp. 434-435.

18. Braudel, (1972), p. 508.

19. See "Large Dollar Payment Flows from New York," in Federal Reserve Bank of New York Quarterly Review, Winter 1987-88.

20. Based on data supplied by the Chicago Mercantile Exchange and the Philadelphia Stock Exchange.

21. See Federal Register, October 23, 1985, pp. 42983-86 for an example of the CFTC's efforts.

22. See The Foreign Exchange Committee (1989), p. 12 for a short discussion of the market.

References

Brooks, Simon, and Keith Cuthbertson and David G. Mayes, 1986, **The Exchange Rate Environment** (Croom Helm, London).

Burdett, Kenneth and Kenneth L. Judd, 1983, Equilibrium Price Dispersion, **Econometrica 51**, 955-969.

Braudel, Fernand, 1972, **The Mediterranean**, (Harper & Row, New York, NY).

Copeland, Thomas E. and Dan Galai, 1983, Information Effects on the Bid-Ask Spread, **Journal of Finance 38**, 1457-1469.

Euromoney Publications, 1982, **The Management of Foreign Exchange**.

Federal Reserve Bank of New York, September 13, 1989, **Summary of Results of U.S. Foreign Exchange Market Survey Conducted in April 1989.** (Press Release).

The Foreign Exchange Committee, 1989, **1988 Annual Report**, (Federal Reserve Bank of New York, New York, NY).

"The Foreign Exchange Market in London," **Bank of England Quarterly Bulletin** November 1989, 531-535.

Garbade, Kenneth, 1982, **Securities Markets** (McGraw-Hill, New York, NY).

J.P. Morgan & Co., 1989, **1988 Annual Report.**

"Large Dollar Payment Flows from New York," **Quarterly Review 12, No. 4, (1987-1988)**, Federal Reserve Bank of New York, 6-13.

Levich, Richard M., 1984, Empirical Studies of Exchange Rates: Price Behavior, Rate Determination and Market Efficiency, in R.W. Jones and Peter B. Kenen, eds: **Handbook of International Economics,**

Volume II, 1984, (North Holland, New York, NY).

Levich, Richard M., 1988, Financial Innovation in International Financial Markets, in Martin Feldstein, ed.: **The United States in the World Economy** (The University of Chicago Press, Chicago, IL).

Taylor, Mark P., 1989, Covered Interest Arbitrage and Market Efficiency, **The Economic Journal 99**, 376-391.

Recent Developments in International Banking
and Finance, S.J. Khoury (editor)

CHAPTER IV

On Political Risk – The Turnover Tax on the Swedish Money and Bond Markets or How to Kill a Market without Really Trying[1]

Johan A. Lybeck

The University of Gothenburg
Sweden

1 Several colleagues have assisted me in getting material for this study. I would like to thank, in particular, Christina Lindenius from Sweden's Central Bank and Dr. Christoph im Obersteg and Patrick Burgy from Schweizerischer Bankverein for their kind help. I would also like to thank the many friends from the Stockholm Options Market OM, SE-Banken and other institutions for the help they gave me in structuring my thoughts during the year that we were striving together -unsuccessfully - to stop the tax from being introduced. I also wish to thank Professor Richard Levich of New York University for comments on an earlier version of the paper. Remaining unclear and improper thoughts are obviously of my own doing.

1. INTRODUCTION AND OUTLINE OF PAPER

The Swedish money market has a relatively short but lively history. From its inception in 1982, the market had already by the spring of 1987 introduced all the major internationally traded instruments: a liquid short and long market in fixed-income instruments (including a large market in commercial paper), futures on several underlying bonds and Treasury bills, options on Treasury Notes, FRN's with both cap's and floor's, a deposit market with FRA's, interest-rate swaps, etc. Liquidity was high, not least because of the immense turnover. In the spring 1987, the average daily turnover on the money and bond market was over SEK40 billion, corresponding to an annual total of ten times the Gross Domestic Product! Of the daily average amounts, about 20 billion was in futures and 5 billion in interest-rate options (interms of underlying values).

In September, 1987, the head of the Trade Union Council (LO) unexpectedly proposed a tax on market turnover in order to "reduce the overly large and socially worthless activities on themoney market". The government immediately agreed, believing that the new tax would mollify the unions into lower wage demands. A tax on money and bond market transactions was accordingly instituted from January 1, 1989, after a minimum of deliberation as a result of the tax, turnover had by the end of 1989 fallen by 95 per cent.

This paper presents the story of the "Rise and Fall of the SwedishMoney and Bond Markets". Of the various financial risks, political risk is easily singled out as the major risk factor and the one that most frequently underlies the more commonly analyzed.

Section 2 presents in brief detail how a very efficient moneymarket with all the internationally available instruments was created in just a few years from 1982 to 1987, under the influence not only of a large budget deficit but also of the active support of the Central Bank and the Government. In section 3 we review the origins of the transactions tax and how it is constructed. Section 4 discusses the a priori effects of the tax in view of the existing literature and known empirical findings. Unfortunately,the area of transactions costs is one where the effects may be obvious but where little empirical work has been done.

This holds a fortiori for the fixed-income market. In section 5 we analyze the effects of the tax on the Swedish markets in terms of lower volumes, increased volatility etc., but also in terms of ways to evade the tax. A formal econometric test of the introduction of the transaction tax is not presented. However, such a formal event study would certainly pin-point the tax as the source of changes in the markets, nothing else of major interest having occurred. A summary of the paper is presented in section 6.2.

2. BACKGROUND - HOW THE MARKET WAS CREATED[1]

Until 1983, the Swedish bond market was characterized by illiquid bonds of complex character. Interest-rate fixes were generally for a period of 5 years, while maturities were of 10-20 years' length. Retractables (call and put possibility at rate resetting) were common. Amortization features, by means of sinking fund or lottery, were common (for housing mortgage bonds in particular). So cal led Priority Bonds (government bonds and bonds issued by the mortgage institutions) were, until December 1986, forced upon banks, pension funds and insurance companies by means of average and marginal liquidity ratios. These bonds held a rate of interest fixed by the government at below-market yields. A listing of new financial instruments introduced into the Swedishmarket appears in Table 1. In 1982, Treasury bills, "Statsskuldvxlar", were introduced and in 1983, a liquid market in standardized Treasury Notes, "Riksobligationer". At the same time, a market for liquid Mortgage Bonds was created along similar lines. These new instruments have resulted in a deeper and less complex market. Treasury Notes and Mortgage Bonds were also the underlying instruments for several futures contracts and one options contract. As the rate of interest of the "Priority Bonds" was refixed at

---

1

For a more detailed presentation of the Swedish money and bond market, see my leaflet written for SwedBank, "The Swedish Capital Market", revised edition", January 1990. This is the most detailed and up-to-date description in existence. A further descriptioon in English is available in European Bond Commission (1989) and in Swedish in Lybeck and Hagerud (1989).

market-rate levels, the share of the bond market that could be regarded as liquid was gradually increased. With their high levels of liquidity and the generally upward-sloping yield curve (see Figure 1), interest from other potential issuers - banks, corporations and local authorities - in issuing bonds has been very small during the 1980's. Instead, their needs have led to a very rapid growth in the market for Commercial Paper. Banks and other corporations have also pioneered an active market in Floating Rate Notes (FRN) and Variable Rate Notes (VRN), where loans of 5-10 years maturity have a 3-month interest rate set from the deposit rate STIBOR (Stockholm InterBank Offered Rate). CAP's and FLOOR's have been added to some of the FRN's. The short-term market was formally started in 1980 with the introduction of Bank CD's, but became a truly liquid money market first with the introduction of marketable Treasury bills in 1982. The gradual improvement of the State's finances has, however, led to a lower volume of issue of bills today. The main volumes in the short-term market are now in commercial paper and in the deposit market. Liquidity in the short market has been enhanced by rating of paper as well as by the introduction of "K-1 Composites" of the highest-grade paper. The connection between the short and the long side of the market is enhanced by an active swap market, where 3-month interest rates (usually the deposit rate, STIBOR) are swapped to 2 to 7 year bond yields, or vice versa.

During the 1980's, the Swedish capital market has been gradually deregulated, as in other countries. The major steps in market deregulation are summarized in Table 2. It is not too much to say, however, that the increased marketability of fixed-income debt has taken place with the active support of the Central Bank and the Government. Until recently, however, the Swedish market has been protected by one of the strictest foreign-exchange controls in Europe. This has had little effect on short-term interest rates inview of the openness of the economy (exports plus imports correspond to over 70 per cent of the Gross Domestic Product,GDP), but it has at times insulated the stock and the bond markets from foreign influences. The elimination of all currency controls - including the bondmarket - took place on July 1, 1989. This means that for the first time in 50 years, foreign investors are able to buy SEK-denominated bonds. The remaining restrictions are of no consequence for the foreign investor, but they do impede competition and efficiency, since they require Swedish residents buying foreign securities to do so through a Swedish bank.

Table 1.

New Instruments on the Swedish Money and Capital Market

	Year of introduction
Certificates of deposit	1980
Treasury bills ("Statsskuldvxlar")	1982
Commercial paper ("certifikat")	1983
Treasury Notes ("Riksobligationer")	1983
Forwards and futures on Treasury Notes and Bills	1985
Interest-rate options on Treasury Notes	1986
Floating Rate Notes (FRN)	1986
Deposit-Market ("STIBOR")	1986
Interest-rate Swaps	1986
CAP's and FLOOR's	1987
Forward-Forwards and Forward-Rate Agreement (FRA)	1987
Standardized FRA's and Swaps (IMM dates)	1988
Standardized Currency Options (USD/DEM)	1988
Standardized Currency Options (USD/SEK)	1989
K-1 Composite Commercial paper	1989
Benchmark Treasury and Mortgage Bonds	1989

Source: own analysis

Table 2

The major steps in the deregulation of the Swedish market

Deregulation of banks' deposit rates	1978
Deregulation of interest rate on corporate bonds	1980
Deregulation of lending rates by insurance companies	1982
Liquidity ratios for banks abolished	1983
Deregulation of banks' lending rates	1985 (May)
Loan ceiling on bank lending abolished	1985 (Nov)
Marginal placement ratios for banks and insurance companies abolished	1986
Relaxation of exchange controls on share transactions	1986-89
Remaining currency controls lifted	1989 (July)

Source: own analysis

During the 1950's, the 1960's and the 1970's, the slope of the yield curve in Sweden was more often negative than positive. To many observers, this indicated an immature and regulated capital market. It may also have been due to the fact that the rapidly growing National Pension Insurance Fund invested mostly in the longer portion of the yield spectrum, driving down long yields. Since 1983, a much more mature market has evolved. Figure 1 showsthe month-by-month development of 3-month Treasury bills and 10-year Treasury Notes. As can be seen, the latter has most often been above the former, i.e., the yield curve has had a positive slope. On average for the total period 1983-88, the yield spread amounted to 25 basis points in effective terms. During 1987-88, the curve was much more positively sloped, with yield spreads of 150 basis points in effective yields. Since then the curve has inverted and shows a downward slope. One reason behind this changemay be the more pessimistic outlook for the economy. Another reason that we examine in this paper is the reversion to a more immature money market after the introduction of the turnover tax. The above description of instruments on the market and of Central Bank policy, together with the description of the yield curve, give several pieces of evidence of how a well-functioning market for fixed-income debt was created in but a few years. Let me tothis add some evidence of market turnover, summarized in Figure 2. Data are only available for Treasury Bills and Treasury Notes and for mortgage bonds (and thus exclude the important markets incommercial paper and deposits, including FRA's), and only from April 1987 on, when the reporting of deals to the Central Bank became compulsory. At this stage, the daily average turnover in Treasury securities was SEK 40 billion, of which SEK 25 billion was interbank and SEK 15 billion for end customers (according to unpublished Central Bank data). Of the total trade, about one-third was in futures. One should add to this a daily average of 5 billion in interest-rate options (in terms of the underlying). Figure 1 and Figure 2

3. THE TURNOVER TAX

The broad lines of the development of the Swedish money marketwere presented in the previous section. To this description should be added

Figure 1. Yield on Swedish 10-year Treasury Notes and 3-month Treasury Bills, January 1983-

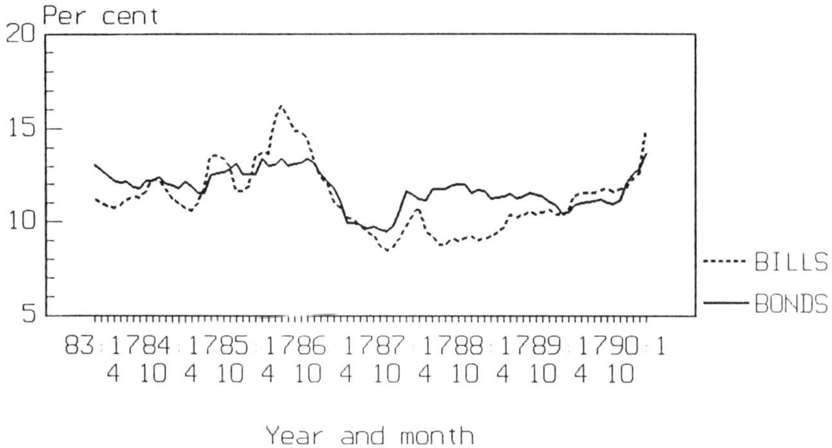

Figure 2. Turnover on the Swedish T-Bill and T-Note Market (SEK Billion) April 1987-March 1990 (daily averages) Source: Bank of Sweden unpublished data

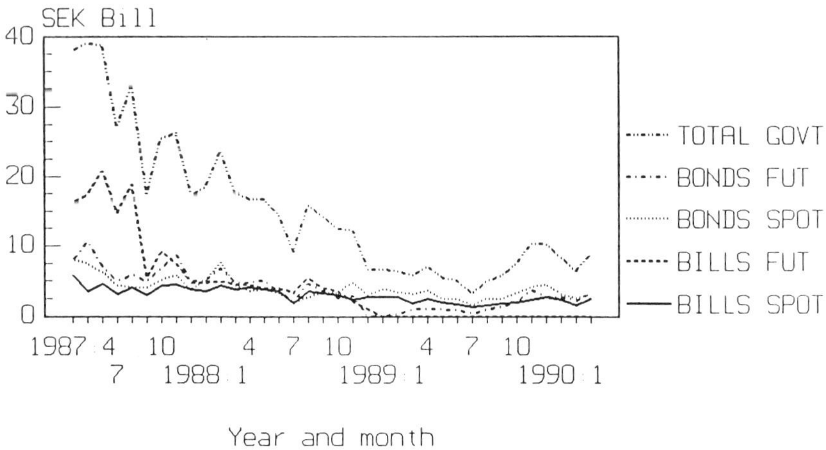

that much of the activity on the market - interbank as well as from end customers - appears to have been speculative in character, caused *inter alia* by the novelty of the market and the absence of internal guidelines for interest-rate risk. From mid-November 1986 to mid-January 1987, bond yields then suddenly rose by almost 300 basis points. As a result, the market was shaken by several losses. The most publicized occurred in the City of Stockholm (a SEK 450 million loss) and the insurance company Folksam (a SEK 300 million loss), both of which had speculated mainly in interest-rate futures and options. Perhaps it was the latter event which caused the Chairman of the Trade Union Council ("LO") Stig Malm to react as he did, since he was, in his capacity as Chairman of the Board of Folksam, severely criticized for the company's losses. Perhaps it was envy from his members of the high salaries paid to the young "financial puppies" (an expression coined at this time and used extensively by Mr.Malm) that forced a reaction. Nevertheless, at the general LO conference, on Monday, September 21, 1987, Mr. Malm suddenly and unexpectedly attacked the financial markets for creating economic instability and excessive wage differentials and for being socially worthless in general, and demanded a tax to stop the excesses of the market. The Finance Minister, Dr. Feldt, was forced to join in the critique and announced during the same conference that a turnover tax was to be proposed for money-market transactions (there already existed a turnover tax on stock-market transactions). This was on the Friday and under repeated angry noises from money-market participants, the Government was forced to work out during that very week-end the proposal that later became law. It was apparent from the proceedings that until then no government officials had even thought of a turnover tax on the money market. The detailed criticism of the capital market and the consequent argumentation for the proposed tax were first worked out by the Economics department of the Trade Union Council during the month following Mr. Malm's speech (LO [1987]). The title of the booklet is significant in its own right: " An 'enough' financial market?"[2] The charges in the booklet were extensive. Without any

---

2 This may not sound English, but it is a literal translation of the just as strangely-sounding Swedish title.

evidence, it was claimed that the financial markets... - "enhance the defects in the fiscal system, thereby leading to unsound developments and erroneous social incentives", - "destabilize real production, e.g. investments, by exaggerating the economy's cyclical tendencies" (op cit, p.18). It was also claimed that since the financial sector is excluded from the VAT levied on other sectors, there was an inherent tendency towards a "too large" financial sector (p.19), a tendency enhanced by the fact that a major part of the activity in the sector consisted of transforming highly taxed (wage) incomes into lower taxed capital gains. It was also claimed (more rightly) that the big winners from the deregulation process were the big corporations, whereas the borrowing and transactions costs of the average household had hardly been affected at all (p.29). In order to minimize the risks that financial markets, driven by speculative motives and too much liquidity, destabilize the economy, the Trade Union Council demanded a "sharp turnover tax" in order to focus on longer horizons for investors.[3]

The government's proposal followed very much in the LO booklet's footsteps but added a new motive; the turnover tax on the moneymarket was necessary in order to create "neutrality" with the stock market, which already had a similar tax.

This is not the place to take exception to the argumentation presented by the Trade Union Council and the Government. I have only wanted to present the political and economic environment in which a well-functioning money market is first created and then just as quickly destroyed.[4]

The turnover tax is, more formally, a tax on all transactions in bearer instruments and on some specifically mentioned registered instruments,

---

3

The Trade Union Council supported its case by invoking an argument from Nobel Laureate James Tobin (1984). "They attract short-term speculators and intermediaries, distract and minimize the importance of economic fundamentals for pricing. I think that Keynes was right in suggesting that we should offer a larger resistence to short-term possession of securities and a larger reward to longer-term investments." (p.35)

4

I have myself been in the forefront in the attempts to stop the tax, with a dozen or so newspaper articles and a professional articles, Lybeck (1988).

such as finance-company paper.[5] The underlying instrument must in this case be meant for general transactions. The underlying must also be an instrument; instrument-less markets are specifically excluded. Forwards and futures, however, are taxed in terms of the underlying transactions volume, even if the gain or loss is settled in cash. For options, the tax is first levied on the premium (at 2 per cent) and then also on the exchange of underlying, if there is delivery. Table 3 presents the tax structure in detail.

Table 3.

The money market turnover tax (for a roundtrip).

The tax is, for securities with a maturity not less than	5 years	0.030 %
	4	0.025 %
	3	0.020 %
"	2	0.015 %
"	1	0.010 %
	4 quarters	0.010 %
	3	0.080 %
"	2	0.060 %
"	1	0.040 %
for securities with a remaining maturity less than	1 quarter	0.020 %
for securities with a remaining maturity less than	45 days	0.010 %

The tax is shown for a round trip, i.e., double the sum for an individual transaction. The tax is levied on the value of the transaction (excluding commissions).

Source: Swedish Law, SFS 1988:781, "Law concerning certain changes in the law 1983: 1053 concerning tax on the turnover on certain securities". The translation is mine.

5

It is perhaps significant that the tax is named - by its proponents and opponents alike - "the puppy tax".

One can note that the tax is graduated according to the approximate risk, since (for par bonds in 13 per cent yield levels), the risk is:

For a note or bill with

5 year's maturity	3.43
4 year's maturity	2.91
3 year's maturity	2.32
2 year's maturity	1.65
1 year's maturity	0.88
3 quarter's maturity	0.66
2 quarter's maturity	0.44
1 quarter's maturity	0.22

By risk is meant price change, in per cent, per percentage pointchange in market rate of interest, i.e., what on the US market is termed "modified duration". See e.g., Fabozzi (1988).

Hence the tax translates approximately into 1 interest-rate basis point, irrespective of maturity. For the Swedish bill and bond market, which both trade according to yield-to-maturity (AIBD definition), the tax thus raises the quoted normal spread from 3 to 4 basis points on bills and from 5 to 6 basis points on bonds.[6]

For interest-rate options, the tax was levied in a different manner, namely 2 per cent (for a round trip) of the premium paid or received. It can be shown that at the time (with the underlying being a five-year Treasury note), this corresponded to around 1 basis point for an option at the money, up to 3 basis points for the deepest-in-the-money option and, of course, to basically nothing for the deepest-out-of-the-money option.

As is the rule in Sweden, the proposal was sent for comments to various institutions (Government bodies, industry associations and lobbying organizations). Out of 37 institutions, 35 were highly negative. The only two organizations to have a positive appreciation of the proposed tax was the Trade Union Council (LO) and the Board of the First Government National Pension Insurance Fund (which is dominated

---

6

These spreads are the normal ones. They have occasionally been increased to 10 basis points.

by blue-collar workers, i.e. LO). The most fiercely negative critique came from the Central Bank. Its well-written comment (published in the collection of comments on the law by the Government but also published in extenso in the Bank of Sweden Quarterly Review, in sharp contrast to normal procedure) focused on the role played in the capital market by liquidity and by government-appointed market makers (in Treasury bills and notes) in order to create this liquidity.

The comment contained a detailed description of how a bank in its market-making role is forced to hedge its portfolio by a series of short-term transactions and warned of the serious consequences for monetary policy and interest-rate stability that would follow if this possibility were to be hampered by the introduction of the tax.[7] [8]

7

"A transactions tax must, by necessity, influence the market-maker system and, in general, the functioning of the money market. If there is a tax on the purchase and sale of securities and also on futures and optiosn, the costs for market makers to creeate a secondary market increase. The cost of hedging interest-rate risk in fixed-income portfolios also rises.

A transactions tax thereby influences the turnover on the market and hence the liquidity in the individual issues. The market-maker system is particularly affected, since it is based on negligible transactions costs. The size cf the effects is naturally a consequence of the height of the tax. The consequences are, however, difficult to quantify. Low turnover and low liquidity also imply raised demands from investors on yield levels.

The imposition of a transactions tax on trade in fixed-income securities also give the market participants an incentive to choose other un-taxed forms of transacting. A multitude of such changes are conceivable. It may be more profitable for banks and other bond dealers to shift from trading for their own accounts to a commission-based brokerage activity for end-customers. Direct loans between investors and borrowers may take the place of securitized lending. The inter-bank market in securities may likewise change into an exchange of [un-taxed] deposits. The magnitude of such changes is naturally caused by the level of the transactions tax. If the shift to alternative forms of transactions becomes extensive, a large part of the present translucency of the money market is lost." (Bank of Sweden, Quarterly Review 1/88, pp. 63-64, my translation).

8

It is even more remarkable to note that the Chairman of the Board of Governors of the Bank of Sweden is by tradition the Under-Secretary of the Treasury, in this instance Mr. Erik Asbrink. In one capacity, Mr. Asbrink wrote the proposed law, in his other capacity signed the vehement opposition to the same law.

The sole response from the government in its final proposal (which then became law) was to half the proposed tax on market-maker transactions. The Government simultaneously introduced the turnover tax to market-maker transactions on shares; previously only customer deals had been taxed (at 2 per cent for a roundtrip).

4. A PRIORI EFFECTS OF THE TAX

From a theoretical point of view, there have been only a few studies on the effects of transactions costs. Most of these have centered on the stock market (e.g. Berkowitz et al. (1988)). A notable exception is Takagi (1987), who shows the effects on Japanese bond markets of the hundred-fold rise in market turnover between 1972 and 1985. As a result, Takagi estimates that transactions costs, as measured by the bid-ask spread, fell by about 80 per cent. The author then goes on to show how market efficiency in terms of the yield structure improved dramatically and conformed much better to economic theory in the form of the expectations hypothesis.

A study of the Swedish stock market (Lindgren and Westlund, 1988) concluded that if the turnover tax were halved (from 2 to 1 percent), it would lead to a volume increase of 50-70 per cent, and by 150 -300 per cent if the tax were to be abolished altogether. Interestingly, Jackson and O'Donnell (1985) suggested identical figures for the British stock market. It is here that we find the reason behind the fact that presently, two-thirds of the turnover on the 16 most widely-traded Swedish shares takes place in London (according to unpublished estimates by the Stockholm Stock Exchange).

The Lindgren and Westlund study thus found that an increase of about 50 per cent in stock-market transactions costs led to a 50 per cent reduction in turnover, for an elasticity of unity (the estimated elasticity varied between 0.85 and 1.35 in different formulations). The introduction of the turnover tax on bond market transactions led correspondingly to an increase in the spread from 3 to 4 basis points for the most traded bonds and hence to an increase in transactions costs by one third.[9] Should this decrease transactions volume by one-third also?

In drawing parallel conclusions for the effects of a turnover tax on the bond market, one must keep in mind *inter alia* the drastic difference between the two markets. One difference pertains to the character of the two markets. The stock market remains to a large extent a speculative market. If a private speculator expects stock prices to rise by 51 per cent (as they did in 1988 in Sweden), a 2 per cent tax is perhaps no major impediment to trade. Since the above-mentioned crashes in 1986-87, the Swedish bond market is however predominantly a hedging market, where position-taking is severely curtailed by position limits (and common sense). A hedging market with its tight spreads can be expected to suffer much more than a speculative market from a tax.

Another difference between the two markets is the degree of substitution. There are no substitute, untaxed, products for a share; stock and stock-index futures and options are also taxed. While Swedish shares have been listed abroad at an increasing frequency in the last few years, it is only since January of 1989 that investment abroad has become deregulated. And already two-thirds of transactions in the shares of the major companies take place abroad!

For the money and bond markets, the possibility to issue and trade abroad is even more recent. On the other hand, there exist more extensive domestic substitutes, as we shall see in the next section.

For both these reasons - the character of the market and the availability of substitutes - an a priori expectation would be that the tax would lead to a much larger impact on the bond market than on the stock market.

Finally, one can also compare the Swedish experience with the documented effects in Switzerland, the only other country to have a transactions tax on the money and bond markets ("dieeidgenossige Stempelabgabe"). Since the tax is not graduated with maturity, it has caused Switzerland to be the only financially highly developed country

---

9

There are no commissions on the Swedish money and bond markets; the dealers live off the spread only. For a survey of market practices in different countries, see Lybeck (1990).

with virtually non-existant short-term markets (for bills or commercial paper). The tax is also estimated (by the Schweizerischer Bankverein) to have had a sharp tendency to lower market turnover, despite the fact that transactions that take place in Switzerland between two foreign parties are (in contrast to Sweden) exempt from the tax, as are market-maker transactions in most cases[10] (also in contrast to Sweden).

5. EFFECTS IN PRACTICE AND SUBTERFUGES

As expected, the most visible effect of the tax has been the dramatic fall in turnover in the Swedish money markets: from a daily average of over SEK 40 billion in the spring of 1987 to around SEK 5 billion by mid-1989 increasing somewhat in latter months (see also Figure 2 above). With regard to the fact that the underlying stock of liquid assets has increased during this period, this corresponds to a decrease in the rate of turnover by 98-99 per cent. The tax elasticity of trading volume on the Swedish money market is thus calculated to be about 3 in contrast to the stock market's unitary elasticity.[11]

Another indication of the decreased market efficiency, in line with the study by Takagi, is the renewed reversal of the term structure relation (see also Figure 1 above). Note that this reversal took place just as the tax was introduced in January, 1989, well before the dramatic deterioration in the Swedish economy by November 1989.

A third effect is the increased interest-rate volatility, visible in particular from November, 1989, onwards when doubts about the Swedish economy have again surfaced. Not only have bond yields risen sharply (from around 11 to around 15 per cent) but daily variations have also become much more notable (with daily movements of 20-30 basis points being common even for bonds). As this is written, the time

---

10

Provided bonds are resold the same day. For further discussion of the Swiss transaction tax, see also Levich and Walter (1990).

11

Since turnover can hardly fall by more than 100 percent, it would be difficult to find an elasticity much larger!

period covered is too short to allow fora meaningful quantitative estimate of increased daily volatility.

While serious in themselves, these effects should be seen in light of the remuneration traditionally given in the Swedish credit markets to different risks. Credit risk has always been badly priced and it is only in recent years, as a result of rating, that there has developed a price difference at all in the market forcommercial paper. Similarly, as noted above, with a yield curvethat traditionally has had a perverse slope, price risk has traditionally been negatively rewarded.

However, liquidity risk has always been very well rewarded. Housing mortgage bonds of the same (5-year) maturity as Treasury 5-year notes and with virtually no credit risk have traded at spreads to Treasuries of up to 100 basis points as late as 1986. With more mature markets and the introduction of interest-rate swaps, these spreads were arbitraged away during 1987 and fell to a stable difference of around 20 basis points. In recent months,the spread has become both more variable and much larger, over 60 basis points.[12] The functioning of the bond market has also suffered. With marketmakers no longer able to live off the spread, given the lower turnover, the National Debt Office has had to start to pay marketmakers in Government debt. Yet several of them have dropped out, leading to a further deterioration in turnover.

For these reasons the expected yield of the "puppy tax" will be much lower than anticipated by the proposal. Instead of bringing an expected SEK one billion a year as the Government proposal calculated, preliminary tax yield calculations revealed by the Deputy Finance Minister in an interview in February said that the tax brought in only SEK 80 million in 1989 (in a total public sector revenue of some SEK 800 billion). Hence it is difficult toclaim, as in Switzerland, that the tax

---

12

These extra, say, 40 points translate to 45 basis points extra for mortgage borrowers, since the bonds issued pay interest annually, while mortgage loans are paid quarterly. With a total stock of fixed-rate mortgages of around SEK 650 billion at the end of 1989 (according to the Monthly Bulletin of Statistics) this translates to an annual extra cost of SEK 3 billion, 0.3 percent of GDP, for the spread loss alone.
To this cost should be added the effect of the tax in raising the average level of interest rates.

cannot be abolished becauseit brings in critical revenues.

A less visible, but just as serious, consequence of the tax has been to make the markets less easy to follow, for the market participants themselves as well as for the supervisory authorities (cf. the cited comment on the tax proposal by the Bank of Sweden). The tax is a tax on bearer instruments; hence one obvious effect has been to revitalize the non-taxed market for debentures (capital-market debentures issued by housing mortgage institutes and finance-market debentures issued by finance companies).

A second subterfuge is increased trade with the issuer, since the tax is a tax on secondary-market transactions and not on issuing activity in the primary market. Hence the FRN market has given way to a VRN market, since a VRN can be putted at par to the issuer at every rate resetting, i.e., every three months.[13]

A third and the major evasion is to turn to the untaxed markets where there is no formal underlying instrument. Hence the deposit market has been vitalized further and FRA's have completely taken over the role once played by Bill futures. Since mid-1989, the FRA market is fully standardized to IMM dates.[14] On the long-term side, interest-rate swaps are gradually taking over the role onceplayed by the active futures market in Treasury Notes and mortgage bonds. However, in both cases, volumes are unknown, since they need not be reported.

To a large extent, the damage has been made even greater by the disfunctional behavior of the supervisory authority, the Bank Inspection Board. After having checked with the National TaxBoard, the Stockholm Options Market was in early 1989 ready to launch futures and options on a synthetic underlying Treasury Note. Since there was

---

13

The FRN market has suffered in particular from the tax, since the authorities have decreed that an FRN pays tax according to its maturity, i.e., 5-10 years, and not according to the rate resetting period, three months, which is of course the proper comparison since it competes with 3-month Treasury bills and 3-month commercial paper.

14

The spot market has difficulty taking over the corresponding spot bill market, however, since the 4 percent cash reserve ratio on deposits is basically equivalent to a tax of about 60 basis points at present yield levels.

formally no underlying paper, the new products would be untaxed The Tax Board had agreed to let it be tax-free. However, at the last moment (at 5 PM on the day before trade was to start) the Bank Inspection Board forbade the product, because it avoided the tax. In doing so, it simultaneously also expressly forbade the introduction of any new product on the market that did not pay the tax (according to a Reuter interview with the Director of the Board). And hence during 1989, innovation on the money market came to a complete standstill.

Since July, 1989, bond transactions with foreign markets are completely liberalized (with the exception of the above-noted rule that Swedish residents must trade through a Swedish-licensed bankor dealer). For this reason one could expect that a large part of the bond market would move abroad. Even if only a few international bond issues in SEK have been issued so far, and foreign-owned, domestically issued, bonds have to physically stay in Sweden, this fact should prove no hindrance to the creation of an active market in interest-rate futures and options on SEK underlying, so long as cash settlement is accepted as the sole means for settlement and not delivery.

6. CONCLUSIONS

During a brief period of perhaps five years, the Swedish capital market went from being one of the most heavily regulated and backwards in Europe to being one of the leading markets, in terms of instruments, turnover and creativity. In two years this whole structure has been destroyed by the turnover tax.

There was no visible motive for the introduction of the tax in thefirst place. The tax goes counter to the development in othercountries. Norway has recently scrapped its (1 per cent) turnovertax on share transactions. Switzerland has recently introducedseveral changes in its tax structure to increase the competitiveability of "Die Finanzplatz Schweiz", namely to completelyliberate from tax any transaction that the "Effektenhndler"(securities dealers) undertake in their own holdings, as well asthe issue and trade of Euro-bonds in Switzerland and all paperwith a maturity less than one year.[15]

The development of the money market and the consequent introduction of a breaking mechanism in the form of the turnover tax conform well to Kane's (1987) recent theory of "competition in regulation". Also the next step, namely the scrapping of the turnover tax on money-market transaction from April 15, 1990, and the halving of the tax on stock transactions to follow on January 1, 1991, are also in line with the dialectics of Kane.[16]

It is interesting to speculate on how much of the market that will return with the scrapping/reduction of the tax. My guess would be that the short-term market will stay at depressed levels of turnover. The main reason is that FRA's have turned out to be a perfect substitute for bill futures, which, as Figure 2 showed, dominated completely the cash market in Treasury bills. For bonds and notes and instruments with these as underlying, I would tend to be more optimistic, since the swap market has not been able to provide a close substitute. The Stockholm Options Market will launch its long-awaited contract (future and futures-style option) on the constant-duration synthetic underlying that was forbidden in early 1989. This contract will be traded in Stockholm and London simultaneously, just as is already the case for Swedishstock-index futures and options.

For cash transactions in shares, I doubt that a halfing of the transactions tax to 1 per cent would do much good. Even a 1 percent tax leads to levels of transactions costs considerably above those in any other developed economy (Roll (1989), Table 3).[17]

15

"Bundesgesetz ueber die Stempelabgaben, Änderung vom 5. Juni 1989".

16

See Kane (1987) for the original statement and e.g., Levich (1990) and Levich and Walter (1989,1990) for recent developments.

17

The only comparable country in Roll's table, Norway, has just abolished its turnover tax completely, as was noted above.

REFERENCES

Berkowitz, S.A., D. E. Logue and E.A. Noser, 1988, The Total Cost of Transactions on the NYSE, *Journal of Finance* 43 , 97-112.European Bond Commission, 1989, The European Bond Markets: An Overview and Analysis for Issuers and Investors (Probus Publishing Co., for the European Bond Commission, Chicago).

Fabozzi, F.J., 1988, Fixed Income Mathematics (Probus Publishing Co, Chicago).

Jackson, P.D. and A.T. O'Donnell, 1985, The Effects of Stamp Duty on Equity Transactions and Prices in the UK Stock Exchange, mimeo, Bank of England.

Kane, E., 1987, Competitive Financial Regulation: An International Perspective, in R. Portes and A. Swoboda, eds., Threats to INternational Financial Stability (Cambridge University Press,London).

Levich, R.M., 1990, The Euromarkets after 1992", in J. Dermine, ed., European Banking After 1992 (Basil Blackwell, London).

Levich, R.M. and I. Walter, 1989, The Regulation of Global Financial Markets", in T. Novelle, ed., New York's Financial Markets (Westview Press, Boulder, Colorado).

Levich, R.M. and I. Walter, 1990, Tax-Driven Regulatory Drag: European Financial Centers in the 1990's, Working Paper IB-90-1, New York University, Stern School of Business.

Lindgren, R. and A. Westlund, 1988, Aktieomsttning och omsttningsskatt. En empirisk studie p svenska data" ("The turnover of stocks and the turnover tax; An empirical study on Swedish data"). Working paper, Stockholm School of Economics.
LO, 1987, An 'Enough' Capital Market? (LO, Stockholm,in Swedish).

Lybeck, J.A., 1988, Are the financial markets too big?" Ekonomisk Debatt 16 (Journal of the Swedish Economic Association), 3-10. (in Swedish).

Lybeck, J.A., 1990, Money and Bond Markets with Emphasis on Europe: Practical Details, mimeo.

Lybeck, J.A. and G. Hagerud, 1989, Penningmarknadens instrument (Rabn & Sjgren, Stockholm).

Roll, R.W., 1989, The International Crash of October 1987, in R.J. Barro et al, Blac Monday and the Future of Financial Markets (Dow Jones Irwin, Homewood, Ill.).

Takagi,S., 1987, Transactions Costs and the Term Structure of Interest Rates in the OTC Bond Markets in Japan", Journal of Money, Credit and Banking 19 ,515-27.

Tobin, J., 1984, On the Efficiency of the Financial System", Lloyds Bank Review, July.

Recent Developments in International Banking
and Finance, S.J. Khoury (editor)

CHAPTER V

Time-Varying Risk Premiums in Forward Exchange Rates and Deviations from PPP

Hossein B. Kazemi

*Dept. of General Business & Finance, School of Management, University of Massachusetts, Amherst, MA 01003. This paper is based on Chapter V of my doctoral dissertation, which was completed at the University of Michigan. I wish to thank G. Dufey, W. Torous, A. Tschoegl, H. Varian and seminar participants at the University of Michigan, and the University of Massachusetts for their comments. I remain responsible for any errors.

I. The Structure of the World Economy

The following assumptions characterize the world economy:

(A.1) **A Two-Country World:** I consider a world economy that consists of two countries, say US and UK. This assumption is relaxed in Section IV. The exchange rate is the price of one UK pound in terms of US dollars and is denoted by S(t). I use subscripts "a" and "b" to denote variables that belong to US and UK investors, respectively.

(A.2) **Perfect Financial Markets:** Financial markets are competitive; trading can take place continuously through time, and there are no taxes or transaction costs.

(A.3) **Consumption Opportunities:** There are K consumption goods, which are traded internationally. $P_i(t)$ denotes the price of consumption good i=1,..,K in terms of US dollars. The law of one price need not hold for consumption goods. That is, the price of consumption good i in terms of UK pounds may or may not be equal to $P_i(t)S(t)$. Thus, there may be deviations from PPP.

(A.4) **Investment Opportunities:** The rates of return on risky securities, the riskless rates of interest, and the exchange rate are endogenously determined. The state of the world economy is completely described by a set of state variables.[3] I assume that the behavior of state variable j, $X_j(t)$, follows an Ito process [e.g., see Merton (1973), and Arnold (1974)] of the following form:

$$dX_j(t) = X_j(t)\alpha_j(t)dt + X_j(t)\phi_j(t)dY_j, \quad j=1,...,N \qquad (1)$$

where $\alpha_j(t)$ is the expected rate of change in state variable j, $\phi_j(t)$ is its standard deviation, and Y_j is a standard Wiener process. I assume that the first K+2 state variables are respectively prices of K consumption goods, US's short-term rate, and UK's short-term rate. Without loss of generality I assume that there are two real risky assets.[4] The return generating process of real asset i=1,2 can be presented as follows:

$$dV_i(t) = [V_i(t)\mu_i(t) - D_i(t)]dt + V_i(t)\sigma_i(t)dZ_i \ , \qquad (2)$$

where $V_i(t)$ is the amount of money invested in asset i=1,2 at time t; $\mu_i(t)$ is the expected rate of return from the investment; $D_i(t)$ is the amount of money added to or withdrawn form asset i; $\sigma_i(t)$ is the standard deviation of the rate of return, and Z_i is a standard Wiener process. Note that because these parameters are functions of the state variables, asset prices do not follow stationary processes. I assume that asset 1 is dollar denominated, while asset 2 is pound denominated. This means that the return generating process displayed in equation (2) presents the dollar return on asset 1 and the pound return on asset 2. Hence, this equation must be adjusted for foreign exchange rate changes to obtain the rates of return on asset 1 and asset 2 in terms of pound and dollar respectively. Investors can also invest in nominal bonds that are risk-free in terms of their home currencies. The rates of return on these bonds are endogenous and are denoted by $r_i(t)$. I use the following notation to describe the movement of the foreign exchange rate:

$$dS(t) = S(t)\gamma_s(t)dt + S(t)\delta_s(t)dY_s(t). \qquad (3)$$

(A.5) **Investor's Choice:** Each investor maximizes the expected value of a time-additive von Neuman-Morgenstern utility of lifetime consumption of the following form,

$$J(W,X,t) = \max_{V_j, C_i} E\left\{ \int_t^T U(C_1,\ldots,C_K,M_1,SM_2,\tau,)d\tau \right\} \qquad (4)$$

subject to the wealth constraint. This expression represents the optimization problem of a US investor. In equation (4), J(W,X,t) is the maximum of the expected utility of lifetime consumption; W is the investor's wealth; E is the conditional expectation operator; C_i is the quantity of consumption good i; M_1 and M_2 are, respectively, the amount of US dollars and UK pounds that the investor holds.[5] Without loss of generality, I assume that the aggregation conditions hold within each country, and hence, I can concentrate on the behavior of only two investorsone from each country [see Rubinstein (1974)].

(A.6) **Wealth Invariant Price Index:** The indirect utility function of a US investor is defined as follows (unless there may be any confusion, subscripts "a" and "b" will be omitted):

$$U(I,P_1,\ldots,P_K,r_1,r_2,\tau) = \max_{C_i, M_i} \Big\{ U(C_1,\ldots,C_K,M_1,SM_2,\tau) + \lambda(I - \sum_i^K C_iP_i - r_1M_1 - r_2SM_2) \Big\}.$$

Note that the budget constraint includes the cost of purchasing consumption goods and the opportunity cost of holding currencies.[6] To obtain a cost of living index, I need to impose further restrictions on utility functions. Define β_i as the percentage that consumption expenditure, I, must change after a change in P_i or r_i, if the investor's indirect utility of consumption is to remain constant. That is,

$$\beta_i = \frac{\partial \ln I}{\partial \ln X_i}\Bigg|_{U=\bar{U}} . \qquad X_i = P_1,\ldots,P_K,r_1,r_2$$

If a wealth invariant price index is to exist, we must have $\beta_i / I = 0$.[7] Assuming that this condition is satisfied, the US investor's price index, ϕ_a , will behave has follows:

$$d\ln\phi_a = \sum_{i=1}^{K} \beta_i d\ln P_i + \beta_{K+1} d\ln r_1 + \beta_{K+2} d\ln r_2.$$

Equation (4) can restated as follows:

$$J(W,\phi_a,X,t) = \max_{V_j, C_i} E\left\{ \int_t^T U(I,\phi_a,\tau)d\tau \right\}.$$

II. The Model

The first order conditions for the expected utility maximization problem discussed in Section I are derived in the Appendix. From equation (A3) we can write the following for a US investor.

$$\gamma_s + r_2 - r_1 = T^{-1}W\ \mathrm{Cov}[W,S] + \sum_{j}^{N} H_j \mathrm{Cov}[X_j,S] \quad (5)$$

where the left hand side represents Fisher open effect, and it is equal to the risk premium in the forward exchange rate; T is the measure of absolute risk tolerance; W is the US investor's wealth; H_j is a measure of the investor's exposure to changes in state variable j. To simplify the notation, I use Cov[x,y] to denote Covariance(dx/x,dy/y).

Equation (5) is a familiar result from multiperiod asset pricing models.[8] According to it, the excess rate of return required by an investor is a function of:

(a) his/her degree of risk tolerance,
(b) his/her exposure to changes in the state variables,
(c) the covariance of the rate of return on the risky asset with the rate of return on the investor's wealth, and
(d) the covariances of the rate of return on the risky asset with changes in the state variables.

In equation (5) the risky asset is a short-term pound denominated riskless bond (it is however risky in terms of dollars). Because capital markets are perfect, interest parity holds, and as a result if the expected rate of change in the exchange rate, gs, is different from the difference between the rate of return on a short-term pound denominated bond and the rate of return on a short-term dollar denominated bond, then the expected future spot rate will also be different from the forward rate [e.g., see Solnik (1974), Deardorff (1979), and Stulz (1981)]. Thus, the left hand side of equation (5) represents the risk premium in a short-term forward rate.[9] For example, if this expression is positive, then the forward rate will be smaller than the expected future spot rate.

The next step in the development of the results is to restate the last N terms on the right hand side of equation (5) in terms of the covariance of the exchange rate with the price index and the remaining state variables.

Proposition 1. If there is a wealth invariant price index, then equation (5) can be expressed as follows:

$$\tau_s + r_2 - r_1 = T^{-1}W_1\{Cov[W_1,S] - Cov[\phi_a,S]\} + Cov[\phi_a,S] + \sum_{j=K+3}^{N} H_j Cov[X_j,S]. \quad (6)$$

Proof: If there is a wealth invariant price index, the last term of equation (5) can be expressed as follows:

$$\sum_{j}^{N} H_j Cov[X_j,S] = -(\partial lnJ_W/\partial ln\phi_a)Cov[\phi_a,S] + \sum_{j=K+3}^{N} H_j Cov[X_j,S].$$

Since J_W is homogeneous of degree negative one in the price index [see Adler and Dumas (1983)], we have $-(\partial lnJ_W/\partial ln\phi a) = W(T^{-1} - 1)$. Combining these two results with equation (4) completes the proof.

The terms inside the curly braces represent the covariance between the rate of change in the exchange rate and the real rate of return on the US investor's wealth.[10] A similar expression can also be obtained for the UK investor; after converting the UK investor's wealth and price index into US dollars, the resulting expression and equation (5) can be aggregated to obtain the following relationship:

$$\tau_s + r_2 - r_1 = (\bar{T})^{-1}\ \bar{W}(\text{Cov}[\bar{W},S] - \text{Cov}[\bar{\phi},S]) \ = \text{Cov}[\hat{\phi},S] + \sum_{j=K+3}^{N} \hat{H}_j \text{Cov}[X_j,S] \qquad (7)$$

where $\bar{W} = W_a + SW_b$, aggregate wealth; $\bar{T} = (T_a + ST_b)$, the measure of aggregate absolute risk tolerance;

$\bar{\phi}$ = a weighted average of the two indices, in which the ratio of each country's wealth to aggregate wealth is the weight [i.e., $d\ln\bar{\phi} = (\bar{W})^{-1}\ (W_a d\ln\phi_a + SW_b d\ln S\phi_b]$; $\hat{\phi}$ = a weighted average of the two indices, in which the ratio of cach country's measure of risk tolerance to aggregate risk tolerance is the weight [i.e., $d\ln\hat{\phi} = (\bar{T})^{-1}\ (T_a d\ln\phi_a + ST_b d\ln S\phi_b)$], and $\hat{H}_j = (\bar{T})^{-1}\ (T_a H_{aj} + ST_b H_{bj})$.

When the distribution of asset returns do not change stochastically through time (i.e., the parameters of equation (2) are only functions of time), the only relevant state variable will be the price index and thus, the last (N-K-2) terms on the right hand side of equation will be zero. In this case I obtain a result similar to those obtained by Grauer, Litzenberger, and Stehle (1976) Kouri (1977), Frankel (1979), and Adler and Dumas (1983).

Proposition 2. Suppose the investment opportunity set is not stochastic through time. Then, the real return from investing in a forward contract will be zero, if the exchange rate is not correlated with the real rate of return on aggregate wealth.

Proof: First, I have to determine the real return on a forward exchange contract, and for this purpose I have to identify the appropriate deflator.

It turns out that in the process of modeling the consumption-investment decisions of the investors I have actually derived the appropriate index for calculating the real return from any security. This index is a weighted average of national price indices in which the measures of risk tolerance serve as the weights; this index was denoted ϕ in equation (7). The left hand side of equation (7) represents the difference between the nominal rate of return on a pound-denominated riskless bond (in terms of dollars) and the nominal rate of return on a dollar-denominated bond; this difference is equal to nominal return on a forward contract. To determine the real return on a forward contract, I must, therefore, consider the difference between the real rate of return on a pound-denominated bond (in terms of dollars) and the real rate of return on a dollar denominated bond. This difference is as follows:

$$\frac{d(SB_2/\hat{\phi})}{SB_2/\hat{\phi}} - \frac{d(B_1/\hat{\phi})}{B_1/\hat{\phi}} = (\bar{\alpha}_s + r_2 - r_1)dt - \mathrm{Cov}[\hat{\phi},S]dt \tag{8}$$

where the right hand side is obtained by using Ito's lemma [e.g., see Arnold (1974)]. We know from equation (7) that the above expression is proportional to the covariance between the real rate of return on aggregate wealth and the rate of change in the exchange rate. I have therefore proved that the forward rate will be a biased estimator of the future spot rate (in real terms) if the exchange rate is correlated with the real rate of return on aggregate wealth, and that the premium is equal to $(\bar{T})^{-1}\bar{W}(\mathrm{Cov}[\bar{W},S] - \mathrm{Cov}[\bar{\phi},S])$.

Here, I seek to identify the conditions under which the foreign exchange rate will be correlated with the real rate of return on aggregate wealth. Clearly, this correlation will be different from zero if the exchange rate is correlated with the real returns on real assets, and, indeed, for various reasons one expects this correlation to be different from zero. For example, corporate profits and dividend income are taxed at their nominal values, and this means that after tax real values are altered whenever before tax real values are not affected by inflation or exchange rate changes. Furthermore, exchange rate changes may alter the relative prices of factors of production and thus, affect real returns on securities.[11]

Therefore, one important source of risk premium in forward

exchange rate is covariability with real returns on real assets. Here, my objective is to determine whether there are other sources of risk premiums in forward exchange rate and whether they are likely to cause time-variation in the size and the sign of the risk premium. Hence, I seek conditions under which there exists a risk premium in the forward rate even though the exchange rate is not correlated with the real returns on real assets. For this purpose I add the following assumption:

(A.7) **Exchange Rate and Real Assets:** I assume that changes in the exchange rate and the real rates of return on real risky assets are not correlated; i.e.,

$$\mathrm{Cov}[V_1/\phi_a, S] = \mathrm{Cov}[V_2/\phi_b, S] = 0 \, .$$

I also use the following notation to represent the behavior of deviations from PPP :

$$d\ln S - (d\ln\phi_a - d\ln\phi_b) = d\ln\epsilon \, , \qquad (9)$$

where $d\ln\epsilon$ represents the movement of deviations from PPP through time.

Proposition 3. If assumptions (A.1)-(A.7) hold and the investment opportunity is not stochastic through time, the real risk premium in the forward exchange rate can be expressed as follows:

$$\pi = (\bar{T})^{-1} \left(F \, \mathrm{Cov}[\epsilon, S] - N_1 \mathrm{Cov}[\phi_a, S] - N_2 \mathrm{Cov}[\phi_b, S] \right), \qquad (10)$$

where P is the real risk premium (i.e., the right hand side of eq. (8)); F is the net foreign investment position of US vis-a-vis UK; N_i is the dollar value of the net supply of nominal assets denominated in the currency of country i.

Proof: See the Appendix.

Before discussing the implications of Proposition 3, let us consider the possible sign of each variable that appears in equation (10).

(a) T, the measure of absolute risk tolerance, is always positive.

(b) F, the net foreign investment position of US, may be positive, negative, or zero.

(c) Cov[ξ,S], the covariance between changes in the exchange rate and changes in deviations from PPP, may be positive, negative, or zero.

(d) N_i i=1,2, the dollar value of the net supply of nominal assets denominated in dollars (i=1) or denominated in pounds (i=2), is likely to positive.

(e) Cov[ϕ_a,S], the covariance between changes in the exchange rate and changes in the US investor's price index, is likely to be positive.

(f) Cov[ϕ_b,S], the covariance between changes in the exchange rate and changes in the UK investor's price index, is likely to be negative.

(g) π, the real risk premium in the forward rate, can be positive, negative, or zero. Note that when π is positive, the forward rate will be smaller than the expected future spot rate.

Equation (10) represents a synthesis of previous work on risk premiums in forward exchange rates. Similar to the studies made by Solnik (1974), Day (1977), and Stulz (1982), the net foreign investment position appears as one of the determinants of the risk premium. Equation (10) also includes the results of Kouri (1977), Frankel (1979), Stulz (1982), and Dornbusch (1983) concerning the effects of the net supplies of outside nominal assets on the magnitude and the direction of the risk premium.

Proposition 4. If (a) deviations from PPP are not correlated with changes in the exchange rate, or (b) the net foreign investment position is zero, then the risk premium will depend on the net supplies of outside nominal assets and the covariances of the exchange rate with the rates of change in the two price indices.

Proof: Let $Cov[\xi,S] = 0$, or $F = 0$.

Then, from equation (10) we have:

$$\pi = -(\overline{T})^{-1} \quad (N_1 Cov[\phi_a,S] + N_2 Cov[\phi b,S]) \; . \qquad (11)$$

This is a generalization of the results presented in Kouri (1977) and Frankel (1979) who show that a risk premium will exist if PPP holds, and if the net supplies of outside nominal assets are different from zero; in the present model, however, PPP may or may not hold. In particular, the net supplies of nominal assets will continue to be the only determinants of the risk premium in the forward rate if deviations from PPP are not correlated with changes in the exchange rate, or if the net foreign investment position is zero.

The effects of a change in the net supplies of outside nominal assets are, however, less than clear for they depend on how strongly the exchange rate is correlated with the price indices of the two countries. For example, if changes in US price index are the major cause of variations in the exchange rate, the risk premium would be significantly affected by a change in the net supply of dollar denominated nominal assets. But, if US has a nonstochastic price index, or its index does not have a major influence on the exchange rate, a change in its net supply of nominal assets will have no effect on the risk premium.

Proposition 5. If (a) there are no outside nominal assets, or (b) if changes in the exchange rate are independent of changes in the two price indices, the risk premium will be proportional to the net foreign investment position of US vis-a-vis UK.

Proof: Let $N_1 = N_2 = 0$, or $Cov[\phi_a,S] = Cov[\phi_b,S] = 0$.

Then, the risk premium will be as follows:

$$\pi = (\overline{T})^{-1} \; F \; Cov[\xi,S] \; . \qquad (12)$$

This is a generalization of the results obtained by Solnik (1974) and Stulz (1982). These studies assume that all changes in the exchange rate are deviations from PPP. However, Proposition 5 demonstrates that the net foreign investment position will be the major determinant of the risk premium only if deviations from PPP are correlated with the exchange rate. But the sign of the risk premium depends on whether US is a net foreign borrower or a net foreign lender, and whether the exchange rate is positively or negatively correlated with deviations from PPP.

Proposition 6. Assuming that $Cov[\phi_a,S] > 0$, $Cov[\phi_b,S] < 0$, then,

(a) the forward rate will tend to overestimate the expected future spot rate if the net supply of dollar-denominated outside nominal assets increases;

(b) the forward rate will tend to underestimate the expected future spot rate if the dollar value of the net supply of pound-denominated outside nominal assets increases; and

(c) the forward rate will tend to underestimate the expected future spot rate if US is a net foreign investor, and the exchange rate is positively correlated with deviations from PPP.

Proof: All three conditions can be observed from equation (10).

Recent empirical studies have pointed out that risk premiums in forward rates may not be constant over time. The determinants of the risk premium were presented in Proposition 3; if I make further assumptions about the variables that appear in equation (10), I can present some testable hypotheses about the direction of the risk premium. For example, the last two terms on the right hand side of equation (10) tend to have offsetting effects; i.e, it is likely that $N_1 Cov[\phi_a,S] \geq 0$, and $N_2 Cov[\phi_b,S] \leq 0$. If these two terms cancel each other, and if the investment opportunity set in not stochastic, then the risk premium can be expressed as follows:

$$\pi = (\overline{T})^{-1} F \, Cov[\varepsilon,S] + \sum_{j=K+3}^{N} \hat{H}_j Cov[X_j,S].$$

Suppose US is a net foreign investor (i.e., F>0). Then, ceteris paribus, the forward rate will be smaller (greater) than the expected future spot rate if the covariance between changes in the exchange rate and changes in deviations from PPP is positive (negative). The sign of the net foreign investment position is not likely to change over a short time interval, while if the exchange rate and deviations from PPP follow nonstationary stochastic processes, the sign of the covariance between would change. Hence, a test of the existence of a time varying risk premium in the forward exchange rate should distinguish between the time intervals that this covariance is positive and the time intervals that it is negative.

III. Extension

The major result of this paper can be extended to a world economy that consists of many countries. Suppose there are M countries indexed by i=1,...,M. Then, the risk premium in the forward rate between country i=2,...,M and country 1 will be as follows (assuming a nonstochastic opportunity set):

$$\pi_i = (\overline{T})^{-1}\left[\sum_{j=2}^{M} F_j Cov[\varepsilon_j,S_i] - \sum_{j=1}^{M} N_j Cov[\phi_j,S_i]\right], \tag{13}$$

where F_j is the net foreign investment position of country 1 vis-a-vis country j; ε_j is the deviation from PPP for the exchange rate between currency j and currency 1; N_j is the net supply of outside nominal assets denominated in the currency of country j in terms of the currency of country 1; S_j is the exchange rate between the currencies of country j and country 1.

Obviously, an empirical test of this more realistic model of the risk premium will be quite complex, since time-variations in risk premiums can be caused by nonstationarity in the covariances of exchange rates with deviations from PPP for all currencies. Therefore, the first step in any empirical test of the model should be to estimate the covariances that appear in equation (13) to see whether they are significantly different from zero.

IV. Concluding Comments

This paper presents a general model of risk premiums in forward exchange rates. I use the rational expectations framework of continuous-time asset pricing models to obtain my results, which show that foreign exchange risk premium is a function of, among other factors, the covariance of the exchange rate with deviations from PPP and national price indices. I also extend these results to the case of many countries. Recent empirical studies have focused on the existence of time-varying risk premiums in forward rates. This paper shows that intertemporal changes in the direction of the risk premium are likely to be caused by changes in the stochastic processes that represent the movements of the exchange rate and deviations from PPP. In particular, over a relatively small time interval [e.g., one year] variations in the direction of the risk premium are likely to be caused by changes in the sign of the covariance between the exchange rate and deviations from PPP.

APPENDIX

A US investor's wealth can be expressed as follows:

$$W(t) = V_1(t) + B_1(t) + M_1(t) + S(t)[V_2(t) + B_2(t) + M_2(t)], \quad \text{(A1)}$$

where $B_i(t)$ $i=1,2$ denote investments in risk-free bonds. Applying Ito's lemma to equation (A1), and using the results of equations (2) and (3), the dynamics of the investor's wealth can be written as follows:

$$dW = V_1[\,(\mu_1 - r_1)dt + \sigma_1 dZ] + SV_2[\,(\mu_2 - r_2 + \sigma_{2s})dt + \sigma_2 dZ]$$

$$+ S(V_2 + B_2 + M_2)[(\gamma_s + r_2 - r_1)dt + \delta_s dY_s] + (W_{r1} - E)\,dt \quad \text{(A2)}$$

In the above equation, σ_{2s} is the covariance of the rate of return on asset 2 with the rate of change in the exchange rate. I have set $-(D_1 + SD_2)$ equal to $\Sigma\, C_iP_i$, which means that consumption expenditures are financed by cash flows from investments. Note that the total opportunity cost of consumption and currency holding, $E = \Sigma\, C_iP_i + r_1M_1 + r_2SM_2$. For further discussion of the budget equation see Merton (1973), Solnik (1974), and Stulz (1981). The maximization problem of the US investor can be solved as follows [e.g., see Fleming and Rishel (1975)]:

$$\max_{B_i, V_i, C_i} \quad \Theta = \left\{ J_t + J_W\mu_W + J_{WW}\sigma_W^2 + \sum_i^N J_i\alpha_i \right.$$

$$\left. + \sum_{i,j}^N J_{ij}\varphi_{ij} + \sum_i^N J_{iW}\varphi_{iW} \right\} = 0 \ .$$

The above expression is the Bellman equation. The first order conditions are obtained as follows:

$$\frac{\partial\Theta}{\partial V_i} = \frac{\partial\Theta}{\partial B_i} = \frac{\partial\Theta}{\partial C_i} = 0 \ .$$

In the above expression, μ_w and σ_w denote the expected return and the standard deviation of return on wealth, respectively; subscripts t, w, and i,j denote partial derivatives of J(W,X,t) with respect to time, wealth, and state variables, respectively; ϕ_{ij} is the covariance between changes in state variables i and j; ϕ_{iw} is the covariance between the return on wealth and changes in state variable i.

The first order conditions for the above problem can be found in Stulz (1981), Hodrick (1981), Cox, Ingersoll, and Ross (1985), and Dufey and Kazemi (1987). One of these conditions that is the basis of my results is as follows (note that Cov[x,y] denotes Covariance(dlnx,dlny):

$$E(\ dSB_2\ /SB_2 - dB_1\ /B_1\ ) = -(\ Cov[J_w,SB_2] - Cov[J_w,B_1]\ )dt. \quad (A3)$$

In this expression the riskiness of a security is equal to the negative of the covariance of its rate of return with the rate of change in the investor's marginal utility of wealth.

Applying Ito's lemma to the marginal utility of wealth, J_w, and noting that the returns on the two bonds are nonrandom, equation (5) is obtained; in equation (5) of the text $H_j = -\partial \ln J_w / \partial \ln X_j$.

Proof of Proposition 3: The proof follows directly from the definition of the investors' wealth and assumption (A.7). Consider equation (6) when Cov[W,S] is expressed as W^{-1} Covariance(dW,dlnS) and the budget constraint (eq. (A1)) is substituted for return on wealth, dW:

$$\gamma_s + r_2 - r_1 = T^{-1}\Big\{ V_1 Cov[V_1, S] + SV_2 Cov[V_2, S]$$

$$+ S(V_2 + B_2 + M_2) Cov[S, S] + (V_1 + SV_2 + B_1 + SB_2$$

$$+ M_1 + SM_2) Cov[\phi_a, S] \Big\} + Cov[\phi_a, S].$$

Taking assumption (A.7) into account and using the definition of deviations from PPP, we will have:

$$\gamma_s + r_2 - r_1 = T^{-1} \{ S(V_2 + B_2 + M_2) Cov[\varepsilon, S] - (B_1 + M_1) Cov[\phi_a, S]$$

$$- (SV_2 + SB_2 + SM_2) Cov[\phi_a, S]\} + Cov[\phi_a, S].$$

A similar equation can be obtained for the UK investor. After converting the UK investor's wealth and price index into US dollars, the resulting equation and the above expression can be aggregated to obtain equation (10).

REFERENCES

Adler, M. and B. Dumas, 1983, "International Portfolio Choice and Corporate Finance: A Synthesis." Journal of Finance 38, 925-983.

Arnold, L., 1974, Stochastic Differential Equations: Theory and Applications (John Wiley & Sons-New York).

Breeden, D. T., 1979, "An Intertemporal Asset Pricing Model With Stochastic Investment and Consumption Opportunities." Journal of Financial Economics 7, 337-352.

------, 1984, "Futures Markets and Commodity Options: Hedging and Optimality in Incomplete Markets." Journal of Economic Theory 35, 275-300.

Cox, J.C., J. Ingersoll, and S. Ross, 1981, "The Relationship Between Forward Prices and Future Prices." Journal of Financial Economics 9, 321-346.

------, 1985, "An Intertemporal General Equilibrium Model of Asset Prices." Econometrica 53, 363-384.

Deardorff, A. V., 1979, "One-way Arbitrage and Its Implications for the Foreign Exchange Markets." Journal of Political Economy 87, 351-364.

Dornbusch, R., 1983), "Exchange Risk and Macroeconomics of Exchange Rate Determination." The Internationalization of Financial Markets and National Economic Policy. Ed. R. Hawkins et al. Greenwich, CT: JAI Press.

Dufey, G. and H. B. Kazemi, 1987, "The Demand and Supply of Forward Exchange Contracts Under Incomplete Information." Paper Presented at Eastern Finance Association meeting, Baltimore, MD.

Fama, E. F. , 1984, "Forward and Spot Exchange Rates." Journal of Monetary Economics 14, 319-338.

Fama, E. F. and A. Farber, 1979, "Money, Bonds, and Foreign Exchange," American Economic Review 69, 269-282.

Fleming, W. H. and R. W. Rishel, 1975), Deterministic and Stochastic Control (Springer Verlag-New York).

Frankel, J., 1979, "The Diversifiability of Exchange Risk." Journal of International Economics 9, 379-394.

------, 1982, "In Search of the Exchange Risk Premium: A Six Currency Test Assuming Mean Variance Efficiency." Journal of International Money and Finance 1, 255-274.

------, 1986, "The Implications of Mean-Variance Optimization for Four Questions in International Macroeconomics." Journal of International Money and Finance 5 (Supplement), 53-75.

------, 1988, "Recent Estimates of Time-Variation in the Conditional Variance and in the Exchange Risk Premium." Journal of International Money and Finance 7, 115-125.

Frankel, J. and R. Meese, 1987, "Are Exchange Rates Excessively Variable?" NBER Macroeconomics Annual. Ed. S. Fisher (MIT Press-Cambridge, MA)

Grauer, F. L. A., R. H. Litzenberger, and R. E. Stehle, 1976, "Sharing Rules and Equilibrium in an International Capital Markets Under Uncertainty." Journal of Financial Economics 3, 233-256.

Hansen L. P. and R. J. Hodrick, 1983, "Risk Averse Speculation in the Forward Exchange Market: An Econometric Analysis of Linear Models." Exchange Rates and International Economics. Ed. J. A. Frankel (University of Chicago Press-Chicago).

Hodrick, R. J., 1981, "International Asset Pricing with Time-varying Risk Premia." Journal of International Economics 11, 573-583.

Hodrick, R. J. and S. Srivastava, 1984, "An Investigation of Risk and Return in Forward Foreign Exchange." Journal of International Money and Finance 3, 5-29.

------, 1986, "The Covariation of Risk Premiums and Expected Future Spot Exchange Rates." Journal of International Money and Finance 5 (Supplement), 5-22.

Hsieh, D., 1984, "Tests of Rational Expectations and no Risk Premiums in Forward Exchange Markets." Journal of International Economics 14, 173-184.

Korajczyk, R. A., 1985, "The Pricing of Forward Contracts for Foreign Exchange." Journal of Political Economy 93, 346-368.

Kouri, P., 1977, "International Investment and Interest Rate Linkage Under Flexible Exchange Rates." The Political Economy of Monetary Reform, Ed. R. Aliber (Macmillan & Co-London).

Levich, R. M., 1979, "The Efficiency of Markets for Foreign Exchange." International Economic Policy: Theory and Evidence, Ed. R. Dornbusch et al. (John Hopkins University Press-Baltimore).

Lucas, R. E., 1982, "Interest Rates, and Currency Prices in a Two-Country World." Journal of Monetary Economics 12, 335-359.

Merton, R. C., 1971, "Optimum Consumption and Portfolio Rules in a Continuous-Time Model." Journal of Economic Theory 3, 373-413.

-----, 1973, "An Intertemporal Asset Pricing Model." Econometrica 41, 867-887.

Rubinstein, M., 1974. "An Aggregation Theorem for Securities Markets."

Journal of Financial Economics 1, 225-244.

Samuelson, P. A. and S. Swamy, 1974, "Invariant Economic Index Numbers and Canonical Duality: Survey and Synthesis." American Economic Review 64, 566-593.

Solnik, B., 1974, "An Equilibrium Model of the International Capital Market." Journal of Economic Theory 6, 500-524.

Stockman, A. C., 1978, "Risk, Information, and Foreign Exchange Rates." Economics of Exchange Rates. Ed. J. A. Frankel et al. (Addison-Wesley-Reading, MA)

Stulz, R. M., 1981, "A Model of International Asset Pricing Model." Journal of Financial Economics 9, 383-406.

-----, 1982, "The Forward Rate and Macroeconomics." Journal of International Economics 12, 285-299.

-----, 1984 "Currency Preferences, Purchasing Power Risks, and the Determination of Exchange Rate in an Optimizing Model." Journal of Money Credit, and Banking 16, 302-316.

NOTES

1. In this paper I examine the relationship between a short-term forward rate and the expected future spot rate. For a discussion of the relationship between forward and futures prices and contracts see Cox, Ingersoll, and Ross (1980).

2. The original discussion of time varying risk premiums is due to Hodrick (1981).

3. Though sources of uncertainty are completely exogenous, investors may use endogenous variables to learn about the state of the world economy; for a discussion of this point in the context of intertemporal asset pricing models see Breeden (1979).

4. By real risky assets I mean claims to productive assets. In contrast, financial securities represent assets that have zero net supply (except in the case of government issued securities), and are created by investors for the purpose of optimal allocation of risk.

5. The inclusion of money balances in utility functions is, of course, a rather crude way to obtain a positive demand for domestic and foreign currencies [e.g., see Stulz (1984)]. Alternatively, one can impose a cash constraint of the type suggested by Lucas (1982). However, the results of the paper will not be significantly affected if this approach is employed.

6. For further discussion of this point see Fama and Farber (1978) and Stulz (1984).

7. See Samuelson and Swamy (1974) and Breeden (1984).

8. See, for example, Merton (1973), Breeden (1979), and Cox, Ingersoll, and Ross (1985).

9. If the two riskless rates of interest do not change stochastically over

time, then my results will also apply to forward contracts with longer maturity; e.g., see Cox, Ingersoll, and Ross (1981).

10. Note that according to Ito's lemma $\text{Cov}[\overline{W},S] - \text{Cov}[\phi_a,S] = \text{Cov}[\overline{W}/\phi_a,S]$, which is the covariance of the real rate of change in aggregate wealth with the rate of change in the exchange rate.

11. I wish to thank the referee for making valuable comments on this point.

Recent Developments in International Banking
and Finance, S.J. Khoury (editor)

CHAPTER VI

Currency Movements and Corporate Pricing Strategy

Anant K. Sundaram

Veena Mishra*

*The authors are with The Amos Tuck School of business Administration at Dartmouth College, and the Indira Gandhi Institute of Development Studies, Bombay, respectively.
We are grateful to an anonymous referee for comments, as well as to Sarkis Khour, and to participants in finance seminars at the Sloan School of Management, the Harvard business School and the Amos Tuck School. An earlier version of this paper was presented at the ORSA/TIMS conference in Washington, D.C., 1988. The first author is grateful to the Tuck Associates Program for support.

I. Introduction

Since the advent of the floating exchange rate regime, substantial real currency movements over the medium term have been common. Such movements offer a firm that sells abroad strategic leeway to make price/ quantity trade-offs that are rarely, if ever, available in domestic markets. For example, with a real depreciation of the home currency, a firm can raise home currency prices, thus improving its profits (compared to the pre-depreciation level), or it can maintain home currency prices and increase its market share relatively costlessly, as the depreciation coupled with maintenance of pre-depreciation home currency prices (with at least the same per-unit profit levels) makes the product cheaper in the foreign currency.

More generally, real currency movements can create operating (sometimes called "real" or "economic") exposure as opposed to merely translation or transaction exposures (**Shapiro (1986); Lessard and Flood (1987)**). The key distinction is that while translation and transaction exposures can be hedged using standard financial instruments and accounting techniques and hence do not affect real cash flows, operating exposures have real cash flow impacts and hence, affect firm value. Firms have to deal with such exposure through variables such as pricing, sourcing from different locations, etc., rather than through financial hedging techniques.

The interest of this paper lies in understanding the pricing behavior of firms operating in foreign markets when the value of currency of their home country undergoes a change. We are interested in examining whether and when firms will adopt a "skimming" pricing strategy (that is, maintain foreign prices at, or close to, the pre-depreciation level) rather than a "penetration" or "market share" pricing strategy (that is, maintain dollar prices at, or close to, the pre-depreciation level). Analogous concepts used in the literature are "pricing-to-market" (**Krugman (1986)**) or "no pass through" (eg., **Dornbusch (1987)**) and "no pricing to market" or "full pass through", respectively.[1].

The post-'84 depreciation of the US dollar brought this question into sharp focus. While much of the evidence remains anecdotal and journalistic, US firms have been observed to adopt the strategy of raising dollar prices (and maintaining foreign currency prices at, or close to, pre-depreciation levels), thus forsaking what appears to be a relatively costless opportunity to gain market share by cutting foreign prices without affecting dollar price profitability[2]. The purpose of this paper is to attempt to explain such pricing behavior, by both extending and integrating previous work.

II. LITERATURE REVIEW

There is a large literature on the application of microeconomic theories relating prices and exchange rates, that goes back at least to early analyses that occur in trade and balance-of-payments theories[3]. These models attempt to examine the impacts of a devaluation on a country's balance of trade, given demand and supply elasticities for exports and imports, using traditional models of market structure (perfect competition as reflected in the "small country" assumption, and monopolist for "large country" assumption; see, for example, **Robinson (1937); Lerner (1944); Harberger (1950); Haberler (1952)**; for a good review, see **Alexander (1959), and Sohmen (1969)**).

Recent additions that explore the question from a firm-level perspective include **Shapiro (1975); Levi (1983); Krugman (1986); Flood (1986); Luehrman (1986); Lessard and Flood (1986); and Dornbusch (1987); Knetter (1989); Fisher (1989); Froot and Klemperer (1989).** All of the studies seek to explain the sensitivity of either (or all of) prices, quantities or profits to changes in the real exchange rate, under different competitive scenarios. The typical model postulates profit maximizing behavior through a quantity adjustment process, the sensitivity of key variables to exchange rate changes being analyzed through comparative statics exercises.

Shapiro (1975) analyzes an "oligopolistic" (but, as **Luehrman (1986)**, points out, a <u>de facto</u> monopolist) multinational in a two-country world, whose prices and costs are affected by a real exchange rate change; **Levi (1983)** considers the cases of perfect competitor and monopolist as both importer and exporter, as does **Fisher (1989)**; **Flood (1986)** considers the cases of perfect competition, monopolistic competition and price discrimination (**Knetter (1989)** also considers the case of a monopolistic price discriminator); **Flood and Lessard (1986)** primarily consider the case of perfect competition. **Froot and Klemperer (1989)** analyze pass-through behavior in a sequential setting, using a model in which the market share of the first period is an additional argument that determines profits in the second period. A detailed review of this literature can be found in **Sundaram and Mishra (1990)**[4].

From the point of view of pricing behavior in foreign markets (given, say, a depreciation), the conclusions are straightforward for the polar cases of a monopolist and a perfect competitor: in the case of a monopolist with constant elasticity of demand and constant marginal costs, there will be full-pass-through of the currency effect (that is, market share pricing, or no pricing to market), since the price-marginal cost relationship remains the same given the demand elasticity; on the other hand, with perfect competition (or infinitely elastic demand) in foreign markets, there will be no-pass-through (that is, firms will follow skimming pricing, or pricing to market, strategies), as the foreign price will remain the same, constrained by competitive forces. These studies also examine the effect of such real currency movements on quantities and profits (the latter being defined as "exposure") and the conclusions are basically that, given a real devalua-tion, the home firm's quantities and profits are affected favorably for its sales abroad. For other forms of competition, a general result is that the extent of pass through will usually lie between the two polar cases.

The model that we develop in this paper integrates and extends a number of these ideas, in a framework of dynamics and imperfect competition. The analysis conducted below examines dynamic economies/diseconomies in the context of the competitors' perception of the currency change being tempo-rary or permanent, and allowing for their products being strategic comple-ments or substitutes. For ease of interpretation, we implicitly assume a depreciation. The primary objective is then to understand whether and when firms will adopt a skimming pricing strategy, rather than a penetration pricing strategy, in the context of generalized demand and cost functions. We also explain a number of results derived in the previous studies using our analytical framework, and discuss extensions to the model (eg., price competition, differentiated products, etc.).

III. THE MODEL

There are two firms--the home country firm and the foreign country firm--that engage in two period quantity competition[5] in a homogeneous[6] product. Each firm is assumed to operate in both periods, and entry is ruled out. Demands across the two periods are not interrelated, but costs can be (more specifically, the second period cost can be affected by quantity sold in the first period). The home and foreign firms' profits, in their respect-ive currencies, are

$$\pi(q_1,q_2,q_{1*},q_{2*})$$
$$= P_1(Q_1)q_1 + P_2(Q_2)q_2 - c_1(q_1) - c_2(q_2,q_1) \quad (1)$$

$$\pi^*(q_1,q_2,q_{1*},q_{2*},e_1,e_2)$$
$$= [P_1(Q_1)q_{1*}]/e_1 + [P_2(Q_{2*})q_{2*}]/e_2 - c_1^*(q_{1*}) - c_2^*(q_{2*},q_{1*}) \quad (2)$$

(variables with asterisks denote those of the foreign firm), where e_1 and e_2 are the exchange rates (number of home currency units per unit foreign currency) for periods 1 and 2 respectively. All currency movements are assumed to be unanticipated. It is possible to account for the interaction between the real and the financial sectors of the economy by considering the effect of interest rate parity; if we define $r > 0$ as the domestic interest rate and $r^* > 0$ as the foreign interest rate, then the interest parity condition will simply be $e_2/e_1 = (1+r)/(1+r^*)$, and the objective functions in (1) and (2) can be rewritten accordingly (we have analyzed this case in detail and there is little change in the results, except that a lot more notation is introduced into the analysis; these results can be had upon request). In what follows, we will assume for simplicity that $r = r^* = 0$.

Since the product is not differentiated[7], the total quantity sold in period $i = 1,2$, is

$$Q_i = q_i + q_{i*} \quad (3)$$

The (inverse) demand function for period i is $P_i(Q_i)$. The first derivatives of prices with respect to all quantities are assumed to be less than zero and the second derivatives greater than zero. Cost in period 2 can be a function of the output in period 1, while the reverse cannot be true[8]. Marginal costs, $c_i'(q_i)$ and $c_i^{*\prime}(q_{i*})$, can be increasing or decreasing; if decreasing, costs are decreasing at a slower rate than the marginal revenue.

In the notation that follows, we will mostly omit the arguments for the sake of brevity. Differentiating (1) and (2) with respect to the individual firms' quantities, the first order conditions are[9]

$$\pi_1 = P_1 + (\partial P_1/\partial q_1)q_1 - (\partial c_1/\partial q_1) - (\partial c_2/\partial q_1) = 0 \tag{4}$$

$$\pi_2 = P_2 + (\partial P_2/\partial q_2)q_2 - (\partial c_2/\partial q_2) = 0 \tag{5}$$

$$\pi_{1*} = [P_1 + (\partial P_1/\partial q_{1*})q_{1*}]/e_1 - \{(\partial c_1^*/\partial q_{1*}) + (\partial c_2^*/\partial q_{2*})\} = 0 \tag{6}$$

$$\pi_{2*} = [P_2 + (\partial P_2/\partial q_{2*})q_{2*}]/e_2 - (\partial c_2^*/\partial q_{2*}) = 0 \tag{7}$$

Totally differentiating the first order conditions gives us

$$\begin{bmatrix} \pi_{11} & \pi_{11*} & \pi_{12} & \pi_{12*} \\ \pi_{1*1} & \pi_{1*1*} & \pi_{1*2} & \pi_{1*2*} \\ \pi_{21} & \pi_{21*} & \pi_{22} & \pi_{22*} \\ \pi_{2*1} & \pi_{2*1*} & \pi_{2*2} & \pi_{2*2*} \end{bmatrix} \begin{bmatrix} dq_1 \\ dq_{1*} \\ dq_2 \\ dq_{2*} \end{bmatrix} = - \begin{bmatrix} \pi_{1e_1} & \pi_{1e_2} \\ \pi_{1*e_1} & \pi_{1*e_2} \\ \pi_{2e_1} & \pi_{2e_2} \\ \pi_{2*e_1} & \pi_{2*e_2} \end{bmatrix} \begin{bmatrix} de_1 \\ de_2 \end{bmatrix} \tag{8}$$

where, for period i (= 1,2),

$$\pi_i = \partial\pi/\partial q_i \tag{9}$$

$$\pi_{i*} = \partial\pi/\partial q_{i*} \tag{10}$$

$$\pi_{ii} = \partial^2\pi_i/\partial q_i^2 \tag{11}$$

$$\pi_{i*i*} = \partial^2\pi_{i*}/\partial q_{i*}^2 \tag{12}$$

$$\pi_{ii*} = \partial^2\pi_{i*}/\partial q_i \partial q_{i*} \tag{13}$$

$$\pi_{ie} = \partial^2\pi_i/\partial q_i \partial e \tag{14}$$

$$\pi_{i*e} = \partial^2\pi_{i*}/\partial q_{i*}\partial e \tag{15}$$

IIIA. Stability Conditions

Define as Δ, the determinant of the matrix of second derivatives of π on the left hand side of expression (8). Then, conditions for the overall stability of the equilibrium of the two-period game will be

$$\pi_{11} < 0;\ \pi_{1*1*} < 0;\ \pi_{22} < 0;\ \pi_{2*2*} < 0, \text{ and} \tag{16}$$

$$\Delta > 0 \tag{17}$$

Further, stability of the markets in each period, separately, will require that the conditions

$$\pi_{11}\pi_{1*1*} - \pi_{11*}\pi_{1*1} > 0, \text{ and} \tag{18}$$

$$\pi_{22}\pi_{2*2*} - \pi_{22*}\pi_{2*2} > 0$$

are also met. We assume throughout that (16)-(18) are met.

IIIB. Strategic Substitutes and Complements

In a paper that integrates many of the recent results in oligopoly theory, BGK systematically analyze how a firm's choice of strategy in one market (or one period) can change the competitor's strategy, affecting the firm's own marginal profitability in that market, or in a second market. Whether the firm's strategy results in costs or benefits depends on two factors: (a) whether the competitor's products are "strategic complements" or "strategic substitutes" and (b) whether the firm can achieve economies or diseconomies between markets (or periods).

Conventional complements and substitutes are defined in terms of the impact of a competitor's strategic choices on the <u>total</u> profits of a firm; for example, with conventional substitutes, an increase in the competitor's quantity will result in a decrease in the firm's profits (the reverse for conventional complements). Strategic substitutes and complements are defined in terms of the impact of a competitor's strategic choices on the *marginal* profitability of the firm: if a more aggressive strategy adopted by one firm lowers the marginal profitability of its competitor, then the product is a strategic substitute; if a more aggressive strategy raises the marginal profitability of its competitor, then the product is a strategic complement. Note that a product can be a conventional substitute, but a strategic complement. While conventional substitutes and complements are defined in terms of the first derivative of a firm's profits with respect to its competitor's (say) quantity, strategic substitutes and complements are defined in terms the second derivative of the firm's profits with respect to its own quantity *and* the competitor's quantity.

In terms of our model, strategic substitutes will imply that

$$\pi_{11*} < 0; \; \pi_{1*1} < 0; \; \pi_{22*} < 0; \; \pi_{2*2} < 0 \qquad (19)$$

while strategic complements will imply that

$$\pi_{11*} > 0; \; \pi_{1*1} > 0; \; \pi_{22*} > 0; \; \pi_{2*2} > 0 \qquad (20)$$

Condition (18) (stability in each market) can be met with the products being either strategic substitutes or strategic complements. Since the signs in (19) and (20) are uniformly positive or negative, the value of Δ will not be affected by the assumption of strategic substitutability or complementarity.

IIIC. Learning

Economies and diseconomies typically arise between markets (or periods) when costs are interlinked. An example of economies across periods is the phenomenon of "learning by doing", where average costs decline as a function of cumulative output. An example of diseconomies across periods is found in "natural resource" models--higher extraction (or larger outputs) in the first period will raise average costs in the second period.

The concept of learning--that is, a firm's costs being a function of its cumulative output--has a long and rich tradition in management literature. In the recent past, there have been many efforts to formally model the concept of learning. Well known examples in the industrial organization literature are those of **Spence (1981)** and **Fudenberg and Tirole (1983)**. In the marketing literature, it appears in the work of **Wernerfelt (1986)**. In a more general sense, the concept of learning is simply that there are joint economies across periods--higher output levels in early periods lead to (average) cost reductions in subsequent periods. Joint diseconomies will imply that higher output levels in early periods lead to higher average costs in later periods. We assume, consistent with a reasonable expectation that ability to learn decreases for higher output levels, that the second derivative of period 2 costs with respect to first period quantity is increasing.

The firm being able to achieve learning will imply that

$$\pi_{12} = \pi_{21} > 0, \text{ and} \tag{21}$$

$$\pi_{1*2*} = \pi_{2*1*} > 0 \tag{22}$$

On the other hand, joint diseconomies will imply that

$$\pi_{12} = \pi_{21} < 0, \text{ and} \tag{23}$$

$$\pi_{1*2*} = \pi_{2*1*} < 0 \tag{24}$$

and, if there are no economies or diseconomies,

$$\pi_{21} = \pi_{12} = \pi_{1*2*} = \pi_{2*1*} = 0 \tag{25}$$

In the results that follow, we will only consider the case of joint economies (ie., presence of learning)[10] or no economies. Also, whenever used, subscript L will denote that the home firm learns and the foreign firm does not; L* that the foreign firm learns but the home firm does not; LL* that both firms learn and NL that neither firm learns (that is, there are neither economies nor diseconomies for either firm)[11]. The magnitude of ▴ (see (17)) will depend on the particular learning scenario assumed (see expressions (9)-(12) in the Appendix, for details).

IIID. Temporary versus Permanent Currency Movement

Krugman (1986) and **Dornbusch (1987)** conjectured that a firm's pricing behavior could depend on whether it expects the currency movement to be temporary or permanent. For example, given a depreciation of the dollar against the yen, a US firm will have no incentive to cut its yen prices (and adopt a market share strategy) if it does not have additional capacity to meet the increased demand. It could, however, build such capacity. But, if such capacity expansion is costly, the decision could depend on whether the US firm expects the depreciation to be temporary or permanent. If the depreciation is expected to be temporary, then the firm will have less of an incentive to lower its yen prices, and is therefore more likely to adopt a pricing-to-market strategy. We formally model the impact of such effects.

A temporary depreciation will imply that

$$de_1 > 0; \; de_2 = 0 \tag{26}$$

while a permanent depreciation will imply that

$$de_1 = de_2 = de > 0 \tag{27}$$

The inequalities will be reversed for appreciation.

IIIE. Analyzing the Model

The basic purpose of this paper is to establish the signs and magnitudes of the derivative of first-period home currency prices with respect to exchange rates under various scenarios. For ease and consistency of inter-pretation, assume that the home currency undergoes a depreciation ($de > 0$). The results for currency appreciation will be exactly the reverse.

If $dP_1/de_1 \geq 0$, the larger it is, the less is the tendency for the firm to pass through currency effects. If $dP_1/de_1 = 0$, it will imply that the firm is adopting a full pass through strategy and if $(dP_1/de_1)(e_1/P_1)^{12} = 1$, it will imply that the firm is adopting a no pass through strategy.

$$dP_1/de_1 = \{dP_1/dQ_1\}\{dQ_1/de_1\}$$

$$= \{dP_1/dQ_1\}\{(dq_1/de_1) + (dq_{1*}/de_1)\}, \quad (28)$$

since $Q_1 = q_1 + q_{1*}$. Recall that $dP_1/dQ_1 < 0$, by assumption. Thus,

$$\text{sgn}[dP_1/de_1] = -\text{sgn}[dQ_1/de_1] \quad (29)$$

At this stage, we introduce some further notation. For i = temporary (T), permanent (P), for j = L, L*, NL, LL* and for k = strategic substitutes (SS), strategic complements (SC),

$dP_1/de_1|_{i,j,k}$ = price response to a depreciation under the scenario of i = T or P, for the learning scenario j and for k = SS,SC. (30)

The case of k = SS is analyzed first. Detailed assessments of signs and comparisons of magnitude are shown in the Appendix. Further, all proofs of propositions are also relegated to the Appendix.

IIIF. Strategic Substitutes and Temporary Depreciation

From expression (8), we can derive the relationships between quantities and exchange rates in the first period[13] (for details, see Appendix, expressions (13) and (14), respectively). The first period price response under a temporary depreciation can then be easily derived from (28) above (see Appendix, expression (15)).

On the firms' quantity responses, we observe the following:

(a) The home firm's quantity rises unambiguously in response to a depreciation, for all j, only if $\pi_{11*} < 0$ and $\pi_{22*} < 0$;

(b) The foreign firm's quantity falls unambiguously in response to a depreciation only for j = NL, L*; the response is ambiguous for j = L, LL*; however, the foreign firm's quantity response is independent of $\mathrm{sgn}(\pi_{11*})$ and $\mathrm{sgn}(\pi_{22*})$.

First, that the home firm's sales abroad increase as the currency depreciates should come as no great surprise. However, note that this result is dependent on the strategic substitutability. If the product is a strategic complement, then the quantity response becomes ambiguous. The foreign firm's quantity response, however, is independent of whether the products are strategic substitutes or complements. Second, the home firm can impact the foreign firm's quantity response negatively or positively, through its ability to achieve learning. The expectation, for the "normal" duopoly case, would have been that the foreign firm's output will always fall--this expectation is generally false. We discuss the intuition behind these conclusions in a later section.

Proposition 1

$dP_1/de_1|_{T,j,SS} > 0$ only if $\pi_{11*} > \pi_{11}$.

For proof, see Appendix.

In the Cournot duopoly case (see, for example, **Dornbusch (1987)**) we may have expected that $dP/de|_{T,j}$ is always greater than 0. This intuition may also derive from the pricing results that obtain for the cases of monopolist and perfect competitor. But proposition 1 tells us that this intuition is not generally true. There will be less than full pass through in a Cournot duopoly only when the strategic term, π_{11*}, is greater than the second derivative of the home firm's profit function. With increasing marginal costs (or if decreasing, the marginal costs are decreasing at a slower rate than the marginal revenue) this condition will hold.

A corollary result that we can derive from the above, from the point of view of pricing strategies is that, when there is no learning, strategic substitutability is necessary to obtain full pass through. Why? Note,

$$dP_1/de_1|_{T,NL} = \{dP_1/dQ_1\}\{(\pi_{1*e}/\blacktriangle)[(\pi_{11*} - \pi_{11})(\pi_{22}\pi_{2*2*} - \pi_{22*}\pi_{2*2})]\} \tag{31}$$

But, full pass through must imply that expression (31) is equal to zero.

This must, however, mean that

$$\pi_{11^*} = \pi_{11} < 0 \tag{32}$$

and hence, the product must be a strategic substitute. An alternative interpretation is that, when there is no learning, full-pass-through is not possible when the product is a strategic complement[14].

We now turn to the relationship between price responses to exchange rate changes under various learning scenarios. The proposition below is obtained by simply examining the signs and relative magnitudes of the individual terms (see Appendix for proof).

Proposition 2

If $\pi_{11^*} > \pi_{1^*1^*}$ and $\pi_{11^*} > \pi_{11}$, then,

$$dP_1/de_1|_{T,L^*,SS} > dP_1/de_1|_{T,NL,SS} > dP_1/de_1|_{T,L,SS} \tag{33}$$

The relationship between $dP_1/de_1|_{T,LL^*,SS}$ and the other terms is ambiguous.

When the depreciation is temporary and the products are strategic substitutes, the scenario of learning for the foreign firm, but no learning for the home firm offers the strongest case for a pass through pricing strategy. The scenario of learning for the home firm, but no learning for the foreign firm offers the strongest case for adopting no pass through pricing strategy. When both firms can learn, the pricing implications are ambiguous. These results are based on the assumption that $\pi_{11^*} > \pi_{11}$ and $\pi_{11^*} > \pi_{1^*1^*}$. With increasing marginal costs (including the marginal costs associated with learning effects) this will obtain. If marginal costs are decreasing, it will require that they be decreasing at a slower rate than marginal revenue (see Appendix). The intuition behind all these results is discussed in section IV.

Detailed expressions for price and quantity responses for strategic substitutes, when the depreciation is permanent, are shown equations (20)-(22), Appendix. By comparing expressions (15) and (22) in the Appendix, we can rewrite the price response in the permanent case as

$$dP_1/de_1|_{P,j} = dP_1/de_1|_{T,j} + \{dP_1/dQ_1\}\{\theta_j\} \qquad (34)$$

The only difference between the temporary and permanent cases is the second term, and the price response will now be dependent also on the sign of θ_j. Examining quantity responses, we can see that the results are exactly similar to the temporary case, and therefore, it must mean that price responses across the various learning scenarios must be also exactly the same as in the temporary case. This insight, along with comparisons between temporary and permanent cases, is summarized in Proposition 3 below (for proof, see Appendix).

Proposition 3

If $\pi_{11*} > \pi_{11}$, then

$$dP_1/de_1|_{P,L*} > dP_1/de_1|_{P,NL} > dP_1/de_1|_{P,L} \qquad (35)$$

$$dP_1/de_1|_{T,NL} = dP_1/de_1|_{P,NL} \qquad (36)$$

$$dP_1/de_1|_{T,L} > dP_1/de_1|_{P,L} \qquad (37)$$

$$dP_1/de_1|_{T,L*} < dP_1/de_1|_{P,L*} \qquad (38)$$

For j = LL*, the relationships are ambiguous.

When the home firm alone can learn, a permanent depreciation will favor a pass through pricing strategy relative to a temporary depreciation. On the other hand, when the foreign firm alone can learn, the home firm has a greater incentive to not pass through currency effects with a permanent depreciation. With no learning for either firm, their strategies become time-independent and hence, the permanence of the depreciation is of no consequence. These results qualify the conjectures in **Krugman (1986)** that there will be a uniformly greater incentive to price to market when the depreciation is expected to be temporary.

IIIH. Strategic Complements

When the product is a strategic complement (and there are no diseconomies), a more aggressive strategy (in our case, a pass through pricing strategy) will invite a more aggressive response from the competitor since π_{ii*} and π_{i*i} will be greater than zero. The impact of strategic complemen-tarity on quantity and price responses will be manifest through the signs of the terms π_{11*} and π_{22*} (they will be greater than zero in the case of strategic complements). Since the signs enter uniformly, none of the Δ_j's will change compared to the strategic substitutes case. The only differences will occur in the numerator. The main result for the case of SC, compared to SS, is summarized in Proposition 4:

Proposition 4

$dP_1/de_1|_{i,j,SC} \geq dP_1/de_1|_{i,j,SS}$, for i = T, P, and j = NL, L, L*, LL*.

The general result is therefore that, compared to the case of strategic substitutes, strategic complementarity will lead to a no-pass-through pricing (or skimming, or pricing to-market) strategy regardless of whether the depreciation is expected to be temporary or permanent, and regardless of the firm's ability to achieve scale economies. The reason for this is that, with strategic complements and a currency depreciation, the home firm's output change will be smaller, while the foreign firm's output will remain the same, compared to the case of strategic substitutes (see expressions (31) and (32), Appendix). However, among products that are strategic complements, price responses bear a similar relationship across learning scenarios as in the case of strategic substitutes.

IV. SUMMARY AND DISCUSSION OF THE RESULTS

Home currency price responses to an exchange rate change are dependent not only on the competitive structure, but also on whether the products are strategic complements or substitutes, whether the currency movement is temporary or permanent, and the firms' ability to achieve learning. The key results of our paper are summarized below:

$$dP_1/de_1|_{P,L*,SS} > dP_1/de_1|_{T,L*,SS} > dP_1/de_1|_{T,NL,SS}$$

$$= dP_1/de_1|_{P,NL,SS} > dP_1/de_1|_{T,L,SS} > dP_1/de_1|_{P,L,SS} \quad (39)$$

$$dP_1/de_1|_{P,L*,SC} > dP_1/de_1|_{T,L*,SC} > dP_1/de_1|_{T,NL,SC}$$

$$= dP_1/de_1|_{P,NL,SC} > dP_1/de_1|_{T,L,SC} > dP_1/de_1|_{P,L,SC} \quad (40)$$

$$dP_1/de|_{.,j,SC} \geq dP_1/de_1|_{.,j,SS} \quad (41)$$

In words, the following conditions favor a pass through pricing (ie., market share pricing or no pricing to market) strategy:

- strategic substitutes
- home firm can achieve scale economies relative to foreign firm
- depreciation is expected to be permanent and home firm can achieve scale economies
- firm is a monopolist

while the reverse set of conditions favor a no-pass-through pricing (skimming or pricing-to-market) strategy. Interestingly, a permanent depreciation offers both the strongest and weakest case for pass through, depending on the firm's ability to learn--when the foreign firm can learn and the home firm cannot, the home firm will not pass through currency effects, but when the home firm can learn and the foreign firm cannot, the home firm will do the opposite. When both firms can learn, we cannot unambiguously discern the pricing response.

That learning by the home firm (and not the foreign firm) will lead it to price to gain market share (compared to the base case of no learning for either firm) is intuitive, since one would expect that it has the incentive to increase its output in the first period in anticipation of a decline in its second period costs.

The reverse incentive (that is, pricing to market) when only the foreign firm can learn but the home cannot, can be explained using a similar intuition. In a situation of permanent depreciation, the home firm will want to prevent a cut in foreign prices (and consequent increase in the foreign firm's output), so that the foreign firm is not able to take advantage of its ability to learn; the incentive to do this is tempered in the case of a temporary depreciation, since foreign prices are going to go back to previous levels anyway.

When both firms learn, the impacts on prices and quantities are ambiguous in relation to the other learning scenarios. The intuition here is probably that the learning effects perhaps cancel each other out, and the outcome may not be very different from the case of no learning for either firm. This is a surmise, because $dP_1/de_1|_{.,LL^*,.}$ is difficult to sign.

Another conclusion that is perhaps worth highlighting, is that we cannot, in general, sign price and quantity movements in response to a depreciation unless we know whether the product is a strategic complement or a substitute. With respect to prices, the assumption of strategic complements will ensure that $dP/de \geq 0$ (that is, the post-depreciation home currency price will be at least at pre-depreciation levels), but the assumption of strategic substitutability will make price responses ambiguous. With respect to quantities, it is the reverse: strategic substitutability is conducive to an increase in quantity sold, while strategic complementarity will make quantity responses of the home firm ambiguous. The intuition behind strategic complementarity leading to no pass through pricing behavior (in the context of a depreciation) could be explained as follows: with Cournot conjectures, note that a more "aggressive" strategy by the home firm entails increasing quantities; if the product is a strategic complement, the foreign firm will retaliate "aggressively" as well, and at least maintain quantities; therefore, the home firm will have less of an incentive to increase quantity sold, and home currency price will fall by less.

What types of competitive situations lend themselves to being strategic substitutes and complements? This categorization will depend on (a) the shape of the demand function; (b) the shape of the cost function and (c) the type of conjecture assumed. For example, we can show that, with Cournot or market share conjectures, linear demand will generally imply strategic sub-stitutes, while constant elasticity demand will generally imply strategic complements; for homogeneous products, demand curves that are convex to the origin will generally favor strategic complements, while demand functions that are concave to the origin will imply strategic substitutes[15].

V. COMPARISONS WITH PREVIOUS RESULTS AND EXTENSIONS OF THE MODEL

Many of the previous results (see section II) in the currency pass through literature can be reinterpreted using the analysis above. Further, the model can be extended in a number of ways to include, for example, differentiated products, Bertrand competition (or other conjectures), price discrimination, more than one home and foreign firm, etc.

A. Comparisons with Previous Results

The case of a monopolist selling abroad is the simplest to analyze. All it would require, in terms of (1) and (2), is that equation 2 will disappear altogether, as will period 2 (alternatively, we can include period 2 and reinterpret the subscripts as "home" and "foreign" markets; if we assumed that PPP obtained, then it would be the case of a bimarket monopolist; if this assumption is not invoked, it would be the case of a monopolistic price discriminator; see below). The profit function in the home currency is

$$\pi \text{ (Monopolist)} = P(q)q - c(q) \tag{42}$$

and the first order condition is

$$\partial\pi/\partial q = P(q) + P'(q)q - c'(q) = 0 \tag{43}$$

which, we can re-express in the form of the Lerner index,

$$P(q)/c'(q) = 1/(1+\eta) \tag{44}$$

where η is the price elasticity of demand[16]. It is now easy to confirm that, with constant demand elasticity and constant marginal cost, the equilibrium home currency price is invariant to the exchange rate change--that is, there will be full pass through.

The profit function for a monopolistic price discriminator (**Flood (1986); Krugman (1986); Knetter (1989)**) operating in the home and foreign markets can be derived from (1) and (2) by allowing (2) to disappear, and treating subscripts 1 and 2 as the home and foreign markets respectively. By definition, we would not require that PPP obtained between the two markets. If we define $P_2{}^*$ as the foreign price, and e as the exchange rate, the profit function is

$$\pi \text{ (Monopolistic price discriminator)} = P_1(q_1) + eP_2{}^*(q_2) - c(q_1+q_2) \tag{45}$$

and the rest of the analysis readily follows. In fact, we can allow for economies between the markets by specifying the cost quite generally as $c(q_1,q_2)$. Thus, we can, for example, examine the impacts of economies of scale induced by a depreciation increasing the quantity sold abroad.

Single period Cournot competition with multiple home and foreign competitors (**Dornbusch (1987)**) can be modelled by allowing period 2 to disappear in (1) and (2), and defining n home firms and n* foreign firms. The profit functions for the ith home firm and the jth foreign firm (ignoring the subscripts for the first period) will be

$$\pi_i = P(Q)q_i - c_i(q_i) \tag{46}$$

$$\pi_j{}^* = [P(Q)q_j{}^*/e] - c_j{}^*(q_j{}^*) \tag{47}$$

Dornbusch assumes that marginal costs (in his case, interpreted as wages) are constant and are similar between home and foreign firms. The first order conditions are, respectively,

$$\pi_{1i} = P(Q) + P'(Q)q_i - c_i'(q_i) = 0 \tag{48}$$

$$\pi_{1*j} = P(Q) + P'(Q)q_j^* - ec_j^{*\prime}(q_j^*) = 0 \tag{49}$$

If we allow for n home firms and n* foreign firms, and define n+n*+1 = N, then, Q = nq + n*q*, and we can easily show that,

$$dP/de = \frac{P'(Q)n^*c^{*\prime}(q^*)}{P'(Q)N + QP''(Q)} \tag{50}$$

We can rewrite (50) as (equation 9' in **Dornbusch (1987), p. 98)**

$$= [n^*c^{*\prime}(q^*)]/[N - \theta] \tag{51}$$

where $\theta = -QP''(Q)/P'(Q)$. We can also rewrite (50) and (51) in terms of the elasticity of prices with respect to exchange rate changes, [dP/de][e/P]. Note that for $N > \theta$, dP/de is always greater than zero if marginal costs are positive.

Finally, the analysis in **Luehrman (1986)** of bimarket duopolists can be obtained by reinterpreting subscripts 1 and 2 as the home and foreign market, respectively, where we define P_1^* and P_2^* as the foreign currency prices in markets 1 and 2. The objective functions are

$$\pi = P_1(Q_1) + eP_2^*(Q_2) - c(q_1,q_2), \text{ and} \tag{52}$$

$$\pi^* = [P_1(Q_1)/e] + P_2^*(Q_2) - c^*(q_1^*,q_2^*) \tag{53}$$

(Luehrman assumes that $c(q_1,q_2) = c(q_1+q_2)$ and $c^*(q_1^*,q_2^*) = c^*(q_1^*+q_2^*)$). By comparing (52) and (53) with (45), we see that Luehrman's analysis is really a generalization of the price discrimination case to quantity setting duopolists, where PPP need not obtain. Further, the concept of "strategic denomination of costs" is simply the terms π_{1e}, π_{2e}, π_{2*e} and π_{2*e} in the matrix of second derivatives.

B. Extensions

The model can be extended (and generalized) in a number of ways. We present the possibilities of a few specific extensions to consider the cases of differentiated products, generalized conjectures (including Bertrand competition), multiple home and foreign firms and interlinked demands. In all cases, we only present the set-up in terms of the objective functions, thus pointing out modelling possibilities.

Differentiated Products

Differentiated products quantity competition will require the specification of four de facto prices and products. Let subscript h denote the home firm's products, and f the foreign firm's products, P_{1h} and P_2h the (home currency) prices of the home firm's products, and P_{1f} and P_{2f} the prices of the foreign firm's products. We require an additional set of assumptions that the products are conventional substitutes (that is, the first derivative of prices with respect to the competitor's quantity is negative). The objective functions will be

$$\pi = P_{1h}(q_{1h},q_{1f})q_{1h} + P_{2h}(q_{2h},q_{2f})q_{2h} - c_1(q_{1h}) - c_2(q_{2h},q_{1h}) \quad (54)$$

$$\pi^* = [P_{1f}(q_{1f},q_{1h})q_{1f}/e_1] + [P_{2f}(q_{2f},q_{2h})q_{2f}/e_2] - c_{1f}(q_{1f}) - c_{2f}(q_{2f},q_{1f}) \quad (55)$$

where the q_{ih} and q_{if} represent the quantities sold by the home and foreign firms in period i.

General Conjectures (including Price Competition)

We follow the generalized framework developed in **Dixit (1986)**. For simplicity of notation, initially assume that the products are homogeneous. The firms' outputs are linked to each other by the conjectural variation relations

(56) $\quad v(q_i,q_{i*}) = dq_{i*}/dq_i \quad$ (home firm), and

(57) $v^*(q_{i*},q_i) = dq_i/dq_{i*}$ (foreign firm)

The analysis in this paper is the Cournot case, where we have assumed that the firm conjectures that its competitor will not alter his output in equilibrium; that is, we have assumed that

$$v(q_i,q_{i*}) = v^*(q_{i*},q_i)) = 0 \tag{58}$$

A competitive equilibrium will result from the conjecture that the (foreign) price will remain constant as the firm's output changes; that is, for the home firm,

$$v(q_i,q_{i*}) = - [\partial P_i/\partial q_i]/[\partial P_i/\partial q_{i*}] \tag{59}$$

and similarly for the foreign firm.

An interesting case to explore fully may be "market share" conjectures. Here, the home firm conjectures that its foreign competitor will counter its output changes with an equiproportionate response; that is,

$$v(q_i,q_{i*}) = q_{i*}/q_i \tag{60}$$

In Bertrand (price) competition, for any meaningful analysis, we would have to assume differentiated products (and thus, we require the subscripts f and h). Here, the (say) home firm conjectures that the foreign firm's price will remain unchanged as it changes its own quantity resulting from a currency movement. That is, for the home firm,

$$v(q_i,q_{i*}) = -[\partial P_{if}/\partial q_i]/[\partial P_{if}/\partial q_{i*}] \tag{61}$$

and similarly for the foreign firm.

With generalized conjectures (and homogeneous products), the home firm's objective function is

$$\pi = P_1(Q_1)q_1 + P_2(Q_2)q_2 - c_1(q_1) - c_2(q_2,q_1) \tag{62}$$

and the first order conditions (including the conjectural variation term), are:

$$\pi_1 = P_1 + q_1\{[\partial P_1/\partial q_1] + [\partial P_1/\partial q_{1*}][v(q_1,q_{1*})]\} - \partial c_1/\partial q_1 - \partial c_2/\partial q_1 \qquad (63)$$

$$\pi_2 = P_2 + q_2\{[\partial P_2/\partial q_2] + [\partial P_2/\partial q_{2*}][v(q_2,q_{2*})]\} - \partial c_2/\partial q_2 \qquad (64)$$

The foreign firm's objective function and first order conditions can be similarly expressed, by using the appropriate subscripts. The rest of the analysis will follow as above.

Multiple Home and Foreign Firms

This is an extension that can be readily made, along the lines of the analysis in **Dornbusch (1987)**. A representative case is shown in (50) and (51), where there are n home firms and n* foreign firms, with $Q = nq + n^*q^*$. dP/de will be now dependent also on the number of firms, and a general result (see **Dornbusch (1987)**) is that dP/de——> 0 as n——> ∞. This is consistent with the pricing intuition for a monopolistic home firm.

Interlinked Demands

The analysis developed in this paper is based on the assumption of interlinked costs, but independent demands, between periods. The addition of interlinked demands--that is, where the demand function in either or both periods is also a function of the prices in the other period--is likely to provide rich additional interpretative possibilities. It would, for example, be possible to model reputation effects such as those discussed in **Krugman (1986)**, where, for example, a firm may refrain from cutting its foreign prices (despite a depreciation) in the first period since it may send negative signals to "status conscious" buyers in the second period--as Krugman points out, "....firms cultivate a reputation over time for being in a certain price range" (p.28). Another avenue that interlinked demands suggest is the possibility of modelling repeat purchase propensity--for example, it may turn out that, for products that can be differentiated to create propensity for repeat purchase, a temporary devaluation offers the opportunity to cut prices to attract new customers; such a firm may thus have the incentive for penetration pricing compared to another firm that cannot create such differentiation.

Areas for Future Research

The foregoing are some first-cut extensions suggested by the framework developed in this paper. One fruitful area for future research will be to develop a general competitive model which explicitly considers the possibi-lity of entry by third firms. For a first pass at this issue, see **Krugman and Baldwin (1987), Baldwin and Lyons (1988)** and **Dixit (1988)**. Another paper that models the impact of third country firms on production decisions of an oligopolistic firm is the early piece of work by **Adler and Stevens (1974)**. In an extension of a still earlier piece of work by **Horst (1971)**, the authors develop a one-period model of an MNC as a Cournot competitor with production and sales in two countries, facing competition from a third country firm. Inter alia, the paper examines the impact of a devaluation on the production versus export decision of an MNC--the major emphasis of the paper is thus on export displacement resulting from a currency devaluation. The modelling methodology adopted is quite similar to the one developed in this paper. As would be expected from this line of analysis, they find, ceteris paribus, that a devaluation of the home currency does lead to an increase in exports relative to foreign production.

Two other important areas for detailed future research include (a) an examination of the effects of exchange rate volatility on pricing of exports and (b) an examination of the effects of exchange rates on pricing behavior when such exchange rate movements are a response to movements in fundamental macroeconomic variables. Non-examination of these issues is a drawback of the present paper (but one that it shares with much of the modelling history in the area of understanding pass-through behavior).

Given the volatile exchange rate environment in recent years, the issue clearly deserves serious examination. However, analyzing this in the context of pricing behavior of oligopolistic firms is likely to be a difficult task. The handful of papers that have examined this issue (for example, **Baron (1976); Hooper and Kohlhagen (1978); Wilson and Takacs (1979); Mann (1989)**) restrict themselves to simpler competitive frameworks (perfect competition or monopolist), or their focus is on the currency invoicing decisions of firms. As noted earlier by **Ethier and Clarke (1972)**, an exporting firm that cannot continuously adjust its price must determine whether it must invoice its exports in the home or the foreign currency. With fixed exchange rates, this choice is obviated. With floating exchange rates, however, the choice of invoicing currency can determine the nature of uncertainty facing the firm. With exports invoiced in the foreign currency, the exporter faces the transaction risk arising from currency conversion; thus, for example, an increase in exchange rate variability can lead to an increase in foreign currency prices. With exports invoiced in the home currency, the exporter faces no transaction risk, though it will face demand risk since it does not know the price at the time the importer makes its purchases; in this case, an increase in exchange rate variability can dec-rease the export price invoiced in the home currency.

This line of analysis, however, has ignored another basic issue, in so far as it assumes, rather than explains, risk averse behavior on part of firms. A typical risk averse firm, for example, is assumed to maximize the expected utility from profits $E(u(\pi))$ (rather than expected profits $E(\pi)$):

$$E(u(\pi)) - E(\pi) \quad \gamma(Var(\pi))^{0.5} \tag{65}$$

where γ measures the degree of risk aversion. Note that for a risk-neutral firm[17], $\gamma = 0$, therefore, $E(u(\pi)) = E(\pi)$. To explain the impact of exchange rate volatility of firm behavior then, an issue that would have to be dealt with in this framework is the reason why Ä would be expected to be greater than zero. Such an explanation must also address two ancillary questions: (a) how much of $Var(\pi)$ is systematic, as opposed to unsystematic, risk? and (b) given the existence of markets for derivative securities to hedge exchange rate uncertainty, why can't firms hedge this risk?

The second major drawback of the line of analysis adopted in this paper (and again, one that is fairly universal) concerns the assumption that exchange rate changes are exogenous. In reality, they are determined by, and move in response to, (expectations of) changes in more fundamental macro-economic variables. A more complete understanding of pass-through behavior therefore requires a fuller understanding of the macroeconomic context in which the firm operates. A recent attempt in this area are that of **Klein (1988)**. The author develops a model of monopolistically competitive firms setting prices under macroeconomic uncertainty, to investigate the link between exchange rate changes and import prices. Exporters cannot observe, but infer, levels of variables relevant to the price setting decision. More specifically, suppose the firm sets its prices in the foreign currency; demand depends not only on the price level, but also income; these variables cannot be observed at the time the firm is setting prices, but must be inferred from past realizations of these variables, as well as past and current exchange rates. Thus, exporters face a signal extraction problem, and pass-through behavior will depend on the underlying stochastic structure of macroeconomic variables (including exchange rates). Such a line of analysis enables us to then distinguish between real and monetary shocks, as well as enables us to model the expectations formation process explicitly. But the modelling sacrifice that is made includes the ability to analyze oligopolistic behavior in detail.

In a general sense, an ideal model will incorporate the impact of exchange rate uncertainty in a generalized competitive framework (ie., imperfect competition, strategic substitutes and complements) and dynamics (ie., temporary versus permanent depreciation, ability to achieve scale economies over time). Such a model will be a significant addition to our understanding of real-world pass-through behavior. While some important beginnings have been made, and while this paper synthesizes and extends many of the previous results, the story of the full impact of real currency movements on corporate pricing strategies is less than fully told.

NOTES

1. This is assuming a depreciation of the home currency. If there is an appreciation, then full pass through will be consistent with skimming pricing behavior, while no pass through will be consistent with penetration pricing behavior (see **Sundaram and Mishra (1990)**).

2. A recent article in the Wall Street Journal (May 15, 1987) suggests that the norm for US firms operating in Japan has been to go for "...profits rather than market share", given the recent devaluation of the dollar. An editorial in Business Week (August 27, 1987) points to similar evidence, and suggests that "....such an approach is short term, whereas US manufacturers should be trying to grab a bigger share of the market..if (they) show price restraint now, they may win bigger markets and profits later". There have been many such reports on exactly the reverse phenomenon on the part of Japanese manufacturers operating in the US--they are seen as holding on to their market shares and restraining dollar prices, despite the dramatic appreciation of the yen during the period 1985-87.

3. The well-known "Marshall-Lerner-Robinson" conditions for stability of exchange rate markets result from this literature.

4. Other models that attempt to explain pass through behavior include those of hysteresis (**Krugman and Baldwin (1987)**, **Baldwin (1988)**, **Dixit (1989)**), those that examine the currency invoicing behavior of firms (**Baron (1976)**, **Hooper and Kohlhagen (1978)**, **Wilson and Takacs (1979)**, **Mann (1989)**) and those that incorporate the effects of macroeconomic uncertainty (**Klein (1989)**. Again, see **Sundaram and Mishra (1990)** for a review of these models.

5. For ease of interpretation, imagine an all-exporter US (home country) firm selling in Japan (foreign country) facing a Japanese competitor whose operations are confined to Japan. All the analysis that follows can be extended quite easily (but at the expense of a lot more algebra) to a two market, two-period case.

6. The assumption of homogeneity is not necessary, but adopted for convenience in analysis. See discussion of extensions to the model, in the last section.

7. If we were to analyze differentiated products, we would require two prices in each period, and the arguments, instead of being additive, will enter quite generally--that is, we would have to model prices as $P_i = P_i(q_i, q_{i*})$ and $P_{i*} = P_{i*}(q_{i*}, q_i)$. In addition, we might impose the condition that the products are conventional substitutes--that is, $\partial P_i/\partial q_{i*} < 0$ and $\partial P_{i*}/\partial q_i < 0$. With homogeneous products, the assumption of conventional substitutes is implicit in the additivity of quantities.

8. As we will explain below, this specification enables us to model the firm's ability to achieve learning (or joint economies through other means) between the two periods. The assumption that quantity sold in the second period does not affect cost in the first period is not necessary, but presumed to be a reasonable interpretation of reality.

9. For the case of Cournot competition, equilibrium prices and quantities will be the same for sequential and simultaneous markets; for conjectures other than Cournot, the first order condition for sequential markets will be based on the total derivative of profits rather than the partial derivative; on this point, see **Bulow, Geanakoplos and Klemperer (1985)** and **Sundaram and Mishra (1989)**.

10. We surmise that for most normal products, the attribute of joint diseconomies between periods will be difficult to interpret or rationalize in terms of real-world analogues. However, interesting (and counter-intuitive) conclusions arise on quantity and price impacts of exchange rate changes, particularly if we consider the possibility of joint economies for one fim and joint diseconomies for the other.

11. Note that this could be interpreted as relative, rather than absolute, learning abilities; all this would require is that we normalize the learning ability of the firm with slower learning to the NL case.

12. This is simply the elasticity of home currency price change with respect to the exchange rate change.

13. We can similarly derive the impact of exchange rate changes on second period quantities and prices. Given our interest basically in first period price responses, we do not further analyze the second period case. Note, however, that the results in the second period will conform to a standard single-period analysis for quantity setting oligopolies.

14. The result that $dP_1/de_1 = 0$ cannot be obtained if both demand and cost functions are linear (see, for example, the quantity setting duopoly analysis of **Dornbusch (1987)**) unless marginal costs are zero (which is ruled out). That is, with linear demand and (positive) constant marginal costs, a duopolist cannot fully pass through the effects of a devaluation.

15. A detailed examination of the relationship between the shape of the demand and cost curves, nature of conjectures, and strategic complementarity or substitutability, can be found in **Sundaram and Mishra (1989)**. A number of these themes are also addressed in **Bulow, Geanakoplos and Klemperer (1985)**.

16. Note that this expression, in terms of the foreign price, is $P^*/c'(q) = 1/[e(1+\eta)]$, where e is the exchange rate; this would correspond to the derivations in **Levi (1983)** and **Flood (1986)**.

17. The assumption of risk-neutral firms is the one that is consistent with the classical theories of finance.

APPENDIX

Recalling equation (8) in text,

$$(1)\qquad \begin{bmatrix} \pi_{11} & \pi_{11^*} & \pi_{12} & \pi_{12^*} \\ \pi_{1^*1} & \pi_{1^*1^*} & \pi_{1^*2} & \pi_{1^*2^*} \\ \pi_{21} & \pi_{21^*} & \pi_{22} & \pi_{22^*} \\ \pi_{2^*1} & \pi_{2^*1^*} & \pi_{2^*2} & \pi_{2^*2^*} \end{bmatrix} \begin{bmatrix} dq_1 \\ dq_{1^*} \\ dq_2 \\ dq_{2^*} \end{bmatrix} = - \begin{bmatrix} \pi_{1e_1} & \pi_{1e_2} \\ \pi_{1^*e_1} & \pi_{1^*e_2} \\ \pi_{2e_1} & \pi_{2e_2} \\ \pi_{2^*e_1} & \pi_{2^*e_2} \end{bmatrix} \begin{bmatrix} de_1 \\ de_2 \end{bmatrix}$$

We rewrite the key relationships in the main text, except that, the signs of the individual variables are shown. A '+' indicates that the variable is positive by assumption or derivation, a '-' that it is negative, a '+/-' indicates a strategic complement if positive and substitute if negative and a '+/0' indicates that there is learning if + or no learning if 0. All of the proofs below simply require us to inspect the signs of each of the terms.

$$(2)\qquad \Delta_{NL} = (\overset{-}{\pi_{11}}\overset{-}{\pi_{1^*1^*}} - \overset{+/-}{\pi_{11^*}}\overset{+/-}{\pi_{1^*1}})(\overset{-}{\pi_{22}}\overset{-}{\pi_{2^*2^*}} - \overset{+/-}{\pi_{22^*}}\overset{+/-}{\pi_{2^*2}})$$

$$(3)\qquad \Delta_{L} = \Delta_{NL} - \overset{-}{\pi_{1^*1^*}}\overset{-}{\pi_{2^*2^*}}\overset{+/0}{(\pi_{12})^2}$$

$$(4)\qquad \Delta_{L^*} = \Delta_{NL} - \overset{-}{\pi_{11}}\overset{-}{\pi_{22}}\overset{+/-}{(\pi_{1^*2^*})^2}$$

$$(5)\qquad \Delta_{LL^*} = \Delta_{NL} + (\overset{+/0}{\pi_{12}}\overset{+/0}{\pi_{1^*2^*}})^2 + (\overset{+/0}{(\pi_{12})^2}\overset{-}{\pi_{1^*1^*}}\overset{-}{\pi_{2^*2^*}} + \overset{+/0}{(\pi_{1^*2^*})^2}\overset{-}{\pi_{11}}\overset{-}{\pi_{22}})$$

$$(\overset{+/0}{\pi_{12}}\overset{+/0}{\pi_{1^*2^*}})^2(\overset{+/-}{\pi_{1^*1}}\overset{+/-}{\pi_{22^*}} + \overset{+/-}{\pi_{11^*}}\overset{+/-}{\pi_{2^*2}})$$

Stability assumes that $\Delta_j > 0$ and $\pi_{ii}\pi_{i^*i^*} - \pi_{i^*i}\pi_{ii^*} > 0$, i = 1,2. Note that the signs or magnitudes of Δ_j's are not affected by whether a product is a strategic complement or substitute, since their signs enter uniformly. Further, $\Delta_{NL} \geq \Delta_L$ and $\Delta_{NL} \geq \Delta_{L^*}$. It is not possible to determine the other relationships unambiguously.

<u>Strategic Substitutes and Temporary Depreciation</u>

- + +/- - - +/- +/-

(6) $dq_1/de_1|_{T,j} = [\pi_{1^*e_1}/\Delta_j]\pi_{11^*}(\pi_{22}\pi_{2^*2^*} - \pi_{2^*2}\pi_{22^*}) +$

- + +/0 +/0 +/-

$[\pi_{1^*e_1}/\Delta_j](\pi_{2^*1^*}\pi_{21}\pi_{22^*})$

We can see that (6) > 0 whenever $\pi_{22^*} < 0$ and $\pi_{2^*2} < 0$.

- + - - - +/- +/-

(7) $dq_{1^*}/de_1|_{T,j} = -[\pi_{1^*e_1}/\Delta_j]\pi_{11}(\pi_{22}\pi_{2^*2^*} - \pi_{22^*}\pi_{2^*2}) +$

- + +/0 +/0 -

$[\pi_{1^*e_1}/\Delta_j](\pi_{21}\pi_{12}\pi_{2^*2^*})$

and thus, (3) < 0 if j = NL,L*. For j = L,LL* it is ambiguous. Further, the sign is not dependent on the sign of π_{ii^*} or π_{i^*i}.

Proof of Proposition 1:

- - + +/- - - - +/- +/-

(8) $dP_1/de_1|_{T,j} = \{dP_1/dQ_1\}\{(\pi_{1^*e_1}/\Delta_j)[(\pi_{11^*} - \pi_{11})(\pi_{22}\pi_{2^*2^*} - \pi_{2^*2}\pi_{22^*})$ +

+/0 +/0 +/- +/0 -

$\pi_{12}(\pi_{2^*1^*}\pi_{22^*} + \pi_{12}\pi_{2^*2^*})]\}$

Thus, (8) > 0 when $\pi_{11^*} > \pi_{11}$.

<QED>

This condition will always obtain when the product is a strategic complement, since then, $\pi_{11*} > 0$ and since $\pi_{11} < 0$ by assumption. With strategic substitutes this condition will generally obtain with increasing marginal costs, since

$$(9) \qquad \pi_{11*} = [\partial P_1/\partial q_1] + q_1[\partial^2 P_1/dq_1^2]$$

$$(10) \qquad \pi_{11} = 2[\partial P_1/dq_1] + q_1[\partial^2 P_1/dq_1^2] - [\partial^2 c_1/\ q_1^2]$$

With decreasing marginal costs, so long as $[\partial P_1/\partial q_1] < [\partial^2 P_1/\partial q_1^2]$--that is, so long as marginal costs are decreasing at a slower rate than the demand curve--then $\pi_{11*} > \pi_{11}$.

Proof of Proposition 2:

Note that since π_{12} and π_{1*2*}, the numerator of dP/de are the same for both NL and L*. However, $\Delta_{NL} > \Delta_{L*}$ and thus,

$$(11) \qquad dP_1/de_1|_{T,L*} > dP_1/de_1|_{T,NL}$$

Comparing the NL and L cases, $dP_1/de_1|_{T,NL} > dP_1/de_1|_{T,L}$ if (after cancelling the common terms and simplifying),

$$(12) \qquad \pi_{11*} > \pi_{1*1*}$$

which will obtain generally if $\partial^2 c_{2*}/\partial q_{1*}^2 > 0$. If it is less than zero, then we would require that it be decreasing at a slower rate than the home firm's demand curve. The ambiguity of the relationship between $dP_1/de_1|_{T,LL*}$ and the dP/de's is easily seen by inspecting the signs. <QED>.

<u>Strategic Substitutes and Permanent Depreciation</u>

(13)

$$dq_1/de_1|_{P,j} = dq_1/de_1|_{T,j} - [\overset{-}{\pi_{2*e_2}}/\overset{+}{\Delta_j}][(\overset{+/-}{\pi_{11*}}\overset{+/0}{\pi_{1*2*}}\overset{-}{\pi_{22}}) + (\overset{-}{\pi_{1*1*}}\overset{+/0}{\pi_{12}}\overset{+/-}{\pi_{22*}})]$$

(14)

$$dq_{1*}/de_1|_{P,j} = dq_{1*}/de_1|_{T,j} + [\overset{-}{\pi_{2*e_2}}/\overset{+}{\Delta_j}][(\overset{-}{\pi_{11}}\overset{-}{\pi_{22}}\overset{+/0}{\pi_{1*2*}}) + (\overset{+/-}{\pi_{1*1}}\overset{+/0}{\pi_{12}}\overset{+/-}{\pi_{22*}}) - \overset{+/0}{(\pi_{12})^2}(\overset{+/0}{\pi_{1*2*}})]$$

(15)

$$dP_1/de_1|_{P,j} = dP_1/de_1|_{T,j} + \{\overset{-}{dP_1/dQ_1}\}\{[\overset{-}{\pi_{2*e_2}}/\overset{+}{\Delta_j}][(\overset{-}{\pi_{11}}-\overset{+/-}{\pi_{11*}})(\overset{+/0}{\pi_{1*2*}}\overset{-}{\pi_{22}}) + (\overset{+/-}{\pi_{1*1}}-\overset{-}{\pi_{1*1*}})(\overset{+/0}{\pi_{12}}\overset{-}{\pi_{2*2*}}) - \overset{+/0}{(\pi_{12})^2}(\overset{+/0}{\pi_{1*2*}})]\}$$

which, for convenience, rewite as

(16) $$= dP_1/de_1|_{Tj} + \{dP_1/dQ_1\}\{\theta_j\}$$

and price responses will also be dependent on the sign of θ_j.

Proof of Proposition 3:

Notice that

(17) $$\theta|_{NL} = 0$$

(18) $$\theta|_L > 0 \text{ if } \pi_{1*1} < 0, \text{ and}$$

$$\Theta\,|_L < 0 \text{ if } \pi_{1*1} > 0$$

(19) $$\Theta\,|_{L*} < 0 \text{ if } \pi_{11*} > \pi_{11}$$

(20) $$\Theta\,|_{LL*} > 0 \text{ if } \pi_{1*1} > \pi_{1*1*} \text{ and } (\pi_{12})^2 > \pi_{22}(\pi_{11} - \pi_{11*})$$

Notice also that Δ_j's remain the same for the temporary and permanent cases.

Comparing (8) with (15), assuming that (17)-(20) are true and noting that Δ_j's remain the same for the temporary and permanent cases, we can readily observe by inspecting signs that

(21) $$dP_1/de_1|_{P,NL} = dP_1/de_1|_{T,NL}$$

(22) $$dP_1/de_1|_{P,L*} > dP_1/de_1|_{T,L*}$$

(23) $$dP_1/de_1|_{P,L} < dP_1/de_1|_{T,L}$$

As before, the relationship between $dP_1/de_1|_{P,LL*}$ and the others is ambiguous. <QED>

Strategic Complements

The impact of strategic complementarity can be seen by noting the signs of the terms π_{ii*} and π_{i*i} (i = 1,2) in (6)-(8) and (13)-(15). The only difference now is that $\pi_{ii*} > 0$ and $\pi_{i*i} > 0$. Further, since the signs enter uniformly in the denominator, the Δ_j's are not affected by the assumption of strategic complementarity.

Proof of Proposition 4:

By inspecting the signs of π_{ii*} and π_{i*i} in (6) and (13), we see that

(24) $dq_1/de_1|_{.,j,SC} \leq dq_1/de_1|_{.,j,SS}$

and similarly, by inspecting the signs of π_{ii*} and π_{i*i} in (7) and (14), we see that

(25) $dq_{1*}/de_1|_{.,j,SC} = dq_{1*}/de_1|_{.,j,SS}$

If (24) and (25) are true, it must be true that

(26) $dP_1/de_1|_{.,j,SC} \geq dP_1/de_1|_{.,j,SS}$

<QED>

REFERENCES

Adler, M. and G. V. G. Stevens, 1974, "The Trade Effects of Direct Invest-ment", Journal of Finance Papers and Proceedings, 29, May, pp. 655-682.

Alexander, S. S., 1959, "The Effects of a Devaluation: A Simplified Synthesis of Elasticities and Absorption Approaches", American Economic Review, 49, 22-42.

Baldwin, R., 1988, "Some Empirical Evidence on Hysteresis in Aggregate US Import Prices", NBER Working Paper No. 2483, January.

Baldwin, R. and R. Lyons, 1988, "Exchange Rate Hysteresis--The Real Effects of Large versus Small Policy Misalignments", Columbia University, October. Baron, D. P., 1976, "Fluctuating Exchange Rates and the Pricing of Exports", Economic Inquiry, 14, September, pp. 425-459.

Bulow, Jeremy I., J. D. Geanakoplos and P. D. Klemperer, 1985, "Multimarket Oligopoly: Strategic Substitutes and Complements", Journal of Political Economy, 93, 488-511.

Clark, P. B., 1973, "Uncertainty, Exchange Rates and the Level of International Trade", Western Economic Journal, 11, September, pp. 302-313.

Dixit, A., 1986, "Comparative Statics for Oligopoly", International Economic Review, 27, 107-122.

Dixit, A., 1988, "Hysteresis, Import Penetration and Exchange Rate Pass-through", Princeton University, March.

Dixit, A., 1989, "Entry and Exit Decisions Under Uncertainty", Journal of Political Economy, 97, 3, pp. 620-638.

Dornbusch, R., 1987, "Exchange Rates and Prices", American Economic Review, 77, 93-106.

Ethier, W., 1972, "International Trade and the Forward Exchange Market", American Economic Review, June.

Flood, E., 1986, "Global Competition and Exchange Rate Exposure", Graduate School of Business, Stanford University, March.

Froot, K. A. and P. Klemperer, 1989, "Exchange Rate Pass through When Market Share Matters", American Economic Review,

Fudenberg, Drew and J. Tirole, 1983, "Learning by Doing and Market Performance", Bell Journal of Economics, 14, 522-530.

Haberler, G., 1952, "Currency Depreciation and Terms of Trade", in Wirtschaftliche Entwicklung und soziale Ordnung, J. Messner and E. Lagler (eds.), Herold Press, Vienna.

Harberger, A. C., 1950, "Currency Depreciation, Income and Balance of Trade" Journal of Political Economy, 58,

Hooper, P. and S. W. Kohlhagen, 1978, "The Effects of Exchange Rate Uncertainty on the Prices and Volumes of International Trade", Journal of Inter-national Economics, 8, pp. 483-511.

Horst, T., 1971, "The Theory of the Multinational Firm: Optimal Behavior Under Different Tariff and Tax Rates", Journal of Political Economy, September/October, pp. 1059-1072.

Klein, M. W., 1989, "Macroeconomic Aspects of Exchange Rate Pass-through", Clark University, April; presented at the session "Economic Exposure to Exchange Rates", Western Economic Association, July.

Knetter, M., 1989, "Price Discrimination by US and German Exporters", American Economic Review, March, pp. 198-210.

Krugman, P., 1986, "Pricing to Market When the Exchange Rate

Changes", NBER Working Paper No. 1926, March.

Krugman P. and R. Baldwin, 1987, "Persistent Trade Effects of Large Exchange Rate Shocks", NBER Working Paper No. 2017, September.

Lerner, A. P., 1944, "The Economics of Control", Macmillan, New York.

Lessard, Donald and E. Flood, 1986, "On the Measurement of Operating Exposure to Exchange Rates: A Conceptual Approach", Financial Management, Spring, 25-36.

Levi, M., 1983, "International Finance", McGraw-Hill, New York.

Luehrman, T. A., 1986, "The Exchange Rate Exposure of a Global Competitor", Harvard Business School, November.

Mann, C., 1989, "The Effects of Exchange Rate Trends and Volatility on Export Prices--Some Industry Examples from Japan, U.S. and Germany", The World Bank, September; presented at the session "Economic Exposure to Exchange Rates", Western Economic Association, July.

Robinson, J., 1937, "The Foreign Exchanges", in Essays in the Theory of Employment, Macmillan, New York; reprinted in American Economic Association, Readings in the Theory of International Trade, Blakiston, Philadelphia, 1950

Shapiro, A. C., 1975, "Exchange Rate Changes, Inflation and the Value of the Multinational Corporation", Journal of Finance, 30, 485-507.

Shapiro, A. C., 1986, "Multinational Financial Management", Allyn and Bacon, Massachusetts (2nd edition).

Sohmen, E., 1969, "Flexible Exchange Rates", University of Chicago Press, Chicago and London (Revised edition).

Spence, A. M., 1981, "The Learning Curve and Competition", Bell

Journal of Economics, 12, 49-70.

Sundaram, A. K. and V. Mishra, 1989, "Strategic Substitutes and Complements, Demand and Cost Functions and Generalized Conjectures--An Exploration of Linkages", Working Paper, The Amos Tuck School of Business Administration, September.

Sundaram, A. K. and V. Mishra, 1990, "Exchange Rate Pass-through and Economic Exposure: A Review", Amos Tuck School of Business Administration Working Paper, March; presented at the session "Economic Exposure to Exchange Rates", Western Economic Association, July 1989.

Wernerfelt, B., 1986, "A Special Case of Dynamic Pricing Policy", Management Science, 32, 1562-1566.

Wilson, J. E. and W. E. Takacs, 1979, "The Differential Responses to Price and Exchange Rate Influences in the Foreign Trade of Selected Countries", Review of Economics and Statistics,

Recent Developments in International Banking
and Finance, S.J. Khoury (editor)

CHAPTER VII

Technical Strategies in Foreign Exchange Markets: An Interim Report

Richard J. Sweeney

Georgetown University

Introduction

Technical analysis has a bad name both with academic financial economists and with a substantial fraction of practitioners. With both groups, the bad repute arises in large part because the evidence seems convincing to many that technical analysis cannot systematically beat the market. The case against technical analysis in foreign exchange markets is not, however, as closed as many think.

Computer simulations provide a substantial, but not incontrovertible, body of evidence that a technical analyst can make ongoing risk-adjusted profits in foreign exchange markets. All of this evidence is based, however, on performance evaluation techniques that assume risk premia are constant over time. Put it another way. Suppose one accepts that the measured profits, found on the basis of assuming constant risk premia, are not somehow mismeasured due to data errors, too low transactions costs and the like. Then, the only way to explain how these measured profits are not economic profits is to insist that the seeming profits are just a reward to time-varying risk premia. In essence, this argument says the analyst buys in on high-risk, high-return days and is out of the asset on low-risk, low-return days, thus earning measured profits but actually receiving only an appropriate return to risk. This paper discusses the evidence that there are measured profits from technical analysis in foreign exchange markets and whether these profits can be explained as due to time-varying risk premia. It does not discuss in any detail the other possible attack on the reported profits, that they arise from data errors, unrealistically low transactions costs, and other sources of mismeasurement.

Many theoretical models imply that time-varying risk premia are not only possible but are perhaps to be expected (Lucas 1978). The evidence that time-varying risk premia explain measured profits is not, however, very convincing. Simply put, there is much evidence that expected returns vary, but little evidence that this is due to variations over time in risk premia. In particular, the relatively few attempts to explain measured profits as due to time-varying risk premia are uniformly unsuccessful.

Section I reviews the evidence that simple technical rules can generate substantial, ongoing risk-adjusted profits in foreign exchange markets if risk premia are assumed constant over time. As backround it includes a discussion of a technique of measuring risk-adjusted profits that is consistent with very many asset-pricing models but requires observations only on rates of return and portfolio weights. As an example, using this technique to evaluate a number of technical trading strategies, Surajaras and Sweeney (1991) report an average risk-adjusted profit of from 3.28%/year to 6.32%/year for a two-thousand day trading period ending in 1986, with these profits highly significant. To supplement the relatively small number of technical studies of foreign exchange markets, this section also offers some discussion of technical analysis in U.S. equities markets. Surprisingly, the results of later studies of these equities markets are much more promising than those of the studies from the 1960s that convinced many observers that technical analysis is a deadend. Thus, the technical studies in equities markets reenforce the evidence in foreign exchange markets.

Section II discusses the evidence that time-varying risk premia exist and that they can explain measured profits to technical analysis in foreign exchange markets. Most of the evidence of time-varying risk premia can equally well be viewed merely as evidence that expected returns vary over time; indeed, the evidence that risk premia vary over time arises mostly under the maintained hypothesis of market efficiency and hence can shed no light on whether markets are inefficient and hence technical analysis might be economically profitable. The few studies that look directly at whether time-varying risk premia can explain measured profits to technical analysis in foreign exchange markets uniformly find little support for this explanation. This failure may, of course, be due to using inadequate models of risk, with better models fully able to explain profits; the question necessarily remains open. At present, however, the practitioner can know only that measured profits in foreign exchange markets have not been explained by current finance models of risk.

Section III offers some conclusions. Using technical analysis to invest in foreign exchange markets is risky, even when diversification is attempted. The evidence seems to be that such approaches can earn economically and statistically significant risk-adjusted profits on an ongoing basis. These profits are found with evaluation techniques that are valid if risk premia are constant. Alternatively, these techniques are valid if the average risk premium on days the investor is "in" the asset is approximately the same as the average on total days. Looked at this way the issue is not whether risk premia vary over time, but whether they vary in such a way that explains profits. So far there is no evidence that time-varying risk premia can be used to dismiss measured profits as not economic profits. If the measured profits are to be dismissed as illusory, perhaps a more successful line of attack is to argue that they may be due to data errors and other types of mismeasurement.

I. Measured Profits from Technical Analysis in Foreign Exchange Markets

Academic financial economists have studied technical analysis in spot, futures and forward foreign exchange markets. Since covered interest rate parity holds to a good first approximation, these markets are not independent. The studies are not mirror images, however, because they focus on instruments of different maturity. Typically, studies of spot markets assume that the investor holds overnight positions. In contrast, forward market studies deal with 30 or 90 day contracts that are held to maturity even if new contracts can be entered into before the old mature.

A. Technical Analysis in Spot Exchange Markets

Soon after the current system of generalized dirty floating exchange rates began in March, 1973, financial economists began studying the efficiency of these markets, using filter rules and other types of technical analysis as one part of their studies. All of the spot market studies discussed here use only current and past values of currencies. Early studies include Dooley and Shafer (1976), Logue, Sweeney and Willett (1978), and Cornell and Dietrich (1978). The latter two studies look for profits by comparing the rates of return on portfolios managed by technical strategies with returns on comparable portfolios where the investor simply buys the foreign assets and holds them. Using buy-and-hold as a benchmark is based on Fama and Blume's (1966) very influential study that convinced many observers that technical analysis could not beat U.S. equities markets. These early foreign exchange market technical studies report rather mixed results, which the authors interpret in various ways regarding the possibilities of making profits. For some periods, some technical strategies and some currencies, there seem to be measured profits. The difficulty in interpreting the results arises because the measured profits seem to be unstable over time, the authors have no statistical test of performance, and they do not handle risk in a satisfactory way.[1] All of these early tests, however, implicitly assume that risk premia on assets are constant over time.

Later work finds evidence of profitability of technical analysis. Dooley and Shafer (1983) find some persistence of economically significant profits by using the same approach as in their earlier (1976) study, but still have no statistical test of the significance of their measured profits.[2] Their approach uses an arbitrage portfolio where the investor puts up no net funds and earns a net return in terms of say dollars equal to the foreign currency's appreciation plus the differential between the foreign and dollar interest rates. They find positive profits on average. They expect to find zero profits if exchange markets are efficient, but this expectation can in general be so only under the assumption of constant risk premia that are all equal to zero, as is explicit in their paper; otherwise an investor long in a high-risk currency and short in a low-risk currency should expect positive measured profits on his arbitrage portfolio.

Sweeney (1986) broke his sample into subperiods, developed a statistical test, and found persistent and statistically significant profits from one period to the next. While he assumed constant risk premia, they did not have to be equal to each other or to zero. Table 1 reports profits Sweeney finds.

A.1. A General Test of Abnormal Performance

As backround to discussion below, it is worthwhile examining the simplest possible version of Sweeney's test. The test does not presuppose that any particular asset pricing model is true, but is consistent with any model that implies that expected excess rates of return are equal in every period to a constant risk premium.[3] Further, the evaluator need observe only the technician's sequences of portfolio weights, not returns on underlying factors that may be measured with error[4], or may be unobservable or not specified in the theory.[5] If the true model were known and the forcing terms known and observed accurately, Sweeney's approach would be inefficient; if these conditions are violated, it is not clear that model-based measures of performance are more efficient.[6]

Suppose that the investor takes dollars as his/her base currency and keeps his funds either in overnight Eurodollars or EuroDMs. S/he uses technical analysis to switch back and forth. Measure the rate of return on any investment as an excess return, the appreciation of the currency plus its interest rate, less the Eurodollar interest rate, implying the (excess) return on dollars is identically zero. When the investor is "in" DMs he puts all his funds in DMs, with a DM weight of unity, and when out the weight is zero, with w_t the weight at time t. The average return to the technical (or filter) strategy is $R_F = (1/T) \Sigma w_t R_t$, where Σ is the summation operator, R_t the return on DMs, and T the number of days in the period examined. The average return to buying and holding the DM is $R_{BH} = (1/T) \Sigma R_t$. Direct comparison of R_F and R_{BH} can be misleading. Suppose the expected value of R each day is g, where g is a risk premium as given by any of a wide range of theories. Then, $ER_F = (1 - f) g$ while $ER_{BH} = g$, where f is the fraction of days the investor is "out" of the DM. Thus, Sweeney uses the test statistic

$$X = R_F - (1 - f) R_{BH},$$

where, conditional on the information available before the evaluation period starts, $EX = 0$. The intuition is that the investor goes in and out of the DM but that in an efficient market with a constant risk premium g, his best guess rate of return each day in is g, giving $EX = 0$.

Further, suppose that the period is over and the evaluator knows that the return to buy-and-hold is R'. Each day during the period, the actual return to being in the DM was $g + e_t$, where e is a zero-mean unforecastable error. The evaluator knows that the average value of e was $e' = R' - g$. Any day that the investor was in during the period, the evaluator now expects to find that he earned R', based on the assumption that while e' was non-zero, all the es were unforecastable.

That is, the evaluator believes that E $(X|R_{BH} = R') = 0$. Thus, knowledge of R' does not call for any adjustment to the test statistic X. This is valuable because it means that the test statistic is fully applicable both in up and down markets.

The standard deviation of X is

$$\sigma_X = \sigma\ [(1 - f)\ f]^{1/2}\ T^{1/2},$$

where σ is the standard deviation of the excess rate of return on the DM. For testing purposes, substitute the sample standard deviation of this rate of return to find the standard error of X. The test clearly depends on the existence of a finite population variance.

Sweeney (1986) forms a test statistic for a portfolio of currencies by taking an equally-weighted average of the Xs for the individual currencies. In essence, this assumes continuous rebalancing of the portfolio. The standard error of the portfolio can be found from the variance of the sum of the Xs, with the covariances of the Xs plausibly either estimated from their sample values or taken as equal to zero.[7]

A more general approach is in Sweeney (1989b), with the above discussion as a subcase. Here the approach takes the deviations of the weight for asset j at time t, w_{jt}, from its average value over the sample, w_j, and compares these deviations with the deviations of the return on j at t, R_{jt}, from the mean of j's return over the sample, R_j, or looks at

$$(w_{jt} - w_j)\ (R_{jt} - R_j).$$

If all risk premia are constant and the expected return on every asset equals its risk premium at all times, the average of these deviations over time, summed across assets, has an expected value of zero, whether this expectation is taken before the period or after the evaluator knows all the R_j. This approach, in effect, takes a constant-weight portfolio (the w_js) as the benchmark, implying continuous rebalancing. It is easy to extend the technique to any arbitrary benchmark (Sweeney 1989b). Surajaras and Sweeney (1991), for example, use as one benchmark an unmanaged portfolio with no rebalancing, so that the benchmark's (initially equal) weights evolve over time as an asset has returns differing from the portfolio's return.

Further, Sweeney (1989b) shows that the technique can be extended to allow for time varying risk premia.[8]

A.2. Profits in a Recent Study of Spot Markets

It is worthwhile examining the results from Surajaras and Sweeney (1991), the latest study of technical trading in spot foreign exchange markets. These authors look at fifteen currencies over 2000 consecutive trading days ending in 1986, and examine multiple trading strategies for any individual currency, as well as two ways of forming portfolios of currencies and two different benchmarks.

In forming portfolios, they use two approaches. One essentially assumes that there is a mutual fund for each of the currencies, with the fund either in the currency or in the dollar; as a benchmark for this case, they simply use an equally-weighted portfolio, implicitly assuming daily rebalancing. No foreign currency can then have more than 1/15th of total funds invested in it. This approach thus gives diversification. On the other hand, it does not exploit very fully whatever profit opportunities are available. Each of the individual funds tends to have its assets lie idle in the Eurodollar account about half the time, where the assets necessarily earn only a zero rate of return; if the technical signals actually give profits, the larger the percentage of time the assets are active, the better. In the other approach to portfolio formation, the investor starts with an equally-weighted portfolio, but puts any funds from a sell signal into a common pool. A buy signal for a currency has the investor allocate all available funds on a pro rata basis to all currencies that get a buy signal that day. Thus, if none of the funds are currently invested and only one currency gets a buy signal, the whole portfolio ends up in this one currency. They call this the variably-weighted approach, in contrast to the equally-weighted approach. Clearly, the variably-weighted approach is a high-risk, high-return approach because it can sometimes produce little diversification. It does, however, have the advantage of keeping the whole portfolio more fully invested in assets where there is the possibility of profits, rather than lying idle in the zero-profit Eurodollar account; empirically, they find the equally-weighted approach has funds active about 50% of the time, the variably-weighted portfolio approach about 86% of the time. For each portfolio formation approach they can use a constant-weight benchmark or an unmanaged, unrebalanced benchmark.

They examine the Alexander (1961, 1964) filter rule, the single moving average strategy and the double moving average strategy to getting in and out of currencies, with all currencies in the portfolio using the same strategy but with each currency having individually tailored triggers (up and down filter sizes, or lag lengths in the moving averages). Further, they look at a so-called mixed approach where each currency uses the strategy (Alexander rule, single or double moving average) that looks best.

Surajaras and Sweeney (1991) use a holdout period to determine in-sample best rules, as measured by the X-statistic discussed above. They then use these "best" rules in a later test sample. They have two contiguous test samples, each 1000 trading days long.

Table 2 gives a sample of their results. Several points deserve discussion. First, these results are from the variably-weighted portfolio approach. Thus, the portfolio can become severely undiversified, leading to high risk. The large standard errors implicit in the t-statistics reflect this risk. Second, the Alexander filter rule does not do nearly as well in the second as the first period. The double and single moving average rules also show some (minor) fall-off in performance from the first to the second period. Surajaras and Sweeney, and also Sweeney and Surajaras (1989), argue that this is not evidence of a trend decline in profitability. Third, the single moving average strategy seems to be the most profitable, but this may well just be a peculiarity of the sample. Thus, the Alexander filter rule that has figured so prominently in academic investigations may be relatively ineffective compared to other strategies.

B. Technical Analysis in Forward Foreign Exchange Markets

This strand of literature starts with the issue of whether the current forward rate, say the 30 day rate, is an unbiased predictor of the value of the spot rate in 30 days. If there is a bias and this bias is partly forecastable, then the investor can take positions that allow measured profits equal to the forecastable component of the bias. Unbiasedness requires an intercept of zero and a slope coefficient of unity in the forecasting equation

$$(1) \qquad \Delta S/S = a + b\,(F - S)/S + u,$$

where S is the current spot exchange rate (number of dollars per unit of foreign currency, so that a rise in S is a depreciation of the dollar, appreciation of the foreign currency), F is the forward exchange rate for a given period (say 30 days), (F - S)/S the forward premium on the foreign currency (discount on the dollar), S/S the actual percentage rate of change over the period covered by F, and u a mean-zero error term that, under rational expectations, is serially uncorrelated and also uncorrelated with F or S. There is substantial evidence that b does not equal unity (Bilson 1981, Fama 1984, Hodrick and Srivastava 1987, Sweeney 1991). This implies not only a bias in the forward premium, but one that varies over time with the premium. Since speculative profits measured as a percentage rate are $(S_+ - F)/S$ where S_+ is the actual spot exchange rate corresponding to F, from (1) this profit rate is

$$(2) \qquad (S_+ - F)/S = a + (b - 1)\,(F - S)/S + u.$$

For zero expected profits, a = b - 1 = 0. The evidence of a non-zero b implies expected profit opportunities that vary over time with the forward premium.

This relationship may not be stable enough over time to allow the investor actually to earn measured profits. Bilson (1981) attempts to earn profits based on using a version[9] of (1) and taking positions based on portfolio optimization techniques. His portfolio holds only forward contracts, however, and is thus very undiversified compared to the average mutual fund. This is important because his performance measure compares profits to the portfolio's risk, here the risk of a fairly undiversified portfolio, rather than to some measure of the premium in the forward rate that would be implied by the systematic risk of an optimally diversified portfolio.[10] He does not update his parameter estimates, either of (1) or of the covariance matrix (needed for the portfolio optimization), over his sample. He finds measured profits, but these tail off towards the end of his test period. He judges these measured profits by comparing them to the standard deviation of his rather undiversified portfolio and arguing that the ratio appears too favorable, though there is no test of this. Hodrick and Srivastava (1984) reexamine Bilson's work with more data, using Bilson's portfolio optimization approach, updating the parameter estimates of (1) as their sample goes on, with (1) expanded to include not only the currency's own premium but also those of other currencies, and find diminished profits compared to Bilson. They conclude that the risk-return trade-off appears both volatile and sensitive to the modeler's strategy, and find that the ratio of profits to standard deviation does not appear impressive to them. Longworth, Boothe and Clinton (1983) use updated versions of (1) to take positions whenever the forecasted coming spot rate differs from the forward rate. They find generally significant profits for the Canadian/US dollars for this and comparable approaches, though their tests ask whether the measured profits are different from zero and hence implicitly assume that there is a zero risk premium in the forward rate.

Unlike Bilson, Sweeney and Lee (1990) find measured profits that are fairly stable over the four quarters of their sample period. They use a 50-period rolling regression estimate of (1) to forecast non-overlapping 30-day changes in the spot exchange rate for 10 major currencies, and for large enough trigger values of (F - S)/S they take buy or sell positions in 67 periods. They treat each buy/sell decision separately, using no portfolio optimization considerations. They report average arithmetic profit rates of 3.53%/year over all currencies; since in about 65% of the cases no position was taken, they also report an arithmetic profit rate of 10.12%/year over those currencies for which positions were taken. Using a modified version of the X-statistic discussed above, they perform a test of the significance of profits--unlike Bilson and Hodrick and Srivastava--and find a t-statistic of 3.23.[11] This test explicitly assumes that the systematic risk premium in each forward rate is constant but does not assume that it is zero (unlike Longworth, Boothe and Clinton). Sweeney and Lee use trigger values (set before examining the data), while the other studies essentially force the investor to take a position every period whether the risk-return tradeoff looks favorable or not.

The difference between (F - S)/S and the expectation of S/S is the bias in the forward premium and is the expected profit rate to taking a position in the forward market. Fama (1984) calls this bias a risk premium, but this is begging the question. While many authors have produced theoretical models where the bias does in fact equal a risk premium, the issue is whether empirically the bias does so. Section II discusses this issue.

C. Technical Analysis in Futures Markets

Cornell and Reinganum (1981) and Hodrick and Srivastava (1985) argue that empirically forward and futures prices for foreign exchange are very close to each other, though theoretical work by Cox, Ingersoll and Ross (1981) shows that the two types of prices can in principle diverge. Based on the previous subsection's discussion, then, it would not be surprising to find that technical analysis of futures prices can lead to measured profits. There has, however, been very little reported work on technical analysis in foreign exchange futures.

Taylor (1986) presents an interesting analysis of futures markets, including those for currencies. He uses a time series forecasting approach, taking buy or sell positions depending on the forecasted profitability being large enough. His approach is geared to finding trends in data that appear to be essentially random as judged by other time series methods. In an out-of-sample simulation on IMM data, he reports that a trading fund investing in three currency futures (pound, DM, Swiss franc) following his strategy would have earned a net return of 23%/year over the three-year period 1979-81, while funds put in a risk-free asset would have earned on average 16%/year, giving adusted average profits of 7%/year.

In his strategies, the number of contracts taken is chosen to make negligible the risk of losing more than the fund's entire capital. He argues that a risk-free asset is the appropriate benchmark because there does not seem to be evidence of a risk premium in currency futures; one might object that buy-and-hold should still be used as a benchmark to normalize for sample-dependent up or down trends (see the above discussion of the X-statistic). Taylor further argues that the particular strategy he pursues with currency futures (his strategy II) is less risky than buy-and-hold because his strategy has the buyer in the risk-free asset a fraction of the overall period; this point is valid, but the strategy's returns must still be compared to buy-and-hold unless both the ex ante risk premium and the ex post price trends are zero.[12] Thus, Taylor's highly interesting results would be more impressive if he had done a comparison to buy-and-hold or had presented data allowing the reader to do so (he gives data on days "in" contracts, allowing inference of the fs).

II. Time-Varying Risk Premia as An Explanation for Measured Profits[13]

Suppose that the measured profits to technical analysis reported above are taken at face value, that is, as not due to measurement error, inaccurate transactions costs, etc. Time-varying risk premia are then needed to explain that these measured profits are really only a reward to risk bearing. Such an eplanation requires, first, evidence of time-varying premia; second, evidence that the ups and downs in the premia (more or less) match the in and out positions that generate the measured profits; and third, evidence that the risk premia and measured profits are commensurate.

Asset pricing models imply that the expected (excess) return to each asset equals a risk premium. Assuming these models are correct, evidence that the expected return is time varying is evidence that the risk premium is time varying. An alternative explanation of such evidence, however, is that the expected return is time varying while the premium is constant (or does not vary pari passu)--this is precisely the opportunity a technician seeks. For example, on average the expected return may equal the risk premium, but with partially forecastable fluctuations above or below the premium. The technician then aims at being in (out) when the expected return is greater (less) than the risk premium.

A. Evidence on Time-Varying Risk Premia

There is a body of model-free empirical evidence supporting the view that expected returns are not constant. For example, in foreign exchange markets, Hansen and Hodrick (1980, 1983) and Hodrick and Srivastava (1984) among many others show that currently available variables are useful in forecasting future profit rates from forward exchange positions; in particular, in explaining values of $(S_+ - F)/S$ they find that lagged values of this variable and also currently observable forward premia are useful. In U.S. equities markets, Poterba and Summers (1988), Lo and MacKinlay (1988) and Fama and French (1988) present evidence that expected rates of return are not constant over time.[14] Such evidence shows that there may well be opportunities for the technician to make measured profits, since it shows that expected returns seem to be time varying.

Showing that risk premia are time varying requires a model of risk. Empirically, models can fail to display time-varying risk premia either because the premia do not vary or because the model is poorly specified. As is usual in efficiency tests, the researcher is examining a joint hypothesis. Even with rejection of the joint hypothesis, a better model may reveal time-varying risk premia that explain measured profits.

Hansen and Hodrick (1983) and Hodrick and Srivastava (1984) model and test for time-varying risk premia in the forward exchange markets. They assume that the expected return to a forward position is equal to the currency's beta times the expected return to a mean-variance-efficient benchmark portfolio. To implement their tests, they assume each currency's beta is constant over time. The expected return on the benchmark portfolio (equal to the risk premium on this portfolio) is allowed to vary, in Hodrick and Srivastava's work as a linear function of the current, observable forward premia on each of the five currencies studied, $pr_t = k_o + \Sigma_j k_j [(F - S)/S]_{j,t}$. They argue, in effect, that if forward premia help predict coming profit rates, it must be because these premia help explain the risk premium on the benchmark portfolio. In essence, their test compares for each of five currencies the unrestricted equation

$$(3) \qquad [(S_+ - F)/S]_i = a_i + \Sigma_j b_{ij} [(F - S)/S]_j + u_i,$$

for a total of 30 parameters, with the restricted system

(4) $[(S_{+} - F)/S]_{i} = B_{i} \{k_{o} + \Sigma_{j} k_{j} [(F - S)/S]_{j}\} + u_{i},$

giving 10 parameters.[15] Hodrick and Srivastava can decisively reject the restricted model relative to the unrestricted. The rejection might be due to the expected returns varying (mostly) independently of the risk premium (allowing potential profits to technical analysis), or to inadequacy of the model. (Giovannini and Jorion (1987) expand this model by letting the betas vary deterministically with the risk free rate; interestingly, they cannot reject the model, though it should be noted that in earlier versions of the work in Hodrick and Srivastava, the data also did not reject the model.) Note that the assumption of constant betas implies that speculative positions of the type in Sweeney and Lee (1980) will change signs only when the premium on the market does. Further, when one currency position changes sign, all must do so. Sweeney and Lee do not find this lock-step pattern in the positions called for by their approach and the data. Hodrick and Srivastava's empirical result that all betas have the same sign further implies that any forward positions the speculator takes should all have the same direction, either all buys or all sells, a pattern not found by Sweeney and Lee.

Sweeney (1991) looks at pound sterling data on forward and spot exchange rates, the same data used in Sweeney and Lee (1990). A UK speculator making a contract to buy Belgian francs for pounds sterling in thirty days, at F_t francs per pound, makes a profit in percentages terms of

$$
\begin{aligned}
(F_t - S_{t+30})/S_t &= (F_t - S_t)/S_t - (S_{t+30} - S_t)/S_t \\
&= (F\text{-}S)/S - S/S = (i_{Bel} - i_{UK}) - S/S \\
&= (i_{Bel} - S/S) - i_{UK},
\end{aligned}
\tag{4a}
$$

where i_{Bel} and i_{UK} are thirty-day Euro dollar rates, i_{Bel} minus i_{UK} is (approximately) equal to (F-S)/S from interest rate parity, and S/S is the percentage increase in the number of francs required to buy one pound or is the rate of depreciation of the franc. i_{Bel}- S/S can be interpreted as the pound-rate-of-return on funds placed in safe Belgian francs, and (i_{Bel} - S/S) - i_{UK} as the excess returns on such an investment relative to putting the funds in a comparable, pound-denominated risk-free asset.[16]

Sweeney's empirical work uses a single-factor model with a market index. The returns to the forward buy contract in (4) are

(5) $$[(i_{Bel} - \Delta S/S) - i_{UK}]_t = B_t [(R_m - i_{UK})]_t + v_t,$$

where B is the speculation's beta and v is a mean-zero random variable orthogonal to the theoretically appropriate market index, R_m. Of course, the return to the opposite speculation of making a forward contract to sell Belgian francs simply changes signs on both sides of the equation, and hence is also described by (5).

Identify all of the bias in the forward premium as a risk premium, RP, and suppose all of RP is due to systematic risk. In the CAPM, the expected return to speculation in any period is then

(6) $$B_t(ER_m - i_{UK})_t = RP_t.$$

Hansen and Hodrick (1983) and Hodrick and Srivastava (1984) view all betas as constant, while allowing variation in the expected excess rate of return on a benchmark portfolio (playing a role like that of ER_m-i_{UK} here). Sweeney takes the other tack, assuming ER_m-i_{UK} is (relatively) constant over the period but the betas can vary and not necessarily together.

Taking the market premium (ER_m-i_{UK}) as constant, (6) says RP_t and B_t vary pari passu. Since neither RP nor B is observable, consider the hypothesis that RP and (F-S)/S vary proportionately, or RP = μ (F-S)/S so

(7) $$B_t = RP_t/(ER_m\text{-}i_{UK}) = \mu\ [(F\text{-}S)_t/S]/(ER_m\text{-}i_{UK}).$$

For ER_m-i_{UK} of 8% on an annual percentage basis, ER_m-i_{UK} is .0067 on a monthly decimal basis. ([F-S]/S and the speculative profit rates are measured as decimal percents per month). What is a reasonable value of μ? Sweeney argues that μ may have values between say 2 and 3; tentatively entertain these values. Then, $\mu/(ER_m$-$i_{UK})$, the slope coefficient on (F-S)/S in (7), is from 300 to 450.[17]

If (8) holds and RP is proportional to (F-S)/S, then from (5) and (7) one can use $[(F-S)/S](R_{mt}-i_{UKt})$ as the independent variable in a market model regression,

(8) $$(F_t - S_{t+30})/S_t = d + g[(F-S)/S]_t\,(R_{mt}-i_{UKt}) + v_t;$$

from the discussion around (7), g should be in the range of 300 to 450. An alternative is to assume systematic risk B is constant as is very often done in estimating market models,

(8') $$(F_t - S_{t+30})/S_t = d + h(R_{mt}-i_{UKt}) + v_t.$$

A market model including both possibilities, that all variations in RP are movements in B as in (7) and that B is constant while RP varies, is (8") $(F_t - S_{t+30})/S_t = d + h(R_{mt}-i_{UKt}) + g[(F-S)/S]_t(R_{mt}-i_{UKt}) + v_t$.

Sweeney reports OLS results for (8) -(8"). The variable R_m is the rate of return on the CRSP value-weighted daily index, aggregated over the exact days in each period and adjusted for pound-dollar exchange rate changes to express R_m as a pound rate of return. Only a daily-returns index could be used to match exactly the periods of the forward contracts, and only the daily CRSP indices were available.

For (8), only five of the nine countries' estimated gs have the correct (positive) sign, and none of these is significant at the 95% confidence level; Germany's g is negative and significant. The average g is only 1.50; the average of the positive gs for is 9.642, at least an order of magnitude less than the expected 300 to 450. The joint hypothesis that all of RP is systematic risk, that RP is proportional to (F-S)/S, and that the market model and market measure used here are adequate, is fairly strongly rejected by the data. (Relaxing the assumption of proportionality of RP to (F - S)/S does not change the results.) The market model with a constant beta as in (8'), fairs poorly. In (8") including both variables makes g positive in six of the nine countries, and significant for the U.S. and Canada. The overall average g is 6.75; the average positive g is 15.21. Sweeney concludes that the model investigated does not uncover time-varying risk premia.

A.1. ARCH Models

Based on Engle's (1982) work on Autoregressive Conditional Heteroskedasticity models, there is a growing literature that looks for time-varying risk premia in foreign exchange as well as stock markets. In one version of Generalized ARCH (GARCH),

$$R_t = a + b\, V_t + e_t, \tag{9}$$

$$V_t = \alpha + \beta\, V_{t-1} + \delta\, (e_{t-1})^2. \tag{10}$$

V is the conditional variance of e and is assumed to depend on the squared lagged value of e as will as its own lagged value, with e_t distributed $N(0,V_t)$[18]. In turn, the expected rate of return depends on V, with this dependence interpreted as a risk premium, along the lines of the CAPM if the asset is the market portfolio or if the asset is an individual stock whose beta varies essentially through changes in own variance. Models where the expected return is influenced by the conditional variance are often called GARCH-M (for "mean").

A number of articles have applied ARCH techniques to characterize the volatility of spot exchange rates. Baillie and Bollerslev (1987) argue that aside from day-of-the-week and holiday effects, daily spot exchange rate data in the 1980's are well described by a simple random walk and a GARCH structure for the conditional variance (or b = 0 in the above model). When they sample the data weekly or monthly, they find a great reduction in the importance of ARCH effects (with the Rs tending towards normality). These results mean that GARCH characterizations, of how risk premia vary to explain speculative profits, must use relatively frequent sampling of data and also imply relatively frequent in and out moves by the investor who makes measured profits. This is true both for the spot and forward exchange rate speculations discussed above, since all of the risk to a forward position comes from movements in the spot rate.

For four major currencies with weekly observations on 30-day forward contracts, Baillie and Bollerslev (1988) estimate the forward profit rate, $(S_+ - F)/S$, as a fourth order MA process[19] where the errors for any currency are GARCH (1,1) and the correlations of errors across currencies are constant (so the covariances change only with the conditional variances). They find this model works relatively well as judged by common specification tests. They then ask whether augmenting this model with own conditional variances improves explanatory power. This specification makes sense in terms of a CAPM if one believes that the correlation of the spot rate with the market is constant and the variance of the rate of return on the market is constant, or rather these two parameters vary little relative to the spot rate's conditional variance. They find that adding these conditional moments seems not to help; they also find that adding other-currency conditional covariances does not improve explanatory power. While the results in other, similar papers vary somewhat, ARCH models seem not to give reasonable representations so far of time varying risk premia in forward markets.

For comparison, consider ARCH applications to other financial markets. In a well known application Bollerslev, Engle and Wooldridge (1988) test the CAPM on the returns (in excess of the 3-month bill rate) of 6-month bills, bonds and the stock market. Since the expected (excess) return on each asset depends in this model on its covariance with the weighted average of all three of the assets (the market, here), they estimate simultaneously a GARCH-M model for all three returns as well as their conditional covariance matrix, finding each moment well represented as a GARCH (1,1) process. According to their estimates, when an asset's conditional covariance with the market rises by unity, its expected return rises by roughly 0.5%, a plausible result in their view[20]. Since forward positions net to zero by definition across the market, adding these to this model would not alter the results for the assets already included, but suggests that equations for forward profit rates should include covariance terms with the market--an insight that Sweeney (1991) tests with no very good results as reported above.

ARCH models intuitively seem very promising in that they give a handle on the potentially time-varying variances and covariances that are crucial in asset pricing theories. Nevertheless, they have certain difficulties. They are subject to great influence of outliers since lagged e^2 enters the variance equation. Further, as Hodrick (1987) argues, a large disturbance may be due to a crisis that is resolved next period, with the model then predicting a large V whereas the resolution gives a below average V. It may be that these problems explain the mixed and mostly unsatisfactory results found from using ARCH in exchange markets; these problems are at least partially remediable, however, so this approach still holds much promise.

Even if the models discussed in this section had found time-varying risk premia, this evidence would have done nothing directly to show that measured profits are not economic profits. For this, the risk premia would have to be shown to vary at times and in size by the amount necessary to explain the technician's profits. Thus, any empirical work hoping to test whether measured profits are economic profits must explicitly include the technician's buy and sell decisions. There are very few efforts in the literature along these lines. Because there are so few, it is worthwhile to look at them, including the few on U.S. equities markets.

B. Tests of Whether Time-Varying Risk Premia Can Explain Measured Profits

Sweeney and Lee (1990) argue that a market model may explain the significant measured profits that they find. They propose that the actual speculative rate of profits to their portfolio in any period, SP, depends on a time-varying beta. If the expected average SP is positive, the average beta must also be positive. To test this, the run the regression

$$SP_t = c + k\ R_{Mt} + w_t,$$

where R_M is the return on the market and w an error term. They argue that while the actual beta varies around the average beta from period to period, these variations are uncorrelated with RM under the assumption of no market forecasting ability on the speculator's part; thus, while an OLS estimate of k is biased in small samples, it is asymptotically unbiased and consistent. Their estimate of k is -.0295 with a t-statistic of .687. They conclude that market risk does not explain measured profits. Bilson and Hsieh (1983) find similar results for a similar experiment using profits from a portfolio strategy similar to the Bilson strategy discussed above.

B.1. Tests for Equities Markets

Since there are so few tests of actual performance of technical analysis, it is worthwhile to look also at those from the US equities markets. Debondt and Thaler (1985) argue that a portfolio of the biggest "losers" over a three-year period will outperform the market in the next three-year period on average, while a portfolio of the biggest winners underperforms. Chan (1988) asks whether the profits that DeBondt and Thaler find for the New York Stock exchange companies they examine can be explained by time-varying betas in a market model. Chan presents evidence that the good performance of past losers can be explained as due to increases in their betas, and similarly for the past winners, *mutatis mutandis*. He uses dummy variable techniques to ask whether shifts in betas or in alphas explain differential performance between the periods, and finds little evidence of intercept effects.

Sweeney (1989c) asks whether time-varying risk premia can explain the measured profits found in Sweeney (1988a) from using very simple technical analysis; Table 3 shows these profits. In order to try to explain them, Sweeney (1989c) considers a fair game version of the market model, where the excess rate of return to stock i at time t (R_{it}) is

$$R_{it} = ER_{it} + B_{it}(R_{Mt} - ER_{Mt}) + e_{it}, \tag{11}$$

where E is the expectations operator conditional on all information available to market participants at time t, B_{it} is the time-varying beta of i on the market, R_{Mt} is the excess rate of return on the market, and e_{it} is the idiosyncratic risk of i. The expected excess rate of return on i, from the CAPM, is

$$ER_{it} = B_{it}(ER_{Mt}). \tag{12}$$

From (12), time variability of ER_{it} arises from variations in B_i and ER_M. Substituting (12) into (11) gives the market model estimating equation

$$R_{it} = B_{it}(R_{Mt}) + e_{it}. \tag{13}$$

In (13), the only time-varying parameter left is B_{it}. Time variations in ER_{Mt} show up in shifts in the mean of R_{Mt} and are not estimatable in the market-model approach (Sweeney and Warga 1986).

Betas might be assumed to vary over a continuum. Sweeney (1989c) makes the simplifying assumption that there are only two values of beta, one high (B') and the other low (B"). With the two-beta regime, (13) becomes

$$(14) \qquad R_{it} = B_i''R_{Mt} + (B_i' - B_i'')\, D_t\, R_{Mt} + e_{it},$$

where D is a dummy variable with value zero on the low-beta days, one otherwise. Operationally, he assumes that the technical buy/sell signals in Sweeney (1988b) can be used to find D.

He sharpens the tests with a plausible alternative hypothesis. Suppose that beta is constant but

$$(12') \qquad ER_{it} = a_i'' + (a_i' - a_i'')\, D_t + B_i\, (ER_{Mt}),$$

where $a_i' > 0$, $a_i'' < 0$. The "a"s cause a gap between the expected return and the premia of priced risk ($B_i\ ER_{Mt}$). The CAPM and all other asset pricing theories predict that no such gap should exist. Intuitively, in the special case where $a_i' = -\ a_i''$ and with the average of days in to total days of about 0.5, (12') says the average expected return on i is explained by systematic risk. Some days, the expected return is less than required by systematic risk, and these are good days to be out. Other days, the expected return is above what is required to compensate for systematic risk, and these are profitable days to be in. Combining the fair-game market model in (11) and the modified pricing equation in (12') gives

$$(14') \qquad R_{it} = a_i'' + (a_i' - a_i'')\, D_t + B_i\, (R_{Mt}) + e_{it}$$

The estimating equation with beta shifts (14) and the estimating equation with time-varying expected returns but constant betas (14') are nested in

(15) $R_{it} = a_i'' + (a_i' - a_i'') D_t + B_i'' (R_{Mt}) + (B_i' - B_i'') D_t (R_{Mt}) + e_{it}$.

If measured profits are due to shifts in expected excess returns that are independent of beta risk, the dummy variable should reveal changes in the intercept but no beta shifts, in which case the measured are true economic profits. Alternatively, if the measured profits are due to time-varying betas, the dummy variable should reveal changes in slopes but no shifts in intercept.

Rather than looking at each of the 50 stocks in each of the 12 years in Table 2, Sweeney looks only at one year, 1973. In estimating (15), Sweeney uses lagged market terms since statistical tests show them necessary at high confidence levels. At conventional significance levels, the data require the dummied slopes for many of the 50 stocks examined. The data also often require intercept dummies. The issue is whether the dummied contemporaneous and lagged slope coefficients can explain measured profits. Whether the lagged coefficients should be considered depends on the rationale for inclusion of lagged market terms. Sweeney argues that whether only the contemporaneous or the contemporaneous plus lagged dummied slopes are examined, the slopes are much too small to explain the measured profits and often have the wrong sign. On the other hand, the dummied intercepts explain on average about 3/4s of the measured profits.

III. Conclusions

There is much academic evidence that technical strategies can make substantial measured profits in foreign exchange markets. On an academic level, the issues are ones of measurement. Are the measures of profits theoretically appropriate? Are the data mismeasured?

Measured profits must be carefully adjusted for risk in order to be economic profits. Some of the papers discussed above do not adjust for risk, and all of them can be charged with making adjustments that are perhaps inadequate and misleading. For example, the X-statistic discussed in section 2 makes an appropriate adjustment for risk if the asset' risk premium is constant over time, and otherwise the adjustment may but need not be inappropriate. Modelling time-varying risk premia is not easy. Further, to show that measured profits are not economic profits, the risk premia must not only vary over time, but must vary more or less in sync with the positions that generate the measured profits and in a magnitude that could explain these profits. Results to date are not encouraging, either for showing time-varying risk premia in foreign exchange markets, or for explaining measured profits to technical analysis.

On a practitioner level, the evidence seems to be that well-crafted technical approaches can generate persistent measured profits. These profits are subject to randomness, however, suggesting using a portfolio of currencies in any technical approach. It is possible that some of the randomness remaining to portfolios of currencies managed with technical approaches can be diversified away. For example, most estimates of foreign exchange betas are small, suggesting that a technical foreign exchange portfolio that is a small part of a well-diversified portfolio might add essentially no risk.

It is not clear that past studies finding little systematic risk in foreign exchange markets are correct. If betas are time varying, for example, but average out to zero, the portfolio manager may arrange to be heavily in currencies just when their risk is high. Further, focussing on market betas may neglect other sources of priced risk (Sweeney and Warga 1986). The possibility of time-varying risk premia is a warning that measured profits may not be economic profits. There is, however, no way at present of showing that the manager who goes after and achieves these measured profits is making a mistake.

The data may have been mismeasured in the technical studies discussed above. It may be that in actual practice, one would have to buy at higher and sell at lower prices than assumed. There are many possible pro and con arguments (Sweeney 1988). The clear answer is that the only way to know for sure is to try with real money in real time on real assets.

FOOTNOTES

* Sullivan/Dean Professor of International Business and Finance, School of Business Administration, Georgetown University, Washington, DC, 20057. Thanks are due to Neal Maroney, Aris Protopapakais and other members of the Claremont Workshop on Monetary and Financial Economics.

1. Sweeney (1986) finds shortcomings with Cornell and Dietrich's (1978) attempt to handle risk with a beta analysis.

2. Hodrick (1987) suggests a rough statistical test of the profits they find and concludes that they do not appear in general to be significant.

3. In a Sharpe-Lintner CAPM, the risk premium for asset j is j's beta on the market times the risk premium on the market. The assumption that j's risk premium is constant over time then requires in general that both the beta and the premium on the market are constant. One way for technical analysis to produce measured profits that are not economic profits is for beta to vary, with the technical strategy having the investor in on high-risk days, out on low-risk days. (Sweeney 1989c) tests this approach to explain profits in US equities markets, while Sweeney (1990) tests this approach for spot foreign exchange markets.) In a Ross APM, j's risk premium is the sum of the product of j's betas on the various risk factors times the factor premia. In general, all of these betas and factor premia must be constant for j's premia to be constant.

4. For example, the observed daily return on the market is surely infected with thin trading problems and hence the true return must be estimated, introducing estimation error.

5. This is a well known difficulty with many APT applications in which factor analysis is used to extract unobservable factors unspecified by the theory.

6. In either Sweeney's approach or in a model-based approach, there remains the problem of mismeasurement in the rates of return on the assets whose simulated trading is studied. In brief, the investor may not be able to buy and sell at the reported prices (even when adjusted for bid-asked spreads as Sweeney does), with the bias systematically going against the investor who buys at a higher and sells at a lower price than reported. See Blume and Stambaugh (1983) for one source of bias.

7. How to treat the covariances depends on whether any positive correlations among the Xs arise from exploitable inefficiencies or simply from crosscorrelations of surprises across returns (Sweeney 1988). In the latter case, the covariances should be included to avoid overstating significance. In the former case, inclusion of the covariances understates significance. Sweeney (1989c) discusses explaining technical profits in U.S. equities markets in terms of a market model with shifting betas and intercepts. Appropriately shifting betas would argue that profits from technical analysis are due to time varying risk premia, while shifting intercepts would argue for exploitable inefficiencies. His evidence is that the shifting intercepts are important and that shifting betas cannot explain profits. The shifting intercepts are positively correlated across stocks. This argues that at least some of the correlation across stocks is due to inefficiency, and significance levels that use the sample covariances of the Xs are understated.

Note that the fact that surprises are correlated across assets can but need not lead to positive correlations of individual Xs. As Sweeney (1988) discusses, this is so because in/out positions tend to get out of sync across assets. For example, if the investor is in half of the assets on a day when the market does very well, this will make his X-statistics look good for these assets but bad for the other assets where he missed out on this good day.

8. The approach can incorporate, for example, the weekend effect if this effect is thought to be associated with time-varying risk premia; if premia are constant over weekends, it would be incorrect to adjust for variations in expected returns of the weekend.

9. Bilson's equation makes a distinction between "large" and "small" forward premia.

10. Foreign exchange betas tend to be small and unstable, indicating that on average this risk may be mostly diversifiable. The point is, Bilson's measure of profits is incorrect in a world where the investor can easily hold a wider portfolio.

The X-statistics discussed here arc risk-adjusted by including buy-and-hold as a benchmark, and are risk-adjusted allowing for the full effects of diversification that go into the expected return on buy-and-hold. The standard errors used to measure significance of the X-statistics are based on a portfolio that holds only currencies. Thus, if some of the risk of these portfolios is diversifiable, the significance of these measured profits is understated.

11. If the covariances of the Xs are set at zero, a possibility discussed in footnote 7 above, the t-statistic is 3.85. This illustrates that often these covariances, though positive on average, have little effect on the significance levels of the measured profits.

12. The X-statistic discussed above uses the weighted average of the return to the technical strategy over all days in the period (thus speaking to Taylor's point that the investor is in the currency less often than under buy-and-hold). In this case, a conditionally constant risk premium and market efficiency imply that the expected average return to the filter is (1 - f)g compared to buy-and-hold's expected average of g. Thus, if the filter measured this way does as well as buy-and-hold, it acutally beats buy-and-hold, <u>if</u> g > 0. If g = 0, then on an ex ante basis the expected return to the filter is zero whether or not adjustment is made for buy and hold, and use of excess returns implicitly uses the risk-free rate as the benchmark. Further, when the market has an ex post trend up or down, even if there is not risk premium and hence no ex ante trend relative to the risk-free

rate, it is important to use buy-and-hold as a benchmark; for example, if the DM rises strongly over a sample, a strategy that has the investor take long positions for some of the period can look very good by itself, but not perhaps relative to buy-and-hold.

13. Hodrick (1987) gives an excellent survey of models of time-varying risk premia, a well as discussing some of the literature on technical analysis in foreign exchange markets.

14. Richardson (1989) argues that overall the Fama and French results are not statistically significant. Cechetti, Lam and Mark (1988) use simulation results to argue that the Fama and French results could easily arise in world of time-varying risk premia.

15. They argue that because the benchmark portfolio is not uniquely determined, they set one of the betas equal to unity rather than estimate it, thus determining the benchmark portfolio. Inspection of (4) makes clear that for any product B_j pr_t, the values of the components are indeterminate. By setting the beta for the French franc equal to unity, they identify pr. With pr identified, they can then estimate the other four betas.

The mean variance efficient benchmark portfolio is in fact identifiable on a theoretical level. Given the risk-free rate for the dollar, there is only on possible benchmark portfolio. The conditional mean-variance frontier is not observable, however. Their issue is econometric rather than one of theory.

16. Thus, even though the world economy's forward positions always aggregate to zero and no money need be put up to enter them, there is an associated excess rate of return that is subject to explanation by asset pricing models.

17. Another way to see that the slope coefficient on [(F - S)/S] R_m must be large is to note that these two variables as well as the profit rate are measured in decimal percent. Thus, if each were 1%/month or .01, the product .0001 might have to explain a profit rate of 1%/month or .01, or the slope coefficient would have to be on the order of 100.

18. e need not be distributed normally; there are a number of papers where it is assumed to follow other distributions.

19. This MA4 is necessary because the weekly forecast errors on overlapping contracts will show up as serially correlated.

20. This slope can be interpreted as a weighted average of individuals' relative risk aversions. Alternatively, it is the ratio of the variance of the return on the market to the expected return on the market. Since the stock market index is never less than 70% of the total market they use, it is interesting to see what the stock index implies. If the standard deviation is 15%/year and the expected excess return is 8%/ year (both reasonable from Ibbotson and Sinquefield data), then the variance/mean ratio is over 28, giving a different impression of the plausibility of the estimated slope.

REFERENCES

Alexander, S. S., 1961, Price Movements in Speculative Markets: Trends or Random Walks, Industrial Management Review 2, 7-26.

_______, 1964, Price Movements in Speculative Markets: Trends or Random Walks, No. 2, Industrial Management Review 5, 25-46.

Bilson, J., 1981, The 'Speculative Efficiency' Hypothesis, Journal of Business 54, 435-51.

_________, and D. Hsieh, 1983, The Profitability of Currency Speculation, NBER Working Paper.

Baillie, R. T., and T. Bollerslev, 1988, A Mulitvariate Generalized ARCH Approach to Modeling Risk Premia in Forward Foreign Exchange Rate Markets, Michigan State University Working Paper.

________, and ________, 1987, The Message in Daily Exchange Rates: A Conditional Variance Tale, Michigan State University Working Paper.

Blume, M. E., and R. F. Stambaugh, 1983, Biases in Computing Returns, Journal of Financial Economics 12, 387-404.

Bollerslev, T., R. F. Engle and J. M. Wooldridge, 1988, A Captial Asset Pricing Model with Time Varing Covariances, Journal of Political Economy (1988).

Chan, K. C., 1988, On the Contrarian Investment Strategy, Journal of Business 61, 147-65.

Cornell, B., and J. K. Dietrich, 1978, The Efficiency of the Market for Foreign Exchange Under Floating Exchange Rates, Review of Economics and Statistics, 111-20.

Cornell, B., and M. Reinganum, 1981, Forward and Futures Prices: Evidence from the Foreign Exchange Markets, Journal of Finance 36, 1035-45.

Cox, J., J. Ingersoll and S. Ross, 1981, The Relation Between Forward Prices and Futures Prices, Journal of Financial Economics, 9, 321-46.

DeBondt, W., and R. Thaler, 1985, "Does the Stock Market Overreact?" Journal of Finance 40, 793-805.

Dimson, E., 1979, Risk Measurement When Shares Are Subject To Infrequent Trading, Journal of Financial Economics 7, 197-226.

Dooley, M. P., and J. Shafer, 1976, Analysis of Short-Run Exchange Rate Behavior: March, 1973 to September, 1975, International finance Discussion Paper No. 124, Federal Reserve Board, Washington.

_________, and _________, 1983, Analysis of Short-Run Exchange Rate Behavior: March, 1973 to November, 1981, in D. Bigman and T. Taya, eds.: Exchange Rate and Trade Instability: Causes, Consequences, and Remedies (Ballinger, Cambridge, MA).

Fama, E. F., 1984, Forward and Spot Exchange Rates, Journal of Monetary Economics, 319-38.

Fama, E. F., and M. E. Blume, 1966, Filter Rules and Stock-Market Trading, Journal of Business 39, 226-41.

Fama, E. F., and K. R. French, 1988, Permanent and Temporary Components of Stock Prices, Journal of Political Economy 96, 246-73.

Giovannini, A., and P. Jorion, 1987, Interest Rates and Risk Premia in the Stock Market and in the Foreign Exchange Markets,

Journal of International Money and Finance 6.

Hansen, L., and R. Hodrick, 1980, Forward Exchange Rates as Optimal Predictors of Future Spot Exchange Rates: An Econometric Analysis, Journal of Political Economy 88, 829-53.

_________, and _________, 1983, Risk Averse Speculation in the Forward Foreign Exchange Market: An Econmetric Analysis of Linerar Models, in J. A. Frenkel, ed.: Exchange Rates and International Macroeconomics (University of Chicago Press for NBER, Chicago, IL).

Hodrick, R., 1987, The Empirical Evidence on the Efficiency of Forward and Futures Foreign Exchange Markets (Harwood Academic Publishers, Chur, Switzerland).

Hodrick, R., and S. Srivastava, 1984, An Investigation of Risk and Return in Forward Foreign Exchange, Journal of International Money and Finance 3, 5-29.

_________, and _________, 1985, Foreign Currency Futures, Journal of International Economics.

_________, and _________, 1986, The Covariation of Risk Premiums and Expected future Spot Exchange Rates, Journal of International Money and Finance 5, S5-S22.

Ibbotson, R. G., and R. A. Sinquefield, 1977, Stocks, Bonds, Bills, and Inflation: The Past and The Future (Charlottesville, VA).

Lo, A. W., and C. A. MacKinlay, 1988, Stock Market Prices Do Not follow Random Walks: Evidence from a Simple Specification Test, Review of Financial Studies 1, 41-66.

Logue, D. E., R. J. Sweeney and T. D. Willett, 1978, The Speculative Behavior of Foreign Exchange Rates During the Current Float, Journal of Business Research 6 , 159-74.

Longworth, D., P. Boothe and K. Clinton, 1983, A Study of the Efficiency of the Foreign Exchange Market (Bank of Canada, Ottawa).

Lucas, R. E., Jr., 1978, Asset Pricing in an Exchange Economy, Econometrica 46, 1429-45.

Poterba, J. M., and L. H. Summers, 1987, Mean Reversion in Stock Prices: Evidence and Implications, Journal of Financial Economics.

Richardson, M., 1989, Temporary Components of Stock Prices: A Skeptic's View, Stanford University GSB manuscript.

Surajaras, P., and R. J. Sweeney, 1991, Profit-Making Speculation in Foreign Exchange Markets (Westview Press, Boulder CO).

Sweeney, R. J., 1986, Beating the Foreign Exchange Market, Journal of Finance 41, 163-82.

________, 1988, Some New Filter Rule Tests: Methods and Results, Journal of Financial and Quantitative Analysis 23, 285-300.

________, 1989a, Evidence on Short-Term Trading Strategies, School of Business Administration, Georgetown University.

________, 1991, Risk Premia In Forward Foreign Exchange Rates: Systematic or Unsystematic? Journal of International.

________, 1989b, Testing Portfolio Performance with Observable Asset Weights, School of Business Administration, Georgetown University.

_________, 1989c, Time-Varying Risk Premia in Equities Markets, School of Business Administration, Georgetown University.

_________, 1990, Time-Varying Risk Premia in Spot Foreign-Exchange Rates," School of Business Administration, Georgetown University.

Sweeney, R. J., and E. J. Q. Lee, 1990, Trading Strategies in Forward Exchange Markets, Advances in Financial Planning and Forecasting 4, JAI Press, forthcoming.

Sweeney, R. J., and P. Surajaras, 1989, The Stability of Speculative Profits in the Foreign Exchanges, in eds.: A Reappraisal of the Efficiency of Financial Markets (Verlag Springer,).

Sweeney, R. J., and A. D. Warga, 1986, The Pricing of Interest-Rate Risk: Evidence from the Stock Market, Journal of Finance 41, 393-410.

Taylor, Stephen, 1986, Modelling Financial Time Series (John Wiley and Sons, New York, NY).

Zarowin, P., 1990, Size, Seasonality and Stock Market Overreaction, Journal of Financial and Quantitative Analysis 25, 113-26.

Recent Developments in International Banking
and Finance, S.J. Khoury (editor)

CHAPTER VIII

Should International Portfolios Be Permanently Hedged?

Michael Adler

Columbia University

Michael R. Granito

J.P. Morgan Investment Management

1. Introduction

International money managers are now grappling with a new twist on an old question: should international portfolios be hedged against exchange rate risk, not selectively as before, nut continuously? Active currency management in this framework becomes the decision to "unhedge". Hedged portfolios should be benchmarked against indices of hedged foreign bonds and stocks.[1]

Interest in this approach has increased with the publication in the May/June 1988 issue of the Financial Analysis Journal of an article by Andre F. Perold and Evan C. Schulman provocatively entitled, "The Free Lunch in Currency Hedging." Their paper makes the following claims:

- There is (or seems to be) evidence that the risk premium on forward exchange positions is zero on the average (over long periods).
- If the forward risk premium is zero, investors do not sacrifice expected return when they reduce volatility by hedging ERR.
- The transaction costs associated with hedging are very small.
- International portfolios should therefore be managed and evaluated on a permanently and fully hedged basis.
- "Fully hedged" in this context means unitary hedge ratios as distinct from "optimal" or regression hedge ratios that may differ from unity.

This reasoning is casual but its bottom line is quite appealing. A hedged international portfolio may indeed offer superior return-risk tradeoffs. The issue in this paper is to determine more precisely when it will. The paper is organized as follows. Section 2 provides a primarily graphical and verbal summary of the optimal asset demands derived in Appendix A. Section 3 together with Appendix B take up the issue of whether the forward risk premium is zero or not and detail the implications of that problem for portfolio managers. Section 4

1

Approximately suitable indexes are in the process of being constructed.

states our conclusions.

2. The Demand for Hedged Portfolios

This section provides a conceptual framework for how one should think about hedging international portfolios against currency risk. A key point is this: assume that portfolio managers want to offer their clients efficient portfolios. In the absence of short selling constraints, they can do so equally well in either of two ways. They can optimize starting with a menu that contains unhedged risky assets and forward contracts or they can start with a list that includes fully hedged stocks and bonds as well as forward contract. The resulting efficient frontiers will be the same.

This means that providing hedged portfolios as a new synthetic investment product offers no potential efficiency gains to investors whose portfolios include forward contracts from the start and are already efficiently diversified. Even if clients' existing portfolios were not efficient, for reasons that include short-selling constraints, introducing a hedge portfolio product might conceivably not add any value. The potential for improved risk-return tradeoffs is not necessarily increased by offering an alternative that managers could have offers before or that clients can replicate for themselves. If, however, clients' portfolio product can prove beneficial as a component of an overall asset-allocation strategy.

2-1. The Pure Theory of Hedging

Let us now turn to these issues more technically. For a representative investor, Appendix A derives the optimal global asset mix consisting of stocks, bonds and forward currency contracts, in each of three scenarios of increasing complexity. The first (Scenario 1) is when the efficient frontier is stationary over time and all assets can be freely traded and sold short. This is the benchmark case. Scenario II retains the stationarity assumptions but introduces a non-traded asset that proxies the effect of short selling constraints. Scenario III allows the efficient frontier to be random which is the most realistic case.

The analysis indicates that investors' holdings of forward currency positions can be represented as the sum of several components. The first reflects that part of the risk-reduction objective which can be achieved by hedging the (optimal) asset portfolio. The second component corresponds to the investor's desire for risk-compensated expected-return enhancement when the forward risk-premium is non-zero. The third reflects the possibility that the investor can obtain additional risk-reduction by using forward currency contracts to hedge inflation. Each of these three components are present even in the simplest case considered, Scenario I. Scenarios II and III contain additional terms. Scenario II necessitates a fourth risk-reduction component which represents the need to hedge risks connected to any non-traded positions that a client's portfolio might be constrained to hold. Scenario III includes a fifth component that reflects the possibility of using currency positions to mitigate the impact of random shifts in the investment environment.

It is quite apparent that, in general, a fully-hedged portfolio is far from optimal. Such a portfolio contains forward exchange positions that represent but partially only the first of the five motives described above. Several extreme assumptions have to be made before one can conclude that full hedging, in and of itself, is optimal.

Specifically the theory shows that offering a client exclusively a fully hedged international global portfolio can completely solve his asset allocation problem only under four stringent conditions. First, inflation must be non-stochastic. Second, there can be no other factors such as political events, policy decisions or technological changes that produce random exogenous information processes or shocks to which prices respond and that are correlated with the exchange rate. Third, the forward risk-premium must be zero at all times. And fourth, domestic and foreign stock and bond prices must be uncorrelated with the exchange rate. All of these conditions are violated empirically.

Consequently, managers should offer their clients at least two additional tactical investment products: portfolios containing risky stocks and bonds as well as forward contracts for hedging inflation and other state variables; and portfolios of forward contracts for disciplined speculation on currencies when not all risk-premia are zero. Such portfolios are in principle easy to compute. Forecasting the inputs is the role of investment research.

2-2. A Practical Course of Action

Actual unhedged portfolios, like international portfolios that confront short selling constraints, are likely to be inefficient. It should therefore be possible to reduce their variances by hedging them without invariably decreasing their expected returns. The key question is whether clients will be unambiguously better off if offered an implementable unitary hedge-ratio strategy for hedging their foreign portfolio. The answer, in general, is negative; but, as optimal demands under short selling constraints are extremely hard to analyze rigorously, it is hard to be precise. The best we can do is to characterize the two additional assumptions that have to be met for fully currency-hedged international portfolios to be clearly beneficial.

The first requirement is that reducing the variance of the international component reduce simultaneously the total variance of the client's overall portfolio. This is most clearly the case when domestic asset returns are independent of the exchange rate. The international portfolios can then be treated in isolation and taken as the only portfolio the client holds. Otherwise the issue should be checked.

The second is that the forward risk-premium over the investment horizon not to be too positive. The reason for this vague statement is most easily made clear graphically.

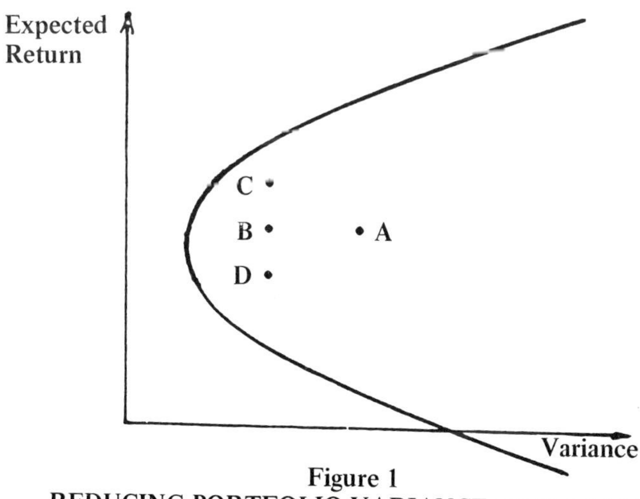

Figure 1
REDUCING PORTFOLIO VARIANCE BY HEDGING

In Figure 1, we start with inefficient portfolio A. Hedging it fully reduces its variance (but falls short of making it efficient both because residual short selling constraints remain and because inflation is stochastic). If the forward risk-premium is negative, expected returns are simultaneously enhanced at point C. In either of these two cases, the investor is unambiguously better off. If the risk-premium is positive, however, point D is reached. Variance reduction now comes at a cost. One cannot say that D is superior to A without first ascertaining that the client would have been willing to sacrifice even more expected returns than the market requires.

Conditional on the first condition being met, in short, a hedged international portfolio product can on balance be an appropriate component of a client's global asset-allocation strategy, The reason is that it will provide efficiency improvements for all domestic clients when the forward risk-premium is negative or zero and for some when the risk-premium is positive, Put differently, the product cannot damage clients on the average if the risk-premium is less than or equal to zero more than half of the time. Risk reduction can of course be improved by using regression rather than unitary hedge ratios where permitted. However, the product can do more harm than good unless it is offered in conjunction with the tactical portfolios described earlier when the risk-premium is positive and when future inflation is uncertain.[2]

3. How To Think About Forward Risk-Premia

A risk-premium that is approximately zero at every instant would be necessary (but not sufficient) to validate a policy of holding only an optimally hedged international portfolio all the time. Unfortunately,

---

2

One caveat is necessary. There is an upper limit to the benefit from hedging which is immediately visible in Figure 1. The variance of an efficient(i.e. a frontier) portfolio cannot further be reduced by hedging without also reducing its expected returns. The potential contribution of a hedged portfolio product clearly diminishes the more nearly efficient the original unhedged portfolio. The degree to which actual portfolios are inefficient, however, is hard to determine empirically.

Perold and Schulman's (1988) casual empiricism notwithstanding, the risk-premium is not continuously zero.[3] This section deals with how to cope with the more complex reality we observe.

A growing body of empirical evidence is quite clear on one central point. The risk-premium for short holding horizons of three months or less, what econometricians call the conditional risk-premium, fluctuates between positive and negative values and is seldom actually zero. The interested reader can refer to the diagrams in Wolff (1987) and Domowitz and Hakkio (1985). Estimated conditional risk-premia reach magnitudes of between four to ten percent in absolute value for the major currencies and have a tendency to persist over time. Such values are too large to ignore. What may but need not converge to zero is the unconditional risk-premium, that is, the average of the conditional risk-premia taken over sufficiently long sample periods that include many observations.

Appendix B should be read integrally with this section. It states in non-mathematical terms why there are solid grounds for expecting precisely the kinds of patterns that the empirical research reveals. Essentially, it provides a framework that links the net excess hedging demand for a currency to the risk-premium. The main results are easiest to see when one makes the not-implausible assumption that traders share expectations which, if not exactly homogenous, are predominantly similar.

In this environment, risk-averse pure speculators who demand the risk premium never trade with each other as all simultaneously want the same side of the transaction. They can trade only with hedgers whose pre-existing positions cause them to want the other side and who are willing to pay a premium for safety. However, hedgers who are willing to pay a premium for Yen would prefer to trade with other hedgers who happen to be willing to pay a premium for US$, before they transact with speculators who demand a premium for buying Yen. When the hedging demand to sell Yen forward exceeds the offsetting

---

3 There are serious flaws in the model specification in Engel (1984), the paper to which they appeal for the implication that the real risk-premium is zero. The model's assumptions effectively rule out the phenomena it is supposed to capture.

hedging demand to buy Yen forward, the net pressure forces the forward rate down to a point sufficiently below the expected spot rate to induce speculators to buy forward Yen and earn premium. Net hedging pressure in the reverse direction produces symmetrically a risk-premium with the opposite sign. To this point a zero risk-premium is ruled out. It is either positive or negative. When the net hedging pressure is zero, both sides are in principle willing to pay for safety: the risk-premium in this case can, but need not necessarily, be zero.

What the foregoing reasoning implies is perhaps startling. The conditional risk-premium need never be zero except by coincidence. What is more , it will get larger in absolute value the greater hedging imbalance as increasingly risk-averse speculators are induced to trade. Nor is there any guarantee that the average over time of the conditional risk premia will be zero: much will depend on the specific sample period and its length. These conclusions do not require homogeneous expectations. They remain robust when beliefs differ but are then harder either to model or to verify empirically.

Additional insight into the forces at work can be gained through the prism of Scenario I in Appendix A. To simplify matters, assume in this connection that U.S. inflation is non-stochastic and that domestic U.S. asset prices are independent of the spot or forward exchange rates. Americans then demand forward exchange for only two purposes: for hedging foreign, say Japanese, stocks and long-term bonds; and for speculation.

Think of the world as consisting of the U.S. and Japan. Suppose now that the Tokyo market is expected to rise. Investors everywhere, including Americans, rebalance their speculative asset portfolios in favor of Japan. These holdings of Japanese stocks and bonds count as pre-established positions. Scenario I then teaches us that the increase in U.S. holdings of Japanese securities is accompanied by a simultaneous proportional increase in U.S. investors' demand for cover in the form of forward Yen sales. Unless the Japanese hedging demand for selling US$ rises equally, the forward rate must fall relative to the expected spot and the risk-premium must increase. If it does, its rise will also induce both U.S. and Japanese investors to increase the speculative demands for buying Yen forward. Say that U.S. investors fail to implement this speculative demand on the mistaken assumption that the risk-premium is zero. Their ex-post returns will clearly suffer especially if the Yen appreciates as a result of the capital flow to Tokyo.

This snapshot example tells us that the risk-premium can be as volatile as expectations themselves. It can change sign as often as expectations change direction. Indeed, hedging pressures are in the nature of being derived demands created in part by simultaneously established speculative positions. The bad news is clear. This is a setting in which it is hard to determine the sign or the size of the risk-premium at any instant. Expectations are not directly observable: they can for the time being only be projected imprecisely from trends, possibly by technical analysis.[4] This difficulty, however, does not mean that the risk-premium can be ignored or, in particular, that it can be presumed to be zero over the relevant holding horizon when in fact it is not. As the example illustrates, making such an assumption can mean suppressing the speculative demand for open forward positions just when it is most needed.

4. Conclusions

The conclusion of our analysis may be summarized as follows.

- Currency hedging by itself cannot produce efficiency gains for international portfolios that are already efficiently diversified in an

---

4

Giovannini and Jorion (1987) reported that "increases in foreign exchange risk-premia are reliably associated with decreases in U.S. interest rates and increases in foreign interest rates." The reason for their discovery is this. If the spot exchange rate were an exact martingale or random walk, with zero drift at any and all instants, the forward risk premium would be precisely equal to the current instantaneous interest differential; and it would be observable. The spot exchange rate however, departs from pure random walk behavior to a random extent and at random intervals. This is what makes the risk-premium both unobservable and hard to estimate.

environment where assets can be sold short. [5] That is, hedging adds nothing in the absence of short-selling restrictions or other constraints that prevent investors from computing and holding efficient portfolios.

- This result is robust independently of whether or not the forward risk premium is zero. Forward exchange contracts or currency options that are equivalent to zero-investment combinations of domestic and foreign bonds are redundant. Introducing redundant assets into an efficient market cannot improve efficiency regardless of how they are priced.

- Being able to short-sell currencies forward may, however, improve the efficiency of any portfolios that is bound by short-selling constraints. In this context, improved efficiency principally means a (risk-reducing) leftward shift of the opportunity set. If actual portfolios are inefficient for this reason, hedging them is likely to be an appropriate component of the solution to the overall asset-allocation problem. How much hedging can help remains an open empirical question.

- Offering hedged portfolios is not the end of the asset allocation story. When their stock-bond portfolios are fully hedged, clients should in theory simultaneously hold naked long or short forward exchange positions for a mixture of tactical purposes that include expected return enhancement as well as hedging other factors such as inflation and other environmental risks. These tactical portfolios are an integral part of the asset-allocation exercise.

- If the short-horizon forward risk-premium is in fact continuously equal to zero, the possibility of expected return enhancement, via the

---

5

Efficiency is improved if the efficient frontier can be moved to the left, that is, if portfolio variance can be reduced at each level of expected portfolio return.

speculative demand for naked forward contracts, disappears.[6] In this particular case, the question of "unhedging" never arises as there is no incentive to speculate regardless of whether or not the hedged portfolio is efficient.[7]

- However, the short-term risk-premium is almost never equal to zero. It is almost always positive or negative. Only its long-run average taken over many investment horizons may converge on zero. In this case, clients may not be well served by a fully-hedged product that does not also emphasize opportunistic, research-based currency management.

- Specifically, the efficiency of actual, fully hedged foreign-asset portfolios and their expected performance is reduced when the risk-premium is sufficiently greater than zero. In this case, any chance of offsetting the negative effect generally depends on having tactical portfolios, containing open forward currency positions, to combine with the hedged international portfolios. Conversely, offering only a fully-hedged product has integrity only if there is conviction that the risk-premium is either zero or completely unforecastable.

- Managers may be in a position to be concerned with their clients' global asset-allocations. Offering a currency-hedged foreign portfolio product is not a good idea unless reducing the variance of the international component simultaneously reduces also the variance of the global portfolio. This is not a result that can be assumed automatically. It must be verified in advance but will often be true.

6

The forward risk premium is the expected currency return in excess of the current forward discount or premium. The currency surprise is the difference between the expected currency return and its subsequent realization.

7

Positions in forward contracts that hedge long positions in stocks and bonds will normally be short. Efficient speculative positions in currencies can be long or short. When the latter are long, they will tend to offset the hedge, giving the appearance of "unhedging".

- When following a strategy of hedging continuously, the optimal hedge ratio is not necessarily unity. Rather, it is the regression coefficient hedge ratio that minimizes portfolio variance. A unitary hedge ratio will be optimal only if exchange rates and foreign asset prices are uncorrelated.

A final note is in order before concluding this report. Tactical portfolios for hedging inflation are part of the manager's arsenal whatever the length of the performance review period. Such products can be of considerable practical importance notwithstanding the fact that the ex-post volatility of the U.S. inflation rate has recently been low. The point is, of course, that fears of future inflation are much more volatile than the time-variance of the actual past inflation rate would suggest. Casual observation suggests that we are currently going through a period of increasing inflationary uncertainty. No economic theory suggests that exchange rates are independent of inflation rates. This means that forward currency contracts together with other asset classes can function usefully as inflation hedges. Hedging inflation is too important a matter to be pushed under the rug in a marginal footnote.[8]

8

Perold and Schulman(1988) argue that inflation uncertainty should be ignored because the volatility of the U.S. inflation rate has been low for several years. They do so apparently because they want to be able to claim that a fully hedged portfolio is all a client needs. Allowing for hedgeble inflation risks appears to modify the full hedge prescription, something they seem to want to avoid. However, as we have shown, a fully-hedged strategy remains optimal provided it is offered in conjunction with additional hedge and speculative portfolios.

Appendix A

Optimal Intertemporal Demands for Risky Assets and Foreign Exchange Futures in an Efficiently Diversified International Portfolio

This appendix derives optimal intertemporal demands for risky assets and foreign currency (FC) hedging instruments. Three scenarios are treated in turn. The first, the benchmark case, is when portfolio choice is completely unconstrained. All assets can be freely traded and sold short. The second proxies the effect of short-selling constraints by allowing some assets to be completely non-tradeable in the spirit of Adler and Detemple (1988). For simplicity, the analysis to this point is restricted to a setting in which the efficient frontier is stationary. The third is a more general treatment, with Brownian motion processes for prices that are functions of exogenous state variables. These allow the efficient frontier to be random. In all cases one can obtain a demand for futures to hedge stocks, a speculative demand and additional hedging demands to hedge inflation plus state variables if there are any.

Following Adler and Dumas (1983), investors evaluate returns in real terms, that is, on an inflation-deflated basis. When inflation is stochastic, even domestic cash is risky and there is no riskless asset. The efficient frontier is then the usual parabola in mean-variance space. Asset demands for the case where inflation is non-random were worked out by Sercu (1980). The efficient set then becomes a line connecting the riskless rate and the tangent portfolio. In what follows, we generalize his results and solve for the composition of the optimal or efficient portfolio at any point on the (possible random) frontier.

The optimal asset demands are always derived from the first-order conditions. In each case they are presented in two equivalent ways. For Scenario I, they are given by equations (A-13) and (A-15); for Scenario II, by (A-21) and (A-22); and for the third, by (A-28) and (A-

29). Both equations in each pair compute the weights in an optimal portfolio consisting of all stocks and long-term bonds, grouped together, and forward contracts.

The first equation in each pair presents these optimal weights in a compact form that identifies the two efficient portfolios from which an investor could construct his entire efficient frontier. The second equation in each pair is merely a decomposition of the first, achieved by partitioning the variance-covariance matrix. The portfolio composition it represents is the same as the first equation. The decomposed form shows that the demand for stocks and long-term bonds is in effect a demand for these assets combined with hedges against currency risks; and the demand for forward currency positions has components that reflect the need to hedge the other assets; to hedge against inflation and other state-variables; and naked forward positions for speculative purposes.

As the asset demands portrayed by each pair are identically the same, they establish the point of departure for thinking about hedged portfolio products. *The variance of an efficient portfolio cannot be reduced further by hedging it against currency risks without decreasing its expected return.* An efficient portfolio is already hedged. What is more, this proposition remains true whatever the size and sign of equilibrium forward risk premia, as these were taken into account from the start.

Scenario I: Optimal Asset Demands in Stationary Efficient Sets Assets are Freely Traded

Stationary efficient frontiers are produced when the moments of all price processes are constant, that is, when there are no exogenous state variables. This section therefore employs log-normal diffusions.

There are N domestic and foreign risky assets whose returns are all stated in a common currency, say US$.[1] Exchange rates are quoted in US terms, that is, (US$/FC), where FC stands for foreign currency. Their diffusions are:

$$\text{(A-1)} \qquad dA_t = A[\mu_a dt + \sigma_a dz_a(t)]$$

where dA is an (N x 1) vector of US$ price changes; A is a diagonal matrix whose diagonal is the vector of US$ prices; μ_a is the constant vector of mean rates of return; $V_{aa} = \sigma_a' \sigma_a$ is the constant variance-covariance matrix and z_a is a vector Weiner process.

In addition, there are L foreign exchange futures contracts, each written on one of the spot exchange rates. These promise delivery at time T of a fixed amount of spot exchange at a futures price fixed ar time 0. They are marked to market (i.e. in effect rewritten) continuously leaving their net value equal to zero at any instant.

Given that spot rates, S, follow vector Wiener processes, we assume here that the (L x 1) vector of settlement prices, F_t, satisfies the stochastic differential equation.

$$\text{(A-2)} \qquad dF_t = F\,[\mu_f dt + \sigma_f dz_f(t)]$$

It is important to note that the specification in (2) all but requires the futures to be priced by arbitrage. This can occur under two conditions: either when domestic and foreign nominal interest rates are constant;or, when they are random, if both term structures are flat and variations in the interest differential are strictly proportional to the spot exchange rate. In either case futures become redundant assets that are perfectly correlated with zero-investment portfolios of foreign bonds (of all maturities) and the domestic riskless asset.[2] In short, given the form of (2) futures replace foreign bonds in the asset menu. The set of risky assets includes only domestic and foreign stocks.

Being rational, investors evaluate future returns in real terms, that is, after deflating nominal returns by their idiosyncratic price index, denoted I for inflation. We assume that the U.S. price index also follows a log-normal process; [3]

$$\text{(A-3)} \qquad dI = I[\mu_i dt + \sigma_i dz_i(t)]$$

As a consequence of inflation uncertainty, there is in general no asset that is riskless in real terms. For example, the real return on the nominally-riskless domestic short term bond follows the process:

$$\text{(A-4)} \qquad R = (r - \mu_i + \sigma_i^2)dt + \sigma_i dz_i(t)$$

Nominal wealth accumulates when the returns on assets and futures exceed outlays on current consumption. The intertemporal nominal wealth constraint is given by:

$$\text{(A-5)}\qquad dW = w'W\frac{dA}{A} + X'dF + [(1 - w'\ell)rW - c]dt$$

where w = the (N x 1) vector of wealth fractions invested in each risky asset and w' is its transpose; X' is the (1 x L) vector of forward exchange positions in contracts that cost nothing to enter but pay off dF continuously thereafter; and ℓ is an (N x 1) vector of ones, the summation operator. Using (A-1) and (A-2), we may write out (A-5) fully as:

$$\text{(A-6)}\qquad dW = [(w'W)\mu_a + X'F\mu_f + (1 - w'\ell)rW - C]dt + w'W\sigma_a dz_a + X'F\sigma_f dz_f$$

To go from nominal to real terms, we define real wealth as Y = W/I. After applying Ito's Lemma, [4]

$$\text{(A-7)}\qquad dY = [(w'W/I)(\mu_a - r\ell - V_{ai}) + (X'F/I)(\mu_f - V_{fi}) + (W/I)(r - \mu_i + \sigma_i^2) - C/I]dt + (w'W/I)\sigma_a dz_a + (X'F/I)\sigma_f dz_f - (W/I)\sigma_i dz_i$$

where V_{ai} and V_{fi} are vectors containing (respectively) the covariances of the risky assets and the futures with inflation.

Each investor solves the program,

$$\text{(A-8)}\qquad \underset{\{w'Y, X'F/I, C/I\}}{\text{Maximize}}\; E\int_t^T U(C/I,s)ds, \text{ subject to (A-7).}$$

Because there are no exogenous state variables, the Bellman equation is:

$$\text{(A-9)}\qquad -J_t = U(C/I,t) + J_y[E(dY)] + 1/2J_{yy}[Var(dY)]$$
$$= U(C/I,t) + J_y[w'Y(\mu_a - r\ell - V_{ai}) + (X'F/I)(\mu_f - V_{fi})$$

$$+ \ (W/I)(r-\mu_i + \sigma_i^2) - C/I]$$

$$+ \ 1/2J_{yy}[(w'W/I,X'F/I)\begin{pmatrix} V_{aa} & V_{af} \\ V_{fa} & V_{ff} \end{pmatrix}\begin{pmatrix} wW/I \\ XF/I \end{pmatrix}$$

$$- 2(W/I)(w'W/I,X'F/I)\begin{pmatrix} V_{ai} \\ V_{fi} \end{pmatrix}]$$

The first order conditions with respect to w'Y and X'F/I provide:

(A-10) $$0 = J_y(\mu_a - r - V_{ai}) + J_{yy}(V_{aa}wW/I + V_{af}XF/I - V_{ai}W/I)$$

$$0 = J_y(\mu_f - V_{fi}) + J_{yy}(V_{fa}wW/I + V_{ff}XF/I - V_{fi}W/I)$$

All the major initial insights emerge from (A-10). The f.o.c. can be solved in three different ways. As all have their basis in the same two equations, they must mean the same thing.

I. First one can solve each f.o.c. separately. Then:

(A-11)

$$wW/I = -\frac{J_y}{J_{yy}} V^{-1}_{aa}(\mu_a - r - V_{ai}) - V^{-1}_{aa}V_{af}XF/I + V^{-1}_{aa}V_{ai}W/I$$

(A-12) $$XF/I = -\frac{J_y}{J_{yy}} V^{-1}_{ff}(\mu_f - V_{fi}) - V^{-1}_{ff}V_{fa}wW/I + V^{-1}_{ff}V_{fi}W/I$$

In (A-11), the term $V^{-1}_{aa}V_{af}XF/I$ says that the investor uses risky assets to hedge his futures positions while the comparable term in (A-12),$V^{-1}_{ff}V_{fa}wW/I$ reveals that futures are used simultaneously to hedge risky assets. These are minimum-variance, regression coefficient hedges in the full amounts of the target demands. However, the full hedge prescription is modified to the extent that assets and futures are used also to hedge inflation risk via $V^{-1}_{aa}V_{ai}$ and $V^{-1}_{ff}V_{fi}$ respectively.

II. Second, we can solve the two conditions in (A-10) simultaneously. Let us further define the quantity, $-Jy/YJ_{yy} = \theta$, as the investor's coefficient of real relative risk tolerance; and the fraction x = (XF/I) (W/I) as the nominal US$ value of foreign currency bought or sold for future delivery taken as a proportion of current nominal wealth. The (A-10) which, in matrix form, is

(A-10)

$$\begin{pmatrix}0\\0\end{pmatrix} = J_y\left[\begin{pmatrix}\mu_a - r\ell\\ \mu_f\end{pmatrix} - \begin{pmatrix}V_{ai}\\ V_{fi}\end{pmatrix}\right] + J_{yy}\left[\begin{pmatrix}V_{aa} & V_{af}\\ V_{fa} & V_{ff}\end{pmatrix}\begin{pmatrix}wW/I\\ XF/I\end{pmatrix} - (W/I\begin{pmatrix}V_{ai}\\ V_{fi}\end{pmatrix}\right]$$

provides,with $V = \begin{pmatrix}V_{aa} & V_{af}\\ V_{fa} & V_{ff}\end{pmatrix}$,

(A-13) $$\begin{pmatrix}w\\ x\end{pmatrix} = \theta V^{-1}\begin{pmatrix}\mu_a - r\ell\\ \mu_f\end{pmatrix} + (1-\theta)V^{-1}\begin{pmatrix}V_{ai}\\ V_{fi}\end{pmatrix}$$

In (A-13), much as in Adler and Dumas (1983), the investor's efficient set can be specified from knowledge of two efficient portfolios. The first, with weight θ, is the one that would be held by an investor with unitary risk tolerance ("the logarithmic-utility investor"). The second is the minimum-variance portfolio that would be chosen by an infinitely risk-averse investor whose $\theta = 0$. This portfolio was labelled the hedge portfolio by Adler and Dumas (1983) as, by construction, it provides the best hedge against inflation.

From (A-13) it might seem as if the only hedging the investor does is against inflation. A better reading of (A-13) in light of what follows, however, is this: in the absence of short-selling constraints there is no need separately to identify demands for futures to hedge stocks. Any so-called hedging of stocks that may be needed is accomplished automatically in the course of computing the optimal demands.

III. This leads us to a third manipulation of (A-10). Following Sercu

(1980), the inverse V^{-1}, of the partitioned variance-covariance matrix can be written out explicitly as:

(A-14)

$$\begin{pmatrix} V_{aa} & V_{af} \\ V_{fa} & V_{ff} \end{pmatrix}^{-1} = \left(\begin{array}{c|c} (V_{aa} - \beta' V_{ff} \beta)^{-1} & -(V_{aa} - \beta' V_{ff} \beta)^{-1} \beta' \\ -\beta (V_{aa} - \beta' V_{ff} \beta)^{-1} & V_{ff}^{-1} + \beta (V_{aa} - \beta' V_{ff} \beta)^{-1} \beta' \end{array} \right)$$

where: β' $= V_{af} V^{-1}_{ff}$ is the NXL matrix of the regression coefficients of the N assets on the L futures; and

$V_{aa} - \beta' V_{ff} \beta$ $= V_{af}$ is the N x N matrix of the residuals of these regressions. this is also the variance-covariance matrix of "hedged" asset returns, that is of asset returns conditional on the forward exchange rate.

Substituting (A-14) into (A-13) and carrying out the multiplication yields the explicit demand equations : 5

(A-15)

$$w = \theta [V^{-1}_{a \cdot f} (\mu_a - r\ell - \beta' \mu_f)] + (1 - \theta) [V^{-1}_{a \cdot t} (V_{ai} - \beta' V_{fi})]$$

$$x = -\beta w + \theta V^{-1}_{ff} \mu_f + (1 - \theta) V^{-1}_{ff} V_{fi}$$

The solution for w in (A-15) is a demand for risky assets that are hedged against exchange risk. Hedged risky assets are held for speculative purposes (the term that depends on expected hedged returns); and to hedge against inflation. Note that $V^{-1}_{af}(V_{ai}-\beta' V_{fi}$ is the N x 1 vector of coefficients obtained by regressing the inflation rate on all N hedged asset returns.

The demand for futures has three components in (A-15). The first is for futures to hedge the (optimal demand for) risky assets. The second is a speculative demand and the third is for futures to hedge inflation. Several comments are in order. First, all the hedge ratios are regression coefficients. They will be unitary for foreign stocks and bonds only if their foreign currency prices are either constant or independent of the forward exchange rate. Second, the speculative demand for futures disappears only if $\mu_f = 0$, the case considered by Perold and Schulman (1988). And third, the demand for futures for hedging inflation has a preference-free component. This is what gives rise to an inflation premium in returns even under risk neutrality.

A major insight from this analysis is that the optimal demands computed from (A-13) and (A-15) are necessarily the same as both are solutions to (A-10). What this means is straightforward. When the opportunity set is stationary, the absence of short selling constraints guarantees that the efficient frontier computed from unhedged asset returns and futures is identical to the one obtained from hedged assets cannot improve efficiency. If clients hold efficient portfolios to begin with, offering them hedged foreign stocks and bonds cannot improve their overall risk-return tradeoffs.

Scenario II. Optimal Asset Demands in Stationary Efficient Sets When Some Position are Non-Tradable.

To complete the first part of this appendix, we add to the asset menu a non-traded position in the spirit of Adler and Detemple (1988). The position may consist of a foreign stock that the investor either cannot or does not want to liquidate or sell short before time t, the hedging horizon. Specifically, the investor is endowed at time o with a position in foreign stock whose foreign currency price at time T, Q_T, is uncertain. This price satisfies the log-normal wiener process:

$$dQ_t = Q_t[\mu_q dt + \sigma_q dz_q(t)] \tag{A-16}$$

In addition, the spot exchange rate is specified exogenously and satisfies a similar process:

$$dS_t = S_t[\mu_s dt + \sigma_s dz_s(t)] \tag{A-16}$$

Total real wealth at maturity is given by:

(A-17) $$Y_T = (W_T + S_T Q_T)/I_T$$

where W_T is defined as before. Even though the non-traded position produces no cash flows before maturity, variations in its present value, $S_t Q_t$, cause the investor to revise his beliefs and modify his intertemporal trading and hedging. His program:

(A-18) $$\underset{\{w'Y, X'F/I, C/I\}}{\text{Maximize}} \quad E\left[\int_t^T U(C/I,s)ds + B(Y_T,T)\right.$$

subject to:[6]

(A-19) $$\begin{aligned} dY = {} & [(w'W/I)(\mu_a - r\ell - V_{ai}) + (X'F/I)(\mu_f - V_{fi}) \\ & + (W/I)(r - \mu_i + V_{ii}) + (SQ/I)(\mu_s + \mu_q + V_{sq} - V_{qi} - V_{si}) \\ & - (C/I)]dt \\ & + (w'W/I)\sigma_a dz_a + (X'F/I)\sigma_f dz_f + SQ(\sigma_s dz_s + \sigma_q dz_q) \\ & -(W/I)\sigma_i dz_i \end{aligned}$$

The Bellman equation in the absence of state variables is, as before,

$$-J_t = U[(C/I),t] + J_y[E(dY)] + 1/2J_{yy}[Var(dY)]$$

The first order conditions with respect to wW/I and XF/I provide the optimal demands for assets and futures:

(A-20)

$$\begin{pmatrix} wW/I \\ XF/I \end{pmatrix} = -\frac{J_y}{J_{yy}} V^{-1}\begin{pmatrix} \mu_a - r\ell - V_{ai} \\ \mu_f - V_{fi} \end{pmatrix} + (W/I)V^{-1}\begin{pmatrix} V_{ai} \\ V_{fi} \end{pmatrix} - (1/I)V^{-1}\begin{pmatrix} V_{a,sq} \\ V_{f,sq} \end{pmatrix}$$

For comparison with (A-15), let us again define $\theta = -J_y/YJ_{yy}$; x= (XF/I)/(W/I); then after dividing by (W/I),(A-20) becomes:

(A-21)

$$\begin{pmatrix} w \\ x \end{pmatrix} = \theta V^{-1}\begin{pmatrix} \mu_a - r\ell \\ \mu_f \end{pmatrix} + (1-\theta)V^{-1}\begin{pmatrix} V_{ai} \\ V_{fi} \end{pmatrix} - (1/W)V^{-1}\begin{pmatrix} V_{a,sq} \\ V_{f,sq} \end{pmatrix}$$

When the opportunity set is and remains intertemporally stationary, the non-tradedness of SQ operates as a constraint. Diagrammatically speaking, the efficient frontier is to the right of that represented by (A-15), where all assets are freely tradable. The effect of introducing a non-traded position is to generate an additional, preference-free demand, the last term in (A-21), for assets and futures to hedge it in an attempt partially to restore unconstrained efficiency.

Recalling (A-14) we can write out the demand equations explicitly as follows:

(A-22)

$$w = \theta[V^{-1}_{a\cdot f}(\mu_a - r\ell - \beta'\mu_f)] + (1-\theta)[V^{-1}_{a\cdot f}(V_{ai} - \beta'V_{fi})]$$
$$- (1/W)[V^{-1}_{a\cdot f}(V_{a,sq} - \beta'V_{f,sq})]$$

$$x = -\beta w + \theta V^{-1}_{ff}\mu_f + (1-\theta)V^{-1}_{ff}V_{ai} - (1/W)V^{-1}_{ff}V_{f,sq}$$

The top row of (A-22) decomposes the demand for risky assets into three parts. The first is a speculative demand for hedged assets. The second is a demand for hedged assets to hedge the non-traded position. The demand for futures in the bottom row of (A-22) now has four components. The first is the demand for futures to hedge the total demand for all risky assets. Futures are then required as part of the speculative demand; to hedge inflation; and to hedge the non-traded position. The difference between (A-22) and (A-15) is the appearance of demands for both assets and futures to hedge the non-traded position.

Additional insight can be obtained from comparing the efficient frontiers that emerge from (A-13), the unconstrained case and (A-21) where a non-traded position exists. In both settings, the requisite two efficient portfolios can be obtained by alternating setting $\theta = 0$, which gives the minimum-variance portfolio, and $\theta = 1$, which produces the so-called log-portfolio.

Risk Tolerance	(A-13)	(A-21)
$\theta=0$	$V^{-1}\begin{pmatrix} V_{ai} \\ V_{fi} \end{pmatrix}$	$V^{-1}\begin{pmatrix} V_{ai} \\ V_{fi} \end{pmatrix} - (1/W)\begin{pmatrix} V_{a,sq} \\ V_{f,sq} \end{pmatrix}$
$\theta=1$	$V^{-1}\begin{pmatrix} \mu_a - r\ell \\ \mu_f \end{pmatrix}$	$V^{-1}\begin{pmatrix} \mu_a - r\ell \\ \mu_f \end{pmatrix} -(1/W)\begin{pmatrix} V_{a,sq} \\ V_{f,sq} \end{pmatrix}$

Clearly, the compositions of both efficient portfolios are shifted by the same amount owing to the introduction of the non-traded position. It can be shown that the unconstrained efficient frontier will unambiguously dominate the constrained frontier unless the non-traded position can be hedged perfectly.

Finally, (A-15) and (A-22) suggest that offering clients hedged foreign stocks and bonds may not be enough, even if the correct regression hedge ratios are used. Additional hedges are required, for inflation and for any non-traded positions. And, of course, unless they insist on holding a minimum-variance portfolio or, alternatively, unless $\mu_f=0$, the speculative demand for futures does not disappear. They should be advised to include naked futures (or their substitute, zero-investment portfolios of domestic and foreign short-term bonds) in their speculative asset demands.

Scenario III. Optimal Asset Demands When the Efficient Set is Random

The section addresses the most general of the cases to be considered. Here we let the opportunity set to be random by allowing the moments of the information processes associated with most prices to be functions of state variables. For notational simplicity, however, we retain the assumption that the price processes of risky assets are log-normal. Specifically, with all variables defined as before.

$$\text{(A-23)} \quad dA = A(\mu_a dt + \sigma_a dz_a) \qquad \text{Risky asset prices}$$

$$dQ = \mu_q(Q,t)dt + \sigma_q(Q,t)dz_q \qquad \text{Non-traded FC price}$$

$$dS = \mu_s(S,t)dt + \sigma_s(S,t)dz_s \qquad \text{Spot exchange rate}$$

$$dF = \mu_f(S,t)dt + \sigma_f(S,t)dz_f \qquad \text{Forward exchange rate}$$

$$dI = \mu_i(I,t)dt + \sigma_i(I,t)dz_i \qquad \text{Domestic price level}$$

In this more general setting with random interest rates, foreign exchange futures will not generally be priced by arbitrage. Were futures contracts to be taken as the hedging instrument, they would not be redundant. The set of risky assets, {A}, would then in principle contain all foreign and domestic stocks and bonds of all maturities, short or long. If, however, the hedging instruments were exchange-traded forward contracts of maturity T, their cash flows, dF, would represent the discounted value of the change in their forward settlement prices. Such contracts, were they to exist, would be perfectly correlated with zero-investment portfolios of pure discount foreign and domestic bonds with the same maturity. The risky-asset menu, {A}, would then have to exclude these portfolios.

The change in nominal wealth is given as before by

$$\text{(A-24)} \quad dW = d(SQ) + w'W(dA/A) + X'dF + [(1-w'\ell)rW - C]dt$$

Setting real wealth, Y=W/I, and applying Ito's lemma while being careful to incorporate the more general diffusions:

$$\text{(A-25)}\quad dY = [(w'W/I)(\mu_a - r\ -V_{ai}/I)+(X'/I)(\mu_f - V_{fi}/I)$$
$$+(W/I)(r-\mu_i/I + V_{ii}/I^2) + (Q/I)(\mu_s-V_{si}/I)$$
$$+(S/I)(\mu_q - V_{qi}/I)+ V_{sq}/I - C/I]dt$$
$$+(w'W/I)\sigma_a dz_a + (X'/I)\sigma_f dz_f + (S/I)\sigma_q dz_q$$
$$+(Q/I)\sigma_s dz_s\ - (W/I_2)\sigma_i dz_i$$

The objective function is precisely the same as (A-18) above. Maximizing (A-18) subject to (A-25) provides the Bellman equation:

$$\text{(A-26)}\quad -J_t = U(C/I,t)+J_y E(dY) + J_i E(dI) + J_s E(dS) + J_q E(dQ)$$
$$+ 1/2J_{yy}\ Var(dY) + 1/2J_{ii}\ Var(dI) + 1/2J_{ss}\ Var(dS)$$
$$+ 1/2J_{qq}\ Var(dQ) + J_{yi}\ cov(dY,dI) + J_{iq}\ cov(dI,dQ)$$
$$+ J_{sq}\ cov(dS,dQ) + J_{ys}\ Cov(dY,dS) + J_{yq} Cov(dY,dQ)$$
$$+ J_{is}\ Cov(dI,dS)$$

where E(dY) is given by the drift term in (A-25) and

$$cov(dY,dI) = (w'W/I)V_{ui} + (X'/I)V_{fi} + (S/I)V_{qi} + (Q/I)V_{si} - (W/I^2)V_{ii}$$

$$cov(dY,dS) = (w'W/I)V_{as} + (X'/I)V_f + (S/I)V_{qs} + (Q/I)V_{ss} - (W/I^2)V_{is}$$

$$cov(dY,dQ) = (w'W/I)V_{aq} + (X'/I)V_{fq} + (S/I)V_{qq} + (Q/I)V_{sq} -$$
$$(W/I^2)V_{iq}$$

$$\mathrm{Var}(dY) = (w'W/I, X'/I)\begin{pmatrix} V_{aa} & V_{af} \\ V_{fa} & V_{ff} \end{pmatrix}\begin{pmatrix} wW/I \\ X/I \end{pmatrix}$$

$$- 2(W/I^2)(w'W/I, X'/I)\begin{pmatrix} V_{ai} \\ V_{fi} \end{pmatrix}$$

$$- 2(w'W/I, X'/I)\left[(S/I)\begin{pmatrix} V_{aq} \\ V_{fq} \end{pmatrix} + (Q/I)\begin{pmatrix} V_{as} \\ V_{fs} \end{pmatrix}\right]$$

+ terms that are independent of the controls

The first order conditions provide:

(A-27)

$$\begin{pmatrix} 0 \\ 0 \end{pmatrix} = J_y\begin{pmatrix} \mu_a - r\ell - V_{ai}/I \\ \mu_f - V_{fi}/I \end{pmatrix}$$

$$+ J_{yy}\left[V\begin{pmatrix} wW/I \\ X/I \end{pmatrix} - (W/I^2)\begin{pmatrix} V_{ai} \\ V_{fi} \end{pmatrix} + (S/I)\begin{pmatrix} V_{aq} \\ V_{fq} \end{pmatrix} + (Q/I)\begin{pmatrix} V_{as} \\ V_{fs} \end{pmatrix}\right]$$

$$+ J_{yi}\begin{pmatrix} V_{ai} \\ V_{fi} \end{pmatrix} + J_{ys}\begin{pmatrix} V_{as} \\ V_{fs} \end{pmatrix} + J_{yq}\begin{pmatrix} V_{aq} \\ V_{fq} \end{pmatrix}$$

As usual, the optimal demands are the solutions to (A-27). The procedure involves solving for (w'W/I,X'/I)' and then, for tractibilty, dividing by real wealth, W/I. This provides the solutions for $w = (wW/I)/(W/I)$ and for a redefined futures decision-variable $\hat{x} = (X/I)/(W/I) = X/W$ which is to be distinguished from $x = XF/W$ in (A-

21). For notational convenience we also define the cross-hedging coefficients $H_y^i = J_{yi}/J_{yy}Y$; $H_{ys} = J_{ys}/J_{yy}Y$; and $H_{yq} = J_{yq}/J_{yy}Y$. As before the coefficient of relative risk tolerance is defined as $\theta = -J_y/J_{yy}Y$. With these conventions in hand, (A-27) produces:

(A-28)

$$\binom{w}{x} = \theta V^{-1}\binom{\mu_a - r\ell}{\mu_f} + [(1/I)(1-\theta) - H_{yi}]V^{-1}\binom{V_{ai}}{V_{fi}}$$

$$-[(S/W) + H_{yq}]V^{-1}\binom{V_{aq}}{V_{fq}} - [(Q/W) + H_{ys}]V^{-1}\binom{V_{as}}{V_{fs}}$$

Recalling (A-14), the demands in (A-28) can be decomposed.

$$w = \theta V^{-1}{}_{af}(\mu_a - r\ell - B'\mu_f) + [(1/I)(1-\theta) - H_{yi}]V^{-1}{}_{af}(V_{ai} - B'V_{fi})$$

$$- [(S/W)+H_{yq}]V^{-1}{}_{af}(V_{aq} - B'V_{fq}) - [(Q/W)+H_{ys}]V^{-1}{}_{af}(V_{as} - B'V_{fs})$$

(A-29)

$$x = -Bw + \theta V^{-1}{}_{ff}\mu_f + [(1/I)(1-\theta) - H_{yi}]V^{-1}{}_{ff}V_{fi}$$

$$- [(S/W) + H_{yq}]V^{-1}{}_{ff}V_{fq} - [(Q/W) + H_{ys}]V^{-1}{}_{ff}V_{fs}$$

The interpretations are much as before, with the addition of cross-hedging terms to protect against adverse shifts of the opportunity set.

Footnotes to Appendix A

[1] The specific content of the risky asset menu depends on what one assumes about interest rates and on the nature of the hedging instrument. If nominal interest rates are random and only FC futures are used for hedging, the set of risky assets can in principle include all domestic and foreign stacks and bonds. In this setting, futures will not be priced by arbitrage, will not be perfectly correlated with spot exchange rates and will therefore not be redundant. However, interest rate randomness may be inconsistent with a log-normal diffusion for futures prices, as is assumed in (2) below, without further restricting the interest rate process itself to be a log-normal diffusion. This last condition, however, violates empirical reality.

[2] Redundancy would be reduced to some extent if, instead of being futures, the hedging instruments were traded forward contracts that were marked to market and rewritten continuously. The daily cash flow associated with such contracts would be equal to the present value of their price change, discounted from their maturity date, T, using the \u.S. interest rate. Even with random interest rates such contracts would be priced by arbitrage. They would be perfectly correlated with zero-investment portfolios of short-term foreign and domestic bonds with maturities equal to the forward contracts' but not, in general, with similar portfolios containing long-term foreign bonds. Were such contracts available, the set of risky assets could contain long bonds in all currencies.

[3] The problems associated with this specification have already been marked by Adler and Dumas (1983, 940-941). Even when all variables including inflation follow non-stationary Ito processes the specification may be inconsistent with equilibrium when investors are heterogeneous.

[4] When Y = W/i, applying Ito's lemma provides:

$$dY = [Y_w E(dW) + Y_i E(dI) + 1/2 Y_{ww} \text{Var}(dW) + 1/2 Y_{ii} \text{Var}(dI)$$

$$+ Y_{wi}\ \mathrm{cov}(dW,dI)]dt + Y_w(w'W\sigma_a dz_a + X'F\sigma_f dz_f) + Y_i I\sigma_i dz_i$$

where:

$Y_w = 1/I$; $Y_i = -W/I^2$; $Y_{ww} = 0$; $Y_{ii} = 2W/I^3$; $Y_{wi} = -1/I^2$; and $\mathrm{cov}(dW,dI) = (w'WIV_{ai} + X'FIV_{fi})dt$.

Expression (A-7) is then obtained by substitution.

[5]Recalling that $V_{af} = V_{aa} - \beta' V_{ff}\beta$, the second row of (A-15) is:

$$x = \theta\{V^{-1}{}_{af}[-\beta(\mu_a - r - \beta'\mu_f)] + V^{-1}{}_{ff}\mu_f\}$$

$$+ (1-\theta)\{V^{-1}{}_{af}[-\beta(V_{ai}-\beta' V_{fi})] + V^{-1}{}_{ff}V_{fi}\}$$

Comparing this expression to the solution for w in the top row produces the form as given:

[6] With a non-traded position in the model, the change in nominal wealth is given by:

$$dW = d(SQ) + w'W(dA/A) + X'dF + [(1-w'\ )rW-C]dt.$$

With $Y = W/I$, the change in real wealth is written as:

$$dY = [Y_w E(dW) + Y_i E(dI) + 1/2Y_{ww}\ \mathrm{Var}(dW) + 1/2Y_{ii}\ \mathrm{Var}(dI)$$

$$+ Y_{wi}\ \mathrm{cov}(dW,dI)]dt + Y_w[w'W\sigma_a dz_a + X'F\sigma_f dz_f$$

$$+ SQ(\sigma_s dz_s + \sigma_q dz_q)] + Y_i I\sigma_i dz_i$$

where the partial derivatives of Y appear in footnote 4. The computation of E(dY) and Var(dY) for use in the Bellman equation is a matter of straightforward but tedious algebra.

Appendix B

Positive, Zero and Negative Forward Risk Premia Under Purchasing Power Parity

Michael Adler

Bhaskar Prasad

This appendix will show that the conditional forward risk-premium can be positive, zero or negative depending on the net hedging pressure in the exchange markets. In fact, a zero risk-premium is less likely than non-zero values despite the evidence that the unconditional risk-premium is zero. The analysis will also help dispel the confusion that underlies assertions that the risk-premium must be zero since an American demands a premium for holding Yen while a Japanese simultaneously demands a premium for holding dollars.

The decomposed asset demands in Appendix A show that any risk-averse agent holds assets in response to two simultaneous motives: a speculative motive and a hedging motive. Let us characterize these motives more precisely.

The speculative motive generates all transactions that increase global portfolio risk. If the agent is risk-averse, he will demand a risk-premium, that is, an increment to expected returns for bearing the extra risk. He will not demand a premium if he is risk-neutral.

The hedging motive produces all transactions that reduce overall portfolio risk. One may think of hedging, that is, the use of offsetting positions in some assets to reduce the risk-contribution to others, also as diversification: the label is unimportant. The hedging motive specifically refers to transactions taken in response to pre-established long or short positions in any or all assets. For example, anyone who sells spot a previously accumulated risky Yen deposit in exchange for less risky US$ cash, or who sells forward a Yen cash flow he expects to receive, is hedging. Risk-neutral agents do not hedge. Risk-averse hedgers are willing to pay a premium for safety but would prefer to receive one were it offered.

These considerations permit us to adopt the following characterization of speculators and hedgers. All are defined by who is on the selling side. This convention enables us subsequently to identify who trades with whom when expectations are homogeneous.

> A Yen speculator sells Yen forward. A US$ speculator sells US$ forward. When the Yen is suddenly expected to appreciate, an erstwhile Yen speculator who now wants to buy Yen forward becomes a US$ speculator, regardless of nationality. The categories are mutually exclusive. By definition, no agent can be simultaneously both a US$ speculator and a Yen speculator.
>
> A Yen hedger is a hedger who sells Yen forward for any of a variety of reasons. He could be an American with a pre-existing Yen asset; or he could be an American who sells Yen forward to hedge domestic assets or to hedge against U.S. inflation; or, finally, he could be a Japanese citizen who buys US$ forward to hedge a pre-established US$ liability or to hedge domestic Japanese assets and Japanese inflation.
>
> A US$ hedger is a hedger who sells US$ forward. This can be an American who buys Yen forward to hedge a Yen liability or to hedge inflation and other assets; or a Japanese who already owns a US$ asset or who wants to hedge his domestic inflation rate and other portfolios.

Thus, for example, a Yen hedger and a Yen speculator both sell Yen forward but for different motives. Moreover, a Yen hedger necessarily can transact only with a US$ hedger or a US$ speculator as by definition a Yen speculator cannot take the other side. Similarly, a US$ hedger trades only with a Yen hedger or a Yen speculator.

Given homogeneous expectations and barring arbitrage opportunities, risk-averse speculators never trade with each other as all want the same side of the transaction at the current price. All demand the risk-premium but, when all want to speculate in the same direction, none can receive it. Under the unanimous speculative pressure, the forward exchange rate moves to the point where finally no one wants to transact. In a purely speculative market with no hedgers there would, therefore, be no transactions at all in this case. The market itself would disappear.

These observations point to the flaw in the seductive reasoning of Giddy (1976) which is still frequently repeated. Giddy posited a market consisting of French speculators and British speculators. He argued that,"if a French speculator is rewarded for taking risk, it follows that a British speculator holding the opposite side of the contract is penalized for taking risk." As this is implausible, he concluded that the equilibrium risk-premium must be zero. Giddy made no assumption about his speculators' beliefs or information but apparently had homogeneous, or at least similar, expectations in mind. His error was to fail to recognize that similar beliefs would drive both speculators to the same side of a transaction which, therefore, would not take place. In Giddy's setting the risk premium would not be zero or any other value as no trade would occur. In our taxonomy, homogeneous expectations causes one class of speculators to disappear. The remaining group cannot trade with itself.

Hedgers must be brought into the picture for a forward market to exist. There is then no difficulty as hedgers are willing to pay the premium that speculators demand. What remains is to describe more precisely the conditions under which the market-risk-premium will be positive, zero, or negative. For this purpose let us define exactly what the risk-premium is.

To tie things down, let all exchange rates be defined in U.S. terms, that is as (US$/FC). To be consistent with financial theory we define the current forward rate, F, as the certainty equivalent of the future spot rate, that is:

(B-1) $$F = E(S) - RP$$

where E(S) is the expected spot rate and RP is the risk-premium. This defines the risk-premium as the difference between the expected spot and current forward rates:

(B-2) $$RP = E(S) - F$$

Speculators demand the risk-premium. We can now determine the sign the risk-premium must have in order to induce speculators to transact in a given direction. From (B-2) we see immediately that:

$$RP > 0 \quad \text{if } F < E(S)$$

To benefit from the expected Yen appreciation the speculator must buy Yen forward, that is, be a US$ speculator. Conversely, US$ speculators can be compensated for their risk and will be induced to transact if the risk-premium is positive. In this case, US$ hedgers may also receive rather than pay the premium while Yen hedgers will pay it.

Again from (B-2), it is obvious that

$$RP < 0 \quad \text{if } F > E(S)$$

Here the Yen is expected to depreciate. To earn the risk-premium, agents must be Yen speculators who sell the Yen forward. Conversely, Yen speculators can be induced to transact if the risk-premium is negative. When it is, Yen hedgers may also receive rather than pay a risk-premium. In this case, US$ hedgers who buy Yen forward will pay the risk-premium.

Exhibit (B-1) sets forth a complete taxonomy of the situations in which a forward currency market exists and the sign of the risk-premium that must be true in each case when expectations are homogeneous. Many squares are blocked out. This is because US$ hedgers can only transact with Yen speculators and hedgers; and Yen hedgers can only

EXHIBIT B-1

The Sign of the Risk Premium Under Homogeneous Beliefs

	1 US $ Speculators	2 Yen Speculators	3 US $ Hedgers	4 Yen Hedgers
US $ A Speculators				• Yen hedgers sell Yen and pay RP. • US $ speculators buy Yen and earn RP, if $F < E(S)$, i.e., if $RP > 0$
Yen B Speculators			• US$ hedgers buy Yen and pay RP. • Yen speculators sell Yen and earn RP if $F > E(S)$, i.e., if $RP < 0$.	
US $ C Hedgers		• US $ hedgers buy Yen and pay RP • Yen speculators sell Yen and earn RP if $F > E(S)$, i.e., if $RP < 0$.		• US $ hedgers buy Yen. • Yen hedgers sell Yen. • Both willing to pay RP. Consistent with $RP \gtreqless 0$
Yen D Hedgers	• Yen hedgers sell Yen and pay RP. • US $ speculators buy Yen and earn RP if $F < E(S)$, i.e., if $RP > 0$.		• Yen hedgers sell Yen • US $ hedgers buy Yen. • Both willing to pay RP. Consistent with $RP \gtreqless 0$.	

trade with US$ speculators and hedgers. The diagonal elements A1,B2, C3 and D4 are empty as by definition the putative traders in these squares want the same side of the transaction. The same is true for A3, B4, C1 and D2. In these cases no trade is possible at current prices. A2 and B1 are crossed out as they are impossible. When expectations are homogeneous no one can be simultaneously a US$ and a Yen speculator.

While hedgers can transact with either speculators or hedgers on the other side, speculators by definition can transact only with hedgers who trade in the opposite direction. Transactions between speculators and hedgers appear on the upward diagonal, in D1,C2, B3 and A4. On this diagonal there are only two independent cases. D1 and A4 represent trades between US$ speculators and Yen hedgers which require a positive risk-premium; and C2 and B3, which portray transactions between Yen speculators and US$ hedgers that will occur only if the risk-premium is negative. In these cases, a zero risk-premium is impossible.

A zero risk-premium is possible only when hedgers transact with each other , as they do in C4 and D3. Such transactions, however, are also consistent with any value of the risk-premium if Yen hedgers' demand for dollars is stronger.

These considerations give rise to the following picture. Under homogeneous expectations, net hedging demands (fear) drive the forward market more strongly than speculation (greed). Similar probability beliefs produce an implicit ordering of transactions in the marketplace. Yen hedgers "prefer" to trade with US$ hedgers who do not demand a premium, and vice-versa. When Yen hedgers want to sell forward more Yen than US$ hedgers want to buy, they will drive the forward rate down to a point sufficiently below the expected spot rate to induce US$ speculators to buy Yen forward to accommodate them. Similarly, when the US$ hedging demand exceeds the Yen hedging demand, the pressure forces the forward rate up to a point where Yen speculators are induced to sell them the Yen they require. In either case, the risk-premium will be larger in absolute value the greater the

Yen hedging $>$ US$ hedging $\Rightarrow$ $F < E(S)$
$\Rightarrow$ $RP > 0$

Buyers of Yen (US$ speculators and hedgers) receive RP.
Sellers of Yen (Yen hedgers) pay RP.

Yen hedging $<$ US$ hedging $\Rightarrow$ $F > E(S)$
$\Rightarrow$ $RP < 0$

Buyers of Yen (US$ hedgers) pay RP, a positive amount.

Sellers of Yen (Yen speculators and hedgers) receive RP.

Yen hedging = US$ hedging $\Rightarrow$ $F = E(S) \pm \delta$,

where $\delta \gtrless 0$ is small

Two fairly strong presumptions emerge from the foregoing analysis. The first is that circumstances under which the market risk-premium either can or must be positive or negative will occur more frequently than those that determine a risk-premium of zero. In fact, a zero risk-premium is never required in any of the market scenarios. It is a possible but not a necessary outcome when the demands of US$ and Yen hedgers more or less offset each other.

The second is that the risk-premium is likely to be volatile. First, hedging demands for forward exchange depend in part on expectations which themselves are volatile. This is evident from the asset demands in Appendix A where the hedging demand for forward contracts is proportional to the size of the total, including the speculative, positions taken in other assets. Second, forward contracts may be taken to hedge inflation and other state variables whose covariances with existing portfolio positions fluctuate. One should, therefore, expect what empirical research finds: conditional risk-premia that are sometimes positive and sometimes negative and that may seem to average to zero over time.

A final note: neither of these conclusions depends in any essential way on expectations being homogeneous. When expectations are portfolio positions fluctuate. One should, therefore, expect what empirical research finds: conditional risk-premia that are sometimes positive and sometimes negative and that may seem to average to zero over time.

A final note: neither of these conclusions depends in any essential way on expectations being homogeneous. When expectations are heterogeneous, the risk-premia can again be positive, zero or negative. What breaks down is our neat ordering of hedgers and speculators in the transaction queue. This means that any empirical attempt to identify net hedging pressures from observed net investment positions may be unsuccessful.[9]

9

For example, if speculators have different beliefs based on different information, they suspect each other and still do not trade with each other. If they have different beliefs based on the same information at least one is making a mistake. Each can demand a premium and think he will get it, but only one actually will. They can trade with each other: the winner gets the premium while the loser is indistinguishable from a hedger and pays it. Mistake-making speculators join hedgers in one direction or the other, making it impossible any longer to say precisely that hedging pressure drives the market. While bad guesses are undoubtedly to be observed in practice, they cannot serve as the foundation for a consistent financial theory. They can, however, confound empirical analysis.

References

Adler, Michael and Bernard Dumas. "International Portfolio Choice and Corporation Finance: A Synthesis." The Journal of Finance, 38 no. 3 (June, 1983), 925-984.

Adler, Michael and Jerome Detemple. "Hedging With Futures in an Intertemporal Portfolio Context." The Journal of Futures Markets, 8 no. 3 (June, 1988), 249-270.

Domowitz, Ian and Craig S. Hakkio. "Conditional Variance and the Risk Premium in the Foreign Exchange Market." Journal of International Economics, 19 no. 1/2 (August, 1985), 47-66.

Engel, Charles M. "Testing for the Absence of Expected Real Profits from Forward Speculation." Journal of International Economics, 17 no. 3/4 (November, 1984), 299-308.

Giddy, Ian H. "An Integrated Theory of Exchange Rate Equilibrium." Journal of Financial and Quatitative Analysis, 11 no. 5 (December, 1976), 883-892.

Giovannini, Alberto and Philippe Jorion. "Interest Rates and Risk Premia in the Stock Market and in the Foreign Exchange Market." Journal of International Money and Finance, 6 no. 1 (March, 1987), 107-123.

Lyons, Richard K. "Tests of the Foreign Exchange Risk Premium Using the Expected Second Moments Implied by Option Pricing." Journal of International Money and Finance, 7 no. 1 (March, 1988), 91-108.

Perold, Andre F. and Evan C. Schulman. "The Free Lunch in Currency Hedging: Implications for Investment Policy and Performance Standards." Financial Analysts Journal, May-June 1988, 45-50.

Sercu, Piet. "A Generalization of the International Asset Pricing Model." Finance: Revue de l'Assocation Francaise de Finance, 1 no. 1 (Juin, 1980), 91-135.

Wolff, Christian C.P. "Forward Foreign Exchange Rates, Expected Spot Rates and Premia: A signal-Extraction Approach." Journal of Finance, 42 no. 2 (June, 1987), 395-406.

Recent Developments in International Banking
and Finance, S.J. Khoury (editor)

CHAPTER IX

A Reexamination of the Benefits to International Diversification

Richard D. Marcus

Associate Professor
University of Wisconsin-Milwaukee

Donald Solberg

Assistant Professor
University of Wisconsin-Milwaukee

Terry L. Zivney

Associate Professor
Clarence E. Harris Chair of Excellence in Business
University of Tennessee at Chattanooga

Acknowledgments: We wish to thank two anonymous reviewers, as well as Sarkis Khoury, Der-Ann Hsu, Harold Klagstad, the participants of the Capital Markets Seminar, University of Wisconsin-Madison, and the Financial Management Association's International Finance session in New Orleans, 1988 for helpful comments. For research assistance, we thank the International Business Center, the Management Research Center, and the Dean's Office of the School of Business Administration, University of Wisconsin-Milwaukee. We wish to thank Distinguished Professor Rosalie Tung, Director of the International Business Center, for funding this research by providing the Ibbotson World Asset Returns data.

Introduction

The 508 point drop of the Dow Jones Industrial Average on October 19, 1987 represented nearly a 23 percent drop in the value of major common stock values in the United States. An investor holding a well-diversified portfolio of U.S. common stocks from the August 25, 1987 market peak through November 11, 1987 would have recorded a 27.8% loss. However, investors in U.S. common stocks did not do significantly worse than internationally-diversified investors. For the same forty-eight day holding period, investors in the U.K. lost 27.2%, France 34.7%, Australia 43.3%, Germany 38.4%, Switzerland 30.5%, and Canada 28.4%.[1] Japan and Italy fared slightly better losing only 19.8% and 18.7%, respectively, over the same holding period. Internationally diversified mutual funds did no better than non-internationally diversified funds. The panic in the U.S. spread faster than a Concord in a tail wind sending the illusion of safety of international diversification into a nose dive.

The interrelationships between markets may be stronger today than in earlier times. Globalization of security markets has meant that I.B.M. stock can trade somewhere in world at any hour, even though it may be after the closing bell in New York. The high correlation among international market returns has prompted a reevaluation of the alleged benefits to international diversification. We will take a somewhat U.S. centric world view by examining the benefits to a typical U.S. investor for investing some of her money internationally.

We assume that her investment horizon is longer than a week or a month. Schlarbaum, Lewellen, and Lease [7] found a mean duration of holding periods for active traders to be 256 days (about 8 months). Earlier tests of the benefits of portfolio risk reduction through international diversification (e.g., Solnik [13, 14]; Joy, Panton, Reilly, and Martin [6]; and Hill and Schneeweis [4]) examined weekly or monthly returns for a handful stocks selected from each country over a few years. The recent availability of Ibbotson's World Asset Returns monthly returns data, along with the older Ibbotson's World Asset Returns annual data, has allowed longer holding periods and more nations to be included in current research.

I. Holding Periods and Time Diversification

Previous studies of international diversification examine cross-sectional benefits within relatively short holding periods (a week or a month). They provide persuasive evidence that investors experience smaller weekly or monthly deviations from average portfolio returns by holding internationally diversified portfolios. Unfortunately, this evidence does not permit the inference that diversification will be equally successful over longer holding periods.

For any given investor, an appropriate measure of risk is defined in terms of deviations from expected returns at the end of the investor's desired holding period. Strictly speaking, the evidence cited above is appropriate only for the examination of weekly or monthly holding periods. The primary justification for examination of shorter periods is pragmatic, rather than economic. The study of shorter holding periods permits a larger number of observations in time series samples. For investors with horizons longer than a week or month, the previous studies provide estimates of variability within the short holding period. While such measures are interesting for many purposes, this "within period" volatility is not necessarily the most relevant measure of risk. In particular, an investor cannot use weekly return data to make inferences about longer period returns.

The emphasis on shorter term horizons may have resulted in a significant bias in the measurement of risk reduction resulting from international diversification. The developing "time diversification" literature of Lloyd and Haney [8] or Lloyd and Modani [9] provides a useful framework for analysis of this bias. Consider the returns of a portfolio of securities. The variance of returns about the long run mean decreases as the number of holding periods increases. Roughly speaking, variance about the long run mean is reduced as the number of holding periods increases because of low serial correlation in security returns. Serial correlations are close to zero in efficient markets. Therefore, increasing the number of holding periods leads to a significant variance reduction. As McEnally [11] has discussed, this evidence does not necessarily imply that risk itself decreases with the number of holding periods. However, the nature of the variance-time relationship does suggest that the variance of any series of returns will be diminished simply by examining more holding periods. Therefore, the relative decrease in variance due to cross-sectional diversification becomes much smaller as the number of periods examined increases.

The relationship between diversification benefits and holding period length has been examined for domestic securities. Lloyd and Modani [9] study the changes in the relative benefits of cross-sectional diversification obtained by adding Treasury bonds, Treasury bills, and corporate bonds to a portfolio of common stocks. These benefits decrease as the investment horizon increases. Their evidence indicates that as the number of holding periods increase, the relative risk reducing benefits of cross-sectional diversification decrease significantly.

II. Market Segmentation

In addition to the well documented variance-time relationship, a second argument provides additional motivation for examination of longer holding periods. At the most fundamental level, correlations among international stock returns are related to a common set of economic variables or factors. Wheatley [15] finds no evidence to suggest that asset prices around the world violate any contemporaneous asset pricing relationships. However, our analysis considers the intertemporal effects of market segmentation.

The analysis in the next section shows, as a result of this intertemporal correlation, that stock returns in different countries will exhibit lower correlations within shorter periods such as a day, week, or month, than within periods such as a quarter or a year. Within such longer periods, barriers to the flow of capital are less significant impediments, and markets tend to be more fully integrated. Therefore factors common to the world economy should explain a greater proportion of each country's variability when the holding period interval is extended.

The relationship between stock returns and real macroeconomic activity in different countries suggests that market segmentation should be examined. For example, an unanticipated increase in the GNP of the U.S. should have an immediate impact on stock prices in the U.S. However, GNP increases in the U.S. should also have a positive impact on the national economies of other countries. Clearly this real impact will occur with a lag as the increase in U.S. income leads to greater U.S. purchases of foreign goods and services. The issue of immediate concern is the reaction of the financial markets in other countries to the anticipated change in real activity. If there are no frictions impeding the flow of information or capital, the stock price reaction in other countries would be instantaneous. But to the extent that such barriers segment international financial markets, there will also be a lag in the financial market.

This phenomenon is not unique to international stock returns. Lo and MacKinlay [10] found strong positive cross-autocovariances among individual company stock returns in the United States, even though each individual security's return is temporally independent. The barriers to the flow of information which could induce such intertemporal cross serial correlations should be even greater across countries than within a single country, however. To the extent that international markets are segmented, short run correlations between returns will be smaller than in frictionless markets. In the short term, legal and institutional barriers as well as information costs may inhibit the flow of both real and financial resources across international boundaries. These costs may well be sufficient to impede short term capital flows, but insufficient to have long run effects.

The increased correlation among returns as holding periods lengthens reduces the risk-reducing benefits of diversification. Clearly, the risk reducing benefits to international diversification will remain as long as returns to stock indices are not perfectly positively correlated. Again, however, the relative reduction in portfolio variance attributable to holding an internationally diversified portfolio may well be much smaller when longer holding periods are studied. Research by Hilliard [5] found complex lagged correlations across international equity market indices. This phenomenon is particularly important to study because longer investment horizons more closely reflect the true holding periods of investors holding equity securities in their portfolios. Unfortunately, no single horizon is relevant for all investors. Therefore, the study examines horizons of varying lengths to document changes in the benefits of diversification as the investment horizon changes.

III. A Model of Diversification and Holding Periods

A central tenet of portfolio theory is the Don't-Put-All-Your-Eggs-in-One-Basket theorem. So long as returns across a given risk class of securities are not perfectly correlated, average portfolio variance declines as N, the number of securities, increases. Recent interest by Reichenstein [12], and Fama and French [1, 2] have demonstrated additional risk-reducing properties of holding securities for longer time periods. If security returns are not positively serially correlated, longer holding periods act much like diversification: longer holding periods emphasize the permanent over the temporary or noisy components of returns in much the same fashion as diversification emphasizes systematic over nonsystematic risk.

These two forms of diversification can be simultaneously introduced in a Markowitz-style model. Suppose there are M securities, where M is large. Let t be an index that rises as the number of intervals in the holding period rises. Each security has a known expected return, $E[R_i(t)]$, and a known standard deviation of returns, $\sigma_i(t)$. Unique to these expressions, both returns and standard deviations depend on the length of holding period, t. Securities of a given holding period many be combined into portfolios. The expected portfolio return, $E[R_p]$, is a weighted average of the $N \leq M$ securities in the portfolio, or N national indices that comprise the portfolio.

$$E[R_p] = \sum_{i=1}^{N} x_i \, E[R_i(t)] \tag{1}$$

The weights are the proportions of funds invested in each of the N securities, where the sum of the weights, $\Sigma x_i = 1$. The portfolio variance, $\sigma_p^2(t)$, in equation 2 is composed of N variances and (N)(N-1) covariances, and the portfolio weights.

$$\sigma_p^2(t) = \sum_{j=1}^{N} \sum_{k=1}^{N} x_j \, x_k \, \sigma_{jk}(t) \tag{2}$$

For the simplifying case of equally-weighted portfolios, the portfolio variance is given in (3).

$$\sigma_p^2(t) = (1/N^2) \sum_{j=1}^{N} \sigma_j^2(t) + (1/N^2) \sum_{j=1}^{N} \sum_{\substack{k=1 \\ k \neq j}}^{N} \sigma_{jk}(t) \quad (3)$$

We can define $\bar{\sigma}^2(t)$ as the mean variance, and define $\bar{\sigma}_{jk}$ as the mean covariance. Using these symbols, the portfolio variance becomes the useful expression (4).

$$\sigma_p^2(t) = (1/N)\ \bar{\sigma}^2(t) + ((N\text{-}1)/N)\ \bar{\sigma}_{jk}(t) \quad (4)$$

Expressions like equation (4) demonstrate the relative importance of covariance over variance in determining the portfolio variance as N rises. Diversification reduces the weight on the first term on the right-hand side of (4) and raises the weight of the second term on the right-hand side. Since $\bar{\sigma}^2(t)$ is always greater than or equal to $\bar{\sigma}_{jk}(t)$, σ_p^2 is non-increasing as N rises.

The time dimension in equation (4) influences the variance of returns for individual securities, as well as the covariance of returns securities. The time diversification literature has emphasized the reduction in variance due to longer holding periods. This implies a typically negative time derivative for the average variance.

$$\partial\bar{\sigma}^2(t)/\ t < 0 \quad (5)$$

Inspection of equation (4) suggests that longer holding periods will lower portfolio variance as the mean holding period variances decline. However, the weight of the covariances of returns, (N-1)/N, is greater than that of the variances. The average covariance may rise or fall over longer holding periods depending on the size and degree of the lagged covariation among securities.

The situation of international diversification is particularly subject to lagged positive correlations among national return indices. As discussed in section II, barriers to capital flows are less significant as the length of time increases. This view is consistent with Hilliard's [5] finding found that international equity markets are linked with lags of variable degrees. Accordingly, it is anticipated that the derivative on mean covariances with respect to holding periods is positive.

$$\partial \bar{\sigma}_{jk}(t)/\partial t \;>\; 0 \tag{6}$$

Differentiating equation (4) with respect to holding periods, t, demonstrates that portfolio variance has two counteracting forces: time diversification reduces variance, and rising covariation increases variance.

$$(\partial \sigma_p{}^2(t)/\partial t) \;=\; (1/N)(\partial \bar{\sigma}^2(t)/\partial t) \;+\; ((N\text{-}1)/N)(\partial \bar{\sigma}_{jk}(t)/\partial t) \tag{7}$$

Diversification of investments across nations, where N now denotes the number of nations, reduces portfolio variance. However, holding a diversified portfolio for longer periods attenuates the impact of diversification whenever the sign of (7) is a net positive. As is shown graphically in Figure 1, diversification reduces portfolio variance as N rises, but the benefits of diversification decline as t, the number of holding periods rises. This means that a 14-country diversified portfolio with t=6 periods may have the same standard deviation as a 2-country portfolio with only t=3 holding period, which is indeed what we find and report in the following section. While this kind of financial risk comparison is unusual, it nevertheless emphasizes the effect that longer time horizons play on "undoing" the risk reducing benefits of diversification.

Figure 1

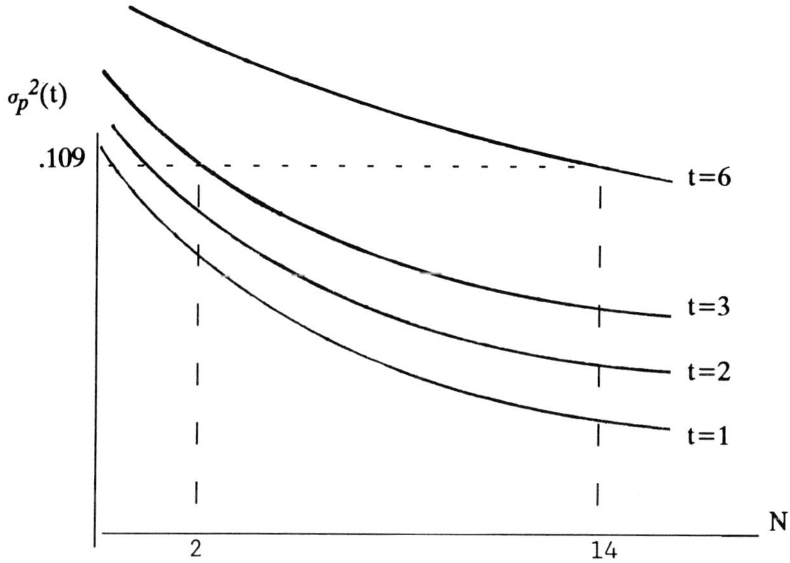

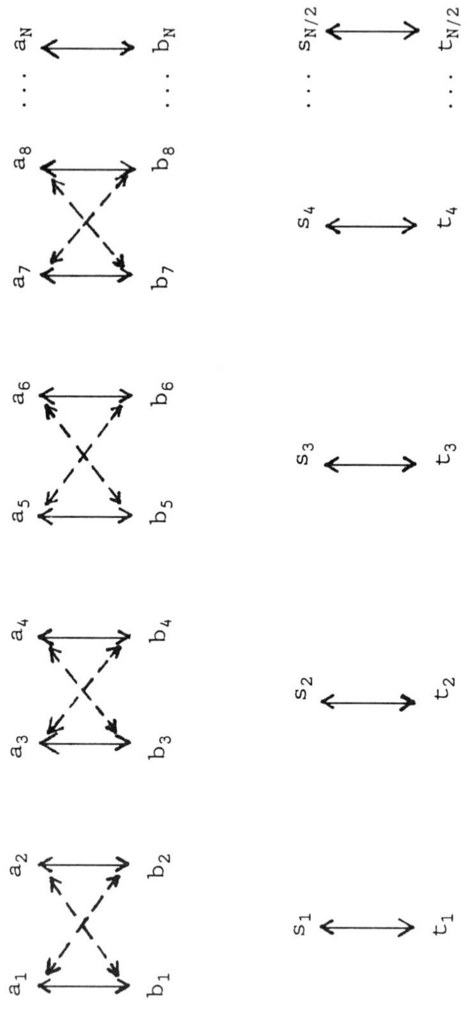
a1 a2 a3 a4 a5 a6 a7 a8 . . . aN
b1 b2 b3 b4 b5 b6 b7 b8 . . . bN
s1 s2 s3 s4 . . . sN/2
t1 t2 t3 t4 . . . tN/2

Figure 2

One particularly useful way to understand the forces at work as the holding period lengthens is to model two time series of returns (a_1, a_2, a_3,...,a_N) and (b_1, b_2,b_3,...,b_N). Each return is for one period. A two-period return is approximately the sum of two single periods; that is, the two period return $s_1 = a_1 + a_2 \cong (1 + a_1)(1 + a_2)-1$, (for a_1 and a_2 small).[2] Similarly, let the two period return for the b-time series be given as $t_1 = b_1 + b_2 \cong (1 + b_1)(1 + b_2)-1$, for small b_1 and b_2. The transformation of the one-period into a two-period time series is illustrated in Figure 2.

A critical element in forming portfolios of series (a and b) is the correlation coefficient, ρ_{ab}, between the two series. The one-period correlation coefficient is given in equation (8).

$$\rho_{ab} = \mathrm{Cov}(a,b)/\sigma_a \sigma_b \qquad (8)$$

The vertical arrows between the (a and b) series in Figure 2 indicate the correlation between these series. If the contemporaneous covariance between short periods in a time series is low, then the correlation coefficient between those series will also be low.

When the same (a and b) series is transformed into two-period returns (s and t) in Figure 2, the correlation coefficient between (s and t) can be decomposed into the several contemporaneous and lagged covariances of the one-period series.

$$\rho_{st} = \mathrm{Cov}(s,t)/\sigma_s \sigma_t = \qquad (9)$$

$$\{\mathrm{Cov}(a_{2k-1},b_{2k-1}) + \mathrm{Cov}(a_{2k-1},b_{2k})$$

$$+\mathrm{Cov}(a_{2k},b_{2k-1}) + \mathrm{Cov}(a_{2k},b_{2k})\}/\sigma_s\sigma_t$$

The numerator of (9) contains four covariances, where k is an integer. Two are the contemporaneous covariances $\mathrm{Cov}(a_{2k-1},b_{2k-1})$ and $\mathrm{Cov}(a_{2k},b_{2k})$, which are identical to the one-period covariances. The sum of these two contem- poraneous covariances should equal $2\rho_{ab}\sigma_a\sigma_b$. The other two covariances are lagged one period. They represent the diagonal dashed arrows between series (a and b) in Figure 2. The sum of these two lagged covariances is $(\rho_{a2k-1,b2k} + \rho_{a2k,b2k-1})(\sigma_a)(\sigma_b)$.

If times series a and time series b are serially uncorrelated, then it is readily proved (see footnote 3) that the two period variance is twice the size of the one period variance; that is, $\sigma_s^2 = 2\,\sigma_a^2$. By applying the square root to both sides we find that $\sigma_s = \sqrt{2}\,\sigma_a$, and a similar reasoning leads to: $\sigma_t = \sqrt{2}\,\sigma_b$. Substituting these expressions into (9) as well as the expressions for the four covariances, the two-period correlation coefficient is shown to be:[4]

$$\rho_{st} = \rho_{ab} + (1/2)[\rho_{a2k-1,b2k-1} + \rho_{a2k,b2k-1}] \qquad (10)$$

This expression demonstrates that the two-period correlation coefficient is larger than the single-period contemporaneous correlation coefficient by the mean of the two lagged correlation coefficients. If the lagged correlation coefficients are positive and important, as argued (due to international market segmentation), then the longer holding periods will exhibit larger correlation between returns. The relative risk reduction resulting from diversification will diminish with these longer holding periods because of their greater covariation.[5]

IV. Data

The empirical results employ equity returns calculated from stock index price series for sixteen different countries. These countries are the prominent industrialized nations in which U.S. investors might consider investing. Along with the United States, their names and descriptive statistics of their returns appear in Table 1.

Table 1 presents exchange-rate adjusted monthly return data for 221 months from February 1970 through June 1988. The monthly mean return is highest, not surprisingly, for Japan. The lowest monthly return was for Switzerland. The standard deviation of monthly returns is six to ten times larger than the mean return. Indeed, the minimum and maximum monthly return often exceeded 20% with some countries experiencing returns in excess of 50%. The country with the lowest standard deviation for its equity markets was the United States. The index for a diversified U.S. portfolio had a standard deviation of 4.9%.

Table 1

Descriptive Statistics of International Monthly Returns

February 1970 through June 1988

Country	Mean Return	Std Dev.	Minimum	Maximum
Australia	.008	.085	-.415	.524
Austria	.007	.049	-.122	.232
Belgium	.010	.069	-.248	.258
Canada	.006	.062	-.237	.161
France	.009	.081	-.221	.579
Germany	.007	.055	-.171	.174
Italy	.005	.089	-.311	.579
Japan	.018	.056	-.131	.140
Netherlands	.007	.055	-.181	.140
New Zealand	.007	.076	-.360	.193
Norway	.011	.088	-.231	.293
Spain	.009	.077	-.288	.203
Sweden	.010	.061	-.186	.180
Switzerland	.002	.074	-.382	.543
United Kingdom	.013	.126	-.573	1.425
United States	.006	.049	-.211	.161

Note: Mean Return is the average monthly price appreciation of each country's index adjusted for exchange rate changes. The standard deviation, minimum, and maximum are descriptive statistics of these monthly exchange rate adjusted returns.

Data for this table were obtained from two different sources. For the period beginning January 1970, and ending December 1980, monthly stock price data were obtained from International Financial Statistics (IFS), a publication of the International Monetary Fund. IFS reports a series of industrial stock index prices for each of the sixteen countries in this sample. From these price series, the price appreciation component of holding period return is computed as the ratio of the stock index value for month t, to the index value for month t-1. The IFS price data therefore permits the calculation of a return series for each of the 131 months from February, 1970 through December, 1980. These returns were then adjusted for exchange rates with the U.S. dollar, using IFS-published monthly exchange rates. Accordingly, they are the monthly returns available to U.S. investors in foreign and U.S. equity markets.

Monthly data for the period January, 1981 through June, 1988 were obtained from the World Asset Returns Module compiled by Ibbotson Associates, Incorporated. The price appreciation components of holding period returns for these additional 90 months, adjusted for exchange rate changes, were appended to the return series computed from the IFS to form a series of 221 monthly returns. The sixteen countries examined in this study represent the intersection of those countries which are reported in both the IFS and Ibbotson series, and which have a complete price series over the entire sample period.

In addition to the monthly data over the 1981-1988 period, the Ibbotson World Asset Returns Module also includes a series of annual returns for each of the sixteen countries. This series begins in 1960, and therefore provides an additional 11 years of data. These additional returns were included in analysis of the annual return series.

The empirical analysis examines changes in the benefits of diversification as return intervals increase. Five different return intervals are examined: monthly, bi-monthly, quarterly, semi-annual, and annual. Regardless of the return interval, the price appreciation component of holding period return is defined as the ratio of the price at the end of the period to the price at the beginning of the period. Each n-month return series is computed as the product of the n one-month returns occurring within each interval.

V. Results

Our model in Section III demonstrates that the correlation coefficients across country returns rise over longer holding periods whenever the lagged correlation coefficients across countries are positive. Table 2 directly examines whether or not the lagged correlation coefficients are positive. This table presents the Pearson correlations between U.S. monthly equity returns (one month lagged) and each of the fifteen other exchange-rate adjusted equity markets around the world. As would be expected, none of the lagged correlations are statistically significant at the .05 level. If lagged correlations were significant, then it would be possible to develop profitable trading rules to exploit this pattern. Our interest is whether these correlations are on average positive. Eleven correlations are positive, whereas four are negative. Assuming the signs followed a Bernoulli process, if the probability of having a positive or negative sign were fifty percent each, the chance of finding eleven or more positive signs is a mere 5.9%.

Also included on Table 2 is the correlation of the United States monthly returns (lagged one month) with an equally-weighted world portfolio (absent the U.S.). The lagged correlation is +0.0329. In some additional work, not reported in Table 2, the world portfolio has a complex lagged correlation structure with the U.S. extending back at least 12 months, with the sixth, eighth, and twelfth month being the most significant.

Our model shows that the correlation coefficients across countries will rise over longer holding periods whenever the lagged correlation coefficients are positive. The natural question is: Do correlation coefficients actually rise as the holding period is lengthened? Figure 3 presents the average correlation coefficients for each holding period from weekly through annual. The horizontal axis displays the number of months in the holding period. The first observation at .25 months represents weekly returns. The weekly average correlation coefficients came from Joy, Panton, Reilly, and Martin [6]. Their data included twelve countries for the years 1963-1972, which gives 66 different correlation coefficients. The monthly, bi-monthly, quarterly, and semi-annual are the average of 120 correlation coefficients for the period February, 1970 through June, 1988. The annual data extends from 1970 to 1987, but due to missing data for New Zealand, only fifteen countries are included. The average correlation coefficients in Figure 3 increase at a decreasing rate. The majority of the increase is accomplished within three to six months. Apparently, the size of the lagged correlations of degree greater than six months is enough to continue the increase in the correlation coefficients for holding periods longer than six months. The average weekly correlation coefficient is 0.1345. At one month, the average correlation coefficient more than doubles to 0.3068. Bi-monthly returns are even more positively correlated, with a correlation coefficient of 0.3796. The quarterly, semi-annual, and annual correlation coefficients are 0.4404, 0.4561, and 0.4462, respectively.

The interpretation of this result is clear. Returns on world equity markets, adjusted for exchange rates, are more closely correlated over longer holding periods. The higher correlation results whenever the time-lagged correlations are on average positive. Portfolio diversification of assets which are more highly correlated will not result in as substantial a risk-reducing benefit as would be the case with asset returns which display lower correlations.

The usual demonstration of the benefits of diversification plots the average portfolio standard deviation or variance of equally-weighted random portfolios of N-securities over increasing numbers of securities. Using the same general methodology, we randomly form without replacement ten portfolios for each N country returns, where N varies from 2 through 15. Since each country's return is already a diversified market index, the benefits of international diversification are already much smaller than forming portfolios of individual securities across countries. For the 16-country portfolio, there is only one portfolio without replacement. For the 1-country portfolio, we used the average of all 16 countries standard deviation. Figure 4 displays the well-known risk-reducing benefits of international diversification. This graph uses one month return data for 221 months. The mean standard deviation declines 44.5% from the typical one-country to the sixteen-country standard deviation.

Forming ten random portfolios without replacement for two-month, three- month, and six-month returns, using the identical methodology for

Table 2

Lagged Correlations of One Month Returns

With U.S. Returns: 1970-1988

Country	Lagged Correlation
Australia	.0524
Austria	.0674
Belgium	-.0155
Canada	-.0244
France	.0428
Germany	.0448
Italy	.0490
Japan	.0782
Netherlands	.0511
New Zealand	.0010
Norway	-.0370
Spain	.0257
Sweden	.0487
Switzerland	.0730
U. K.	-.0699
World Portfolio (Equally-Weighted Excluding U.S.)	.0329

Note: Lagged correlations are the correlation coefficients between the exchange rate adjusted returns in the U.S. last month and exchange rate adjusted returns in 15 other countries in this month for 221 months. World Portfolio is the correlation coefficient between the U.S. last month and the exchange rate adjusted return of an equally-weighted 15 country portfolio.

Figure 3

Mean Correlation Coefficients

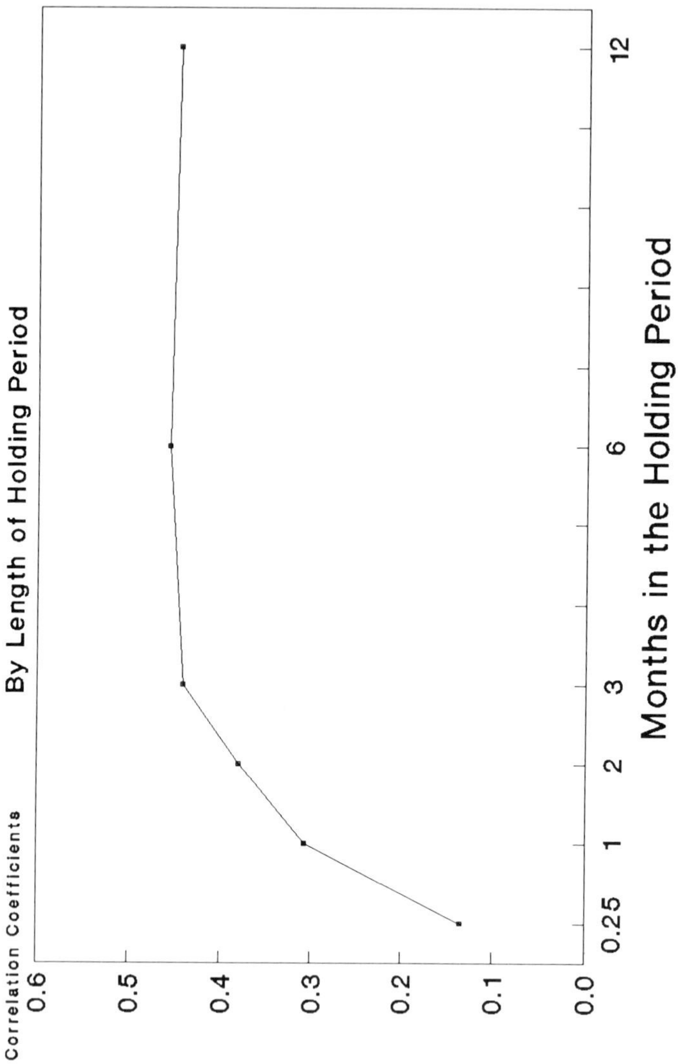

one-month returns, is also plotted on Figure 4. Two month returns, r_2, are generated as the product of two exchange-rate adjusted returns, r_t, as in the formula:

$$r_2 = [(1+r_{t-1})(1+r_t)-1]. \qquad (11)$$

The number of observations for two-month returns declines from 221 to 110. Here the risk-reducing benefits are attenuated as only a 40.0% reduction in standard deviation is effected. Figure 4 uses this same approach for quarterly and semi-annual data. Returns for these longer holding periods extend the formula in (11) for additional months. The sample size declines for each successive lengthening of the holding period. The risk reduction for quarterly and semi-annual diversification are 36.7%, and 40.4%, respectively.

For the annual data on Figure 4, exchange-rate adjusted annual returns for 1960-1987 were used to provide 28 years of data. The risk-reducing benefits decline to a mere 29.1 percent reduction for annual data over the period 1960-1987 for which Ibbotson annual data is available. In nontechnical language, the graphs are <u>flatter</u> as the holding period is extended. The greater covariation found for longer holding periods acts to attenuate the risk-reducing benefits of diversification internationally. Nevertheless, Figure 4 continues to be downward sloping indicating that there remains substantial benefit to international diversification.

For comparison also on Figure 4 includes the U.S. only portfolio over each of these holding periods. This represents the non-internationally diversified portfolio available to U.S. investors. The exact data is presented in Table 3. For one-month returns, the U.S. only portfolio has a standard deviation of 4.9%, whereas the standard deviation of the 16-country portfolio is 4.1%. International diversification gives favorable comparisons with the U.S. only portfolio for two-month and quarterly returns. However, Figure 4 visually demonstrates the interesting result that for holding periods of six-months or longer, non-international diversification dominates international diversification with respect to standard deviation. For the annual data, the U.S. only data offers a standard deviation of 16.9% with an average return of 11.1% over this 28 year period, whereas the

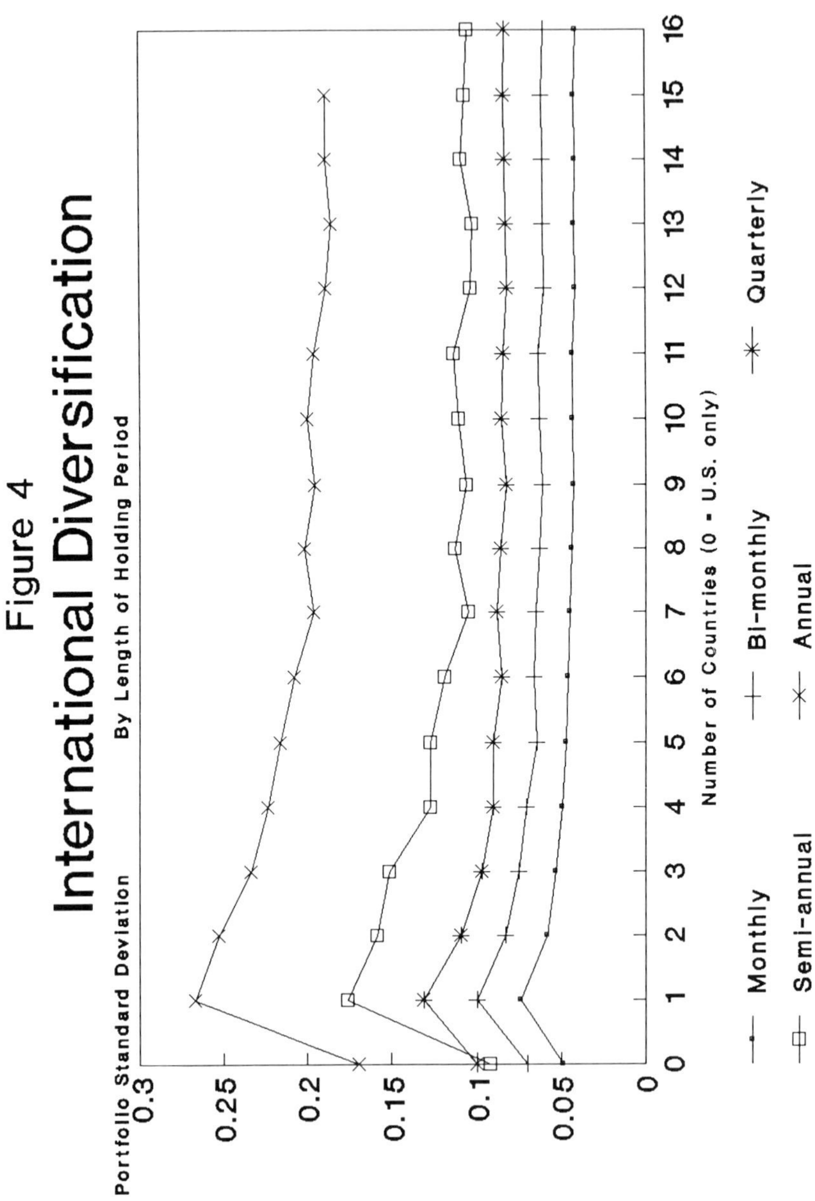
Figure 4
International Diversification
By Length of Holding Period
Portfolio Standard Deviation
0.3
0.25
0.2
0.15
0.1
0.05
0
0 1 2 3 4 5 6 7 8 9 10 11 12 13 14 15 16
Number of Countries (0 = U.S. only)
Monthly
Bi-monthly
Quarterly
Semi-annual
Annual

Table 3

International Diversification by Length of Holding Period

No. of Countries	One Month	Two Months	Three Months	Six Months	Twelve Month
U.S. only	0.0490	0.0700	0.1000	0.0920	0.1690
1	0.0739	0.1000	0.1311	0.1762	0.2665
2	0.0585	0.0829	0.1092	0.1588	0.2524
3	0.0533	0.0750	0.0972	0.1516	0.2333
4	0.0497	0.0706	0.0901	0.1274	0.2235
5	0.0472	0.0646	0.0902	0.1272	0.2160
6	0.0463	0.0661	0.0852	0.1188	0.2080
7	0.0452	0.0651	0.0880	0.1049	0.1961
8	0.0438	0.0629	0.0858	0.1126	0.2018
9	0.0427	0.0615	0.0827	0.1063	0.1954
10	0.0435	0.0628	0.0854	0.1107	0.1998
11	0.0436	0.0637	0.0843	0.1131	0.1959
12	0.0417	0.0603	0.0821	0.1035	0.1890
13	0.0421	0.0607	0.0826	0.1021	0.1855
14	0.0417	0.0609	0.0832	0.1091	0.1889
15	0.0420	0.0615	0.0838	0.1065	0.1890
16	0.0410	0.0600	0.0830	0.1050	

Note: Each entry is the mean portfolio standard deviation of ten random equally-weighted portfolios. The U.S. only portfolio is given first. The 1 portfolio is the mean standard deviation of the 16 individual countries. The time period is 2/70 through 6/88 for the one month through the six month holding period. For the annual holding period, the time was 1/60 to 6/88, and New Zealand is excluded.

15-country equally- weighted portfolio including the U.S. has a higher standard deviation of 18.9% with a higher exchange rate adjusted return of 14.2%. A diversified U.S. investors' standard deviation is higher with international diversification over longer holding periods because (1) the foreign markets display greater inherent volatility than the U.S., and (2) the correlation among markets increases as the holding period is increased.

VI. Conclusions

Diversification across international markets offers well-known risk-reducing benefits in the same fashion as diversification domestically reduces portfolio return variance. Portfolio standard deviation is cut nearly in half for one-month returns by diversifying across 16 industrialized security markets. However, these benefits are greatly attenuated when the time horizon is extended to bi-monthly, quarterly, semi-annual, or annual returns. The risk reduction of diversification is cut to 29.1% for annual holding periods.

We demonstrate that the correlation coefficient across countries for longer holding periods is a function of the contemporaneous (one-month) correlation coefficient, each market's one-month standard deviation, and lagged correlation coefficients across markets. If the lagged correlation coefficients are generally positive, the longer holding period correlation coefficient across countries will be greater than the correlation coefficient found for shorter holding periods.

We find that the correlation coefficients do rise as the holding period is lengthened. This implies that international diversification is relatively less valuable for investors with longer investment horizons. International diversification continues to offer risk-reducing benefits for six-month and annual holding periods; however, the non-internationally diversified U.S. only portfolio has lower overall return standard deviation.

NOTES

[1]Michael R Sesit, "Crash Highlights Perils of Linked Market," Wall

Street Journal, Friday, November 13, 1987, p. 8, gives data for ten countries.

[2]This is only an approximation as the product, $(a_1)^*(a_2)$, compounds interest on interest in the exact formula. However, the product is very small and can be ignored. The presentation is simplified by this approximation and the conclusions are not altered.

[3]Young [16] provides a proof. Assume a security with price P undergoes a large number of transactions per period. Assuming a finite variance, the distribution Y(t) of price changes for a two-unit period has form:

$$Y(t) = (\ln P_2 - \ln P_0) = (\ln P_2 - \ln P_1) + (\ln P_1 - \ln P_0)$$

which is the sum of the two unit intervals. If we assume that the unit intervals are each serially independent, the central limit theorem implies that the distribution will have a variance which is twice as large as the variance of the unit interval. Similar reasoning shows the variance of a three period holding period to be equal to three times the unit variance if returns are serially uncorrelated. In general, if each period is independent, the holding period variance for t periods is:

$$\sigma_t^2 = t\sigma_1^2$$

where σ_1^2 is the unit interval variance.

[4]If series a and b are perfectly correlated and returns within each series are serially uncorrelated, then the lagged correlation coefficients must be zero. However, if series a and b are not perfectly correlated but the returns within each series are serially uncorrelated, then the lagged correlation coefficients may be negative, positive, or zero. As a proof, suppose Cov(s,t) > 0. In that case:

$$\{Cov(a_{2k-1},b_{2k-1}) + Cov(a_{2k-1},b_{2k}) + Cov(a_{2k},b_{2k-1}) + Cov(a_{2k},b_{2k})\} > 0$$

Then the two contemporaneous covariances must be greater than the negative of the two lagged correlation coefficients:

$$Cov(a_{2k-1},b_{2k-1}) + Cov(a_{2k},b_{2k}) > -Cov(a_{2k},b_{2k-1}) - Cov(a_{2k-1},b_{2k})$$

This condition can be met if the lagged covariances are positive, negative, or zero.

[5]This result holds whether serial correlation across the unit returns is positive or negative. If there is positive serial correlation, then Young [16] showed that $\sigma_s^2 > 2\ \sigma_a^2$. In this case the correlation coefficient in (10) will be slightly smaller. If serial correlation is negative, as some of the time diversification literature suggests, then the two-period correlation coefficient is even larger. In either case, the larger and and more positive are the lagged correlation coefficients ($_{a2k-1,b2k-1}$, $_{a2k,b2k-1}$), the greater will be correlation coefficients for longer holding periods.

REFERENCES

1. Eugene F. Fama and Kenneth R. French. "Permanent and Temporary Components of Stock Prices." Journal of Political Economy 96 (April 1988), 246-273.

2. Eugene F. Fama and Kenneth R. French. "Forecasting Returns on Corporate Bonds and Common Stocks." Working Paper No. 220, University of Chicago, (December 1987).

3. Lawrence Fisher and James H. Lorie. A Half Century of Returns on Stocks and Bonds. Chicago: The University of Chicago Graduate School, 1977.

4. Joanne Hill and Thomas Schneeweis. "International Diversification of Equities and Fixed Income Securities." Journal of Financial Research 6 (Winter 1983), 333-343.

5. Jimmy E. Hilliard. "The Relationship Between Equity Indices On World Exchanges." Journal of Finance 34, (March 1979), 103-114.

6. O. Maurice Joy, Don B. Panton, Frank K. Reilly, and Stanley A. Martin. "Co-Movements of International Equity Markets." The Financial Review 11 (February 1976), 1-20.

7. Gary G. Schlarbaum, Wilbur G. Lewellen, and Ronald C. Lease. "Realized Returns of Common Stock Investments: The Experience of Individual Investors." Journal of Business, 51 (1978), 299-325.

8. William P. Lloyd and Richard L. Haney. "Time Diversification: Surest Route to Lower Risk." The Journal of Portfolio Management 6 (Spring 1980), 5-9.

9. William P. Lloyd and Naval K. Modani. "Stocks, Bonds, Bills, and Time Diversification." The Journal of Portfolio Management 9 (Spring 1983), 7-10.

10. Andrew W. Lo and A. Craig MacKinlay. "When are Contrarian Profits Due to Stock Market Overreaction?" Working Paper, November 1988.

11. Richard W. McEnally. "Time Diversification: Surest Route to Lower Risk?" The Journal of Portfolio Management 11 (Winter 1985), 24-26.

12. William Reichenstein. "On Standard Deviation and Risk: The Time Horizon Has a Lot to do With Perceived Risk." The Journal of Portfolio Management 13 (Winter 1987), 39-40.

13. Bruno H. Solnik. "Why Not Diversify Internationally Rather than Domestically?" Financial Analysts Journal 30 (June/July 1974), 48-54.

14. Bruno H. Solnik. "The International Pricing of Risk: An Empirical Investigation of the World Capital Market Structure." Journal of

Finance 29 (June 1974), 365-78.

15. Simon Wheatley. "Some Tests of International Equity Integration." Journal of Financial Economics 21 (1988), 177-212.

16. William E. Young. "Random Walk of Stock Prices: A Test of the Variance-Time Function." Econometrica 39 (September 1971), 795-812.

Recent Developments in International Banking
and Finance, S.J. Khoury (editor)

CHAPTER X

Linkages of National Stock Markets: Statistical Evidence Before, During and After the October 1987 Crash

A.G. Malliaris

Jorge L. Urrutia*

* Dr. A.G. Malliaris is the Walter F. Mullady, Sr. Professor of Business Administration, Department of economics and Dr. Jorge L. Urrutia is Assistant Professor, Department of Finance, both at Loyola University of Chicago. We are deeply indebted to Professors Paul Newbold, C.W.J. Granger, and Michael K. Salemi for useful conversations and suggestions and to anonymous referees of this journal for detailed suggestions on two earlier versions. We also thank numerous colleagues for constructive comments among whom we wish to mention Monzurul Hoque, Panos Evangelou, Marc Hayford and George Kaufman. Finally we are grateful to Wichai Saenghirunwattana for extensive research and computational assistance.

Introduction

THE U.S. GREAT BULL MARKET OF THE 1980'S began on August 12, 1982, when the Dow Jones Industrial Average (DJIA) index closed at 776.92. After that and for five consecutive years the market continued to climb until it reached a peak on August 25, 1987, when the DJIA closed at 2722.42. Over these five years the DJIA gained 1945.50 points, that is, it more than tripled in value. On October 19, 1987, the equity market crashed. On that day, the New York Stock Exchange experienced the greatest one-day drop in stock prices in history. Actually the DJIA dropped 508 points from the closing price on Friday, October 16 of 2246.74 to the closing price on Monday, October 19 of 1738.74. This was a drop of 22.6% in a single day. (As a reference, recall that the one day drop in the October 1929 crash was only 12.8%). In addition, on the so-called Black Monday more than 600 million shares were traded on the NYSE. This figure was twice as large as the previous one-day volume record.

Black Monday was the climax of the market crash, but the crash did not occur instantly and without warning. Indeed, between October 5 and October 16, the DJIA dropped from 2640.18 to 2246.74, that is, a drop of 15% or about 400 points. Subsequent days also showed low prices and record levels of trading volume. However, the market recovered quickly and by Thursday October 26, 1987, the DJIA recorded a large point increase.

As Roll (1988) points out, the October 19, 1987 equity market crash has created at least one new industry: the production of explanations for the crash. Among the most popular explanation is the one known as the "twin tower" theory. According to this theory, the U.S. trade deficit and the U.S. budget deficit appear to be a possible cause of the crash. Followers of the twin tower theory argue that the economic reality in the U.S. did not justify the steadily climbing stock prices of the 1982-1987 bull market and that the market crash had to occur, sooner or later. Others claim that the real cause of the crash could be found at the over-inflated equity prices generated through a speculative bubble during the earlier period of the bull market. Roll (1988) elaborates on both of these possible explanations.

Other popular explanations refer to the US market's institutional structures and practices, such as portfolio insurance, program trading, the micro structure of the organized exchange specialists, margin rules, and the absence of trading suspension and limitations on price movements. In fact, several commission reports about the crash such as, The Task Force Report (1988), are centered around these institutional forms. In this respect Roll (1988), Leland and Rubinstein (1988), Miller and associates (1987), among others, found no strong evidence that institutional structures and practices were the main cause of the crash. In addition, commission reports, as the one prepared by Miller and associates (1987) for the Chicago Mercantile Exchange refuted the general consensus that trading in futures markets was the cause of the domestic increase in trading volume and price volatility in the equity market. More about the October market crash, its possible causes, and criticisms of the proposed explanations and suggested recommendations may be found in Greenwald and Stein (1988), Grammill and Marsh (1988), Leland and Rubinstein (1988), Harris (1989), and Blume, MacKinlay and Terker (1989).

The 1980's have witnessed an increasing internationalization of financial markets. Therefore, it was not surprising that the crash affected also markets in Europe and Asia. Indeed, the most important markets around the world displayed dramatic declines on October 19 and October 20. Roll (1988) indicates that, with few exceptions, several countries experienced most of their declines prior to the opening of the U.S. market on October 19, 1987. The most important exception is Japan whose drop on October 19 was much smaller than that of New York. However, on Tuesday October 20, the Nikkei index dropped almost 15%. Moreover, Roll claims that prices fell first in non-Japanese Asian stock markets. In addition, several markets continued to fall through the end of October. This information seems to suggest that the crash may not even have started in the United States.

Statistics presented by Roll (1988) show a great disparity of returns and low correlation coefficients for a large number of financial markets for the most recent period just prior to the crash. However the correlation coefficients between various markets increased dramatically during October 1987. Furthermore, the returns for major markets were all negative on the month of the crash. That is, the only month when all markets moved together was October,1987. Roll concludes that the market crash was caused by some international "trigger" or underlying fundamental factor, and not by the institutional defects of the United States market. In fact, the global fall of equity markets in October 1987 suggests that the markets may feed on each other, and that some causal relationship between markets may exist.

Finally, a questionnaire survey conducted by Shiller (1987) indicates that U.S. institutional investors believed that news of the drop of the U.S. stock prices and the subsequent self-amplifying sequence of reactions to price declines were the primary cause of the October crash. Also a survey of institutional investors in Japan conducted by Shiller, Konya and Tsutsui (1987) suggested that events in the United States were the proximate source of the market crash in Japan.

The international fundamental common factor proposed by Roll suggests the hypothesis that the crash was initiated in non-Japanese Asian markets and from there was expanded to Europe, the United States, and finally reached Japan. The several commission reports and the survey of American and Japanese institutional investors, on the other hand, seem to indicate that the world crash started in the United States and then expanded to European and Asian markets.

The purpose of this paper is to test these two opposite hypotheses. In fact, this paper attempts to throw some light on the linkages of major national stock market indexes. The questions of causality or lead-lag relationships are empirically investigated for four major equity markets: New York, Tokyo, London, and Frankfurt. Causality tests based on the Granger and the Modified Sims models are conducted for time periods before, during and after the October 1987 market crash. The rest of the paper is organized as follows: section I contains the description of the two tests of causality used in the paper; section II describes the data and explains the design of the empirical tests; section III presents and discusses the major results of the tests; and finally section IV summarizes the conclusions of our study.

I. Tests for Granger Causal Ordering

Our empirical tests are based on the Granger and the Modified Sims tests of causality. Therefore, a brief description of these tests is desirable.

The causal tests of Granger and Sims are essentially tests of the predictive ability of time series models. A time series $\{Y_t\}$ causes another time series $\{X_t\}$ if present X can be predicted better by using past values of Y than by not doing so, other relevant information, including the past of X, being used in either case. More formally, let $\sigma^2(X/U_t)$ be the variance of X given the information in the universe accumulated since time t-1 and let $\bar{U}$ and $\bar{U}-\bar{Y}$ be the information in the universe with past values of Y included and excluded, respectively.

The following definitions are of interest:

i) Unidirectional causality:

If $\sigma^2(X/\bar{U}) < \sigma^2(X/\bar{U}-\bar{Y})$,

then Y is causing or leading X, denoted by $Y \rightarrow X$.

ii) Bi-directional or feedback:

If $\sigma^2(X/\bar{U}) < \sigma^2(X/\bar{U}-\bar{Y})$,

$\sigma^2(Y/\bar{U}) < \sigma^2(Y/\bar{U}-\bar{X})$,

then feedback is occurring, denoted by $Y \leftrightarrow X$.

iii) Instantaneous or contemporaneous causality:

If $\sigma^2(X/\bar{\bar{Y}}) < \sigma^2(X/\bar{U})$,

where $\bar{\bar{Y}}$ indicates the current value of Y, we say that instantaneous causality, denoted by $Y_t \rightarrow X_t$ is occurring.

A description of several testable forms of Granger's causality can be found in Pierce and Haugh (1977), Geweke et al (1982), and Guilkey and Salemi (1982).

1. The Granger Test

The simple causal model of the Granger test (1969) is

$$X_t = c_0 + \sum_{i=1}^{m} a_i Y_{t-i} + \sum_{j=1}^{m} b_j X_{t-j} + \epsilon_t \tag{2-1}$$

$$Y_t = \delta_0 + \sum_{i=1}^{m} \alpha_i X_{t-i} + \sum_{j=1}^{m} \beta_j Y_{t-j} + \mu_t \, . \tag{2-2}$$

The definition of causality given above implies that Y is causing X provided some a_i is not zero in equation (2-1). Similarly, X is causing Y if some α_i is not zero in equation (2-2). If both of these events occur, there is a feedback. The F-statistic is calculated by estimating the above expression in both unconstrained and constrained forms (full and reduced models) and may be written as:

$$F_1 = \frac{(SSE_r - SSE_f) \; / \; m}{SSE_f \; / \; (T-2m-1)}$$

where

SSE_r, SSE_f	=	Residual sum squares of the reduced and full models, respectively.
T	=	Total number of observations.

F_1 follows a χ^2/m distribution and corresponds to a Wald test because the SSE_f, the unrestricted regression statistic, rather than SSE_r, the restricted statistic, is used to estimate the residual variance (see, i.e., Guilkey and Salemi (1982), Schmidt (1976), and Geweke, Meese, and Dent (1983)).

A more general model with contemporaneous causality can be constructed by including the current values of X and Y in equations (2-1) and (2-2), respectively. The contemporaneous equation models imply that X and Y may affect each other contemporaneously through a_0 and

a_0. However, the null hypotheses with contemporaneous causality differ from those which test Granger causality because they allow the coefficient at lag zero to enter the model. The null hypotheses with contemporaneous causality are tested with an F-statistic. Indeed, the possibility of "instantaneous causality" is ruled out in tests of Granger causality. Authors, such as Granger (1969), Geweke (1978), Koch and Ragan (1986), and Kawaller, P. Koch and T. Koch (1987), provide detailed discussion of this approach.

2. The Modified Sims model

Theorem 2 of Sims (1972) establishes that when causality runs from X to Y we can expect that no future values of X would enter the regression of Y on current and past X. Sims' test of causality consists in regressing Y on past and future values of X, and, if causality runs from X to Y only, the regression coefficients of future values of X should be insignificantly different from zero as a group. Because the residuals are generally serially correlated, a feasible generalized least squares estimator or an ad hoc prefilter must be employed in such applications of the Sims test.

There is a variation of the Sims test suggested by Geweke et al. (1983) described in detail by Guilkey and Salemi (1982). This variation is known as the Modified Sims test and it corrects for serial correlation by including lagged values of Y in the regression rather than using the generalized least squares procedure of the Sims test. The Modified Sims test is based on OLS estimation of

$$Y_t = c_0 + \sum_{i=-LF}^{LL} a_i X_{t-i} + \sum_{j=1}^{m} b_j Y_{t-j} + \epsilon_t \tag{2-3}$$

The test that Y does not cause X is the test that $a_i = 0$ for $i = -1,...,-LF$. Equation (2-3) is estimated in unconstrained and constrained forms and the test of no causality is based on the following statistic:

$$F_2 = \frac{(SSE_r - SSE_f) \ / \ LF}{SSE_f \ / \ (T-LF-LL-P-2)} .$$

F_2 follows a χ^2/LF distribution (see, i.e.,Guilkey and Salemi (1982)).

Similarly, the test that X does not cause Y is the test that $\alpha_i = 0$, for i = -1,...,-LF in the following regression:

$$X_t = \delta_0 + \sum_{i=-LF}^{LL} \alpha_i Y_{t-i} + \sum_{j=1}^{m} \beta_j X_{t-j} + \mu_t \tag{2-4}$$

II. Sample Selection and Design of The Empirical Tests

The data sample corresponds to daily closing prices for the following major equity market indexes: the New York S&P 500, the Tokyo Nikkei, the London FT-30, and the Frankfurt DAX. The prices have been collected from the Wall Street Journal for the time period April 22, 1987 through December 31, 1988. All data for the foreign indexes have been converted to a common base: the US dollar using the spot exchange rates reported in the Wall Street Journal for the corresponding data. Lack of available data causes a synchronization problem between the closing stock indexes and foreign exchange rates.

Our purpose is to investigate the lead-lag relationships between the four market indexes before, during, and after the market crash. To do this we have divided the data into three sets:

i) April 22, 1987 through September 22, 1987: i.e.,the period before the market crash;

ii) September 23, 1987 through November 23, 1987: i.e.,the period of the market crash;

iii) November 24, 1987 through December 31, 1988: i.e.,the period after the market crash.

Note that we use September 23, 1987 to November 23, 1987 as the period of the market crash to have enough observations for our causality tests.

Tests of unidirectional, bi-directional or feedback, and contemporaneous causal relationships are constructed for the three data sets. The causality tests are based on the unconstrained and constrained forms of the Granger and Modified Sims models presented in equations (2-1) through (2-4), assuming 5 lags.

Testing for lead-lag relationships between international markets presents a problem of data synchronization due to time-zone shifts.

Since we use close-to-close daily prices and returns in our empirical tests, the observations really line up like this:

<---- R(Tokyo,t) ----- X ----- R(Tokyo,t+1) ---->
<---- R(New York,t) --*-- X ----- R(New York,t+1) -->

For example, the Tuesday NY return (NY Monday close to NY Tuesday close) overlaps with the Wednesday Tokyo return (Tokyo Tuesday close to Tokyo Wednesday close). Therefore, a world surge which occurs at time * will show up in time t in New York return and the time t+1 Tokyo return, but if something happens in Tokyo at time t will show in New York also at time t. We have solved the synchronization problem by making the necessary adjustments of the data. For instance, equations (2-1) and (2-2) for New York and Tokyo look like this:

$$R_t^{NY} = c_0 + \sum_{i=1}^{m} a_i R_{t-i}^{T} + \sum_{j=1}^{m} b_j R_{t-j}^{NY} + e_t$$

and,

$$R_{t+1}^{T} = \delta_0 + \sum_{i=1}^{m} \alpha_i R_{t-i}^{NY} + \sum_{j=0}^{m} \beta_j R_{t-j}^{T} + \mu_t$$

where

R_t^{NY} = S&P 500 Market Index return at time t

R_{t+1}^{T} = Nikkei Market Index return at time t+1.

Similar adjustments were made in testing for lead-lag relationships among other markets. Specifically, European market indexes today impact the U.S. market today but the Japanese market is impacted the following trading day. Also, today's activity in the New York market affects European and Japanese markets the following day. Finally activities in the Japanese markets impact European and American markets the same day.

One important problem we have to deal with in this paper is cointegration. Engle and Granger (1987) show that if two nonstationary variables are cointegrated, a vector autoregression in the first differences is misspecified. For example, if New York and Tokyo prices are both nonstationary (follow random walks), but the first differences of each price are stationary, it is said the prices are integrated of order one, i.e. ~ I(1). Now, if the difference between the New York price and the Tokyo price (or any linear combination) is stationary, they are said to be cointegrated. The presence of cointegration can cause the Granger causality tests of equations (2-1) through (2-4) to be misspecified. Therefore, it is necessary to test for cointegration before we run the causality tests. If cointegration is found, an error-correcting model must be constructed.

III. Empirical Tests and Analysis of the Results

Table 1 presents the correlation coefficients between the returns on the four indexes. In computing these correlations we used same day data. Since we did not adjust for the differences in closing times of the exchanges our correlations are biased downwards and should be interpreted as lower bounds. It is interesting to notice that in the period previous to the market crash, the correlation coefficients were generally small and statistically insignificant. During the period of the crash, the correlation coefficients are larger, positive and significant in a statistical sense. For the period after the market crash only the coefficients associated with London are statistically significant. In general, the correlation coefficients are small. Our results agree with the modest correlations found by Roll (1988) for a broader sample of equity indexes. They also support Roll's findings of an increase of these coefficients during the crash. Dwyer and Hafer (1988) using monthly data for the past 31 years, also find no evidence that the levels

TABLE 1
Correlation Coefficients of Daily Returns for Major Stock Market Indexes - US Dollar

A. - Time Period April 22, 1987 - September 22, 1987.

	New York	Tokyo	London
Tokyo	0.10476[a] (0.2829)[b]		
London	-0.22635 (0.0191)	0.05342 (0.5847)	
Frankfurt	0.04476 (0.6471)	-0.08481 (0.3851)	0.15630 (0.1079)

B. - Time Period September 23, 1987 - November 23, 1987.

	New York	Tokyo	London
Tokyo	0.09782 (0.5429)		
London	0.44106 (0.0039)	0.55454 (0.0002)	
Frankfurt	0.39910 (0.0097)	0.50527 (0.0008)	0.68663 (0.0001)

C. - Time Period November 24, 1987 - December 31, 1988.

	New York	Tokyo	London
Tokyo	0.03545 (0.5663)		
London	0.35352 (0.0001)	0.16002 (0.0092)	
Frankfurt	-0.01711 (0.7820)	0.03869 (0.5314)	0.08272 (0.1803)

a. - Pearson Correlation Coefficient
b. - Prob.$>|R|$ under H_0:RHO=0

of stock market indexes for the U.S., Japan, Germany and the United Kingdom are related. Schollhammer and Sand (1987) for daily data of national stock prices from January 1, 1981 through June 30, 1983 find correlation coefficients that are generally low. Khoury, Dodin and Takada (1987) find that the U.S.equity market leads those of Canada, Europe and Japan.

The remaining of this section presents the tests of integration and cointegration, and the Granger and Sims tests of causality.

1. Test Whether is Integrated

As Engle and Granger (1987) point out economic time series must commonly be differenced before the assumption of stationarity can be presumed to hold. To test whether $\ln P_t$ is integrated we run the following Augmented Dickey-Fuller regression:

$$\ln P_t - \ln P_{t-1} = b_0 + b_1 \ln P_{t-1} + \sum_{j=2}^{4} b_j (\ln P_{t-j+1} - \ln P_{t-j}) + \epsilon_t \quad (5)$$

The null hypothesis of the unit root is $H_0{:}b_1 = 0$; that is, $\ln P_t$ is integrated.

The results presented in Table 2 indicate that the null hypothesis cannot be rejected at the 5% or 10% significance level. Thus, $\ln P_t$ is integrated or nonstationary.

2. Test Whether $R_t = \ln(P_t/P_{t-1})$ is Integrated

Given that $\ln P_t$ is nonstationary we proceed to test whether the return, $R_t = \ln(P_t/P_{t-1})$ is stationary. To test whether the returns are integrated we run the following Augmented Dickey-Fuller regression:

$$R_t - R_{t-1} = b_0 + b_1 R_{t-1} + \sum_{j=2}^{4} b_j (R_{t-j+1} - R_{t-j}) + \epsilon_t \quad (6)$$

The null hypothesis of unit root is $H_0{:}b_1=0$. Thus, R_t is integrated. The results presented in Table 3 show that the null hypothesis is rejected at the 5% or 10% significance level. We conclude that the market index returns are stationary and prices are integrated of order one, i.e. $P_t \sim I(1)$.

3. Test for Co-integration between $\ln P_{1t}$ and $\ln P_{2t}$

Engle and Granger (1987) propose several test statistics for testing the null of no-cointegration. In this paper we use the Durbin-Watson statistic and the Dickey-Fuller test. In fact, Engle and Granger (1987) recommend the Durbin-Watson test for its simplicity and indicate that the Dickey-Fuller statistic is more powerful than the Augmented Dickey-Fuller test when it is known that the system is first order (as in our case). The D-W tests of cointegration are based on the following cointegration regression:

$$\ln P_{1t} = b_0 + b_1 \ln P_{2t} + \epsilon_t \qquad (7)$$

The null hypothesis of no-cointegration is $H_0{:}b_1=0$.

Table 4 presents the results of the D-W tests of cointegration. We can observe that the null of no-cointegration is rejected at the 5% or 10% level of significance for all the cointegration regressions corresponding to the sample period of September 23, 1987 through November 23, 1987. We conclude that the logarithms of the prices are cointegrated during the period of the crash. For the period after the crash the null of non-cointegration cannot be rejected. For the period before the crash we obtained mixed results.

The Dickey-Fuller test of cointegration consists of running first the following cointegrating regression:

$$\ln P_{1t} = c_0 + c_1 \ln P_{2t} + \epsilon_t \qquad (8)$$

and then running the following auxiliary Dickey-Fuller regression on the residuals of (4-4):

$$\epsilon_t - \epsilon_{t-1} = -b_1 \epsilon_{t-1} + \mu_t \qquad (9)$$

The null hypothesis is $H_0{:}b_1=0$; that is, $\ln P_{1t}$ and $\ln P_{2t}$ are not cointegrated.

Table 5 exhibits the results of the Dickey-Fuller test of cointegration. The results are mixed and, in general, the null of no-cointegration is rejected less often than in the D-W test, especially for the period during the crash.

Given that the results of the tests of cointegration are mixed we have proceeded as follows: When there is conclusive evidence that the

TABLE 2

Dickey-Fuller Tests Results:
Test Whether ln P_t is integrated

	b_0	b_1	b_2	b_3	b_4
A. - Sample Period : April 22, 1987 - September 22, 1987 (n = 103)					
New York	0.2038	-0.0354	0.0176	0.0983	0.0086
	(0.1113)	(0.0194) (-1.82)	(0.0986)	(0.0979)	(0.0970)
Tokyo	0.6130	-0.1191	-0.4591	-0.2608	-0.0896
	(0.3518)	(0.0684) (-1.74)	(0.1098)	(0.1127)	(0.1000)
London	0.6909	-0.0867	0.1750	-0.1023	0.0912
	(0.2809)	(0.0353) (-2.46)	(0.0960)	(0.0970)	(0.0961)
Frankfurt	0.4992	-0.0853	-0.6757	-0.4416	-0.2096
	(0.3828)	(0.0656) (-1.30)	(0.1089)	(0.1168)	(0.0984)
B. - Sample Period: September 23, 1987 - November 23, 1987 (n = 41)					
	b_0	b_1	b_2	b_3	b_4
New York	0.2485	-0.0455	0.0248	-0.1287	-0.0649
	(0.3116)	(0.0554) (-0.82)	(0.1679)	(0.1653)	(0.1673)
Tokyo	1.3556	-0.2636	-0.2175	-0.0930	0.1761
	(0.7465)	(0.1450) (-0.82)	(0.1900)	(0.1833)	(0.1655)
London	0.3322	-0.0427	0.4013	-0.3126	0.3945
	(0.2703)	(0.0343) (-1.25)	(0.1524)	(0.1554)	(0.1523)
Frankfurt	0.0553	-0.0112	-0.0123	-0.2780	0.1206
	(0.2265)	(0.0394) (-0.30)	(0.1689)	(0.1613)	(0.1680)

C. - Sample Period : November 24, 1987 - December 31, 1988 ($n=264$)

	b_0	b_1	b_2	b_3	b_4
New York	0.3058	-0.0547	-0.2082	-0.1086	-0.0273
	(0.1283)	(0.0230) (-2.38)	(0.0629)	(0.0634)	(0.0617)
Tokyo	0.0864	-0.0158	-0.4185	-0.1899	-0.0622
	(0.0555)	(0.0104) (-1.52)	(0.0619)	(0.0661)	(0.0617)
London	0.3388	-0.0431	0.0653	-0.1190	0.0207
	(0.1215)	(0.0155) (-2.78)	(0.0616)	(0.0610)	(0.0614)
Frankfurt	0.0211	-0.0029	-0.0737	0.0159	0.0005
	(0.0506)	(0.0087) (-0.33)	(0.0626)	(0.0628)	(0.0625)

Notes

- Regressions are of the form:

$$\ln P_t - \ln P_{t-1} = b_0 + b_1 \ln P_{t-1} + \sum_{j=2}^{4} b_j (\ln P_{t-j+1} - \ln P_{t-j}) + \epsilon_t$$

- Standard errors are in parentheses below coefficients (for b_1 the t-statistic is also shown in parentheses)
- n corresponds to the sample size
- The null hypothesis is $b_1=0$ (ln P_t is integrated)

The rejection regions for each sample are the set of values of the t-statistics below the following $\tau\mu$ statistics obtained from Fuller (1976) for a test of size 0.05 and 0.10:

Sample size	5%	10%
50	-2.93	-2.60
100	-2.89	-2.58
250	-2.88	-2.57

The null cannot be rejected at the 5% or 10% significant level: ln P_t is integrated (ln P_t is nonstationary)

TABLE 3

Dickey-Fuller Tests Results:
Test Whether $R_t = \ln P_t/P_{t-1}$ is integrated

A. - Sample Period : April 22, 1987 - September 22, 1987 (n = 102)

	b_0	b_1	b_2	b_3	b_4
New York	0.0938	-1.0140	0.0214	0.1232	0.1153
	(0.1016)	(0.1882)(-5.39)	(0.1632)	(0.1387)	(0.0983)
Tokyo	0.0690	-2.1113	0.5603	0.2219	0.0659
	(0.3446)	(0.3116)(-6.78)	(0.2590)	(0.1843)	(0.1004)
London	0.1447	-0.9423	0.1278	-0.0098	0.1057
	(0.1321)	(0.1811)(-5.20)	(0.1589)	(0.1283)	(0.0986)
Frankfurt	0.2277	-3.1814	1.3722	0.7450	0.2965
	(0.2788)	(0.3371)(-9.44)	(0.2785)	(0.1914)	(0.0960)

B. - Sample Period: September 23, 1987 - November 23, 1987 (n = 40)

	b_0	b_1	b_2	b_3	b_4
New York	-0.6183	-1.0172	0.0307	-0.0920	-0.1797
	(0.7427)	(0.3575)-2.85	(0.2968)	(0.2317)	(0.1649)
Tokyo	-0.1407	-1.4874	0.0777	-0.1428	-0.0353
	(0.6378)	(0.4678)(-3.18)	(0.4031)	(0.2959)	(0.1773)
London	-0.4627	-0.6641	0.0999	-0.2808	0.1429
	(0.4952)	(0.2468)-2.69	(0.2371)	(0.1814)	(0.1635)
Frankfurt	-0.9527	-1.2475	0.2304	-0.0677	0.0443
	(0.5536)	(0.3756)(-3.32)	(0.3204)	(0.2376)	(0.1669)

C. - Sample Period : November 24, 1987 - December 31, 1988 (n=263)

	b_0	b_1	b_2	b_3	b_4
New York	0.0896	-1.7209	0.4707	0.3090	0.2114
	(0.0973)	(0.1513) (-11.37)	(0.1269)	(0.0965)	(0.0604)
Tokyo	0.2312	-1.7019	0.2756	0.0800	0.0118
	(0.1000)	(0.1727) (-9.85)	(0.1442)	(0.1053)	(0.0589)
London	0.0501	-0.9541	0.0041	-0.1155	-0.1130
	(0.0678)	(0.1267) (-7.53)	(0.1080)	(0.0851)	(0.0617)
Frankfurt	0.4289	-1.0703	-0.0058	0.0076	0.0053
	(0.3721)	(0.1305) (-8.20)	(0.1126)	(0.0913)	(0.0621)

Notes

- Regressions are of the form:

$$R_t - R_{t-1} = b_0 + b_1 R_{t-1} + \sum_{j=2}^{4} b_j (R_{t-j+1} - R_{t-j}) + \epsilon_t$$

- Standard errors are in parentheses below coefficients (for b_1 the t-statistic is also shown in parentheses)
- n corresponds to the sample size
- The null hypothesis is $b_1 = 0$ (R_t is integrated)

The rejection regions for each sample are the set of values of the t-statistics below the following τ_μ statistics obtained from Fuller (1976) for a test of size 0.05 and 0.10:

Sample Size	5%	10%
50	-2.93	-2.60
100	-2.89	-2.58
250	-2.88	-2.57

The null is rejected at the 5% or 10% significant level: R_t is not integrated (R_t is stationary or ln P_t is stationary in the first differences).

TABLE 4
Durbin-Watson Tests of Cointegration
Cointegration Regression:

$$\ln P_{1t} = b_0 + b_1 \ln P_{2t} + \epsilon_t$$

$$H_0 : b_1 = 0 \qquad (\ln P_{1t} \ and \ \ln P_{2t} \ are \ not \ cointegrated)$$

A:- Sample Period : April 22, 1987 - September 22, 1987

Dependent Variable	Independent Variable	b_0	b_1	DW*
New York	Tokyo	5.6503(12.06)	0.0150(0.17)	0.039
Tokyo	New York	5.0449(8.51)	0.0171(0.17)	0.493
New York	London	2.2445(2.52)	0.4377(3.90)	0.071
London	New York	6.3122(14.98)	0.2872(3.90)	0.135
New York	Frankfurt	0.9190(2.49)	0.8240(13.02)	0.932
Frankfurt	New York	1.5582(4.74)	0.7468(13.02)	1.428
Tokyo	London	7.0295(7.03)	-0.2371(-1.89)	0.518
London	Tokyo	8.6612(23.19)	-0.1370(-1.89)	0.128
Tokyo	Frankfurt	5.1531(8.12)	-0.0018(-0.02)	0.493
Frankfurt	Tokyo	5.8427(13.09)	-0.0014(-0.02)	0.535
Frankfurt	London	3.2997(3.77)	0.3187(1.90)	0.564
London	Frankfurt	6.6107(14.24)	0.2307(2.90)	0.132

B:- Sample Period : September 23, 1987 - November 23, 1987

Dependent Variable	Independent Variable	b_0	b_1	DW*
New York	Tokyo	-3.9526(-2.58)	1.8582(6.24)	0.827
Tokyo	New York	3.6369(15.04)	0.2690(6.24)	1.408

New York	London	-1.4020(-3.10)	0.8917(15.49)	0.650
London	New York	2.4519(7.02)	0.9646(15.49)	0.598
New York	Frankfurt	0.2693(0.61)	0.9327(12.05)	0.452
Frankfurt	New York	0.9841(2.50)	0.8452(12.05)	0.404
Tokyo	London	2.8543(10.25)	0.2914(8.23)	1.509
London	Tokyo	-3.3438(-2.46)	2.1778(8.23)	0.877
Tokyo	Frankfurt	3.4947(13.77)	0.2884(6.51)	1.200
Frankfurt	Tokyo	3.5643(-2.50)	1.8053(6.51)	0.571
Frankfurt	London	-1.1346(-3.26)	0.8725(19.69)	0.366
London	Frankfurt	1.9000(6.27)	1.0415(19.69)	0.363

C:- Sample Period : November 24, 1987 - December 31, 1988

Dependent Variable	Independent Variable	b_0	b_1	DW*
New York	Tokyo	3.8197(34.14)	0.3289(15.67)	0.297
Tokyo	New York	-2.8685(-5.48)	1.4711(15.67)	0.191
New York	London	2.0148(4.56)	0.4533(8.06)	0.154
London	New York	5.4086(17.85)	0.4378(8.06)	0.078
New York	Frankfurt	5.2634(173.61)	0.0566(10.94)	0.215
Frankfurt	New York	-25.0389(-8.88)	5.5371(10.94)	0.093
Tokyo	London	-4.4641(-5.25)	1.2478(11.52)	0.070
London	Tokyo	6.4124(51.43)	0.2695(11.52)	0.101
Tokyo	Frankfurt	4.6472(72.10)	0.1173(10.62)	0.055
Frankfurt	Tokyo	-7.8532(-6.10)	2.5651(10.62)	0.040
Frankfurt	London	-15.0436(-3.20)	2.6580(4.43)	0.023
London	Frankfurt	7.6959(222.74)	0.0263(4.43)	0.069

Note: t-statistics in parentheses
*DW crit at 5% = 0.386, at 10% = 0.322

TABLE 5
Dickey-Fuller Tests of Cointegration

Cointegration Equation:

$$\ln P_{1t} = c_0 + c_1 \ln P_{2t} + \epsilon_t$$

Dickey-Fuller Regression:

$$\epsilon_t - \epsilon_{t-1} = -b_1 \epsilon_{t-1} + \mu_t$$

$H_0: b_1 = 0$ ($\ln P_{1t}$ *and* $\ln P_{2t}$ *are not cointegrated*)

Dependent Variable	Independent Variable	Regression Coefficient, STD error and t-statistic in parentheses*		
		Sample Period		
		4/22/87-9/22/87	9/23/87-11/23/87	11/24/87-12/31/88
New York	Tokyo	0.0233	0.4427	0.1489
		(0.0191)(1.22)	(0.1284)(3.45)	(0.0324)(4.59)
Tokyo	New York	0.2469	0.7176	0.0971
		(0.0639)(3.87)	(0.1514)(4.74)	(0.0263)(3.69)
New York	London	0.0355	0.3281	0.0762
		(0.0257)(1.38)	(0.1179)(2.78)	(0.0239)(3.20)
London	New York	0.1038	(0.2989)	0.0430
		(0.0347)(2.99)	(0.1143)(2.61)	(0.0170)(2.53)

New York	Frankfurt	0.4677	0.2260	0.1132
		(0.0822)(5.69)	(0.1020)(2.22)	(0.0278)(4.08)
Frankfurt	New York	0.7151	0.1903	0.0441
		(0.0934)(7.66)	(0.0991)(1.92)	(0.0187)(2.36)
Tokyo	London	0.2627	0.7746	0.0332
		(0.0652)(4.03)	(0.1532)(5.06)	(0.0163)(2.03)
London	Tokyo	0.1070	0.4702	0.0523
		(0.0336)(3.19)	(0.1313)(3.58)	(0.0194)(2.70)
Tokyo	Frankfurt	(0.2471)	0.6132	0.0357
		(0.0639)(3.37)	(0.1467)(4.18)	(0.0143)(2.50)
Frankfurt	Tokyo	0.2690	0.3003	0.0185
		(0.0662)(4.06)	(0.1146)(2.62)	(0.0123)(1.51)
London	Frankfurt	0.1053	0.1693	0.0425
		(0.0342)(3.08)	(0.0945)(1.79)	(0.0160)(2.65)
Frankfurt	London	0.2820	0.1624	0.0060
		(0.0676)(4.17)	(0.0966)(1.68)	(0.0095)(0.63)

*DF crit at 5% = 3.37, at 10% = 3.03

TABLE 6
Granger Causality Tests

Models

$$I)\quad Y_t = \delta_0 + \sum_{i=1}^{5} \alpha_i X_{t-i} + \sum_{j=1}^{5} \beta_j Y_{t-j} \qquad (X \Rightarrow Y)$$

$$II)\quad X_t = c_0 + \sum_{i=1}^{5} a_i Y_{t-i} + \sum_{j=1}^{5} b_j X_{t-j} \qquad (Y \Rightarrow X)$$

A: Sample Period: April 22, 1987 - September 22, 1987

Direction of Causality	*a_i, α_i Regression Coefficients, STD errors and t-statistics in parentheses* $i=1$	$i=2$	$i=3$	$i=4$	$i=5$	χ^2 $H_0: \sum_{i=1}^{5} a_i = 0$; $\sum_{i=1}^{5} \alpha_i = 0$
New York ⇒ Tokyo	0.5326 (0.3440) (1.55)	0.0818 (0.3329) (0.25)	0.0835 (0.3354) (0.25)	-0.0968 (0.3298) (-0.29)	0.2430 (0.3267) (0.74)	0.63
Tokyo ⇒ New York	-0.0237 (0.0289) (-0.82)	-0.0499 (0.0332) (-1.51)	0.0475 (0.0348) (1.36)	0.0515 (0.0345) (1.49)	-0.0202 (0.0306) (-0.66)	2.59
New York ⇒ London	-0.1871 (0.1361) (-1.38)	0.3312 (0.1350) (2.45)	-0.0423 (0.1385) (-0.31)	-0.1806 (0.1406) (-1.29)	0.0494 (0.1404) (0.35)	1.88

London ⇒ New York	-0.0679 (0.0874) (-0.78)	0.0131 (0.0896) (0.15)	0.0113 (0.0885) (0.13)	0.0215 (0.0863) (0.25)	-0.1160 (0.0829) (-1.40)	0.52
New York ⇒ Frankfurt	0.7422 (0.1934) (3.84)*	0.8010 (0.1878) (4.27)*	0.3774 (0.1933) (1.95)*	0.4567 (0.1946) (2.35)*	0.5278 (0.1927) (2.74)*	9.74*
Frankfurt ⇒ New York	-0.0208 (0.0376) (-0.55)	-0.0228 (0.0479) (-0.48)	-0.0447 (0.0503) (-0.89)	0.0106 (0.0464) (0.23)	-0.0155 (0.0368) (-0.42)	0.61
London ⇒ Tokyo	-0.2311 (0.2581) (-0.90)	-0.1141 (0.2600) (-0.44)	-0.0527 (0.2554) (-0.21)	-0.3008 (0.2536) (-1.19)	-0.1152 (0.2444) (-0.47)	0.63
Tokyo ⇒ London	0.0815 (0.0373) (2.19)*	-0.0138 (0.0443) (-0.31)	0.0046 (0.0460) (0.10)	0.0034 (0.0439) (0.08)	-0.0058 (0.0382) (-0.15)	1.55
Frankfurt ⇒ Tokyo	-0.0088 (0.1141) (-0.08)	-0.0441 (0.1426) (-0.31)	0.0323 (0.1507) (0.21)	0.0233 (0.1420) (0.16)	0.1562 (0.1144) (1.37)	0.64
Tokyo ⇒ Frankfurt	-0.0349 (0.0857) (-0.41)	-0.0509 (0.097[illegible]) (-0.52)	-0.0035 (0.1004) (-0.03)	0.0420 (0.0974) (0.43)	0.0682 (0.0845) (0.81	0.22
London ⇒ Frankfurt	-0.2920 (0.2287) (-1.28)	-0.0787 (0.2328) (-0.34)	-0.0899 (0.2286) (-0.39)	0.2763 (0.2261) (1.22)	0.2340 (0.2271) (1.03)	1.11
Frankfurt ⇒ London	-0.0566 (0.0486) (-1.17)	-0.0859 (0.0592) (-1.45)	-0.0510 (0.0625) (-0.82)	-0.0376 (0.0592) (-0.64)	-0.0028 (0.0470) (-0.06)	0.53

χ^2 crit at 5% = 11.07, at 10% = 9.24

TABLE 6 (cont.)
Granger Causality Tests

Models

$$I)\quad Y_t = \delta_0 + \sum_{i=1}^{5} \alpha_i X_{t-i} + \sum_{j=1}^{5} \beta_j Y_{t-j} \qquad (X \Rightarrow Y)$$

$$II)\quad X_t = c_0 + \sum_{i=1}^{5} a_i Y_{t-i} + \sum_{j=1}^{5} b_j X_{t-j} \qquad (Y \Rightarrow X)$$

B: Sample Period: September 23, 1987 - November 23, 1987

Direction of Causality	a_i, α_i *Regression Coefficients, STD errors and t-statistics in parentheses* $i=1$	$i=2$	$i=3$	$i=4$	$i=5$	χ^2 $H_0: \sum_{i=1}^{5} a_i = 0;\ \sum_{i=1}^{5} \alpha_i = 0$
New York ⇒ Tokyo	0.4234 (0.1762) (2.40)*	0.3733 (0.1838) (2.03)*	0.3805 (0.1795) (2.12)*	0.4134 (0.1829) (2.26)*	0.4987 (0.1925) (2.59)*	3.48
Tokyo ⇒ New York	-0.1418 (0.3197) (-0.44)	-0.1098 (0.3713) (-0.30)	-0.0875 (0.3770) (-0.23)	-0.5938 (0.4072) (-1.46)	-0.2002 (0.2787) (-0.72)	0.56

New York ⇒ London	-0.1246 (0.1576) (-0.79)	0.1572 (0.1549) (1.02)	0.0642 (0.1438) (0.45)	-0.2089 (0.1474) (-1.42)	0.2973 (0.1395) (2.13)*	1.85
London ⇒ New York	-0.5642 (0.3709) (-1.52)	0.2617 (0.3666) (0.71)	-0.1483 (0.3301) (-0.45)	0.3819 (0.3345) (1.14)	-0.1721 (0.2719) (-0.63)	0.64
New York ⇒ Frankfurt	0.0284 (0.1630) (0.18)	0.0936 (0.1634) (0.57)	0.0183 (0.1697) (0.11)	-0.1542 (0.1700) (-0.91)	0.1047 (0.1700) (0.62)	0.52
Frankfurt ⇒ New York	-0.5105 (0.2995) (-1.70)	-0.1018 (0.3215) (-0.32)	-0.3914 (0.3166) (-1.24)	0.0664 (0.3110) (0.21)	-0.6961 (0.2623) (-0.37)	0.73
London ⇒ Tokyo	-0.2441 (0.1801) (-1.36)	-0.0658 (0.2141) (-0.31)	-0.0638 (0.2318) (-0.28)	-0.3716 (0.2507) (-1.48)	0.0487 (0.2468) (0.20)	1.36
Tokyo ⇒ London	0.3019 (0.2367) (1.28)	0.3010 (0.2358) (1.28)	0.1485 (0.2453) (0.61)	0.4000 (0.2473) (1.62)	-0.0692 (0.2268) (-0.31)	1.34
Frankfurt ⇒ Tokyo	-0.0135 (0.1983) (-0.07)	0.2098 (0.2608) (0.80)	0.1807 (0.2762) (0.65)	-0.1990 (0.2614) (-0.76)	-0.1261 (0.2186) (-0.58)	0.79
Tokyo ⇒ Frankfurt	-0.0567 (0.2241) (-0.25)	-0.1787 (0.2435) (-0.73)	0.0249 (0.2582) (0.10)	0.3049 (0.2501) (1.22)	0.2351 (0.2491) (0.94)	0.56
London ⇒ Frankfurt	0.5588 (0.2395) (2.33)*	-0.0630 (0.2574) (-0.25)	0.4407 0.2645) (1.66)	-0.0956 (0.2506) (-0.38)	0.4483 (0.2397) (1.87)	1.71
Frankfurt ⇒ London	-0.4571 (0.2315) (-1.98)*	-0.0046 (0.2362) (-0.02)	-0.2397 (0.2557) (-0.94)	0.0174 (0.2361) (0.07)	-0.2259 (0.2409) (-0.94)	0.84

χ^2 crit at 5% = 11.07, at 10% = 9.24

TABLE 6 (cont.)
Granger Causality Tests

Models

$$I)\quad Y_t = \delta_0 + \sum_{i=1}^{5} \alpha_i X_{t-i} + \sum_{j=1}^{5} \beta_j Y_{t-j} \qquad (X \Rightarrow Y)$$

$$II)\quad X_t = c_0 + \sum_{i=1}^{5} a_i Y_{t-i} + \sum_{j=1}^{5} b_j X_{t-j} \qquad (Y \Rightarrow X)$$

C: Sample Period: November 23, 1987 - December 31, 1988

Direction of Causality	a_i, α_i Regression Coefficients, STD errors and t-statistics in parentheses $i=1$	$i=2$	$i=3$	$i=4$	$i=5$	χ^2 $H_0: \sum_{i=1}^{5} a_i = 0$; $\sum_{i=1}^{5} \alpha_i = 0$
New York ⇒ Tokyo	0.0463 (0.0625) (0.74)	0.0299 (0.0632) (0.47)	-0.0689 (0.0633) (-1.09)	0.0338 (0.0631) (0.54)	-0.0600 (0.0625) (-0.96)	0.89
Tokyo ⇒ New York	-0.0073 (0.0608) (-0.12)	0.0038 (0.0659) (0.06)	0.0751 (0.0658) (1.14)	0.0667 (0.0624) (1.07)	-0.0644 (0.0555) (-1.16)	1.03

New York ⇒ London	-0.0165 (0.0467) (-0.35)	0.0133 (0.0468) (0.29)	-0.0163 (0.0468) (-0.35)	0.0382 (0.0466) (0.82)	-0.0611 (0.0465) (-1.31)	0.70
London ⇒ New York	0.0529 (0.0953) (0.56)	-0.0082 (0.0948) (-0.09)	-0.0184 (0.0952) (-0.19)	0.1634 (0.0945) (1.73)	-0.0138 (0.0953) (-0.15)	0.68
New York ⇒ Frankfurt	0.0397 (0.2384) (0.17)	0.1480 (0.2403) (0.62)	0.1115 (0.2413) (0.46)	0.1799 (0.2398) (0.75)	-0.0162 (0.2372) (-0.07)	0.19
Frankfurt ⇒ New York	0.0010 (0.0163) (0.06)	-0.0054 (0.0164) (-0.33)	-0.0070 (0.0164) (-0.43)	0.0116 (0.0164) (0.71)	0.0015 (0.0163) (0.09)	0.16
London ⇒ Tokyo	0.1759 (0.092) (1.91)	0.0102 (0.0916) (0.11)	-0.0093 (0.0924) (-0.10)	0.0995 (0.0916) (1.09)	-0.1528 (0.0914) (-1.67)	1.38
Tokyo ⇒ London	-0.0022 (0.0446) (-0.05)	0.0056 (0.0490) (0.11)	-0.0073 (0.0493) (-0.15)	-0.0509 (0.0461) (-1.10)	-0.0089 (0.0405) (-0.22)	0.32
Frankfurt ⇒ Tokyo	0.0048 (0.0169) (0.28)	-0.0130 (0.0169) (-0.77)	0.0017 (0.0169) (0.10)	0.0091 (0.0168) (0.54)	0.0006 (0.0166) (0.04)	0.20
Tokyo ⇒ Frankfurt	0.1377 (0.2337) (0.59)	-0.6717 (0.2541) (-2.64)*	-0.2707 (0.2561) (-1.06)	-0.1768 (0.2429) (-0.73)	0.2036 (0.2165) (-0.94)	2.13
London ⇒ Frankfurt	0.5171 (0.3440) (1.50)	-0.2444 (0.3417) (-0.72)	0.1555 (0.3443) (0.45)	0.0314 (0.3418) (0.09)	-0.0180 (0.3432) (-0.05)	0.56
Frankfurt ⇒ London	-0.0047 (0.0115) (-0.41)	0.0001 (0.0115) (0.01)	-0.0013 (0.0115) (-0.11)	0.0179 (0.0115) (1.56)	0.0045 (0.0115) (0.40)	0.55

χ^2 crit at 5% = 11.07, at 10% = 9.24

TABLE 7
Tests of Contemporaneous Causality

Models

$$I)\quad Y_t = \delta_0 + \sum_{i=0}^{5} \alpha_i X_{t-i} + \sum_{j=1}^{5} \beta_j Y_{t-j} \qquad (X \Rightarrow Y)$$

$$II)\quad X_t = c_0 + \sum_{i=0}^{5} a_i Y_{t-i} + \sum_{j=1}^{5} b_j X_{t-j} \qquad (Y \Rightarrow X)$$

A: Sample Period: April 22, 1987 - September 22, 1987

Direction of Causality	a_i, α_i *Regression Coefficients, STD errors and t-statistics in parentheses* *i=0*	*i=1*	*i=2*	*i=3*	*i=4*	*i=5*	F_1^* $H_0: \sum_{i=0}^{5} a_i = 0; \sum_{i=0}^{5} \alpha_i = 0$
New York ⇒ Tokyo	0.5531 (0.3392) (1.63)	0.5151 (0.3410) (1.51)	-0.0194 (0.3356) (-0.06)	0.1153 (0.3329) (0.35)	0.0161 (0.3340) (0.05)	0.2192 (0.3240) (0.68)	0.98
Tokyo ⇒ New York	0.0244 (0.029) (0.85)	-0.0096 (0.0331) (-0.29)	-0.0406 (0.0345) (-1.18)	0.0520 (0.0347) (1.49)	0.0540 (0.0343) (1.57)	-0.0187 (0.0304) (-0.61)	2.31*
New York ⇒ London	0.2128 (0.1327) (1.60)	-0.1897 (0.1349) (-1.41)	0.3136 (0.1343) (2.34)*	-0.0428 (0.1373) (-0.31)	-0.1472 (0.1409) (-1.05)	0.0535 (0.1392) (0.38)	2.02*

London ⇒ New York	-0.1542 (0.0842) (-1.83)	-0.0261 (0.0888) (-0.29)	-0.0223 (0.0896) (-0.25)	0.0284 (0.0871) (0.33)	0.0029 (0.0848) (0.03)	-0.1301 (0.0808) (-1.61)	1.06
New York ⇒ Frankfurt	0.6515 (0.1867) (3.49)*	0.7684 (0.1823) (4.2[illegible])*	0.7457 (0.1776) (4.20)*	0.4225 (0.1825) (2.32)*	0.5614 (0.1857) (3.02)*	0.4918 (0.1818) (2.71)*	11.17*
Frankfurt ⇒ New York	0.0018 (0.0381) -0.046	-0.0194 (0.0492) (-0.39)	-0.0216 0.0544 (-0.40)	-0.0438 (0.0535) (-0.82)	0.0111 (0.0476) (0.23)	-0.0156 (0.0372) (-0.42)	0.51
London ⇒ Tokyo	0.0261 (0.2660) (0.10)	-0.2356 (0.2635) (-0.89)	-0.1096 (0.2655) (-0.41)	-0.0552 (0.2581) (-0.21)	-0.2977 (0.2570) (-1.16)	-0.1137 (0.2462) (-0.46)	0.52
Tokyo ⇒ London	0.0526 (0.0368) (1.43)	0.1117 (0.0427) (2.62)*	0.0060 (0.0458) (0.13)	0.0138 (0.0460) (0.30)	0.0083 (0.0438) (0.19)	-0.0041 (0.0380) (-0.11)	1.65
Frankfurt ⇒ Tokyo	0.1371 (0.1140) (1.20)	0.0982 (0.1444) (0.68)	0.0328 (0.1559) (0.21)	0.0803 (0.1555) (0.52)	0.0488 (0.1432) (0.34)	0.1391 (0.1150) (1.21)	0.78
Tokyo ⇒ Frankfurt	0.0031 (0.0867) (0.04)	-0.0332 (0.0982) (-0.34)	-0.0499 (0.1015) (-0.49)	-0.0030 (0.1018) (-0.03)	0.0421 (0.0980) (0.43)	0.0683 (0.0851) (0.80)	0.19
London ⇒ Frankfurt	0.3844 (0.2244) (1.71)	-0.3671 (0.2305) (-1.59)	-0.0147 (0.2333) (-0.06)	-0.1179 (0.2268) (-0.52)	0.3175 (0.2250) (1.41)	0.2555 (0.2250) (1.14)	1.43
Frankfurt ⇒ London	0.0810 (0.0479) (1.69)	0.0065 (0.0609) (0.11)	-0.0391 (0.0648) (-0.60)	-0.0211 (0.0643) (-0.33)	-0.0210 (0.0594) (-0.35)	-0.0110 (0.0468) (-0.23)	(0.93)

$F^{crit}_{6,89}$ at 5% = 2.22, at 10% = 1.85

TABLE 7 (cont.)
Tests of Contemporaneous Causality

Models

$$I)\quad Y_t = \delta_0 + \sum_{i=0}^{5} \alpha_i X_{t-i} + \sum_{j=1}^{5} \beta_j Y_{t-j} \qquad (X \Rightarrow Y)$$

$$II)\quad X_t = c_0 + \sum_{i=0}^{5} a_i Y_{t-i} + \sum_{j=1}^{5} b_j X_{t-j} \qquad (Y \Rightarrow X)$$

B: Sample Period: September 23, 1987 - November 23, 1987

Direction of Causality	a_i, α_i *Regression Coefficients, STD errors and t-statistics in parentheses* $i=0$	$i=1$	$i=2$	$i=3$	$i=4$	$i=5$	F_1^* $H_0: \sum_{i=0}^{5} a_i = 0$; $\sum_{i=0}^{5} \alpha_i = 0$
New York ⇛ Tokyo	0.5184 (0.0708) (7.32)*	0.3275 (0.1046) (3.13)*	0.3295 (0.1085) (3.04)*	0.3801 (0.1058) (3.59)*	0.2057 (0.1114) (1.85)*	0.3017 (0.1166) (2.59)*	17.28*
Tokyo ⇛ New York	-0.1169 (0.3214) (-0.36)	-0.2111 (0.3763) (-0.56)	-0.1457 (0.3897) (-0.37)	-0.0946 (0.3833) (-0.25)	-0.6071 (0.4151) (-1.46)	-0.2115 (0.2847) (-0.74)	0.48
New York ⇛ London	0.3266 (0.1391) (2.35)*	0.0247 (0.1595) (0.16)	0.2244 (0.1466) (1.53)	0.1802 (0.1423) (1.27)	-0.1388 (0.1400) (-0.99)	0.3098 (0.1295) (2.39)*	2.71*

London ⇒ New York	1.1593 (0.2216) (5.24)*	-0.4714 (0.2588) (-1.75)	0.5138 (0.2695) (1.91)	-0.3017 (0.2405) (-1.26)	0.3846 (0.2419) (1.59)	-0.2206 (0.1969) (-1.12)	5.59*
New York ⇒ Frankfurt	0.3836 (0.1293) (2.96)*	0.1265 (0.1480) (0.86)	0.1764 (0.1473) (1.20)	0.1136 (0.1536) (0.74)	-0.1702 (0.1506) (-1.13)	0.1166 (0.1505) (0.78)	2.02*
Frankfurt ⇒ New York	0.6956 (0.2644) (2.63)*	-0.2578 (0.2894) (-0.89)	0.1385 (0.3069) (0.45)	-0.4063 (0.2886) (-1..41)	-0.0340 (0.2860) (-0.12)	-0.2707 (0.2481) (-1.09)	1.89
London ⇒ Tokyo	0.6731 (0.1695) (3.97)*	0.0697 (0.2003) (0.35)	0.5838 (0.2037) (2.87)*	0.0250 (0.2009) (0.13)	0.2298 (0.2047) (1.12)	0.0330 (0.1853) (0.18)	4.33*
Tokyo ⇒ London	0.4489 (0.1267) (3.54)*	0.1278 (0.1850) (0.69)	0.1842 (0.1944) (0.95)	0.0823 (0.2004) (0.41)	-0.3072 (0.2128) (-1.44)	0.1111 (0.2095) (0.53)	3.68*
Frankfurt ⇒ Tokyo	0.412[illegible] (0.1986) (2.08)*	0.0782 (0.22[illegible]7) (0.35)	0.0223 (0.2499) (0.09)	-0.0132 (0.2449) (-0.05)	0.2486 (0.2381) (1.04)	0.1614 (0.2382) (0.68)	1.24
Tokyo ⇒ Frankfurt	0.4978 (0.1332) (3.74)*	0.3551 (0.1921) (1.85)	0.3259 (0.2190) (1.49)	0.0639 (0.2317) (0.28)	-0.1941 (0.2173) (-0.89)	0.0078 (0.1852) (0.04)	3.28*
London ⇒ Frankfurt	0.7101 (0.1285) (5.53)*	0.0743 (0.1899) (0.39)	0.3314 (0.1947) (1.70)	0.0671 (0.1981) (0.34)	0.1194 (0.1806) (0.66)	0.2810 (0.1714) (1.64)	7.98*
Frankfurt ⇒ London	0.7081 (0.1289) (5.49)*	-0.1287 (0.174[illegible]) (-0.74)	0.2842 (0.1749) (1.63)	-0.0805 (0.1828) (-0.44)	0.1139 (0.1684) (0.68)	-0.0813 (0.1721) (-0.47)	6.43*

$F^{crit}_{6,28}$ at 5% = 2.42, at 10% = 1.98

TABLE 7 (cont.)
Tests of Contemporaneous Causality

Models

$$I)\quad Y_t = \delta_0 + \sum_{i=0}^{5} \alpha_i X_{t-i} + \sum_{j=1}^{5} \beta_j Y_{t-j} \qquad (X \Rightarrow Y)$$

$$II)\quad X_t = c_0 + \sum_{i=0}^{5} a_i Y_{t-i} + \sum_{j=1}^{5} b_j X_{t-j} \qquad (Y \Rightarrow X)$$

C: Sample Period: November 24, 1987 - December 31, 1988

Direction of Causality	a_i, α_i *Regression Coefficients, STD errors and t-statistics in parentheses* $i=0$	$i=1$	$i=2$	$i=3$	$i=4$	$i=5$	F_1^* $H_0: \sum_{i=0}^{5} a_i = 0; \sum_{i=0}^{5} \alpha_i = 0$
New York ⇛ Tokyo	0.0431 (0.0639) (0.68)	0.0576 (0.0648) (0.89)	0.0374 (0.0642) (0.58)	-0.0642 (0.0637) (-1.01)	0.0435 (0.0648) (0.67)	-0.0610 (0.0626) (-0.97)	0.82
Tokyo ⇛ New York	0.0221 (0.0611) (0.36)	0.0022 (0.0662) (0.03)	0.0081 (0.0671) (0.12)	0.0766 (0.0660) (1.16)	0.0671 (0.0625) (1.07)	-0.0640 (0.0556) (-1.15)	0.87
New York ⇛ London	-0.0278 (0.0467) (-0.60)	-0.0264 (0.0478) (-0.55)	0.0062 (0.0471) (0.13)	-0.0208 (0.0470) (-0.44)	0.0297 (0.0478) (0.62)	-0.0640 (0.0463) (-1.38)	0.66

London ⇛ New York	0.5075 (0.0838) (6.06)*	0.0231 (0.0893) (0.26)	0.0529 (0.0893) (0.59)	-0.0182 (0.0891) (-0.20)	0.1020 (0.0890) (1.15)	-0.0341 (0.0893) (-0.38)	6.76*
New York ⇛ Frankfurt	0.2677 (0.2394) (1.12)	0.0667 (0.2455) (0.27)	0.1562 (0.2436) (0.64)	0.1150 (0.2431) (0.47)	0.2043 (0.2450) (0.83)	-0.0575 (0.2379) (-0.24)	0.33
Frankfurt ⇛ New York	0.0004 (0.0164) (0.02)	0.0010 (0.0164) (0.06)	-0.0054 (0.0164) (-0.33)	-0.0070 (0.0164) (-0.43)	0.0116 (0.0163) (0.71)	0.0015 (0.0164) (0.09)	0.14
London ⇛ Tokyo	0.1662 (0.0912) (1.82)	0.1719 (0.0915) (1.88)	0.0330 (0.921) (0.36)	-0.0104 (0.0919) (-0.11)	0.0194 (0.0913) (0.87)	-0.1638 (0.0912) (-1.80)	1.71
Tokyo ⇛ London	0.1260 (0.0432) (2.94)*	0.0557 (0.0432) (1.16)	0.0348 (0.0493) (0.70)	0.0047 (0.0488) (0.10)	-0.0457 (0.0455) (-1.01)	-0.0064 (0.040) (-0.16)	1.69
Frankfurt ⇛ Tokyo	-0.0043 (0.0170) (-0.26)	0.0045 (0.0170) (0.26)	-0.0129 (0.0170) (-0.76)	0.0017 (0.0169) (0.10)	0.0091 (0.0168) (0.54)	0.0006 (0.0167) (0.03)	0.18
Tokyo ⇛ Frankfurt	0.1906 (0.2338) (0.82)	0.2185 (0.2540) (0.86)	-0.6348 (0.2583) (-2.46)*	-0.2580 (0.2567) (-1.01)	-0.1738 (0.2431) (-0.71)	-0.2002 (0.2167) (-0.92)	1.89
London ⇛ Frankfurt	0.3996 (0.3444) (1.16)	0.4993 (0.344[illegible]) (1.45)	-0.1969 (0.3439) (-0.57)	0.1510 (0.3441) (0.44)	-0.0115 (0.3436) (-0.33)	-0.0424 (0.3436) (-0.12)	0.69
Frankfurt ⇛ London	0.0133 (0.0687) (1.16)	-0.0037 (0.0115) (-0.32)	-0.0001 (0.0115) (-0.01)	-0.0013 (0.0115) (-0.11)	0.0180 (0.0115) (1.56)	0.0047 (0.0115) (0.41)	0.68

$F^{crit}_{6,251}$ at 5% = 2.10, at 10% = 1.77

TABLE 8
Modified Sims Causality Tests

Models

$$I)\quad Y_t = c_0 + \sum_{i=-5}^{5} a_i X_{t-i} + \sum_{j=1}^{5} b_j Y_{t-j} \qquad (Y \Rightarrow X)$$

$$II)\quad X_t = \delta_0 + \sum_{i=-5}^{5} \alpha_i Y_{t-i} + \sum_{j=1}^{5} \beta_j X_{t-j} \qquad (X \Rightarrow Y)$$

A: Sample Period: April 22, 1987 - September 22, 1987

Direction of Causality	*a_i, α_i Regression Coefficients, STD errors and t-statistics in parentheses* $i=-5$	$i=-4$	$i=-3$	$i=-2$	$i=-1$	$i=0$	χ^2 $H_0: \sum_{i=-5}^{0} a_i = 0;\ \sum_{i=-5}^{0} \alpha_i = 0$
New York ⇒ Tokyo	0.0397 (0.0347) (1.14)	-0.0289 (0.0393) (-0.74)	0.0340 (0.0402) (0.85)	0.0099 (0.0404) (0.25)	0.0507 (0.0387) (1.30)	0.0515 (0.0351) (1.47)	1.34
Tokyo ⇒ New York	-0.6531 (0.3809) (-1.74)	0.2473 (0.3627) (0.68)	1.0149 (0.3654) (2.78)	-0.5259 (0.3812) (-1.38)	-0.6434 (0.4002) (-1.61)	0.5243 (0.4031) (1.30)	2.63
New York ⇒ London	0.0424 (0.0807) (0.53)	-0.0787 (0.0822) (-0.96)	0.0054 (0.0836) (0.07)	0.1928 (0.0829) (2.33)*	-0.1295 (0.0850) (-1.52)	0.1743 (0.0873) (2.00)*	1.80

London ⇒ New York	-0.2672 (0.1373) (-1.95)*	-0.0416 (0.1344) (-0.31)	0.1483 (0.1334) (1.11)	-0.0142 (0.1333) (-0.11)	-0.2128 (0.1374) (-1.55)	-0.2470 (0.1357) (-1.82)	1.20
New York ⇒ Frankfurt	0.0717 (0.0432) (1.66)	0.0977 (0.0492) (1.99)	0.0858 (0.0558) (1.57)	0.1595 (0.0574) (2.78)	0.1648 (0.0601) (2.74)	0.1167 (0.0625) (1.87)	2.44
Frankfurt ⇒ New York	-0.3693 (0.3346) (-1.10)	0.2430 (0.3223) (0.75)	-0.1261 (0.3038) (-0.42)	0.0712 (0.3145) (0.23)	-0.0855 (0.3148) (-0.27)	0.1200 (0.3096) (0.39)	0.46
London ⇒ Tokyo	-0.0226 (0.0475) (-0.48)	-0.0820 (0.0541) (-1.51)	-0.0682 (0.0566) (-1.21)	-0.0090 (0.0566) (-0.16)	-0.0545 (0.0539) (-1.01)	0.0262 (0.0492) (0.53)	0.87
Tokyo ⇒ London	-0.2910 (0.3131) (-0.93)	-0.0744 (0.2994) (-0.25)	-0.1159 (0.3121) (-0.37)	-0.5307 (0.2977) (-1.78)	0.05091 (0.3051) (1.67)	0.1156 (0.3098) (0.37)	1.41
Frankfurt ⇒ Tokyo	0.2291 (0.1060) (2.16)*	0.1089 (0.1180) (0.92)	0.1183 (0.1205) (0.98)	0.0423 (0.1201) (0.35)	-0.0015 (0.1169) (-0.01)	0.0916 (0.1090) (0.84)	1.02
Tokyo ⇒ Frankfurt	0.1131 (0.1388) (0.82)	0.2195 (0.1753) (1.25)	0.2302 (0.1938) (1.19)	0.1392 (0.2005) (0.69)	0.0377 (0.2026) (0.19)	-0.0271 (0.2020) (-0.13)	0.39
London ⇒ Frankfurt	0.1182 (0.2405) (0.49)	-0.0487 (0.2469) (-0.20)	0.1739 (0.2466) (0.71)	-0.3493 (0.2448) (-1.43)	-0.1656 (0.2428) (-0.68)	0.3687 (0.2449) (1.51)	0.74
Frankfurt ⇒ London	0.0718 (0.0508) (1.42)	0.0981 (0.0629) (1.56)	0.0640 (0.0699) (0.92)	0.0132 (0.0724) (0.18)	-0.0614 (0.0733) (-0.84)	0.0137 (0.0734) (0.19)	0.97

χ^2 crit at 5% = 11.07, at 10% = 9.24

TABLE 8 (cont.)
Modified Sims Causality Tests

Models

$$I)\quad Y_t = c_0 + \sum_{i=-5}^{5} a_i X_{t-i} + \sum_{j=1}^{5} b_j Y_{t-j} \qquad (Y \Rightarrow X)$$

$$II)\quad X_t = \delta_0 + \sum_{i=-5}^{5} \alpha_i Y_{t-i} + \sum_{j=1}^{5} \beta_j X_{t-j} \qquad (X \Rightarrow Y)$$

B: Sample Period: September 23, 1987 - November 23, 1987

Direction of Causality	a_i, α_i *Regression Coefficients, STD errors and t-statistics in parentheses* $i=-5$	$i=-4$	$i=-3$	$i=-2$	$i=-1$	$i=0$	X^2 $H_0: \sum_{i=-5}^{0} a_i = 0;$ $\sum_{i=-5}^{0} \alpha_i = 0$
New York ⇒ Tokyo	-0.2184 (0.0808) (2.70)*	-0.0112 (0.0923) (-0.12)	0.2311 (0.1035) (2.23)*	0.0966 (0.0892) (1.08)	0.1923 (0.0935) (2.06)*	1.2029 (0.0887) (13.56)*	3.32
Tokyo ⇒ New York	-0.0709 (0.0570) (-1.24)	0.1014 (0.0578) (-1.75)	0.0367 (0.0634) (0.58)	-0.0778 (0.0602) (-1.29)	-0.0179 (0.0603) (-0.30)	0.0654 (0.0562) (1.16)	1.37
New York ⇒ London	0.4792 (0.2319) (2.07)*	-0.5258 (0.2092) (-2.51)*	0.5783 (0.2522) (2.29)*	-0.2054 (0.2757) (-0.75)	0.1831 (0.2515) (0.73)	0.6993 (0.2433) (2.87)*	2.25

London ⇒ New York	-0.0216 (0.0981) (-0.13)	0.0758 (0.0944) (0.80)	0.0005 (0.0954) (0.01)	0.0044 (0.0943) (0.05)	-0.0983 (0.0955) (-1.03)	0.3421 (0.0937) (3.65)*	0.26
New York ⇒ Frankfurt	0.6766 (0.3649) (1.85)	-0.0550 (0.3477) (-0.16)	0.1300 (0.3238) (0.40)	0.1003 (0.2610) (0.38)	0.0504 (0.2513) (0.20)	1.0330 (0.2731) (3.78)*	0.71
Frankfurt ⇒ New York	-0.0217 (0.0953) (-0.23)	0.0003 (0.0899) (0.01)	-0.0335 (0.0903) (-0.37)	0.0274 (0.0935) (0.29)	-0.1080 (0.0925) (-1.16)	0.2205 (0.0954) (2.31)*	0.34
London ⇒ Tokyo	0.0961 (0.1077) (0.89)	0.1170 (0.1025) (1.14)	0.0357 (0.1192) (0.30)	0.0778 (0.1293) (0.60)	-0.0288 (0.1256) (-0.23)	0.3923 (0.1180) (3.32)*	0.61
Tokyo ⇒ London	0.0963 (0.1565) (0.62)	-0.3328 (0.1632) (-2.04)	0.2107 (0.1875) (1.12)	-0.0138 (0.2062) (-0.07)	-0.0371 (0.2185) (-0.17)	0.7252 (0.2327) (3.12)*	1.34
Frankfurt ⇒ Tokyo	0.1648 (0.1238) (1.33)	0.1775 (0.1313) (1.35)	0.0681 (0.1470) (0.46)	-0.1110 (0.1440) (-0.77)	0.0449 (0.1401) (0.32)	0.3695 (0.1366) (2.70)*	0.90
Tokyo ⇒ Frankfurt	0.2313 (0.2711) (0.85)	-0.4063 (0.2425) (-1.68)	0.1476 (0.2009) (0.74)	0.0156 (0.1908) (0.08)	0.0556 (0.2007) (0.28)	0.5191 (0.2044) (2.54)*	0.79
London ⇒ Frankfurt	0.3633 (0.2234) (1.63)	0.1103 (0.1919) (0.58)	0.0934 (0.1824) (0.51)	0.0770 (0.1624) (0.47)	0.1732 (0.1725) (1.00)	0.9008 (0.1812) (4.97)*	1.23
Frankfurt ⇒ London	-0.1656 (0.1512) (-1.10)	0.0781 (0.1515) (0.52)	-0.0119 (0.1692) (-0.07)	0.1460 (0.1665) (0.88)	-0.1780 (0.1709) (-1.04)	0.7040 (0.1728) (4.07)*	0.66

χ^2 crit at 5% = 11.07, at 10% = 9.24

TABLE 8 (cont.)
Modified Sims Causality Tests

Models

$$I)\quad Y_t = c_0 + \sum_{i=-5}^{5} a_i X_{t-i} + \sum_{j=1}^{5} b_j Y_{t-j} \qquad (Y \Rightarrow X)$$

$$II)\quad X_t = \delta_0 + \sum_{i=-5}^{5} \alpha_i Y_{t-i} + \sum_{j=1}^{5} \beta_j X_{t-j} \qquad (X \Rightarrow Y)$$

C: Sample Period: November 24, 1987 - December 31, 1988

Direction of Causality	*a_i, α_i Regression Coefficients, STD errors and t-statistics in parentheses* $i=-5$	$i=-4$	$i=-3$	$i=-2$	$i=-1$	$i=0$	χ^2 $H_0: \sum_{i=-5}^{0} a_i = 0;$ $\sum_{i=-5}^{0} \alpha_i = 0$
New York ⇒ Tokyo	-0.0924 (0.0634) (-1.46)	0.0054 (0.0692) (0.08)	-0.1027 (0.0698) (-1.47)	-0.0520 (0.0699) (-0.74)	0.0237 (0.0690) (0.34)	0.0229 (0.0668) (0.34)	1.19
Tokyo ⇒ New York	-0.0872 (0.0712) (-1.23)	0.0181 (0.0725) (0.25)	0.0473 (0.0732) (0.65)	0.0434 (0.0727) (0.60)	-0.0402 (0.0750) (-0.54)	0.0343 (0.0742) (0.46)	0.60
New York ⇒ London	-0.1154 (0.0872) (-1.32)	-0.0767 (0.0876) (0.88)	-0.0118 (0.0881) (-0.13)	0.0516 (0.0877) (0.59)	-0.0036 (0.0870) (-0.04)	-0.0407 (0.0871) (-0.47)	0.54

London ⇒ New York	0.0121 (0.0415) (1.29)	0.0634 (0.0426) (1.49)	0.0014 (0.0431) (0.03)	-0.0040 (0.0427) (-0.09)	0.0235 (0.0436) (0.54)	0.2599 (0.0435) (5.98)*	0.52
New York ⇒ Frankfurt	-0.0045 (0.0168) (-0.27)	0.0097 (0.0158) (0.57)	0.0086 (0.0169) (0.51)	0.0094 (0.0169) (0.56)	0.0013 (0.0169) (0.08)	0.0188 (0.0168) (1.12)	0.19
Frankfurt ⇒ New York	0.1106 (0.2440) (0.45)	0.2243 (0.2487) (0.90)	0.0010 (0.2522) (0.00)	-0.0577 (0.2517) (-0.23)	0.0210 (0.2572) (0.08)	0.0294 (0.2555) (0.12)	0.22
London ⇒ Tokyo	-0.0694 (0.0430) (-1.62)	0.0100 (0.0471) (0.21)	-0.0065 (0.0478) (-0.14)	0.0146 (0.0477) (0.31)	0.0999 (0.0471) (2.12)*	0.1100 (0.0460) (2.39)*	1.68
Tokyo ⇒ London	0.1315 (0.0977) (1.35)	-0.0273 (0.0980) (-0.28)	-0.0161 (0.0983) (-0.16)	0.0150 (0.0976) (0.15)	-0.0040 (0.0977) (-0.04)	0.2525 (0.0966) (2.61)*	0.40
Frankfurt ⇒ Tokyo	-0.0378 (0.2390) (-0.16)	0.1283 (0.2604) (0.49)	0.0926 (0.2641) (0.35)	-0.1341 (0.2635) (-0.51)	0.0307 (0.2602) (0.12)	-0.0351 (0.2519) (-0.14)	0.22
Tokyo ⇒ Frankfurt	-0.0097 (0.0179) (-0.55)	-0.0027 (0.0179) (-0.15)	-0.0001 (0.0179) (-0.01)	-0.0529 (0.0179) (-2.95)*	0.0024 (0.0182) (0.13)	0.0130 (0.0182) (0.72)	1.84
London ⇒ Frankfurt	0.0025 (0.0116) (0.22)	0.0029 (0.0115) (0.25)	0.0023 (0.0116) (0.20)	-0.0062 (0.0116) (-0.54)	0.0167 (0.0115) (1.45)	0.0145 (0.0116) (1.26)	0.54
Frankfurt ⇒ London	0.1494 (0.3514) (0.43)	0.5220 (0.3511) (1.49)	-0.0356 (0.3539) (-0.10)	0.0959 (0.3505) (0.27)	-0.1489 (0.3516) (-0.42)	0.3377 (0.3512) (0.96)	0.52

χ^2 crit at 5% = 11.07, at 10% = 9.24

variables are not cointegrated; that is, the D·W and the Dickey-Fuller statistics both cannot reject the null hypothesis of no-cointegration, we conduct the causality tests by running the regressions (2-1) through (2-4). However, if the D-W or the Dickey-Fuller statistics or both reject the null, we conclude that the variables are cointegrated and, therefore the regressions (2-1) through (2-4) are misspecified. We correct the regressions by incorporating the residuals from the cointegrating regression (4-4) as an additional independent variable in all regression equations (2-1) through (2-4).[**] For instance, equations (2-1) and (2-2) become:

$$X_t = c_0 + \sum_{i=1}^{m} a_i Y_{t-i} + \sum_{j=1}^{m} b_j X_{t-j} + d\hat{e}_{t-1} + u_t$$

$$Y_t = \delta_0 + \sum_{i=1}^{m} \alpha_i X_{t-i} + \sum_{j=1}^{m} \beta_j Y_{t-j} + \delta_1 \hat{e}_{t-1} + \nu_t$$

where $\hat{\epsilon}_{t-1}$ are the residuals from regression (4-4).

4. Granger Causality Tests

The results of the Granger causality tests are presented in Table 6. As the ^{2} statistics indicates the null hypothesis of no-causality cannot be rejected and practically no lead-lag relationships are detected for any of the three subperiods.

In addition, for the periods before and after the crash most of the individual regression coefficients are not different from zero at the 5% significance level, except New York leading Frankfurt in the precrash period. For the period of the crash, September 23, 1987 - November 23, 1987, the individual regression coefficients are also not significantly different from zero at the 5% level, except for the case of New York leading Tokyo.

[**] We thank Professor Paul Newbold for suggesting these error-correcting regressions.

5. *Tests of Contemporaneous Causality*

The results of the contemporaneous causality are shown in Table 7. As it was indicated earlier, the tests generated in Table 7 are not exactly Granger's tests, because the regressions include also the current values of the variables. In general, no contemporaneous causality is detected for the periods before and after the crash. However, an increase in contemporaneous causality is observed during the period of the crash. In effect, all of the a_0 and α_0 coefficients are significantly different from zero at 5% level for the September 23, 1987 - November 23, 1987 time period. However, we should interpret these results with caution. In effect the significant contemporaneous coefficients reported in Table 7 could merely indicate that some shock caused both markets to move in the same direction. Put differently, significance may be due to correlation between markets rather than causality.

The rejection of the null hypothesis of no causality in Table 7 also indicates an increase in lead-lag relationships during the period of the crash. In effect, we can observe that New York leads Tokyo and Frankfurt, and we have feedback between New York and London, London and Tokyo, and London and Frankfurt.

6. *Modified Sims Causality Tests*

The results of the Modified Sims' causality tests are presented in Table 8. In general, these results are similar to those found for the Granger's causality tests, which agrees with Geweke, Meese and Dent (1983) who claim parity between Wald tests of the Granger and Sims types.

From Table 8 we can observe that lead-lag relationships are practically nonexisting for the periods before and after the crash. However, contemporaneous causality is found for the period of the crash, September 23, 1987 - November 23, 1987. In addition, the statistical significance of the individual regression coefficients suggests that New York led Tokyo and London during the period of the crash.

IV. Summary and Conclusions

This paper attempts to detect lead-lag relationships between four major equity market indexes: New York S&P 500, Tokyo Nikkei, London FT-30, and the Frankfurt DAX. The study covers the time period April 22, 1987, when the Wall Street Journal started reporting international stock market indexes, through December 31, 1988. For analytical purposes the information is divided in three data sets covering the time periods before, during and after the market crash. Unidirectional, feedback and contemporaneous causality are analyzed based on the Granger and the Modified Sims tests. We test two hypotheses: (i) the crash was initiated in the United States and (ii) the crash was initiated overseas.

The Granger's tests find little causality relationships between the four market indexes for the periods before, during and after the market crash of October, 1987. The exception is New York leading Tokyo, during the period of the crash. However, the additional tests designed to detect possible linkages indicate that contemporaneous causality was present during the period of the crash, September 23, 1987 through November 23, 1987. Moreover, these tests also show that during the period of the crash there was an increase in causality, with New York leading Tokyo and Frankfurt, and feedback between New York and London, London and Tokyo, and, London and Frankfurt. The Modified Sims tests also suggest contemporaneous causality during the period of the crash. In addition, the Modified Sims tests indicate that New York led Tokyo and London during the period of the crash. However, the significant coefficients can be due to correlation rather than causation.

In summary, the tests suggest that New York appears to have played an important role during the October, 1987 market crash. Tokyo, on the other hand, appeared to lag the other markets. Nevertheless, contemporaneous causality was also present during the period of the crash. Our empirical results indicate, partially, that the United States played a leading role during the crash; but, at the same time, we observed strong simultaneous causality and even feedback between markets.

REFERENCES

1. Blume, M.E., A. Craig MacKinlay and Bruce Terker, 1989, "Order Imbalances and Stock Price Movements on October 19 and 20, 1987" Journal of Finance, 44, pp. 827-848.

2. Brady, Nicholas (chairman), James Cotting, Robert Kirby, John Opel, Howard Stein, and Robert Glauber, 1988, Report of The Presidential Task Force on Market Mechanisms.

3. Dickey, D.A., and W.A. Fuller, 1981, "Likelihood Ratios Statistics for Autoregressive Time Series with a Unit Root", Econometrica, 49, pp. 1057-1072.

4. Dwyer, G.P. and R.W. Hafer, 1988, "Are National Stock Markets Linked?" Review of the Federal Reserved Bank of St.Louis, pp. 3-14.

5. Engle, R. and C.W.J. Granger, 1987, "Co-integration and Error Correction: Representation, Estimation, and Testing", Econometrica, 55, pp. 251-276.

6. Gammill, James, and Terry A. Marsh, 1988, "Trading Activity and Price Behavior in the Stock and Stock Index Futures Markets in October 1987", Journal of Economic Perspectives, 2, pp. 25-44.

7. Geweke, John, 1978, "Testing the Exogeneity Specification in the Complete Dynamic Simultaneous Equations Model", Journal of Econometrics, 6, pp. 163-185.

8. Geweke, John, Richard Meese and Warren Dent, 1983, "Comparing Alternative Tests of Causality in Temporal Systems", Journal of Econometrics, 21, pp.161-194

9. Guilkey, David K., and Micheal K. Salemi, 1982, "Small Sample Properties of Three Tests for Granger Causal

Ordering in a Bivariate Stochastic System", The Review of Economics and Statistics, pp. 668-680.

10. Granger, C.W.J., 1969, "Investigating Causal Relations by Econometric Models and Cross Spectral Methods", Econometrica, 37, pp. 428-438.

11. Greenwald, Bruce and Jeremy Stein, 1988, "The Task Force Report: The Reasoning Behind the Recommendations", Journal of Economic Perspectives, 2, pp. 3-23.

12. Harris, Lawrence, 1989, "The October 1987 S&P 500 Stock-Futures Basis", Journal of Finance, 44, pp. 77-99.

13. Kawaller, Ira, Paul Koch and Timothy Koch, 1987, "The Temporal Price relationship between S&P500 Futures and the S&P500 Index", The Journal of Finance, 42, pp. 1309-1329.

14. Khoury, Sarkis, Bajis Dodin and H. Takada, 1987, "Multiple Time-Series Analysis of National Stock Markets and their Structure: Some Implications", Recent Developments in International Banking and Finance, 1, pp. 169-186.

15. Koch, Paul, and James Ragan, 1986, "Investigating the Causal Relationship between Wages and Quits: An Exercise in Comparative Dynamics," Economic Inquiry, 24, pp. 61-83.

16. Leland, Hayne, and Mark Rubinstein, 1988, "Comments on the Market Crash: Six Months After," Journal of Economic Perspectives, 2, (Summer 1988), pp. 45-50.

17. Ljung, G.M., and G.E.P. Box, 1978, "On a Measure of Lack of Fit in Times Series Models", Biometrika, 65, pp. 297-303.

18. Miller, Merton H., John D. Hawke, Jr., Burton Malkiel and Myron Scholes, 1987, "Preliminary Report of the Committee of Inquiry Appointed by the Chicago Merchantile Exchange

to Examine the Events Surrounding October 19, 1987", Chicago Merchantile Exchange.

19. Pierce, David A., and Larry D. Haugh, 1977, "Causality in Temporal Systems: Characterizations and a Survey", Journal of Econometrics, 5, pp. 265-293.

20. Roll, Richard, 1988, "The International Crash of October, 1987", Working Paper No. 9240, University of California, Los Angeles.

21. Schmidt, Peter, 1976, Econometrics (New York: Marcel Dekker, Inc.,).

22. Schollhammer, Hans and O.C. Sand, 1987, "Lead-Lag Relationships Among National Equity Markets: An Empirical Investigation", Recent Developments in International Banking and Finance, 1, pp. 149-168.

23. Shiller, Robert J., 1987, "Investor Behavior in the October, 1987 Stock Market Crash: Survey Evidence", NBER, Working Paper No. 2446.

24. Shiller, Robert J., Fumiko Konya and Yoshiro Tsutsui, 1988, "Investor Behavior in the October, 1987 Stock Market Crash: The Case of Japan", NBER, Working Paper No. 2684.

25. Sims, C., 1972, "Money, Income and Causality", American Economic Review, 62, pp. 540-552.

Recent Developments in International Banking
and Finance, S.J. Khoury (editor)

CHAPTER XI

Information and Price Adjustment Processes: A Comparison of U.S. and Japanese Stocks

Aswath Damodaran

Graduate School of Business
New York University

INTRODUCTION

Portfolio managers in the United States have increasingly turned to stocks listed on foreign markets in recent years both to augment returns and to reduce risk. In spite of the success of these international diversification efforts, many investors remain wary of foreign stocks because of the perception that the markets they trade on are not as efficient as the U.S. exchanges. While there is fairly widespread agreement among financial economists that an efficient market is one in which information is reflected quickly in prices, there is remarkably little evidence on whether the price adjustment process is indeed slower on foreign markets.

This paper develops a simple measure for the price adjustment coefficient, from returns data, for various return intervals, and uses it to compare the speed of price adjustment on stocks in the S&P 500 with those in the Nikkei 500. The derivation of the measure draws on the description of the return process contained in Amihud and Mendelson(1987) as a combination of an intrinsic value adjustment factor and a noise term, and uses the information in various return intervals to arrive at the estimate of the adjustment coefficient.

The approach developed here is used to estimate price adjustment coefficients for the firms that comprise the S&P 500, trading on the New York Stock Exchange, and those firms that comprise the Nikkei 500, trading on the Tokyo Stock Exchange, using five years of daily returns data, from January 1983 to December 1987. We find strong evidence that price adjustment processes are very different for the two groups. While there is some evidence of lagged price adjustment for stocks in the S & P 500, Japanese stocks, on average, seem more prone to price overreaction, leading to higher daily return volatility and lower variance ratios. The fact that prices adjust much more quickly to new information for Japanese stocks may be viewed as evidence that Japanese markets are more efficient, though this has to be weighed against the higher volatility induced by market overreaction.

Section 1: The Efficiency of International Stock Markets

Researchers examining the efficiency of foreign security markets relative to the U.S. markets have generally used one of two approaches. In the first, the time series of stock price and return data is examined to see whether there are significant deviations from normality and randomness. In the second, stock price reactions to significant news announcements - for instance, earnings and dividends announcements- are studied to determine the speed with which prices reflect the new information.

Fama (1964) used daily closing price data for 30 U.S. companies and concluded that while there are some deviations from normality in short-period returns (in terms of serial correlation and runs) the differences are not significant from either a statistical or an investment point of view. Similar studies in other countries find significant deviations from normality in daily and weekly returns. Dryden (1969) and Brealey (1970) find evidence of significant positive correlation (0.16 to 0.30) for the ETA (all-share) London index. Conrad and Juttner (1973) arrive at a similar conclusion for their sample of German stocks. Jennergren and Korsvold(1974) investigate 45 Norwegian and Swedish stocks and find significant positive correlation in daily returns (0.10 to 0.20) and conclude that "the random walk hypothesis is probably not a very accurate description of share price behavior" on these markets. Solnik (1973) in a comprehensive examination of 234 securities from 8 European stock markets found that while the serial correlation coefficients are quite small (less than .04), deviations from the random walk are slightly more apparent in the European data. Errunza and Losq (1985) extend this analysis to include ten less-developed countries (LDC) and report that these markets exhibit slightly higher positive correlations in returns than the European or U.S. markets.

A series of studies have examined market reaction to earnings announcements in the United States. Studies of quarterly earnings announcements (Watts(1978), Joy et al.(1977)) have generally concluded that they contain information, since positive (negative) surprises, on average, evoke positive (negative) market reactions. Other studies (Patell and Wolfson(1985), Woodruff and Senchack(1988)) note that price adjustments are not instantaneous and that the adjustment process takes anywhere from a few hours (for larger firms) to a few days (for smaller firms). Since daily return and transactions data is not freely available for foreign markets, there have been relatively few attempts to do similar studies in these markets. Forsgardh and Hertzen (1974) examine the price reactions to earnings announcements on the Swedish stock market and find that while some of the price adjustment occurs in the month preceding the announcement week, the main price adjustment occurs in connection with the report. Elton and Gruber (1990) examine stock price reactions to earnings reports for Japanese stocks and conclude that analysts' estimates are incorporated in stock prices but that changes in estimates are incorporated with a lag.

This paper extends the study of foreign market efficiency in two directions. First, while most of these studies conclude that foreign markets are less efficient than U.S. markets, there is little consensus on the reasons for the inefficiencies. The positive serial correlation in short-interval returns evidenced by stocks in most foreign markets may be caused by a slower price adjustment process, infrequent trading and/or data averaging. This paper attempts to measure the speed of the price adjustment process, and by so doing provides some explanations for the idiosyncratic behavior of foreign markets. Second, most empirical studies of foreign markets have been constrained by the paucity of data on foreign stocks and sample sizes are fairly small, making it difficult to draw strong conclusions or make relevant comparisons with the U.S. markets. This paper uses a relatively large database of stock prices (Daily price data for five years for five hundred large Japanese companies) and compares their stock price behavior with that of stocks in the S&P 500 over the same time period. Hence we are able to make much stronger comparisons between the two markets.

Section 2: A Partial Price-Adjustment Model

a. The Estimation of Price Adjustment Coefficients

We start with the simple model of price behavior described in Amihud and Mendelson , which distinguishes between the intrinsic value V_t and the observed price P_t by allowing for market-structure noise or information noise as well as imperfect price adjustments to value changes.

$$P_t - P_{t-1} = g\,[V_t - P_{t-1}] + u_t \qquad (1)$$

where V_t and P_t are in logarithms and g is the price adjustment coefficient[1] $[0 \le g \le 2]$. The last term u_t is a noise term, the magnitude of which is determined by information-related factors (such as liquidity trading and noisy information) and market-structure related factors (such as the bid-ask spread, dealer inventory positions and the discreteness of stock prices). We assume, as they do, that u_t has mean zero and variance σ^2, but assume, unlike them, that the presence of the bid-ask spread induces negative serial correlation[2] in this noise term.

The price adjustment coefficient as defined here has several appealing features. It enables us to distinguish between and define some traditional interpretations of market efficiency--

[1] This is a measure of how quickly prices adjust to all information, market-wide as well as firm-specific.

[2] If we assume, as Roll(1984) does, that there is an equal probability of the stock ending at the bid or the ask price the correlation induced by the bid-ask spread will be - 0.5. Amihud and Mendelson assume that the noise term is i.i.d.

$$g = \begin{Bmatrix} 0\text{: No price adjustment to information} \\ <1\text{: Partial adjustment to information} \\ =1 \text{ Full adjustment to new information} \\ >1 \text{ Overreaction to new information} \end{Bmatrix}$$

Following Amihud and Mendelson, we assume that the intrinsic value time series $\{V_t\}$ follows a random walk process with drift[3]:

$$V_t = V_{t-1} + e_t + m \tag{2}$$

where m represents the expected return for the return interval, and $\{e_t\}$ are i.i.d. random variables, independent of u_t, with mean zero and finite variance v^2. They go on to show that

$$Var(R_t) = \frac{g}{2-g} v2 + \frac{2}{(2-g)} \sigma^2 \tag{3}$$

where,

$Var(R_t)$ = Variance in observed return time series

To derive our measure of g, we intend to use the variances in different return intervals. To do so, we define R_{jt} to be the returns in time interval t where each interval is of length j. Then equation (3) can be written as follows:

$$Var(R_{jt}) = \left[\frac{g_j}{2-g_j} jv^2 + \frac{2}{(2-g_j)} \sigma^2\right] \tag{4}$$

where $Var(R_{jt})$ is theariance in observed return time series of returns of interval j and g_j is the price adjustment coefficient for j-interval returns. Note that v^2 is linear in j because $\{e_t\}$ is an i.i.d. random variable, and $\{e_t\}$ and $\{u_t\}$ are assumed to be independent of each other. The noise variance becomes a smaller component[4] of the total return variance as the return interval is increased because of the negative serial correlation induced by the bid-ask spread.

Assume that a sequence of n observed unit-interval returns $\{R_{11}, R_{12} .... R_{1n}\}$ is used to estimate the variances for different return intervals (j=1,2,...k). Then the general formulation for the variances can be written as follows:

$$Var(R_{1t}) = \left[\frac{g_1}{2-g_1} v2 + \frac{2}{(2-g_1)} \sigma^2\right]$$

---

[3] By making this assumption, we ensure that the variance increases linearly with the return intervals. Alternative descriptions of the intrinsic value process can be accomodated by the model though the calculations of the price adjustment coefficients become more tedious.

[4] The noise variance remains unchanged as the return interval is extended, but becomes a smaller component of the overall variance because of the negative serial correlation in the spread. If the spread is only a portion of the total noise variance, the noise variance may increase as the return interval is extended, though less than proportionately.

$$\mathrm{Var}(R_{1t}) = \left[\frac{g_1}{2-g_1} v^2 + \frac{2}{(2-g_1)} \sigma^2\right]$$

$$\mathrm{Var}(R_{kt}) = \left[\frac{kg_k}{2-g_k} v^2 + \frac{2}{(2-g_k)} \sigma^2\right] \tag{5}$$

The price adjustment coefficients in these variance calculations for the longer return intervals, j=2,3,....k, can be written as functions of the unit-interval coefficient,

$$g_2 = g_1 + [g_1(1-g_1)/2]$$

$$g_3 = g_1 + [(2g_1(1-g_1) + g_1(1-g_1-g_1(1-g_1)))/3]$$

Note that the prices adjust much more completely to information (g_j is closer to one) as the return interval is extended and markets are provided more time to assimilate and react to information. We illustrate this in figure 1, where we examine the effects of return intervaling on price adjustment coefficients for different values of g_1, ranging from 0.6 to 1.2.

While the range of values for g_1 is large, there is rapid convergence to one for the price adjustment coefficients for longer return intervals (For instance, g_{20} is close to one for all the initial values of g_1). This is of some comfort to use since we assume for purposes of our analysis that k is of sufficient length to allow g_k=1. Then we can rewrite Var(R_{kt}) and its component parts as

$$\mathrm{Var}\,(R_{kt}) = k\,v^2 + 2\,\sigma^2$$

$$\sigma^2 = -\mathrm{Cov}\;(R_{kt},\, R_{kt-1}) \tag{6}$$

$$v^2 = \frac{\mathrm{Var}\,(R_{kt}) + 2\,\mathrm{Cov}\,(R_{kt}, R_{kt-1})}{k} \tag{7}$$

Note that the noise variance is measured by the serial covariance in returns and that (6) is the Roll measure of the bid-ask spread, since the spread is the only source of noise in his model and g is assumed to be equal to one.

The assumption that g_k=1 buys us a great deal since the difference between the variance in unit-return returns and the equivalent variance in k-interval returns can be written as follows:

$$\mathrm{Var}(R_{1t}) - \frac{\mathrm{Var}(R_{kt})}{k} = v^2\left[\frac{g_1}{(2-g_1)} - 1\right] + 2\,\sigma^2\left[\frac{1}{(2-g_1)} - \frac{1}{k}\right] \tag{8}$$

Substituting for v^2 and σ^2 from (6), we get

FIGURE 1: PRICE ADJUSTMENT COEFFICIENTS AND RETURN INTERVALING

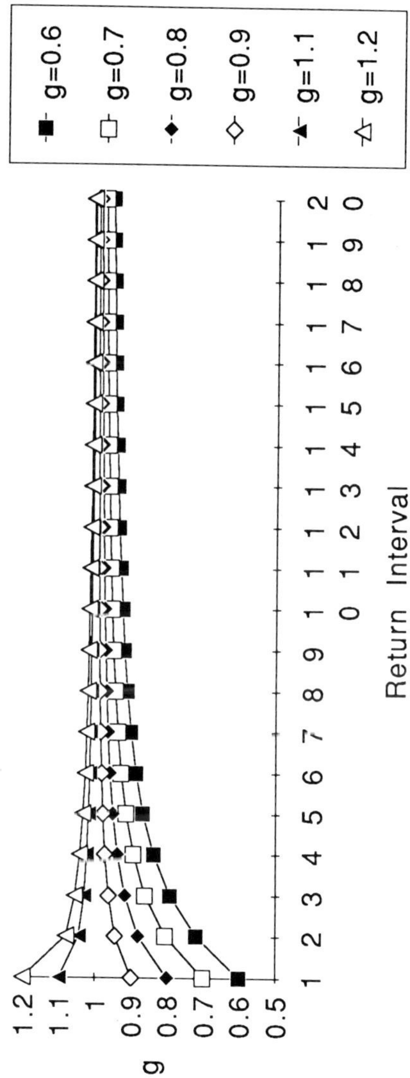

$$\text{Var}(R_{1t}) - \frac{\text{Var}(R_{kt})}{k} =$$

$$\left(\frac{\text{Var}(R_{kt}) + 2\,\text{Cov}(R_{kt}, R_{kt-1})}{k}\right)\left[\frac{g_1}{(2-g_1)} - 1\right] - 2\,\text{Cov}(R_{kt}, R_{kt-1})\left[\frac{1}{(2-g_1)} - \frac{1}{k}\right]$$

$$= 2\left(\frac{\text{Var}(R_{kt}) + 2\,\text{Cov}(R_{kt}, R_{kt-1})}{k}\right)\left[\frac{(g_1-1)}{(2-g_1)}\right] - 2\,\text{Cov}(R_{kt}, R_{kt-1})\left[\frac{1}{(2-g_1)} - \frac{1}{k}\right]$$

Solving through for g, we get

$$g_1 = \frac{2\left[\text{Var}(R_{1t}) + \text{Cov}(R_{kt}, R_{kt-1})\right]}{\left[\text{Var}(\frac{R_{kt}}{k}) + \text{Var}(R_{1t}) + \frac{2\,\text{Cov}(R_{kt}, R_{kt-1})}{k}\right]}$$

Similarly we can solve for $g_2, g_3 \ldots\ldots g_{k-1}$ with the following general formulation--

$$g_j = \frac{2\left[(\frac{\text{Var}(R_{jt}}{j}) + \text{Var}(\frac{R_{kt}}{k})(j-1) + \frac{\text{Cov}(R_{kt}, R_{kt-1})}{j}\right]}{(\frac{\text{Var}(R_{jt}}{j}) + \text{Var}(\frac{R_{kt}}{k})(2j-1) + \frac{2\,\text{Cov}(R_{kt}, R_{kt-1})}{k}} \qquad (9)$$

Equation (9) helps us estimate the price adjustment coefficients for return intervals until j=k-1, and requires no information beyond that available in the time series of unit-interval returns data.

There are three critical assumptions that we make that enable us to arrive at our formulations for the price adjustment coefficients. The first is that the intrinsic value $\{V_t\}$ process is i.i.d. and follows a random walk. While this is not an uncommon assumption in other papers in this area, it is difficult to justify stationarity in the process for very long period returns (such as annual or three-year returns). Consequently, the longest return interval that we use in our empirical tests of equation (9) is twenty days[5]. The second is that the noise terms and intrinsic value processes are independent, an assumption of convenience that may be set aside if one is willing to explicitly model the covariance between the two processes. The third is that the price adjustment coefficient approaches one as the return interval is extended. This assumption is justifiable on both intuitive and empirical grounds. It seems reasonable to assume that giving financial markets more time to adjust to new information will result in a more complete price adjustment process. Studies of earnings announcements also seem to indicate that any lags due to incomplete price adjustment last a few days at the most (and can generally be measured in hours for larger firms). Furthermore, as figure 1 indicates the price adjustment coefficient for longer intervals approaches one rapidly even for very low or very high values of g_1.

---

[5] Twenty trading days corresponds roughly to a month of returns.

b. Issues related to Estimation

While equation (9) provides us with a measure of the price adjustment coefficient, there are several issues related to estimation that need to be addressed prior to empirically testing its usefulness. The first relates to the unit measure for unit-returns since the empiricist has a choice of transactions data, daily returns or even longer return periods. While longer period returns may not meet our requirements of stationarity in the intrinsic value process, returns over very short intervals (such as fifteen minutes) may be too noisy to provide precise estimates. There is also the possibility that it would be difficult to disentangle the effects of mean reversion from price adjustment effects when longer return intervals are used. Our choice of daily returns for the empirical tests is ultimately driven by practical considerations, since transactions data is not freely available. However, applying the model to transactions data may be an interesting extension to examine intraday price adjustment coefficients.

The second issue relates to the limiting interval. Since we assume full price adjustment by this interval, the assumption is a key one and determines the magnitude of the estimated price adjustment coefficients. Studies of market reactions to earning surprises generally find that prices adjust fully to the information in the announcement within a few days for most firms and within a few hours, or overnight, for some large firms. Drawing on the price adjustment paths graphed in figure 1 for different value of g_1, we choose an limiting interval of twenty days to conduct our tests, but examine the sensitivity of our results to other limiting intervals[6].

The third issue relates to the precision and unbiasedness of the estimates obtained from equation (9). Harris (1988) notes that the covariances obtained from daily returns are biased upwards, probably because of positive correlation in the intrinsic value process. Another problem arises from the use of overlapping data to estimate the variances in different return intervals. Richardson and Smith (1988) note that using the same observation numerous times to estimate the sample variance-covariance matrix induces substantial dependence in the elements of the matrix, and results in the underestimation of the standard errors of the estimates. By taking covariances from the limiting interval returns, we mitigate the first problem somewhat, but the estimates for individual firms remain noisy. To avoid the second problem, we report the average price-adjustment coefficients for fairly large subsamples of stocks, since the estimators are much more reliable when large crosssectional samples are used.

The efficacy and robustness of this approach to estimating price adjustment coefficients was tested, using a series of simulations, each of which generated 1250 price observations from known values of σ^2, v^2 and g_1. Equations (6), (7) and (9) were used to obtain the corresponding

---

[6] If $g_{20} \neq 1$, the estimates we obtain for g_1 through g_{19} will be biased, downwards if $g_{20} < 1$, and upwards if $g_{20} > 1$.

estimates from the generated price data with 20 days used as the limiting interval. While the estimates were noisy for individual simulations, the averages obtained over 100 simulations were close to true values.

Section 3: Empiral Methods and Results

a. Sample and Data Sources

The data for the stocks in the S&P 500 index was obtained from the CRSP daily returns database. Only those stocks in the index with returns data available from January 1, 1983 to December 31, 1987 were used in our analysis. The data for the stocks in the Nikkei 500 index was obtained from the NEEDS data base of daily stock prices for Japanese stocks, provided by the Nikkei Databank Bureau. This data base has daily price data (in Yen) from 1978 to 1987 for 2530 stocks listed on the various Japanese exchanges. Again, only those stocks in the Nikkei 500 index with data available from January 1, 1983 to December 31, 1987 are used in the study, and prices are converted into returns.

b. Methodology

To test the efficacy of the model in estimating price-adjustment coefficients, we use daily returns from January 1, 1983 to December 31, 1987. For each firm, we estimate the variances in returns with return frequencies ranging from one day to twenty days--

$$Var(R_{jt}) = \frac{1}{(\frac{n}{j}-1)}\left[\sum_{t=1}^{n/j} (R_{jt} - \widehat{R}_j)\right]$$

where n is the number of daily returns, j is the return intervaling frequency (j=1,2,3,...... 20), R_{jt} is the Return in interval t and $\widehat{R}_j$ is the average return for j-interval returns over the entire time period. We estimate the covariances in twenty-day returns using non-overlapping returns:

$$Cov(R_{kt}, R_{kt-1}) = \frac{1}{(\frac{n}{k}-2)}\left[\sum_{t=1}^{n/k} (R_{kt} - \widehat{R}_k)(R_{kt-1} - \widehat{R}_k)\right]$$

Summary statistics for the variances and covariances for daily, five-day and twenty-day returns are reported for the Nikkei and S&P 500 indices in Table 1.

The contrast between the two groups when return intervals are lengthened is evident in the t and χ^2 statistics reported in the last two columns of Table 1. On average, while daily return variances are very similar to monthly return variances for stocks in the S & P 500, daily return variances are about 15% higher than monthly return variances for Japanese stocks. Concurrently, while the Nikkei stocks have significantly higher daily return variances than the S&P stocks, the monthly return variances of stocks are not significantly different. The behavior of covariances as return intervals are extended is also

TABLE 1: RETURN INTERVALING EFFECTS ON VARIANCES AND COVARIANCES
S & P 500 AND NIKKEI 500 INDICES: 1983-87
CROSSSECTIONAL AVERAGES OF FIRM-SPECIFIC ESTIMATES

	S & P 500			NIKKEI 500			DIFFERENCE: S&P - NIKKEI		
Interval	Mean	Std Error	Median	Mean	Std Error	Median	Mean	T statistic	χ^2 Stat
VARIANCE									
Daily	0.000457	0.000010	0.000416	0.000539	0.000009	0.000502	0.0865	1.78	72.01**
Five-day	0.000444	0.000010	0.000396	0.000487	0.000010	0.000442	0.0196	0.78	16.73**
Ten-day	0.000469	0.000012	0.000415	0.000476	0.000011	0.000422	0.0095	0.79	0.69
Twenty-day	0.000461	0.000013	0.000406	0.000482	0.000013	0.000413	0.0009	0.13	1.68
COVAR.									
Daily	0.000023	0.000001	0.000022	-0.000021	0.000002	-0.000023	0.000044	18.09	307.08**
Five-day	-0.000002	0.000008	-0.000012	-0.000092	0.000010	-0.000098	0.000089	6.90	69.03**
Ten-day	-0.000303	0.000024	-0.000238	0.000028	0.000028	-0.000003	-0.000331	-8.77	85.26**
Twenty-day	-0.000182	0.000020	-0.000303	0.000059	0.000023	0.000114	-0.000242	-7.77	46.37**

** Significant at 99% level   * Significant at 95% level

(1) The trading days from 1/1/83 to 12/31/87 were used to calculate the variances and covariances.

(2) The crosssectional standard errors are reported for the estimates.

(3) The implied daily variances in the longer intervals are reported.

(4) The t statistic tests the hypothesis that the means of the two groups are equal.

(5) The Wilcoxon rank sum statistic is reported and is distributed χ^2 with one degree of freedom.

TABLE 2: PRICE ADJUSTMENT COEFFICIENTS - S&P 500 AND NIKKEI 500 STOCKS: 1983-87
CROSSSECTIONAL AVERAGES OF FIRM-SPECIFIC ESTIMATES

	S&P 500			NIKKEI 500			S & P 500 - NIKKEI 500		
Interval	Mean	Std Error	Median	Mean	Std Error	Median	Mean	$t[g_{sp}=g_{Nik}]$	χ^2 Stat
1 day	0.9272	0.0156	0.7357	1.1230	0.0184	1.1254	-0.1958	8.07	42.04**
2 days	0.9282	0.0100	0.8067	1.0508	0.0113	1.0802	-0.1226	8.10	42.06**
3 days	0.9688	0.0045	0.9236	1.0261	0.0052	1.0306	-0.0573	8.30	55.90**
4 days	0.9827	0.0025	0.9613	1.0173	0.0029	1.0168	-0.0346	9.00	72.73**
5 days	0.9891	0.0016	0.9765	1.0105	0.0020	1.0085	-0.0214	8.33	60.48**
6 days	0.9962	0.0011	0.9907	1.0072	0.0015	1.0040	-0.0110	5.83	29.19**
7 days	1.0011	0.0008	0.9975	1.0069	0.0011	1.0053	-0.0058	4.13	14.41**
8 days	0.9949	0.0007	0.9929	1.0055	0.0009	1.0044	-0.0106	9.45	82.41**
9 days	0.9939	0.0006	0.9924	1.0022	0.0007	1.0005	0.0083	8.99	76.20**
10 days	1.0005	0.0004	0.9992	1.0019	0.0005	1.0012	-0.0014	2.10	3.60
11 days	0.9974	0.0004	0.9963	1.0017	0.0005	1.0004	-0.0033	6.34	38.73**
12 days	0.9945	0.0004	0.9936	1.0014	0.0005	1.0003	-0.0069	6.27	117.46**
13 days	0.9959	0.0003	0.9952	1.0020	0.0004	1.0012	-0.0061	6.24	114.41**
14 days	1.0045	0.0003	1.0041	1.0012	0.0004	1.0004	0.0033	0.45	49.45**
15 days	0.9973	0.0003	0.9974	1.0004	0.0003	0.9984	-0.0031	7.22	46.85**
16 days	0.9980	0.0003	0.9975	1.0022	0.0004	1.0014	-0.0042	9.22	79.57**
17 days	0.9972	0.0003	0.9971	1.0014	0.0003	1.0012	-0.0042	9.28	100.36**
18 days	0.9982	0.0002	0.9979	1.0005	0.0003	0.9998	-0.0023	6.56	35.51**
19 days	0.9978	0.0002	0.9977	1.0010	0.0003	1.0007	-0.0032	9.05	71.46**
20 days	1.0000	0.0000	1.0000	1.0000	0.0000	1.0000	0.0000	0.00	-

** Significant at 99% level   * Significant at 95% level

(1) The price adjustment coefficients are estimated using equation (9). We set $g_j=0$ if $g_j<0$, and $g_j=2$ if $g_j>2$.
(2) The standard errors are estimated crosssectionally.
(3) Daily returns are the unit intervals. The limiting interval is set equal to twenty days.
(4) The percentage of the sample with price adjustment coefficients greater than one is reported. (** Significant at 99% confidence level)

different across the two groups. Covariances are positive for daily returns but become more negative as the return interval is increased to twenty days for stocks in the S&P 500, while the reverse is true for Japanese stocks. We will explore potential reasons for these differences in the next section.

Fama and French (1987) present evidence of mean reversion in longer term return intervals, which can cause negative covariances for these return intervals. In addition, time variation in the risk premia can also cause negative covariances in longer return intervals. Most of the extant literature on mean reversion and time variation in the risk premium is based upon examination of much longer return intervals (semi-annual, annual, five-year returns etc.) than those used in this paper. Lo and MacKinlay (1988) examine weekly and monthly returns on the equally-weighted CRSP index from 1962 to 1985 and find no evidence of mean reversion in these return intervals. Since the longest return interval that we use in our study is twenty days, it seems reasonable to argue that the bid-ask spread is a much more important determinant of the covariances in these intervals[7].

c. Comparison of Price Adjustment coefficients

The variances and covariances are used in equation (9) to estimate price adjustment coefficients for return intervals ranging from one to twenty days for each firm in the sample. The crosssectional averages of these coefficients are summarized and reported for the S&P 500 and Nikkei 500 sub-samples in Table 2.

Some interesting results emerge from this table. There is some evidence of a lagged price adjustment for stocks in the S&P 500, with about 92% of new information being reflected in prices by the end of the day on which it is released. In contrast, there is evidence of market overreaction for the Japanese stocks, with one-day to three-day price adjustment coefficients significantly greater than one. To illustrate that these differences are not due to outliers, we report the same pattern in the median statistics for the price adjustment coefficients. Both the t statistics, testing the hypothesis that means of the two groups are equal, and chi-squared statistics, from a Wilcoxon rank sum test, indicate that the differences across the two groups are significant at the 99% level. If we define speed of adjustment in terms of the speed with which the price adjustment coefficients converge to one, the median statistics seem to indicate that prices adjust slightly more quickly for Japanese stocks than for the S&P 500 stocks.

We illustrate the differences in the speed of the price adjustment process for firms in the S&P 500 and Nikkei 500 indices further in figure 2.

---

[7] The size of the covariances are also consistent with this assertion. While Fama and French report that 25 to 40 percent of the variation in longer-horizon returns is predictable from past returns, we find much smaller negative covariances and correlations in the twenty-day returns for the S&P 500 stocks, and positive covariances and correlations for Japanese stocks.

FIGURE 2: PRICE ADJUSTMENT COEFFICIENTS AND RETURN INTERVALS: S&P 500 VS NIKKEI 500

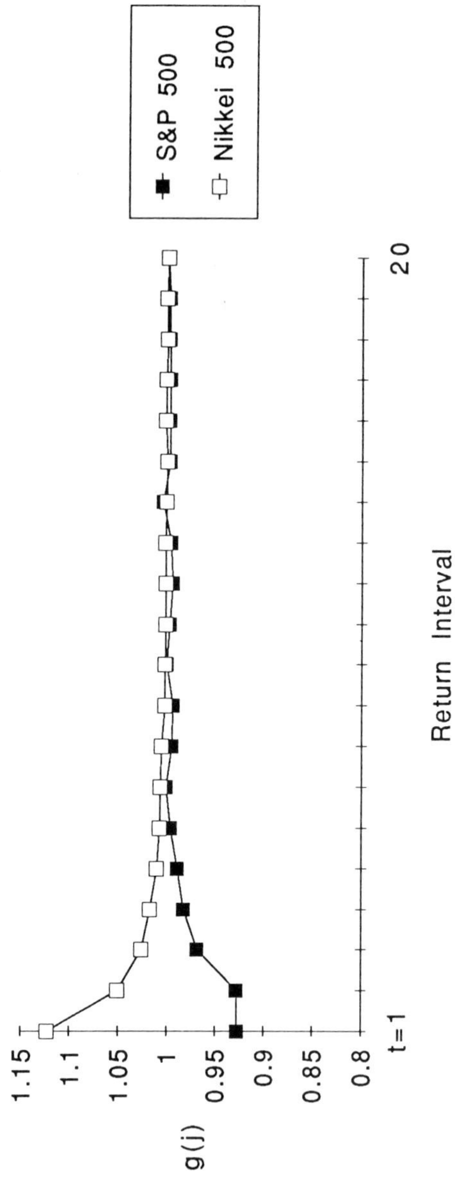

The lagged price adjustment evidenced by the S&P 500 stocks and the market overreaction in the Japanese stocks may help resolve some of the differences across the two groups in the behavior of variances as return intervals are lengthened. As equation (3) in the prior section indicates, lagged price adjustment ($g_1<1$) will result in lower daily return variances while market overreaction ($g_1>1$) leads to higher daily return variances, which is consistent with our finding that Japanese stocks have higher daily return volatilities than the S&P 500 stocks. Since price adjustment coefficients approach one as the return interval is lenghtened, the differences across the two groups in the variances in ten-day and twenty-day returns are much smaller.

The reasons for the differences in price adjustment behavior are not clear. While we would have expected the stocks in the S&P 500, which have more private information generated[8] and disseminated about them by analysts and iinstitutions, to have much speedier price adjustment paths and be more likely to evidence market overreaction than stocks in the Nikkei 500, the reverse seems to be true in the data. One explanation may be that private information is impounded in prices through extensive insider trading in Japanese stocks. Since other investors can learn from these trades, albeit noisily, about the information, prices may reflect the information just as effectively. This explanation would also be consistent with the market overreaction observed on Japanese stocks, if one is willing to accept the arguments of some (French and Roll (1986)) that trading sometimes results in prices overshooting true values.

d. Relationship to Variance Ratios

The use of variances estimated using different return frequencies is not new to financial economics, though the interpretation given in this paper may be different from that given in others. Campbell and Mankiw(1987) and Cochrane (1987) use variance ratios to examine the temporary components in the time-series of macro-economic variables. Fama and French (1987) use variance ratios as well as regressions to conclude that there were large temporary components in long-period stock returns. French and Roll (1986) and Damodaran (1985) use variance ratios to examine the effects of information noise on stock return variances, and interpret high ratios of daily variance to longer return-interval variance to mean more noisy private information. Lo and MacKinlay (1988), in addition to using variance ratios to test the random walk hypothesis, also examine the asymptotic distribution of the ratio statistic.

---

[8] There are two reasons for believing that S&P 500 stocks have more information produced on them that Nikkei stocks. First, public disclosure requirements are much more stringent in the United States than in Japan for publicly traded stocks. As an example, insider trading and holdings do not have to registered with the regulatory authorities in Japan. Second, the number of analysts (and analyst reports) on Wall Street following the S&P 500 stocks vastly exceeds the number of analysts following the Nikkei 500.

ratios on Japanese stocks can be attributed to the fact that price adjustment coefficients are, on average, greater than one for these stocks. To illustrate this, we reestimate variance ratios by manipulating equation (3) to estimate the intrinsic variance from different return intervals:

$$\text{Adjusted Variance ratio (j)} = \frac{\left[\left(\frac{2-g_j}{g_j}\right)\text{Var}(R_{jt}) - \frac{2}{g_j}\text{Cov}\,(R_{jt},R_{jt-1})\right]}{\left[\left(\frac{2-g_1}{g_1}\right)\text{Var}(R_{1t}) - \frac{2}{g_1}\text{Cov}\,(R_{1t},R_{1t-1})\right]}$$

The adjusted variance ratios reveal no significant differences across stocks in the two indices.

In summary, there seem to be clear differences in the price behavior of stocks in the S&P 500 and the Nikkei 500. Surprisingly, Japanese stocks seem to adjust much more quickly to new information and are also more like to overreact, leading to higher daily return variances and lower variance ratios. While the speedier price adjustment can be viewed as evidence that Japanese markets are more efficient than U.S. stocks markets, it has to be weighed against the higher volatility in prices induced by the tendency to overreact to new information. If, in fact, the speedier price adjustment in Japanese markets is caused by insider trading, there are sobering implications for foreign portfolio managers who invest in Japanese stocks. First, those portfolio managers who invest in Japanese stocks primarily for diversification purposes and do not expend the resources or have the contacts[9] to acquire inside information will find themselves at a disadvantage trading with better-informed Japanese investors. Second, the perception that Japanese stocks are more stable than U.S. stocks may be false, since the former have higher daily return volatility over the time period of this analysis and are also more likely to over-react to new information.

Conclusion

Extending the basic model of returns developed in Amihud and Mendelson, we derive a simple measure of firm-specific price-adjustment coefficients that draws on the information in return processes. The approach is used to estimate the price adjustment coefficients of all firms comprising the S&P 500 and the Nikkei 500. We find that stocks in the S&P 500, on average, tend to have lagged price adjustment processes, while the Japanese stocks exhibited a tendency to overreact in response to new information.

---

[9] The difficulties that foreign investors may face in acquiring insider information and competing on an 'even playing field' with Japanese investors may operate as a significant barrier to foreign investment in Japanese markets.

References

Amihud, Y. and H. Mendelson., 1987, " Trading Mechanisms and Stock Returns: An Empirical Investigation." Journal of Finance 42 , 533-553.

Amihud, Y. and H. Mendelson., 1989, "Index and Index-Futures Returns" Working paper, New York University.

Brealey, R.A., 1970, "The distribution and independence of successive rates of return from the British equity market." Journal of Business Finance 2, pp 29-40.

Campbell, J. and G. Mankiw, 1987, "Are Output Fluctuations Transitory?" Quarterly Journal of Economics 102 , 857-880

Cochrane, J., 1987, "How Big is the Random Walk in GNP?" Working Paper, University of Chicago

Conrad, K. and D.J. Juttner., 1973, "Recent Behavior of stock market prices in Germany and the random walk hypothesis." Kyklos 26, pp 576-599.

Damodaran, A., 1985, "Economic Events, Information Structure and the Return-Generating Process." Journal of Financial and Quantitative Analysis 20, pp 423-434.

Diamond, D.W. and R.E. Verrecchia., 1986, "Constraints on short-selling and Asset price adjustment to private information." Journal of Financial Economics 17, pp 5-26.

Dryden, M., 1969, "Share Price Movements: A Markovian Approach," Journal of Finance, pp 49-61.

Elton, E.J. and M.J. Gruber., 1990, "Analysts' Expectations and Japanese Stock Prices." in Elton and Gruber eds., Japanese Capital Markets (Harper and Row).

Errunza, V.R. and E. Losq., 1985, "The Behavior of Stock Prices on LDC markets," Journal of Banking and Finance 9, pp 561-575.

Fama, E. , 1965, "The Behavior of Stock Market Prices," Journal of Business, pp 34-104.

Fama, E. and K.R. French., 1987, "Permanent and Temporary Components of Stock Prices." Working paper, University of Chicago.

Forsgardh, L. and K. Hertzen., 1975, "The adjustment of stock prices to new earnings information; A study of the efficiency of the Swedish stock market " in Elton and Gruber eds., International Capital Markets (North-Holland, Amsterdam).

French, K.R. and R. Roll., 1986, "Stock Return Variances: The Arrival of Information and the Reaction of Traders." Journal of Financial Economics 17, pp. 5-26.

Harris, L., 1989, "The Power of the Roll Serial Covariance Bid/Ask Spread Estimator." Working Paper, University of Southern California.

Jennergren, L.P. and P.E. Korsvold., 1975, "The non-random character of Norwegian and Swedish stock market prices." in Elton and Gruber eds., International Capital Markets (North-Holland, Amsterdam).

Jennings, R.H. and L.T. Stark., 1981, "Earnings Announcements, Stock Price Adjustment and the Existence of Options Markets." Journal of Finance 41, pp 43-61.

Lo, A.W. and A.C. MacKinlay., 1988, " Stock Market Prices Do Not Follow Random walks: Evidence from a Simple Specification Test." The Review of Financial Studies 1, pp 41-66.
Patell, J.M. and M.A. Wolfson., 1984, "The Intraday Speed of Price Adjustment of Stock Prices to Earnings and Dividend Announcements." Journal of Financial Economics 13, pp. 223-252.
Richardson, M. and T. Smith., 1988, "On Tests for Serial Dependency of Returns" Working paper, Stanford University.
Roll, R., 1984, "A Simple Implicit Measure of the Effective Bid-Ask Spread in an Efficient Market." Journal of Finance 39, pp 1127-39.
Solnik, B.H., 1973, "Note on the validity of the random walk for European stock prices." Journal of Finance 28, pp 1151-1159.
Woodruff, C.S. and A.J. Senchack., 1988, "Intraday Price-Volume Adjustments of NYSE Stocks to Unexpected Earnings." Journal of Finance 43, pp. 467-492.

Recent Developments in International Banking
and Finance, S.J. Khoury (editor)

CHAPTER XII

Valuation of Swaps

Suresh Sundaresan[1]

This research was initiated when I spent a year at the Derivative Products Research Group at Shearson Lehman Hutton and I thank Jacques Rolfo for his support during that time. Doug Breeden and Sanjiv Sharma offered valuable comments on different drafts of this paper.

---

1 Columbia University. I thank the seminar particpants at Columbia University, Duke University, Ohio State University, Unviersity of Texas at Austin and the European Finance Association Meetings for their comments and suggestions. I am responsible for any remaining errors.

1 Introduction

Transactions in which two parties agree to make to each other periodic payments computed on the basis of specific interest rates on a *notional principal* amount are known as interest rate swaps. In most interest rate swaps, the payment made by one counterparty is based on a *floating rate of interest such as the London Interbank Offered Rate or LIBOR,* while the payment made by the other counterparty is based on a *fixed rate of interest or a different floating interest rate.* Participants in the swap market use interest rate swaps to transform one type of interest liability into another. The swap transaction is used as a tool to manage their interest rate exposure or to lock in a predetermined profit level. In Figure 1, the basic structure of interest rate swap is depicted. Counterparty A borrows in the floating rate market (say, at LIBOR plus 2%) which is reset every year and counterparty B in the fixed rate market (say, at 12%). They then enter into a swap transaction in which B pays A floating rate swap payments (say, LIBOR plus 1%) and A pays B fixed rate swap payments (say, 13%). With the swap transaction, the borrowing cost of A is 14% and the borrowing cost of B is LIBOR. The swap will turn out to be beneficial if A's borrowing cost in the fixed rate market exceeds 14% and B's borrowing cost in the floating rate market exceeds LIBOR. Usually, the floating rate borrower (A) will be a corporation and the fixed rate borrower (B) will be a bank. If the bank is in a better position to monitor and manage the risks of A, then a bilateral contract such as swap may benefit both parites. For example, B may have an informational advantage relative to the typical floating rate lender. Moreover, B is in the business of evaluating the risks of borrowers and as a result may have acquired greater monitoring and risk management skills over time. In addition, B also has an equilibrium supply of borrowers with differing borrowing requirements. As a result, his search costs are perhaps lower in identifying and matching two counterparties with complementary borrowing needs. For this service, he typically gets a fee. The advantages of better information and lower transactions costs (of monitoring, for instance) are reflected in the swap transaction. Figure 2 depicts the basic structure of a matched swap transaction that typically results in the swap market. The foregoing observations suggest that it is necessary to admit differential information and costs of monitoring and search to rationalize a swap transaction. The focus of this paper, however, is to provide a contingent claims framework towards the valuation of swaps. As a result, we will not model informational asymmetries or costs in this paper.

Given the foregoing observations, it is not surprising that conceptually, swaps have been regarded as forward contracts on interest rates. See, Bicksler and Chen (1986) for instance. This view, while essentially correct, oversimplifies the complexities of swaps. A swap in which floating payments are exchanged for fixed payments may be regarded as a portfolio of forward contracts on the floating index, *only if the reset dates and payment dates coincided.* Frequently, this condition may not be met. When there is a lag between the reset date and the payment date, swap is *a portfolio of random number of forward contracts, where the randomness arises from the uncertainty in future discount functions*. Moreover, these forward contracts are on interest rates or yields and not on prices. Since the transformation from price to yield is *nonlinear*, the valuation of forward contracts on yields is not a simple extension of the valuation of forward contracts on prices. In some swap contracts, floating payments depend on *averages of past yields* creating possible path dependencies. In others, the floating streams are either subjected to a ceiling or floor. In addition, most swap contracts provide counterparties with options such as the ability to cancel the contract, ability to extend the contract, etc. There is also a growing market in which participants trade options on swaps. Yet another dimension of swaps is that there is a positive probability of default. These aspects are taken up in this paper.

1.1 Literature Review and Unresolved Issues

The valuation of floating rate payments has received some attention recently in the academic literature. Cox, Ingersoll and Ross (1980) and Ramaswamy and Sundaresan (1986) have developed arbitrage-free models of pricing floating rate payments. In their paper, Ramaswamy and Sundaresan (1986) developed a continuous time model of pricing floaters which may be subject to default risk. The model accommodated

Figure 1

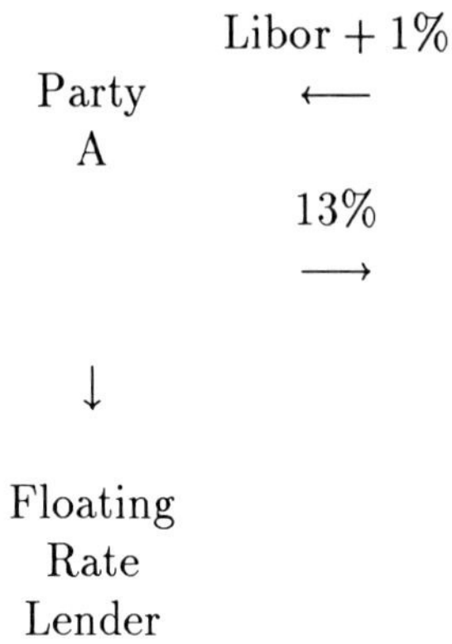

Figure 2

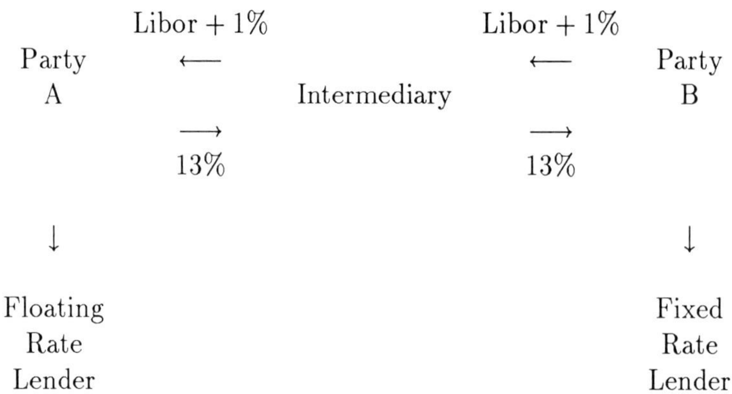

collars, drop lock and conversion features, but required continuous resets and payments. Interest rate swaps which is a gigantic market as described earlier, has also begun to attract formal analysis in the literature. See Bicksler, et al. (1986), Smith, et al. (1986, 1988) and Turnbull (1987), for instance. In a recent paper, Cooper and Mello (1988) have studied the default risk of swaps. They study, in a partial equilibrium setting, the default risk of swaps, spreads due to default and possible wealth transfers due to swaps. We view their contribution as complementing many of the issues relating to swaps that are studied in our paper. In this paper, a framework is developed for the valuation of swaps. Although the paper will primarily focus on interest rate swaps, the insights are applicable to many other swap contracts. The novel aspects of this paper which distinguishes it from other contributions mentioned earlier are:

(i) The model admits discrete reset dates. This generalization is important, for all floaters are reset at periodic intervals. Monthly, quarterly and semi-annual resets are fairly common. (ii) Reset dates may differ from payment dates. In reality, there is typically a lag between the payment date and the reset date. (iii) The maturity of the index to which the floating payments are indexed may differ from the delay between payment and reset dates. Currently many floating rate indices are used: Prime, 30 days LIBOR, 90 days LIBOR and 3 month Treasury bills are some of the indices that are frequently used in swaps. (iv) The term structure of interest rates is stochastic. The Cox, Ingersoll and Ross (1985) term structure model is used to generate *nominal* discount functions and price swaps. Existing models of swaps have not used this term structure framework to accommodate the features cited earlier. (v) The procedure developed here is *path independent* and compositionally easy to implement. (vi) Swaps in which averages of past yields are used are also valued as are foreign currency swaps and options on swaps. These generalizations are made in an arbitrage-free framework.

1.2 Overview of Paper

In the rest of this section some notations and conventions are developed. Section 2 provides several model independent results concerning pricing swaps and implementing them. But to price swaps which may have features such as lags, averages, etc, it is necessary to have a model of the term structure of interest rates. In section 3 we develop a framework to value interest rate swaps and currency swaps. We use the arbitrage-free term structure model Cox, Ingersoll and Ross (1985) although *any* arbitrage-free model of the term structure may be used. Procedures are sketched for valuing floating rate payments which are linked to averages of past index yields. Section 4 provides a framework for the valuation of options on swaps. In section 5, we present an approach to the valuation of swaps that are subject to credit risk.

1.3 Definitions and Notations

We begin by defining some notations and conventions.

A sequence of floating rate payments is defined by the following attributes:

- A sequence of reset dates denoted by s_i for $i = 1,2,...N$. The reset frequency is implicitly defined by this sequence.

- A sequence of payment dates associated with each reset dates and denoted by $t_p(s_i) \geq s_i$ for $i = 1,2,...N$. When $t_p(s_i) = s_i$, reset dates coincide with payment dates.

- A payment rule which defines the index (to which payments are linked) and the spread relative to the index. Let the price at t of a default-free discount bond paying a dollar at $s > t$ is denoted by $b(t,s)$. Let $y(s_i)$ be the index yield at the reset date s_i, and τ is the time to maturity of the index.

  Note that the index yield, $y(s_i)$ may be expressed in terms of the underlying state variable using the following definition. This is annualized LIBOR using money market conventions.

$$y(s_i) = \frac{1}{\tau} \times \left(\frac{1}{b(s_i, s_i + \tau)} - 1\right) \qquad (1)$$

Define $\{\hat{y}(s_i)\} = \{y(s_i)\} \times \tau$. Let δ be the spread over the index. Then the total payments on the payment date $t_p(s_i)$ will be $\hat{y}(s_i) + \delta$. The time to maturity of the index is denoted by τ.

The present value operator at date t on a random future cash flow, Y, to be received at T_i will be denoted by $PV_t\,[Y; T_i]$.

A sequence of fixed rate payments is defined by the following attributes:

A sequence of payment dates indexed by $t_p(s_i)$ where i = 1, 2,... N.

The dollar payments, C.

Definitions

Single Period Swap: Consider a floater which has one future payment. At $t_p(s_i)$, the floater will pay an amount $\hat{y}(s_i) + \delta$. This is equivalent to a payment of $b(s_i, t_p(s_i)) \times (\hat{y}(s_i) + \delta)$ at s_i. What is the fixed payment, C, at $t_p(s_i)$, such that

$$PV_t\left[C; t_p(s_i)\right] = PV_t\left[(\hat{y}(s_i) + \delta) \times b(s_i, t_p(s_i)); s_i\right]?$$

The pair $\{C, \hat{y}(s_i)\}$ constitutes a single period swap. *The concept of a single period swap turns out to be a key primitive in the valuation of multi-period swaps and floating rate instruments with discrete reset and payment dates.*

Multi Period Swap: An *interest rate swap* is an exchange of a sequence of fixed payments, {C}, with a sequence of floating payments, $\{\hat{y}(s_i) + \delta$, as defined earlier, such that

$$\Sigma_{i=1}^{i=N} PV_t\left[C; t_p(s_i)\right] = \Sigma_{i=1}^{i=N} PV_t\left[\hat{y}(s_i) + \delta; t_p(s_i)\right]$$

If the reset dates and payment dates coincide, then the multi period swap is a portfolio of single period swaps each of which is a forward contract on the floating index. If the dates do not coincide, then the multi period swap is a portfolio of *random number*, $b(s_i, t_p(s_i))$, of forward contracts with payments brought back to the reset dates.

In the next section, we consider the problem of pricing and implementing swaps.

2 Model independent results

The results in this section relate the value of any sequence of floating rate payments to a sequence of deterministic rate payments. We will begin this section by focusing on Eurodollar futures as a mechanism for implementing swaps. In this section alone, it will be assumed that Eurodollar futures are not marked-to-market. For the sake of simplicity, the reset dates are assumed to be the payment dates. Furthermore, Eurodollar futures are assumed to mature in reset dates.

2.1 Swap Pricing with Eurodollar Futures

Let t be the current date, s_1 be the maturity date of the nearest Eurodollar futures contract and s_2 be the maturity date of the next Eurodollar futures contract. Let $H_t(s_i)$ be the Eurodollar futures price at date t maturing on s_i. The time to maturity of the underlying deposit is 90 days for Eurodollar futures contract.

Define $r_t(i) = 100 - H_t(s_i)$ as the *implied interest rate* at time t for the maturity date s_i. The next proposition shows that the futures prices provide a mechanism for pricing swaps. *The key here is to recognize that Eurodollar futures are actually futures contracts on rates, $y(s_i)$, (LIBOR) as opposed to futures contracts on prices. Thus, they are the natural vehicles for implementing and hedging LIBOR-based swaps.*

The next result stresses this fact and shows how Eurodollar futures may be used to transform a floating sequence into a fixed sequence.

Proposition 1

The swap rate, r_t, for the sequence of London Interbank Offered Rates, $\{y(s_1), y(s_2)\}$ paid at s_1 and s_2 respectively, is a convex combination of the implied interest rates, $r_t(1)$ and $r_t(2)$, *determined at t from the term structure of futures prices.*

The payoff from a short position in futures contract is $H_t(s_i)$ - $H_{si}(si)$ which is the same as $y(s_i)$ - $r_t(i)$ by the convergence of Eurodollar futures to LIBOR.[1] The Eurodollar futures price converges to LIBOR at maturity according to the following rule:

$$H_{s_i}(s_i) = 100 - y(s_i).$$

It is costless to enter into futures contracts. Therefore,

$$PV_t\left[y(s_i) - r_t(i); T_i\right] = 0$$

This implies that PV_t $[y(s_i); s_i]$ = PV_t $[r_t(i); s_i]$. Thus an individual should be indifferent between receiving the floating payment $y(s_i)$ and the known payment $r_t(i)$ at s_i. No-arbitrage requirement implies that

[1] In reality, the futures prices are quoted in basis points. Each basis point change denotes $25. As a result, the futures price changes have to be multiplied by 2500 to arrive at the corresponding change in the interest rates at maturity. We have ignored this to simplify exposition.

$$PV_t\left[\hat{r}_t; s_1\right] + PV_t\left[\hat{r}_t; s_2\right] = PV_t\left[r_t(1); s_1\right] + PV_t\left[r_t(2); s_2\right]$$

Casting the above relationship in terms of pure discount functions, we get:

$$(b(t,s_1) + b(t,s_2))\hat{r}_t = b(t,s_1)r_t(1) + b(t,s_2)r_t(2)$$

Let $b(t,T_i) = 1/1+R(t,T_i)$, then it follows that

$$\hat{r}_t = \alpha \times r_t(1) + (1-\alpha) \times r_t(2), \tag{2}$$

where

$$\alpha \equiv \frac{1 + R(t,T_2)}{2 + R(t,T_1) + R(t,T_2)}.$$

Thus, the fixed sequence $\hat{r}$ is equivalent to the floating sequence $\{y(s_1), y(s_2)\}$ and therefore constitutes a swap at equilibrium. This is the swap rate when the LIBOR at reset dates s_i is paid without a lag. The swap rate depends on the term structure of interest rates. The swap rate r is a *convex combination of the interest rates implied by the term structure of Eurodollar futures prices.* Thus, we have shown that the Eurodollar futures prices contain the swap pricing information.

To implement a swap, which assures the investor the sequence $\{r_t(1), r_t(2)\}$, it is sufficient to sell a *strip of Eurodollar futures:* sell one of each at t and pay the LIBOR at the maturity dates of futures.

2.2 Risk of Floaters and Swaps

Let us consider now the swap pricing problem when the payment date differs from the futures maturity dates. We now assume that $\tau_p \equiv t_p(s_i) - s_i = \tau$.

Consider a floater which pays $\hat{y}(s_i)$ at $t_p(s_i)$. The value of this floater is given by

$$V(t, s_i) = b(t, s_i) - b(t, t_p(s_i)).$$

This result is true in very general settings and was shown in Smith, et al. (1986). We present this result here to highlight the effect of the lag between reset and payment dates on the equilibrium swap rate. The arbitrage proof works as follows: sell a discount bond maturing on $t_p(s_i)$ and use the proceeds to partly finance the purchase of a discount bond which matures on s_i. At s_i, receive \$1 from the maturing bond and buy a time deposit maturing on $t_p(s_i)$. The total proceeds at $t_p(s_i)$ may be used to cover the short position by buying back the other discount bond which now sells at par. The return on this strategy as of $t_p(s_i)$ is LIBOR (which prevailed at s_N) which is exactly what the floater would have provided. So to preclude arbitrage, the value of the floater must be equal to $b(t,s_i)$ - $b(t,t_p(s_i))$. Thus the floater is significantly less risky than the fixed rate sequence. If the floater pays a face value of \$1 at maturity, then it must sell for $b(t,s_i)$.

Note that if there are N reset dates, and if s_{i+1} - s_i = τ, then the value of such a floating sequence without principal at maturity is simply given by $b(t,s_1)$ - $b(t,t_p(s_N))$. If the floater pays a face amount of 1 at par, then it will sell for $b(t,s_1)$, *irrespective of its maturity.* Note that as the frequency of resets increases, the risk of the floater decreases. Although all our arguments apply only to default free floaters, the concept is similar for bank or corporate floaters and swaps which entail some credit risk. The results above suggest that a risk measure of a floater of any maturity is the time to the next reset date. Thus the "quality spread" for a floater could be relatively small when compared to a fixed rate note of same maturity.

Consider a swap in which floating payments are made under the following conditions:

1. τ is the maturity of the floating index.

2. s_{i+1} -s_i = τ, where s_1 is the first reset date after t.

3. $t_p(s_i)$ = s_{i+1}.

Let the fixed payments c be made on $t_p(s_i)$ for i= 1,2,...N. Then at time t when the swap contract is initiated, the value of the swap must be zero. The value of c which will cause this to happen, by the analysis above, is given by:

$$c = \frac{[b(t, s_1) - b(t, t_p(s_N))]}{\Sigma_{i=1}^{i=N} b(t, t_p(s_i))}. \tag{3}$$

A comparison of (2) and (3) should indicate the differences in the swap rates due to differences in reset date and payment dates. In (2), it is necessary to know the Eurodollar futures prices because they contain (by virtue of their settlement feature) information about the current value of receiving LIBOR on the settlement date without any lag. In (3), it is sufficient to know the pure discount functions.

Note that we were able to value the swap with no term structure assumptions. At any time t' > t, the swap may have a negative or positive value. In general, the interest rate swap value, S(t') is given by:

$$S(t') = b(t', s_1) - b(t', t_p(s_N)) - c\Sigma_{i=1}^{i=N} b(t', t_p(s_i)).$$

On a reset date, note that the sensitivity of the swap contract is identical to that of a fixed rate note which pays c on payment dates $t_p(s_i)$ plus the face amount on $t_p(s_N)$.

In reality, floaters have many other features: floaters may have an index whose maturity may not necessarily coincide with τ_p. Some floaters pay the amount on the reset dates. Many floaters have payments that are linked to averages of past index yields with floors and ceilings. In addition, the presence of credit risk may pose additional complications. In order to satisfactorily handle these features, it becomes necessary to use a specific term structure model for swap valuation. We proceed to do this in the next section.

3 Valuation of swaps with a term structure model

In this section, a simple model of swap valuation is developed using the Cox, Ingersoll and Ross (1985) term structure model for generating default-free discount functions. The approach is sufficiently general that any other stochastic term structure model may be imbedded in it. In the context of this section, the swap valuation is performed for arbitrary reset dates and payments dates.

The term structure model of Cox, Ingersoll and Ross (1985) is based on the following key assumption:

> The model assumes that the short-rate follows a mean-reverting stochastic process as shown below:
>
> $$dr = \kappa(\mu - r)dt + \sigma\sqrt{r}dz \qquad (4)$$
>
> In the equation above, κ is the speed of adjustment, μ is the long--run mean rate of interest and $\sigma^2 r$ may be viewed as the variance of changes in interest rates. Furthermore, [z(t),t > 0] is a standard Wiener process.

Prices of discount bonds in the Cox, Ingersoll and Ross (1985) model are specified as follows: Let the current time be denoted by t, then a bond paying $1 at time s should be priced as

$$b(t,s) = A(s-t)e^{-B(s-t)r_t} \qquad (5)$$

where the functions $A(\tau_d)$ and $B(\tau_d)$ are as defined below:

$$A(\tau_d) = \left(\frac{2\gamma e^{(\kappa+\gamma+\lambda)\tau_d/2}}{2\gamma + (\kappa+\gamma+\lambda)(e^{\gamma\tau_d}-1)}\right)^{2\kappa\mu/\sigma^2}$$

$$B(\tau_d) = \frac{2(e^{\gamma\tau_d}-1)}{2\gamma + (\kappa+\gamma+\lambda)(e^{\gamma\tau_d}-1)}$$

$$\gamma = \sqrt{(\kappa+\lambda)^2 + 2\sigma^2}$$
$$\tau_d = s - t$$

In the discount function formula above λ may be interpreted as factor risk premium. In this stochastic term structure environment, we proceed to value floating rate sequences which have discrete reset dates and payment dates.

3.1 A Framework for valuing swaps

Consider a contract that pays $\hat{y}(s_i)$ at $t_p(s_i)$. This terminal payoff is equivalent to receiving $b(s_i, t_p(s_i))$ X $\hat{y}(s_i)$ at s_i. The value of this contract, $V(t, s_i)$, satisfies the following partial differential equation:

$$V_t + V_r(\kappa(\mu - r) - r\lambda) + \frac{1}{2}V_{rr} r\sigma^2 - Vr = 0 \qquad (6)$$

The contract value function satisfies the initial condition shown below:

$$V(s_i, s_i) = b(s_i, t_p(s_i)) \times \hat{y}(s_i) \qquad (7)$$

3.1.1 Interest rate swap valuation

A sequence of floating rate payments, $\{\hat{y}(s_i)\}$, paid at $t_p(s_i)$ may be priced by the following procedure.

1. For each $t_p(s_i)$, calculate $V(t, s_i)$ by solving the valuation equation (6) subject to the initial condition (7) shown above.

2. The value of the sequence, $\{\hat{y}\}(s_i)\}$, denoted by V(t,

$\{\hat{y}_t\}(s_i)\})$ is obtained by the summation of individual value functions as shown below:

$$\Sigma_{i=1}^{i=N} V(t, s_i)$$

The swap terms may then be solved by equating the present value of a sequence of fixed rate payments, {C} with the value of the floating rate sequence as follows:

$$\Sigma_{i=1}^{i=N} PV_t \left[C; t_p(s_i) \right] = \Sigma_{i=1}^{i=N} V(t, s_i)$$

This procedure demonstrates clearly the relationship between the valuation of interest rate swaps and that of floating rate payments. The same idea may be applied for currency swap transactions in which *principal amounts are also exchanged.*

3.1.2. Currency swap valuation

In a currency swap, initially (at the time of swap agreement) firm A agrees to receive \$X from firm B and pays a certain amount Y of British Sterling. This part of the transaction is clearly a bilateral forward contract. In addition, the firms agree to reverse

these transactions at the end of the term of the swap and during the term, the firms exchange predetermined interest payments. Let {x}, paid at $t_p(s_i)$ be the dollar payments and let {y}, paid at $t_p(s_i)$ be the Sterling payments. These interest payments may either be floating are fixed. For the purposes of illustration, we will treat the interest payments to be fixed, but denominated in their respective currencies. Let P_t be the spot exchange rate at t (in dollars per Sterling). The exchange of \$X for Y units of British Sterling at the end of the term of the swap, $t_p(s_N)$ may be valued as follows:

$$X \times b(t, t_p(s_N)) \equiv Y \times b^*(t, t_p(s_N)) \times P_t.$$

So a complete valuation of the currency swap may be carried out as follows:

$$V_t(\{x\}) + X \times b(t, t_p(s_N)) \equiv V_t(\{y\}) + Y \times b^*(t, t_p(s_N)) \times P_t.$$

The value of interest payments may be first found by determining the present value using the discount functions and then mapping them to the currency of choice using the current spot exchange rate. If the interest payments are floating, then the valuation procedure developed earlier may be applied to each payments to determine their present values.

We now proceed to apply this framework to price floaters and swaps.

3.2 Straight Floaters and Swaps

For two cases of interest, we proceed to develop closed form solutions.

3.2.1. Reset date coincident with payment date

In this section, we assume that $t_p(s_i) = s_i$. With this assumption, condition (7) becomes:

$$V(s_i, s_i) = \hat{y}(s_i) \tag{8}$$

For this special case, the proposition below provides a closed form solution to $V(t,s_i)$. We define $\tau_f = s_i - t$. In this case, the holder of the security receives LIBOR on the day the rates are posted. This is to be contrasted with swaps in which the LIBOR is posted on the reset date but is paid in *arrears* on the payment date.

Proposition 2

The value, $V(t,s_i)$, of a floating payment at s_i is given by the formula below:

$$V(t, s_i) = g(\tau_f)e^{-h(\tau_f)r_t} - b(t, s_i),$$

where,

$$g(\tau_f) = \frac{1}{A(\tau)}\left(\frac{a_1 e^{\theta_1 \tau_f} + e^{(\theta_1-\gamma)\tau_f}}{(1+a_1)}\right)^{-2\kappa\mu/\sigma^2},$$

$$h(\tau_f) = \frac{2}{\sigma^2}\left(\frac{a_1\theta_1 e^{\gamma\tau_f} + (\theta_1 - \gamma)}{(1 + a_1 e^{\gamma\tau_f})}\right),$$

$$\theta_1 = \frac{1}{2}[-(\kappa + \lambda) + \gamma],$$

$$\gamma = ((\kappa + \lambda)^2 + 2\sigma^2)^{1/2} > 0,$$

and

$$a_1 = -\frac{\frac{\sigma^2}{2}B(\tau) + (\theta_1 - \gamma)}{\theta_1 + \frac{\sigma^2}{2}B(\tau)}.$$

The swap terms may be found by requiring that $V(t,s_i) = c \times b(t,s_i)$ and solving for c as

$$c = \frac{\left(g(\tau_f)e^{-h(\tau_f)r_t} - b(t,s_i)\right)}{b(t,s_i)}.$$

The pair $\{c,\hat{y}(s_i)\}$, constitutes a swap at equilibrium.

The formulae derived above was used to value LIBOR-based swaps for the following parameter configuration.

$$\kappa = 0.70; \mu = 0.07; \sigma = 0.078; \lambda = -0.20.$$

These parameter values permit both upward sloping and downward sloping term structure environments. The floating leg of the swap is assumed to pay 90 day LIBOR every quarter with no lag between reset and payment dates. We considered swaps with a life of 1 to 5 years.

Table 1 provides a summary of swap valuation.

Table 1: **SWAP VALUATION–NO LAG**

90 day Libor	1 Year Swap	2 Year Swap	3 Year Swap	4 Year Swap	5 Year Swap
5.00%	6.36%	7.03%	7.57%	7.99%	8.33%
6.00%	7.18%	7.74%	8.19%	8.55%	8.84%
7.00%	7.99%	8.45%	8.82%	9.11%	9.34%
8.00%	8.81%	9.17%	9.45%	9.67%	9.85%
9.00%	9.63%	9.89%	10.08%	10.24%	10.36%
10.00%	10.45%	10.61%	10.72%	10.81%	10.88%
11.00%	11.28%	11.33%	11.36%	11.38%	11.40%
12.00%	12.11%	12.05%	12.00%	11.96%	11.92%
13.00%	12.93%	12.78%	12.65%	12.54%	12.45%
14.00%	13.76%	13.51%	13.30%	13.12%	12.98%
15.00%	14.60%	14.24%	13.95%	13.71%	13.51%

The shape of the term structure affects the terms of the swap significantly. *When interest rates are low, (say, 90 day Libor is at 5\%), the term structure is upward sloping and the fixed rate compensation is an increasing function of the life of the swap.* At that level of LIBOR, difference between the fixed rate compensation for 1 year swap and five year swap is slightly less than 200 basis points. When the LIBOR level is 9\%, the term structure is nearly flat and the difference between the fixed rate compensation for 1 year and 5 year swap becomes 73 basis points *With inverted yield curve, (say, at a LIBOR of 15\%), the fixed rate compensation is a decreasing function of the life of the swap.*

The swap terms did not change significantly when the variance parameter was changed. It appears as if the expectations of LIBOR play a more central role in the valuation of swaps than the volatility of the rates.

Holding the life of swap fixed, it is seen that increases in LIBOR have relatively bigger effect on short-term swaps than they do on long-term swaps: an increase of 100 basis points in LIBOR from an initial level of 10\% causes the fixed rate compensation for a 1 year swap to go up by 83 basis points, whereas the compensation for a 5 year swap goes up only by 52 basis points.

The sensitivity of swap exchange rates to the speed of adjustment is illustrated in Table 2 for a swap term of 5 years. Clearly the location of the interest rate relative to the long run mean and the speed of its adjustment to the mean play an important part in determining the swap the exchange rates. The conclusions were similar for swaps with a life of less than 5 years.

Table 2: **SENSITIVITY OF SWAP VALUES**

90 day Libor	$\kappa = 0.30$	$\kappa = 0.70$	$\kappa = 0.90$
5.00%	8.49%	8.33%	8.17%
6.00%	9.26%	8.84%	8.52%
7.00%	10.03%	9.34%	8.88%
8.00%	10.81%	9.85%	9.23%
9.00%	11.59%	10.36%	9.59%
10.00%	12.37%	10.88%	9.95%
11.00%	13.16%	11.40%	10.31%
12.00%	13.95%	11.92%	10.68%
13.00%	14.74%	12.45%	11.04%
14.00%	15.55%	12.98%	11.41%
15.00%	16.35%	13.51%	11.79%

As the speed of adjustment increases, the fixed rate compensation required for a given level of 90 day LIBOR decreases, irrespective of the shape of the term structure of interest rates. This decrease is much more pronounced at higher level of LIBOR, where the tendency to be pulled towards a lower long run mean dominates the fixed rate compensation. We also simulated the impact of volatility of interest rates on swap spreads for a five year swap. Increases in volatility appear to increase the swap spreads, but not by much.

Corollary 1

The value, $V(t,s_N)$, of a floating payment $\hat{y}(s_N)$ plus a face amount of 1 at s_N is given by the formula below:

$$V(t, s_N) = g(\tau_f)e^{-h(\tau_f)r_t}$$

The interest rate risk of this floater may be defined by its elasticity $-\frac{\partial V_f}{\partial r}\frac{1}{V_f}$ which is given by $h(\tau_f)$. The precise quantification of the floater's interest rate risk (exposure) is an important outcome of the model. The interest rate elasticity is found to be increasing in time to the next reset date of the floater. Of particular interest is the impact that the frequency of resets has on the value of the floater and its interest rate risk. As the frequency of resets increases, holding the maturity fixed, we found that the floater became less sensitive to interest rate changes. As the time to next reset date increases, the interest rate sensitivity of the floater was found to increase as well.

3.2.2 Reset date differs from payment date

In this more general case, the swap valuation formula becomes a bit more complicated. This case is similar to receiving LIBOR in arrears and is closer to the spirit of interest rate swaps.

Proposition 3

When the reset date differs from the payment date, so that $t_p(s_i) - s_i = \tau$, the valuation function is given by the formula below:

$$V(t, s_N) = g_1(\tau_f)e^{-h_1(\tau_f)r_t} - g_2(\tau_f)e^{-h_2(\tau_f)r_t}.$$

where

$$h_1(\tau_f) = \frac{2}{\sigma^2}\left(\frac{\Gamma_1\theta_1 e^{\gamma\tau_f} + \theta_2}{\Gamma_1 e^{\gamma\tau_f} + 1}\right),$$

$$g_1(\tau_f) = \frac{A(\tau_p)}{A(\tau)}\left(\frac{\Gamma_1 e^{\theta_1\tau_f} + e^{\theta_2\tau_f}}{1 + \Gamma_1}\right)^{-2\kappa\mu/\sigma^2},$$

$$h_2(\tau_f) = \frac{2}{\sigma^2}\left(\frac{\Gamma_2\theta_1 e^{\gamma\tau_f} + \theta_2}{\Gamma_2 e^{\gamma\tau_f} + 1}\right),$$

$$g_2(\tau_f) = A(\tau_p)\left(\frac{\Gamma_2 e^{\theta_1\tau_f} + e^{\theta_2\tau_f}}{1 + \Gamma_2}\right)^{-2\kappa\mu/\sigma^2},$$

$$\gamma = ((\kappa + \lambda)^2 + 2\sigma^2)^{1/2},$$

$$\theta_1 = [-(\kappa + \lambda) + \gamma]/2,$$

$$\theta_2 = \theta_1 - \gamma,$$

$$\Gamma_1 = \frac{\frac{\sigma^2}{2}[B(\tau_p) - B(\tau)] - \theta_2}{\theta_1 - \frac{\sigma^2}{2}[B(\tau_p) - B(\tau)]},$$

and

$$\Gamma_2 = \frac{\frac{\sigma^2}{2}B(\tau_p) - \theta_2}{\theta_1 - \frac{\sigma^2}{2}B(\tau_p)} = -\frac{\theta_2}{\theta_1}e^{\gamma\tau_p}.$$

When $= \tau_p = \tau$, the formula may be simplified considerably as:

$$V(t, s_i) = b(t, s_i) - b(t, t_p(s_i)).$$

Table 3 provides the exchange terms for swaps which are identical in every way except that the lags vary from 1 month to about 3 months.

The terms of this swap are identical to the terms specified in the swap corresponding to table 1, except that we are now considering a lag in the actual payment date relative to the reset date. Both fixed and floating legs are assumed to be paid with a lag. Three lag periods were considered: 1 month, 2 months and 3 months. As the table indicates, the lag does not have a significant impact on the pricing of swaps. Table 3 reports our findings for a five year swap, although results were similar for swaps with a life of less than 5 years.

Corollary 2

The value, $V(t,s_i)$, of a floating payment $\hat{y}(s_i)$, plus a face amount of 1 at $t_p(s_i)$ is given by the formula below:

$$V(t,s_i) = g_1(\tau_f)e^{-h_1(\tau_f)r_t} - g_2(\tau_f)e^{-h_2(\tau_f)r_t} + b(t,t_p(s_i))$$

The interest rate risk of this floater may be defined by its elasticity $-\frac{\partial V_f}{\partial r}\frac{1}{V_f}$ which may be computed using corollary 2 above.

Note that on any reset date (when $\tau_f =$ 0), if the index maturity τ coincides with τ_p, the floater value V_f goes to par. This follows from corollary 2 by setting $\tau_p \equiv \tau$ and $\tau_f = 0$. When τ coincides with τp, the value of the floater is given by

$$V_f(t,s_N) = b(t,s_N)$$

Thus the floater behaves like a discount paper maturing on the next reset date. Thus the duration risk measure of any floater, *regardless of its time to maturity* is simply the time to its next reset date.

Together, the three propositions provide mechanisms for valuing swaps under different assumptions. Crucial to the use of these models are reliable estimates of the parameters $(\kappa,\mu,\lambda,\sigma^2)$. Recent advances in the estimation of these parameters due to Gibbons and Ramaswamy (1987) may be used to obtain reliable estimates of these parameters.

Table 3: **EFFECT OF LAGS ON SWAP VALUATION**

90 day LIBOR	1 Month Lag	2 Month Lag	3 Month Lag
5.00%	2.08%	2.08%	2.08%
6.00%	2.21%	2.21%	2.20%
7.00%	2.34%	2.33%	2.33%
8.00%	2.46%	2.46%	2.46%
9.00%	2.59%	2.59%	2.59%
10.00%	2.72%	2.72%	2.71%
11.00%	2.85%	2.85%	2.84%
12.00%	2.98%	2.98%	2.98%
13.00%	3.11%	3.11%	3.11%
14.00%	3.24%	3.24%	3.24%
15.00%	3.38%	3.37%	3.37%
16.00%	3.51%	3.51%	3.51%
17.00%	3.65%	3.64%	3.64%
18.00%	3.79%	3.78%	3.78%
19.00%	3.92%	3.92%	3.92%
20.00%	4.06%	4.06%	4.05%

3.3 Floating sequences which are averages of past index yields

Consider a floating rate note which pays at t_p, the amount $\lambda_1\hat{y}\}(s_1) + \lambda_2\hat{y}(s_2)$. This is equivalent to buying λ_1 units of a floater which pays at t_p, the amount $\hat{y}(s_1)$ and λ_2 units of a floater which pays at t_p, the amount $\hat{y}(s_2)$. Extension to a sequence of such floating payments is direct. Many floaters issued by commercial banks and financial companies in the United States have such coupon rules: for example, many of these floaters have rules in which the coupon paid on any payment date is an arithmetic average of the Treasury bill yields which prevailed on three successive auctions prior to the associated reset dates. The pricing of floaters with collars also proceeds along the lines proposed in this paper. Currency swaps, puttable swaps and extendible swaps may also be valued using the procedure described in this paper. Caps on LIBOR may also be priced in a similar manner.

3.4 Foreign currency swaps

We illustrate the pricing of foreign currency swaps with both fixed and floating interest rate arrangements. As explained in section 3.1.2, the foreign currency swap valuation may be carried out only by using a fully specified model of the term structure of interest rates in *both* domestic economy and foreign economy. No assumptions are needed, however, concerning the evolution of spot exchange rates. Consider a foreign currency swap that was entered into by two counterparties sometime ago. Let counterparty A be required to repay X U.S dollars at time T and let counterparty B be required to pay Y British pounds on the same date. In addition, let A be required to pay a sequence (of U.S.dollars) $\{x_i\}$ at times s_i and let B be required to pay (British pounds) $\{y_i\}$ at times s_i. The value of the swap to counterparty A at t, S(t), is the present value of projected receipts minus the present value of projected payments. We computed the value of the swap in British pounds.

$$S(t) = b^*(t,T) \times Y + \Sigma_{i=1}^{i=N} b^*(t,s_i)y_i - P_t[b(t,T) \times X - \Sigma_{i=1}^{i=N} b(t,s_i)x_i]$$

where P_t is the spot exchange rate in pounds per dollar. If the agreed upon interest rates were keyed to floating indexes, the currency swap valuation will proceed as detailed in section 3.1.2. There is one special case for which it is possible to get a simple valuation formula. This corresponds to a situation in which the payment lag is exactly equal to the time between two successive reset dates. For example, let counterparty A pay 90 day LIBOR in U.S. dollars every 3 months with a payment lag of 3 months. Let counterparty B pay 180 day LIBOR in Sterling every 180 days with a lag of 180 days. Let A pay B \$X and receive from B Y sterling on the final day $t_p(s_N)$. We know that the value, of the stream (excluding principal) paid by A is equal to $b(t,s_1) - b(t,t_p(s_N))$, where, s_1 is the first reset date and $t_p(s_N)$ is the last payment date for interest. Similarly, the value of the stream (excluding principal) paid by B is given by $b^*(t,s_1) - b^*(t,t_p(s_N))$. Then, the value of this currency-interest rate swap to counterparty A is given by:

$$S(t) = [b^*(t, s_1) - b^*(t, t_p(s_N))] \times P_t - [b(t, s_1) - b(t, t_p(s_N))] + Y \times b^*(t, T) \times P_t - X \times b(t, T).$$

4 Valuation of Options on Swaps

There is a growing dealers market for options on swaps both in the United States and abroad. This section will provide a framework for pricing them. Consider a contract which provides the following option: The investor at his or her option may convert a floating sequence, $\{\hat{y}\}(s_i)\}$, to a fixed sequence, $\{C\}$, on or before a predetermined date T. Let S(t), be the swap value at time t. Then the value, V of the swaption satisfies the following partial differential equation.

$$V_t + V_r(\kappa(\mu - r) - r\lambda) + \frac{1}{2}V_{rr}r\sigma^2 - Vr = 0 \quad (9)$$

The option on swaps must satisfy the condition shown below at maturity:

$$V(T) = \max[0, S(T)] \quad (10)$$

To complete the specification of pricing options on swaps, we must solve endogenously for the *free boundary* problem of optimal early exercise of such options. Let r^* be the critical interest rate at which the optimal exercise takes place. Then at r*, the following requirement must be met.

$$V(s) - S(s).$$

Although most swaptions are structured as European options we calculated values of both American and European swaptions for the following parameter set:

$$\kappa = 0.70; \mu = 0.07; \sigma = 0.078; \lambda = -0.20.$$

The valuation procedure was implemented and the results are shown in the next two tables. The options were assumed to have a time to maturity of 30 days. The strike rate for the option was set at 6.0%. In other words, the holder of this option has the right to enter into a swap in which he will be obliged to pay 6.0% (annualized) every quarter and will have the right to receive 90 day LIBOR every quarter. Obviously, as the LIBOR level increases, the option becomes extremely valuable. At a LIBOR level of 6.00% and below, both European and American options on swaps are nearly identically priced. But as LIBOR increases, the early exercise feature of American options on swaps begins to dominate the pricing: at a LIBOR level of 12.00%, American options are worth about 5 basis points more than their European counterpart. In table 5, the options premia are reported when the underlying swaps have different terms. Quite clearly, options on swaps with longer term to maturity are at least as valuable as options on swaps (which are otherwise identical) with shorter term to maturity.

Table 4:

AMERICAN VERSUS EUROPEAN SWAPTIONS

90 DAY LIBOR	EUROPEAN CALL	AMERICAN CALL
2.00%	0.04468	0.04468
3.00%	0.06266	0.06267
4.00%	0.08032	0.08042
5.00%	0.09749	0.09854
6.00%	0.11420	0.11810
7.00%	0.13046	0.13891
8.00%	0.14627	0.16026
9.00%	0.16165	0.18187
10.00%	0.17661	0.2037
11.00%	0.19116	0.22573
12.00%	0.20531	0.2476
13.00%	0.21908	0.26749
14.00%	0.23253	0.28264
15.00%	0.24581	0.29309

5 Default risk in swaps

The problem of default risk in interest rate swaps may not be a severe one for a number of reasons.

1. Interest rate swaps exclude principal payments in general and as a result eliminate one important dimension of default.

2. Swaps entail *an exchange* of floating sequence with fixed sequence. In the event of default, the investor who stood to receive floating payments is also relieved of his obligation to pay fixed payments. Thus the nature of the swap contract makes the default risk less severe in general.

Table 5: **OPTIONS ON DIFFERENT SWAPS**

90 DAY LIBOR	1 YEAR SWAP	3 YEAR SWAP	5 YEAR SWAP
2.00%	0.0000	0.0031	0.0447
3.00%	0.0001	0.0144	0.0627
4.00%	0.0012	0.0287	0.0803
5.00%	0.0047	0.0429	0.0975
6.00%	0.0097	0.0568	0.1142
7.00%	0.0152	0.0705	0.1305
8.00%	0.0206	0.0838	0.1463
9.00%	0.0260	0.0969	0.1617
10.00%	0.0313	0.1096	0.1766
11.00%	0.0366	0.1221	0.1912
12.00%	0.0418	0.1343	0.2053
13.00%	0.0469	0.1463	0.2191
14.00%	0.0520	0.1580	0.2325
15.00%	0.0571	0.1696	0.2458

3. The swap contract may be structured to minimize the impact of default risk. *For the same present value of floating obligations*, by requiring more collateral, more frequent resets and payments, the swap may be made less risky.

4. In addition, a counterparty to a swap contract may default on swaps when the swap has a positive value to him, simply because the circumstances which lead to bankruptcy are unrelated to the swap's risk-return pattern.

Smith, et al (1988) in their paper argue that the default risk is a lot less for an additional reason as well: if the intermediary has a well diversified swap book, then roughly half of the book will contain swaps in which the intermediary receives floating rate and pays fixed, whereas the other half has a complementary cashflow pattern. Thus through proper diversification, this risk could be managed better.

The treatment of default risk in swaps renders the problem less tractable, in general. In Ramaswamy and Sundaresan (1986), the concept of an
instantaneous default premium was used to value floaters prone to default risk. Let x be the instantaneous default premium and let x evolve as shown below:

$$dx = \kappa_x(\mu_x - x)dt + \sigma_x\sqrt{x}dz_x \tag{11}$$

We assume that the processes $\{z(t), z_x(t)\}$ are uncorrelated to keep the problem tractable. The value of a fixed rate note is determined according to the Local Expectations Hypothesis (LEH) as shown below.[2] This way of accommodating the default premium differs from the procedure used by Merton (1974) and has been used to keep the problem tractable.

$$E_t\left(\frac{db(t,s)}{b(t,s)}\right) = (r_t + x_t)dt \tag{12}$$

The fixed rate note's price satisfies the valuation equation shown below:

$$b_t + b_r\kappa(\mu - r) + \frac{1}{2}b_{rr}r\sigma^2 - b(r+x) + b_x\kappa_x(\mu_x - x) + \frac{1}{2}b_{xx}x\sigma_x^2 = 0 \tag{13}$$

The value of the fixed rate note is then given by the formula shown below:

$$b(t,s) = H(\tau)e^{-B(\tau_f)r_t - C(\tau_f)x_t} \tag{14}$$

where,

$$C(\tau_f) = \frac{2}{{\sigma_x}^2}\left(\frac{\Gamma_x\theta_{x1}e^{\gamma_x\tau_f} + \theta_{x2}}{\Gamma_x e^{\gamma_x\tau_f} + 1}\right),$$

---

[2] See Cox, Ingersoll and Ross (1981) for a discussion of this hypothesis.

$$H(\tau) = \left(\frac{2\gamma e^{(\kappa+\gamma)\tau_f/2}}{2\gamma + (\kappa+\gamma)(e^{\gamma\tau_f}-1)}\right)^{2\kappa\mu/\sigma^2} \times \left(\frac{2\gamma_x e^{(\kappa_x+\gamma_x)\tau_f/2}}{2\gamma_x + (\kappa_x+\gamma_x)(e^{\gamma_x\tau_f}-1)}\right)^{2\kappa_x\mu_x/\sigma_x^2},$$

$$\gamma_x = (\kappa_x^2 + 2\sigma_x^2)^{1/2},$$

$$\theta_{x1} = [-\kappa_x + \gamma_x]/2,$$

$$\theta_{x2} = \theta_{x1} - \gamma_x,$$

and

$$\Gamma_x = \frac{-\theta_{x2}}{\theta_{x1}}.$$

The function $C(\tau_f)$ measures the elasticity of the fixed rate note with respect to the instantaneous default premium.

The value of a floater which pays $y(\tau)$ at $t_p(s_N)$ where we assume that $t_p(s_N)$- $s_N = \tau$, also obeys the valuation equation shown above. The initial condition is

$$V(N, s_N) = b(s_N, t_p(s_N)) \times \hat{y}(s_N)$$

The initial condition above may be rewritten as follows:

$$V(N, s_N) = 1 - b(s_N, t_p(s_N))$$

The value of the floating payment may be expressed as shown below:

$$V(t, s_N) = b(t, s_N) - \hat{H}(\tau_f)e^{-h_2(\tau_f)r_t - \hat{C}(\tau_f)x_t} \tag{15}$$

where

$$\hat{C}(\tau_f) = \frac{2}{{\sigma_x}^2}\left(\frac{\Gamma_{x2}\theta_{x1}e^{\gamma_x\tau_f} + \theta_{x2}}{\Gamma_{x2}e^{\gamma_x\tau_f} + 1}\right),$$

$$\Gamma_{x2} = \frac{\frac{\sigma_x^2}{2}C(\tau) - \theta_{x2}}{\theta_{x1} - \frac{\sigma_x^2}{2}C(\tau)},$$

and

$$\hat{H}(\tau_f) = H(\tau)\left(\frac{\Gamma_2 e^{\theta_1\tau_f} + e^{\theta_2\tau_f}}{1 + \Gamma_2}\right)^{-2\kappa\mu/\sigma^2} \times \left(\frac{\Gamma_{x2}e^{\theta_{x1}\tau_f} + e^{\theta_{x2}\tau_f}}{1 + \Gamma_{x2}}\right)^{-2\kappa_x\mu_x/\sigma_x^2}.$$

The function $\hat{C}(\tau_f)$ measures the elasticity of the floater with respect to the instantaneous default premium. The properties of swaps under default risk may now be examined using the results developed above.

5.1 Swap Spreads Over Treasuries

The formulation in the previous section was used to determine the spreads over Treasuries. In each case, we have considered different levels of instantaneous default premium. The common parameters used in the analysis are:

$$\kappa = 0.50; \mu = 0.07; \sigma = 0.078; \lambda = 0.0.$$

$$\kappa_x = 0.50; \mu_x = 0.02; \sigma_x = 0.078$$

We have also assumed that the underlying index is 90 day LIBOR and that there is a payment lag of 90 days in the swap structure. It is assumed that the time to next reset is 90 days.

In addition to these parameter values, we need to specify the current spread x. We chose spread levels of x=0.01, x=0.02 and 0.03.

As the life of the swap increased, it was found that the swap rates increased in general. For low levels of x, the term structure of default premia is upward sloping as $x < \mu_X$. Thus the spreads are unambiguously increasing with the term of the swap. For high levels of x the term structure of default premia is downward sloping. This effect dominates for short-term swaps thereby producing higher spreads for shorter dated swaps. The results of this section clearly demonstrates that the swap spreads embody both the term structure of LIBOR and the term structure of default premia. The quantification of their interaction was made possible by the specific assumptions that were employed in this section concerning the structure of the problem. For a different approach to the treatment of credit risk in swaps the reader is referred to Cooper and Mello (1988).

6 Conclusion

The concepts developed in this paper are useful in the pricing of interest rate swaps in particular and other types of swaps in general. Many of the contractual provisions in the swap contracts are easily accommodated in the framework. The techniques may also be used in measuring the interest rate sensitivity of floating rate notes, the relationship between risk and frequency of resets, the delay in payment from the reset dates, etc.

References

1. Boris Antl, (1986), Editor "Swap Finance," Euromoney publications., Volumes I and II.

2. J. Bicksler and A. H. Chen, (1986), "An Economic analysis of Interest rate swaps", *The Journal of Finance*, 41, **3**, 645-655

3. I. Cooper and A.S. Mello, (1988), "The Default Risk Of Swaps", WP\#2111-88, Sloan School of Management, Working Paper, November (1988)

4. J. C. Cox, J. E. Ingersoll, Jr., and S. A. Ross, "An Analysis of Variable Rate Loan Contracts," *The Journal of Finance, Vol.* **XXXV,** *No.* **2**, (May 1980), 389--403.

5. J. C. Cox, J. E. Ingersoll, Jr., and S. A. Ross, "A Re-examination of Traditional Hypotheses about the Term Structure of Interest Rates," *The Journal of Finance, Vol.* **XXXVI,** *No.* **4,** (September 1981) 769--799.

6. J. C. Cox, J. E. Ingersoll, Jr., and S. A. Ross, "A Relation between Forward Prices and Futures Prices," *Journal of Financial Economics, Vol.* **9**, (1981), 321--346.

7. J. C. Cox, J. E. Ingersoll, Jr., and S. A. Ross, "A Theory of the Term Structure of Interest Rates," *Econometrica, Vol.* **53,** *No.* **2**, (March 1985), 385--407.

8. R. C. Merton, "On The Pricing of Corporate Debt: The Risk Structure of Interest Rates",, *Journal of Finance, Vol.* **29**, (May 1974), 449--470.

9. K. Ramaswamy and S. M. Sundaresan, "The Valuation of

Floating-Rate Instruments, Theory and Evidence," *Journal of Financial Economics, Vol.* **17**,(1986), 251--272.

10. C. Smith, C. W. Smithson and L. M. Wakeman, (1986), "The evolving market for swaps", *Midland Corporate Finance Journal,* **3**, 20-32.

11. C. Smith, C. W. Smithson and L. M. Wakeman, (1988), "The market for interest rate swaps", *Financial Management,* **Winter**, 34-44.

12. S. M. Turnbull, (1987), "Swaps: Zero sum game?", *Financial Management,* **Spring,** 15-21

13. J. G. Whittaker, (1987), "Interest rate swaps: Risk and regulation", *Economic Review of the Federal Reserve Bank of Kansas City, March, 3-13.*

14. *"Swaps Monitor", Volume* **1**, Number 17, May (1988).

Recent Developments in International Banking
and Finance, S.J. Khoury (editor)

CHAPTER XIII

Exchange Rate Jumps and Currency Options Pricing

Alan L. Tucker

Assistant Professor
School of Business and Management
Temple University
Philadelphia, PA

The author thanks two anonymous referees for helpful comments, and the Philadelphia Stock Exchange for data assistance.

Introduction

Bodurtha and Courtadon [7] report that an American, stationary-parameter currency options pricing model (OPM) exhibits a time-to-maturity bias: as option maturity increases, the overpricing of in-the-money and at-the-money currency options first decreases and then increases slightly. These mispricing patterns are consistent with the possibility that part of the exchange rate risk comes from random jumps in the spot currency price, suggesting that Merton's [14, 15] OPM may be more appropriate for valuing these options. Also, Shastri and Wethyavivorn [22], using the methodology of Rubinstein [18], report that currency return variances implied from a stationary-parameter currency OPM exhibit patterns (across maturities and exchange rate-exercise price ratios) most consistent with a mixed-jump process for currency returns. Akgiray and Booth [1] and Jorion [12] document the existence of a significant jump structure in exchange return series. Finally, Tucker and Pond [26] report that the mixed-jump process describes daily currency returns better than several alternative distributional processes, including the scaled-t, general stable Paretian, and compound normal models.

Merton's [14,15] OPM, which admits jumps in the underlying process, predicates that total price changes are comprised of two types of changes: (a) normal price vibrations caused by marginal information events satisfying a local Markov property; and (b) abnormal price vibrations caused by information shocks satisfying an antipathetical jump process defined in continuous time. The Black and Scholes [5] OPM, which does not admit jumps, assumes that price changes are described by a standard Ito process with constant mean and variance. The purpose of this study is to compare these two models for the pricing of foreign currency options. Thus, this study is similar to that of Ball and Torous [3], who contrast these models for the pricing of common stock call options. While Ball and Torous do provide statistical evidence consistent with the existence of lognormally distributed jumps in a majority of the daily returns of common stocks, they find no operationally significant differences between the Black-Scholes and Merton model prices. However, Ball and Torous also establish that significant discrepancies between model prices may occur if the underlying return process is dominated by large jumps that occur infrequently. This may be true for the sample path of currency returns, given central bank intervention and exchange rate realignment by the European Economic Community. This study is developed in the following sections. Section I provides a brief literature review. The transactions data used in the empirical tests are described in section II. The statistical estimation of the mixed-jump process is conducted in section III. A brief discussion comparing the two options pricing models is contained in section IV. Section V provides the principle empirical results, while section VI. Section V provides the principle empirical results, while section VI provides a summary and conclusions.

I. Literature Review

The recent academic literature concerning currency options minics earlier stock options literature, focusing on market efficiency and options valuation. Most studies employ transactions data supplied by the Philadelphia Stock Exchange (PHLX), the world's leading trader of listed American currency options.

Empirical tests of the efficiency of the currency options market are conducted by Bodurtha and Courtadon [6], Shastri and Tandon [19], and Tucker [24], among others. These tests are of two types: (a) arbitrage tests, where violations of rational pricing conditions, like Put-Call Parity, are investigated; and (b) hedge tests, where the profitability of trading rules, based on differences between model and observed prices, is investigated. All three of the above studies perform arbitrage tests; Tucker also conducts a hedge test of market efficiency. Each study supports the notion of currency options market efficiency, finding few violations of rational pricing conditions and no economic profits from trading rules after controlling for the effects of bid-ask spreads, price synchronization, market depth, and transaction costs.

Several studies, including Bodurtha and Courtadon [7], Goodman, Ross and Schmidt [10], Shastri and Tandon [20], and Tucker [24], report that a European currency options valuation model often misprices PHLX-traded call options. For instance, Goodman et. al. report model prices deviating typically 12-16% from observed prices for the period January 1983 through October 1983. A resolution for this mispricing has yet to emerge. For instance, Bodurtha and Courtadon continue to report mispricing when employing synchronous transactions data and an American valuation model solved via numerical methods. Specifically, Bodurtha and Courtadon report average absolute percentage pricing errors of 19.12% and 19.13% for the European and American models, respectively, when applied to 3,326 call currency options for the period February 1983 through September 1983. Thus data nonsynchronization and the application of a European model to American options data do not appear to be the root-cause of the mispricing. Shastri and Tandon [21] report a similar result using a simulation analysis.

Alternative currency options pricing models that allow for deviations from normality for currency return distributions also have failed to substantially improve pricing accuracy. For instance, Tucker, Peterson and Scott [25] report that a constant elasticity for variance model, wherein currency return variance is allowed to vary intertemporally with exchange rate levels, fails to outperform the simpler, constant-variance European currency OPM for predictive intervals of greater than three trading days. Shastri and Wethyavivorn [23] report that a generalized currency options model exhibits pricing improvement of less than .5% beyond that exhibited by the European model. This generalized model uses an Edgeworth series expansion (see Jarrow and Rudd [11]). Borensztein and Dooley [8] report that a pure jump currency OPM outperforms a model based on normality, but only for deeply out-of-the-money options. McCulloch [13] develops a currency OPM with log-stable uncertainty, but does not test the model employing trade data. Finally, Jorion [12] provides an illustration of how a mixed-jump model may improve pricing accuracy, but does not test the model employing actual trade data.

Two other studies involving currency spot options merit discussion. Peterson and Tucker [17] find that proportional deviations between observed exchange rates and simultaneous exchange rates implied from out-of-the-money currency call options are a direct and statistically significant determinant of subsequent currency returns. Further, these authors report that the added information impounded in highly levered out-of-the-money options can be utilized in a trading rule to generate abnormal economic profits. This affirms the hypothesis that informed traders, seeking to optimize the returns to information, trade in more levered markets. In short, currency option prices appear to lead exchange rates. Ogden and Tucker [16] empirically test contingent claims pricing models for American currency spot and futures options. They report a substantial number of violations of relative pricing conditions governing these related contingent claims. Most of these violations are substantial enough to imply riskless arbitrage profits. These violations may be attributable to either intermarket inefficiency or model misspecification.

II. Data

The transactions data used to test the Merton and Black-Scholes models are American currency call options traded on the PHLX for the period June 13, 1983 through June 16, 1986. There are five currencies upon which options are traded throughout this period: the British pound (BP), Canadian dollar (CD), Deutsche mark (DM), Japanese yen (JY), and the Swiss franc (SF). These transactions data contain the time of trade (to the minute) as well as trade price, exercise price, maturity, and trade volume. Underlying interbank exchange rates are reported at the exact clock time of each option trade. Thus, the data exhibit complete synchronization of option prices and underlying exchange rates.[1]

Option inception occurs on the Monday preceding the third Wednesday of the contract month, either March, June, September or December. Thus, there are thirteen inception dates over the period: June 13, 1983, September 19, 1983, December 19, 1983, ..., June 16, 1986. Options traded on these dates exhibit 3, 6 or 9-month maturities.[2] Hence, a total of 195 currency option "contracts" are used in the empirical tests: five currencies at three maturities at thirteen inception dates. Of course, each contract exhibits various exercise prices. Exercise price intervals are .01¢ for the JY, 1¢ for the CD, DM and SF, and 5¢ for the BP. In total, there are 1,196 call options traded on the thirteen inception dates. This study compares the Merton and Black-Scholes models for pricing these 1,196 options.

U.S. and foreign interest rates are required for the option pricing models. Eurocurrency rates obtained from the London Financial Times are used. Eurocurrency rates are available for maturities of 7 days, 1,

2, 3, 6, and 12-months. For 9-month options, averages of the 6 and 12-month rates reported on the inception dates are used.

Finally, exchange rate series are required to estimate the process parameters for Merton's mixed-jump model. For each inception date, daily exchange rates for the previous two years are employed. For instance, for the first inception date, June 13, 1983, daily rates for the period June 13, 1981 through June 12, 1983 are used to estimate the process parameters. These exchange rate series are obtained from 3:00 p.m. Eastern time rates reported in The Wall Street Journal.

III. Estimation of the Mixed-Jump Process

The mixed-jump diffusion process is represented by the following stochastic differential equation:

$$dS/S = \alpha dt + \sigma dZ + dq, \qquad (1)$$

where S = the exchange rate

α = the instantaneous expected return on a holding of the foreign currency

σ^2 = the instantaneous variance of this holding's return, conditional on no arrivals of abnormal information

dZ = a standardized Wiener process

q = a Poission process which is independent of dZ

λ = the intensity of the Poission process, defined as the mean number of abnormal information arrivals per unit time.

It is assumed that upon the arrival of abnormal information there is an instantaneous jump in the exchange rate of size Y, independent of dZ. The jump size has a posited distribution given by $\ln(Y) \sim N(\mu, \delta^2)$.

Ball and Torous [2] provide a maximum likelihood procedure to estimate the parameters of this mixed-jump diffusion process. Their procedure requires that the mean logarithmic jump size, μ, equals zero, implying a symmetric return distribution.[3] Also, abnormal information arrivals are modeled by a Bernoulli jump process.[4] The resultant loglikelihood function is given by:

$$\ln L(\underline{x}, \underline{\theta}) = \sum_{i=1}^{m} \ln\left(\sum_{n=0}^{\infty} \frac{e^{-\lambda}\lambda^{n}}{n!} \phi(x_i;\alpha, \sigma^2 + n\delta^2)\right), \tag{2}$$

where

$$\phi(x_i;\alpha, \sigma^2 + n\delta^2) = (2\pi(\sigma^2 + n\delta^2))^{-\frac{1}{2}}\exp(-(x_i - \alpha)^2/2(\sigma^2 + n\delta^2))$$

$\underline{x} = (x_1, x_2, \ldots, x_m)$, the daily exchange-return series

$\underline{\theta} = (\lambda, \sigma^2, \delta^2, \alpha)$, the parameter vector.

The parameter vector $\underline{\theta}$ is obtained by maximizing equation (2). To do so, a multidimensional Newton-Raphson iterative procedure is employed. An upper bond of ten for the infinite summation is sufficient to ensure covergence and meaningless truncation errors.

Table I provides parameter estimates associated with the first inception date in the sample, June 13, 1983. That is, these estimates are obtained by maximizing equation (2) for the daily currency return series June 13, 1981 through June 12, 1983. Similar parameter estimates obtain for the other twelve inception dates. The small values of λ and σ^2, combined with the reported values of δ^2, suggest that daily currency returns exhibit infrequent but large lognormally distributed jumps. Thus Merton's OPM may exhibit superior forecasting than the Black-Scholes OPM for foreign exchange call options.

Table I also provides likelihood ratio test results for the presence of a jump structure in the sampled currency returns. The likelihood ratio test statistic, Λ, is given by

$$\Lambda = -2(\ln L(\underline{x}, \underline{\theta}) - \ln L(\underline{x}, \underline{\gamma})), \tag{3}$$

Where $\underline{\theta}$ is the maximum likelihood estimate under the mixed-jump diffusion process specification, and $\underline{\gamma}$ is the parameter vector estimate corresponding to the absence of a jump structure (= 0). Under the null hypothesis of normally distributed daily currency returns, has an asymptotic chi-square distribution with two degrees of freedom. The test statistic is significant at the .05 level for every currency, indicating the presence of a jump component. Similar results obtain for the other twelve inception dates.

IV. A Comparison of the Two Pricing Models

The Black-Scholes currency call OPM is given by:

$$c(\sigma^2;\ S,X,r,r^*,T) = e^{-r^*T}S\cdot N(d) - e^{-rT}X\cdot N(d-\sigma\sqrt{T}), \quad (4)$$

where $d = [\ln(S/X) + (r - r^* + (\sigma^2/2))T]/\sigma\sqrt{T}$

C = the price of the currency call option

S = the underlying spot exchange rate

X = the exercise price

r = the U.S. riskless rate of interest

r^* = the foreign riskless rate of interest

σ = the instantaneous standard deviation of the returns on a holding of foreign currency

T = the time to option maturity expressed as a fraction of a year

N (•) = the standard normal cumulative distribution function.

Equation (4) is an adaptation of the stock OPM of Black and Scholes [5], provided by Biger and Hull [4] and Garman and Kohlhagen [9]. The major transformation in the adaptation of the stock OPM to value currency options is the substitution of exchange rates for stock prices.

Thus, the percentage change of exchange rates is assumed to follow a diffusion process with constant mean and variance.

Now suppose an investor employs equation (4) to price currency call options when currency returns actually follow the mixed-jump process of equation (1). If the investor has a sufficiently long time series of exchange rates such that the resultant estimate of the variance per unit time, v^2, corresponds to the actual jump-diffusion process' total variance, $\sigma^2 + o^2$, then the Black-Scholes value of the call option is given by $F_e(v^2;S,X,r,r^*,T) = C(v^2;S,X,r,r^*,T)$.

Merton's [14, 15] currency call option valuation model is given by:

$$F(\sigma^2,\lambda,\delta^2;S,X,r,r^*,T) = \sum_{n=0}^{\infty} \frac{e^{-\lambda T}(\lambda T)^n}{n!} F_e((\sigma^2 + n\delta^2/T); S,X,r,r^*,T). \quad (5)$$

Equation (5) assumes (a) that $E[Y] = 1$, implying that there is no effect, on average, upon the underlying currency's return from any particular jump, and (b) that the jump component represents diversifiable risk.

Both Merton [15] and Ball and Torous [3] investigate the conditions on the actual underlying security price process such that the Black-Scholes value, $F_e(v^2;S,X,r,r^*,T)$, diverges from the Merton value, $F(\sigma^2,\lambda,\delta^2;S,X,r,r^*,T)$. They find that the Black-Scholes value (i.e., the investor's appraised value of the call option) may potentially overprice or underprice the appropriate Merton call value. Specifically, the appraised Black-Scholes call value can slightly underprice in-the-money ($S/X > 1$) and out-of-the-money ($S/X < 1$) call options, and can substantially overprice all call options if the underlying security return process is predominated by extremely large jumps that occur infrequently. Thus the investor's misspecification of the currency return process may have important impacts on currency call options pricing.

V. Empirical Results

Table I provides evidence consistent with the existence of lognormally distributed jumps in the sampled currency returns. An investor ignoring this jump structure may misprice currency call options. To assess this, the Merton and Black-Scholes models are applied to the sample of 1,196 PHLX-traded currency call options. Given a zero expected logarithmic jump, $\mu = 0$, the Merton model is:

$$F(\sigma^2,\lambda,\delta^2;S,X,r,r^*,T) = \sum_{n=0}^{\infty} \frac{e^{-kT}(kT)^n}{n!} \cdot \tag{6}$$

$$C((\sigma^2 + n\delta^2/T);\ S,X,(r + n((1/2)\delta^2)/T-\lambda(e^{(1/2)\delta^2}-1)),r^*,T)$$

Where $K = \lambda \exp(1/2)\delta^2$. The corresponding Black-Scholes model remains as follows:

$$F_e(v^2;S,X,r,r^*,T) = C(v^2;S,X,r,r^*,T). \tag{7}$$

Equation (6) requires that the jump component is diversifiable. If so, then a regression of the jump intensity (λ) onto the market return should yield a statistically insignificant slope coefficient (β). To investigate this, a simple time-series regression is estimated separately for each of the five currencies. Recall there are thirteen inception dates in the empirical sample of currency options, so for each currency is estimated thirteen times. Thus each separate regression consists of thirteen observations. The market return for each estimation period is the total return (adjusted for dividends and stock splits) for the Center for Research in Securities Prices (CRSP) Value-Weighted Index. Table II reports the results of the regression analysis. For every currency the estimated slope coefficient (β) is statistically insignificant. Further, the F-statistics are insignificant. Thus the assumption that jumps are uncorrelated with the market appears to be warranted.

Table III provides average absolute percentage pricing errors for the Black-Scholes and Merton models when applied to the 1,196 currency call options. Average absolute percentage pricing errors are the averages of absolute percentage differences between model and market prices.[5] These errors are categorized by currency, maturity, and

TABLE I

Parameter Estimates for the Mixed-Jump Diffusion Process

Currency	λ	$\sigma^2 \times 10^4$	$\delta^2 \times 10^4$	$\alpha \times 10^2$	Λ
British Pound	0.138 (0.211)	1.241 (0.422)	6.866 (4.895)	0.033 (0.099)	37.11*
Canadian Dollar	0.144 (0.158)	1.350 (0.450)	7.005 (3.211)	0.040 (0.102)	42.08*
Deutsche Mark	0.109 (0.081)	0.971 (0.089)	5.539 (2.008)	0.037 (0.124)	22.70*
Japanese Yen	0.036 (0.086)	0.518 (0.126)	4.790 (3.774)	0.020 (0.052)	18.56*
Swiss Franc	0.082 (0.111)	1.077 (0.334)	5.921 (4.035)	0.031 (0.094)	19.44*

Notes: The standard errors of the estimates are given in parentheses. Estimates are generated using daily currency returns for the period June 13, 1981 through June 12, 1983. The likelihood ratio statistic, Λ, tests the mixed-jump process against the null hypothesis of normality, and is distributed $\chi^2_{(2)}$. As asterick (*) indicates statistical significance at the .05 level.

boundary status in panels A, B, and C, respectively. The Merton model errors are much smaller, regardless of the categorization. Indeed, the Merton model errors are significantly lower, at the .05 level, then the corresponding Black-Scholes model errors for every categorization.[6]

The overall average absolute percentage pricing errors for the Black-Scholes and Merton models are 13.60% and 7.26%, respectively. The difference in these overall errors is statistically significant at the .05 level. Thus the Merton model exhibits significantly less pricing error than the Black-Scholes model. The improvement in forecast accuracy offered by the Merton model is substantial; the Merton model's pricing error is nearly one-half of that exhibited by the Black-Scholes model.

VI. Summary and conclusions

Recent empirical evidence, including Bodurtha and Courtadon [7], Shastri and Wethyavivorn [22], Jorion [12], and Tucker and Pond [26], suggests that foreign exchange price changes may exhibit a significant jump structure. Employing daily exchange-return series, this study provides empirical evidence consistent with the existence of lognormally distributed jumps for five major trading currencies. These jumps are large and occur infrequently, implying that the Merton [14, 15] model, which admits such jumps in the underlying return process, may outperform the Black-Scholes [5] model for valuing foreign exchange options. This hypothesis is tested empirically using 1,196 currency call options traded on thirteen inception dates spanning the period June 13, 1983 through June 16, 1986. The results strongly suggest that the Merton model is superior. The Merton model exhibits significantly lower pricing errors across currencies, option maturity, and boundary status. Overall, the Merton model exhibits nearly half of the forecast error documented for the Black-Scholes model. And this improvement in pricing accuracy may be even more pronounced should the mixed-jump process parameters be more precisely estimated (ie. have lower standard errors perhaps through the use of longer time series). Thus investors who ignore the jump structure may substantially misprice currency call options. An interesting topic for future research concerns whether the added pricing information offered by the Merton model may be utilized profitably in a trading rule.

TABLE II

Estimated Slope Coefficients and F-Statistics

Currency	β	F-statistic
British Pound	.0031	0.23
	(.2416)	
Canadian Dollar	.0040	0.46
	(.3029)	
Deutsche Mark	.0037	1.17
	(.1959)	
Japanese Yen	.0021	0.55
	(.1622)	
Swiss Franc	.0019	0.25
	(.1843)	

Notes: The standard errors of the estimates are given in parentheses. The slope coefficients (β) are generated from a simple Ordinary Least Squares regression of the currency's jump intensities ( ) onto the returns of the CRSP Value-Weighted Index. None of the slope coefficients or F-statistics are significant at the .10 level. Similar results were obtained when estimating coefficients using the Generalized Method of Moments, which allows for a conditional heteroscedastic error term.

TABLE III

Average Absolute Percentage Pricing Errors for the Black-Scholes and Merton Currency Call Option Models

Panel A: By Currency

Currency	Black-Scholes	Merton
British Pound (198)	11.91	6.54*
Canadian Dollar (72)	8.87	4.41*
Deutsche Mark (359)	14.05	7.22*
Japanese Yen (263)	16.26	7.91*
Swiss Franc (304)	13.00	7.90*

Panel B: By Maturity

Maturity	Black-Scholes	Merton
Three Months (470)	11.76	6.40*
Six Months (446)	12.67	6.17*
Nine Months (280)	18.18	10.45*

Panel C: By Boundary Status

Boundary Status	Black-Scholes	Merton
In-the-Money (658)	14.23	7.46*
Out-of-the-Money (538)	12.84	7.02*

Notes: Average absolute percentage pricing errors are the averages of absolute percentage differences between model and market prices. Sample sizes are in parentheses. An asterisk indicates that the Merton model errors are significantly lower than the corresponding Black-Scholes model errors, at the .05 level

Footnotes

1. The currency options employed are American, whereas the models tested are European. No American version of Merton's [14, 15] mixed-jump model exists. Still, the analysis of competing European models may be considered appropriate for two reasons. First, prices predicted by American and European currency option models are similar. Recall that Bodurtha and Courtadon [7] report average absolute percentage pricing errors of 19.12% and 19.13% for European and American models, respectively, and that Shastri and Tandon [21] employ a simulation analysis and demonstrate that European and American model values are nearly identical for currency call options. Second, note that in the comparison of two European models, any bias due to the probability of premature exercise and the associate premium is not particular to either model. Thus both models, Black-Scholes and Merton, are subject to the same (small) early exercise bias.

   As a diagnostic test, the analysis conducted here for the American currency options is also applied to a sample of European currency options traded on the Chicago Board of Trade. Specifically, European options having inception dates March 17, 1986 and June 16, 1986 are tested. The data used are transactions data where the underlying spot rate is recorded at the same clock time of the option trade. The results using these data (not reported) are similar to those based on the larger sample of American currency call prices.

2. The PHLX recently began trading shorter-term currency option contracts.

3. Tucker and Pond [26] cannot reject the null hypothesis of

symmetry for the daily return distributions of the five currencies studied here.

4. A Bernoulli jump process implies that, at most, one abnormal information arrival occurs over a fixed interval of time. For small intervals, the Bernoulli model converges to the Poisson model.

5. Percentage errors are computed to control for price levels. Absolute dollar pricing errors will be smaller for shorter-term, out-of-the-money currency options since such options already exhibit small prices.

6. The significance test employed for results in table III is the matched-pair t-test. Similar results obtain when employing a nonparametric signs rank test.

References

1. Akgiray, V. and G. Booth, "Mixed Diffusion-Jump Process Modeling of Exchange Rate Movements," Review of Economics and Statistics 70 (November 1988), 631-637.

2. Ball, C. and W. Torous, "A Simplified Jump Process for Common Stock Returns," Journal of Financial and Quantitative Analysis 18 (March 1983), 53-65

3. Ball, C. and W. Torous, "On Jumps in Common Stock Prices and Their Impact on Call Option Pricing," Journal of Finance 40 (March 1985), 155-173.

4. Biger, N. and J. Hull, "The Valuation of Currency Options," Financial Management 12 (Spring 1983), 24-28.

5. Black, F. and M. Scholes, "The Pricing of Options and Corporate Liabilities," Journal of Political Economy 81 (May/June 1973),

637-653.

6. Bodurtha, J. and G. Courtadon, "Efficiency Tests of the Foreign Currency Options Market," Journal of Finance 41 (March 1986), 151-162.

7. Bodurtha, J. and G. Courtadon, "Tests of the American Option Pricing Model on the Foreign Currency Options Market," Journal of Financial and Quantitative Analysis 22 (June 1987), 153-167.

8. Borensztein, E. and M. Dooley, "Options on Foreign Exchange and Exchange Rate Expectations," International Monetary Fund Staff Papers 34 (December 1987), 643-680.

9. Garman, M. and S. Kohlhagen, "Foreign Currency Option Values," Journal of International Money and Finance 3 (December 1983), 231-236.

10. Goodman, L., Ross S. and F. Schmidt, "Are Foreign Currency Options Over-valued? The Early Evidence of the Philadelphia Stock Exchange," Journal of Futures Markets 5 (Fall 1985), 349-359.

11. Jarrow, R. and A. Rudd, "Approximate Option Valuation for Arbitrary Stochastic Processes," Journal of Financial Economics 10 (September 1982), 347-369.

12. Jorion, P., "On Jump Processes in the Foreign Exchange Markets," Review of Financial Studies (forthcoming, 1990).

13. McCulloch, J., "Foreign Exchange Option Pricing with Log-Stable Uncertainty," in Recent Developments in International Banking and Finance, S. Khoury and A. Ghosh (eds.), 1987, 231-245.

14. Merton, R., "Option Pricing When Underlying Stock Returns are

Discontinuous," Journal of Financial Economics 3 (January/March 1976a), 125-144.

15. Merton, R., "The Impact on Option Pricing of Specification Error in the Underlying Stock Price Returns," Journal of Finance 31 (May 1976b), 333-350.

16. Ogden, J. and A. Tucker, "The Relative Valuation of American Currency Spot and Futures Options: Theory and Empirical Tests," Journal of Financial and Quantitative Analysis 23 (December 1988), 247-258.

17. Peterson, D. and A. Tucker, "Implied Spot Rates as Predictors of Currency Returns: A Note," Journal of Finance 43 (March 1988), 247-258.

18. Rubinstein, M., "Nonparametric Tests of Alternative Option Pricing Models Using All Reported Trades and Quotes on the 30 Most Active CBOE Option Classes from August 23, 1976 Through August 31, 1978," Journal of Finance 40 (June 1985), 455-480.

19. Shastri, K. and K. Tandon, "Arbitrage Tests of the Efficiency of the Foreign Currency Options Market," Journal of International Money and Fiance 4 (December 1985), 455-468.

20. Shastri, K. and K. Tandon, "Valuation of Foreign Currency Options: Some Empirical Tests," Journal of Financial and Quantitative Analysis 21 (June 1986a), 145-160.

21. Shastri, K. and K. Tandon, "On the Use of European Models to Price American Options on Foreign Currency," Journal of Futures Markets 6 (Spring 1986b), 93-108.

22. Shastri, K. and K. Wethyavivorn, "The Valuation of Currency Options for Alternative Stochastic Processes," Journal of Financial Research 10 (Winter 1987), 283-293.

23. Shastri, K. and K. Wethyavivorn, "Pricing of Foreign Currency Options for Arbitrary Stochastic Processes," Working Paper, University of Pittsburgh, 1988.

24. Tucker, A., "Empirical Tests of the Efficiency of the Currency Option Market," Journal of Financial Research 7 (Winter 1985), 275-285.

25. Tucker, A., Peterson, D. and E. Scott, "Tests of the Black-Scholes and Constant Elasticity of Variance Currency Call Option Valuation Models," Journal of Financial Research 11 (Fall 1988), 201-213.

26. Tucker, A. and L. Pond, "The Probability Distribution of Foreign Exchange Price Changes: Tests of Candidate Processes," Review of Economics and Statistics 70 (November 1988), 638-647.

Recent Developments in International Banking
and Finance, S.J. Khoury (editor)

CHAPTER XIV

Exchange Rate Uncertainty and Precommitment in Symmetric Duopoly: A New Theory of Multinational Production

Sarkis J. Khoury

University of California, Riverside

David Nickerson

University of British Columbia

Venkatraman Sadanand

University of Guelph

We would like to thank Lanny Arvan, Steve Ambler, Russ Boyer, Alison Butler, Marsha Courchane, Alberto Giovannini, Asha Sadanand, Bill Schworm, Barbara Spencer, three anonymous referees and seminar participants at the 1989 Annual Meetings of the Canadian Economics Association, the University of British Columbia, and the University of Waterloo for their comments on an earlier version of this paper. Partial research support for the second author was provided by the Centre for International Business Studies at the University of British Columbia. The usual disclaimer applies.

I. Introduction

The dramatic increase in exchange rate volatility during the last decade has focussed attention on the influence of random exchange rate fluctuations on corporate behavior in concentrated industries. One aspect of this influence concerns the observation that leading firms in such industries frequently tend to be multinational in character, while their rivals remain purely domestic. Another aspect concerns the increasingly common phenomenon of foreign sourcing of production by domestic firms, in which dominant firms in one economy frequently choose to produce part or all of their product abroad and then export the commodity to their home economy for domestic sale. [1]

Several rationales for multinationalism and the foreign sourcing of production among industry leaders have appeared in both academic journals and the business press. The most obvious explanation for foreign production sourcing involves the opportunity for cheap production abroad as a result of a belief in the persistant strength of domestic currency. The emergence of certain firms as multinationals can subsequently be explained through the presence of some inherent asymmetry between rival firms in an industry. The possession by one firm of some internal advantage, such as proprietary knowledge from research expenditures or superior management and marketing techniques, could yield a substantial cost advantage over both foreign and domestic rivals and allow it to become an industry leader. Other asymmetries between firms which could induce multinational production include differential access to foreign subsidy programs, imperfect domestic capital markets, or the desire by certain domestic firms to secure access to a foreign economy, under the expectation of future trade barriers, for eventual sales in the foreign market. Yet another explanation for multinationalism and the foreign

[1] Examples of this latter phenomenon include American firms, such as Apple, choosing to produce some lines of personal computers in Taiwan for sale in the US, or Japanese firms, such as Honda, producing automobiles in the US for ultimate sale in Japan.

sourcing of production involves the hedging of exchange rate risk through the diversification of production locations. While all of these explanations are plausible, each relies, in some measure, on either the exogenous existence of explicit or implicit asymmetries between rival firms in an industry, or on a corporate aversion to risk and associated imperfections in domestic and international capital markets.

When the industry producing for the domestic market is concentrated, however, multinational production may arise among completely *symmetric*, *risk-neutral* firms and may underlie the *endogenous* emergence of industry leadership. Foreign production sourcing can occur precisely because uncertainty over real exchange rates offers a *purely strategic* motive for initially symmetric, risk-neutral domestic oligopolists to precommit to foreign production for domestic sale. A decision to incur a fixed investment cost and credibly commit to foreign production in advance may, as a result of random exchange rate fluctuations, offer a domestic firm a lower marginal cost of production and the opportunity to obtain the increased expected profits associated with being a Stackelberg leader in the domestic market. This advantage of precommitment, however, must be weighed against the opportunity cost of precommitment, which involves surrendering the option to remain flexible under such uncertainty and to select a production location and production volume after the resolution of that portion of exchange rate uncertainty which is relevant for current production and investment decisions.

Our objective in this paper is to proffer this new explanation of multinational production. We examine the role of exchange rate randomness in creating endogenous industry leadership, through strategic precommitment to multinational production, in the context of a symmetric duopoly with risk-neutral firms. We analyze a stylized model of an industry in which each firm can produce its commodity domestically, under certain demand and cost conditions, or, by incurring a fixed cost, credibly precommit to foreign production and domestic sale under cost uncertainty induced by a random real exchange rate. When decisions concerning production volume and location are made simultaneously, a domestic firm must assess the tradeoff between precommitting to a volume of foreign production under uncertainty and possibly obtaining the position of a Stackelberg leader in the industry, or remaining flexible and waiting until short-run exchange rate uncertainty is resolved to make its decision about production location, at the cost of possibly becoming a follower to its rival in the industry.

The optimal precommitment decision under exchange rate uncertainty is characterized by a unique symmetric sequential equilibrium in mixed strategies with respect to the *timing* of the selection of production location by the symmetric domestic duopolists in our model. When the fixed cost of exercising the option to engage in foreign production is small relative to the expected cost advantage of foreign production created by the randomly fluctuating exchange rate, each firm will select a positive probability of foreign production sourcing, thereby obtaining the leadership advantage of precommitment, but, as long as there is some uncertainty about the exchange rate, both firms will not, with certainty, exercise their option to produce abroad. Such randomization in the timing of the production location decision implies that exchange rate uncertainty can induce multinational production, even among firms that are entirely risk-neutral and display an initial symmetry, and that foreign production is, for purely strategic reasons, quite naturally associated with the endogenous emergence of industry leadership.

While this paper considers a novel source of influence of exchange rate uncertainty on strategic and irreversible decisions about the foreign sourcing of production, it is related to earlier literature concerning the existence of multinational firms and also to recent literature examining the implications of precommitment and irreversibility for domestic market structure.

Several theories rationalize the existence of multinational firms in a deterministic economy. These include the ***industrial organization*** theory of direct foreign investment, most notably associated with Caves (1971) and Hymer (1976), in which firms in oligopolistic industries are argued to possess intangible, firm-specific assets, such as management and marketing techniques and proprietary knowledge from research expenditure, which give them an advantage over rivals in foreign markets; the ***eclectic*** theory of Dunning (1973), (1977), in which it is argued that some firms possess unique firm-specific assets which can be fully utilized only through combination with factor inputs specific to a foreign economy; and the ***internalization*** theory, primarily owing to the work of Rugman (1980), (1981), (1986), in which reputational effects and other considerations can create advantages for the creation of foreign subsidiaries by a domestic firm, relative to its licensing the production of its commodity by autonomous foreign firms. Each of these theories reflect a common assumption that multinational firms emerge from the ***asymmetric*** possession by some firms of unique nonmarketable assets. These assets have a public-good component, which induces multi-plant scale economies, giving those firms which possess them a potential cost advantage over both foreign and domestic rivals and, in the presence of tariffs or international transportation costs, an obvious incentive to engage in direct foreign investment. Grosse (1985) provides an early description of some game theoretic aspects of multinational production and sales, while Buckley and Casson (1981), Helpman (1984), Horstmann and Markusen (1987), Grossman and Helpman (1988) and Butler (1989) provide rigorous models of the incentives created for foreign direct investment by the possession of firm-specific assets.

An alternative explanation for the practice of foreign production sourcing, offered by Hodder and Jucker (1985), Shapiro (1987), and others, relies directly on the presence of randomness in (real) exchange rates. Firms which exhibit risk-averse behavior may choose to diversify their production between for-

and who may produce this good either domestically or abroad. [2] Such firms have two aspects to their production decisions. They must decide on the volume of production they wish to sell to domestic consumers and they must also choose a domestic or foreign location for their production. [3] The option to produce the commodity abroad can be exercised, for each of these firms, by incurring a certain plant–specific cost G. [4] This expenditure, which is analogous to the exercise price of a financial option, represents the general fixed costs of activating a foreign plant for production. The presence of such a cost allows, as in Helpman (1984), Horstmann and Markusen (1987) and Dixit (1988), for the potential existence of plant-specific scale economies, which the firm must balance against potential reductions in the marginal costs of foreign production created by a randomly fluctuating exchange rate.

The fixed cost G of activating a foreign plant for production also, however, has *strategic* significance in our model, because it allows the firm which incurs it to credibly precommit to an aggressive production and sales strategy in the domestic mar-

---

[2] Since our analysis examines the potential influence of multinational production on *domestic* market structure, we refrain from explicit consideration of the symmetric problem of domestic (foreign) multinationals serving a foreign (domestic) market through the creation of a local subsidiary. Our results will also, however, apply identically to that case. We also assume, following Helpman (1984), Markusen (1984), Horstmann and Markusen (1987) and others, the implicit existence of firm–specific sunk costs, representing the value of activities internal to the established firm, such as research, management and marketing. Such sunk costs allow us to distinguish between a firm and its plants, and, in order to retain our focus on the strategic behavior of incumbent duopolists, are assumed to of a magnitude sufficient to preclude entry into the domestic market by new firms.

[3] Although firms are, in general, free to share production intended for domestic sale between domestic and foreign plants, the presence in our model of constant marginal production costs implies that each firm will optimally produce at only one plant. This assumption, traditional in the literature on multinational firms, allows us to clearly exposit the purely strategic aspects of foreign production sourcing and can readily be relaxed without qualifying any of our results.

[4] The analogous expenditure for maintaining the domestic plant is, following Horstmann and Markusen (1987) and others, assumed to have already been incurred by each of the domestic firms or, alternatively, to be negligible relative to the cost G of investing in the foreign plant.

ket. [5] The strategic value of such a precommitment depends crucially on its credibility, as perceived by the rival firm, since only a credible precommitment will influence the production and sales strategy adopted by this rival. Credibility requires any ex ante decision to incur a cost of producing abroad to be an irreversible action. A firm, consequently, may choose to sign binding contracts to make its precommitment credible, which, in the context of our model, involves making an irreversible investment G to activate the foreign plant under exchange rate uncertainty. [6]

The real exchange rate e is assumed to be the unique source of uncertainty facing firms in our duopoly. [7] The stochastic value of this exchange rate which is relevant for current production decisions is revealed exogenously at a certain time. Periods 1 and 2 respectively refer to the periods before and after the common observation of the realization of the exchange rate. The timing of this revelation allows for the existence of two distinct periods enabling firms to precommit to a volume and location of production. [8] The costs of domestic production, as well as the

---

[5] We assume that the only extant source of uncertainty faced by firms in our model is real exchange rate uncertainty and, consequently, the only precommitment device available to these firms is the option each holds to produce abroad. This assumption is made because real exchange rate fluctuations are the purest theoretical example of relative price changes and also because, for many American and Canadian firms, real exchange rate volatility was the predominant source of uncertainty during the last several years.

[6] A recent case of multinational corporate behavior which is entirely compatible with such a strategic interpretation is that of Ford Motor Company, which has recently engaged in extensive and irreversible commitments to the foreign sourcing of production components and which, most remarkably, precommited to binding design and engineering contracts with the Japanese automaker Mazda in the development of the new Ford Escort model. Details of this episode appear in Treece and Borrus (1990).

[7] Although no real distinction between the real and nominal exchange rates is necessarily implied by our model, this distinction is empirically useful when applying our theoretical results to the analysis of real corporate behavior. We are grateful to a referee for also pointing out that the value of incurring the cost G of exercising the option to produce abroad should be measured with respect to real exchange rate uncertainty, and that fluctuations in the real rate have a greater tendency toward mean-reversion than do nominal exchange rate fluctuations. See Coughlin and Koedijk (1990) and Meese and Rogoff (1988) for evidence regarding this latter point.

[8] While games of a finite number of periods, such as the one analyzed in this paper and those commonly employed in the study of industrial organization, allow us to explicitly consider the role of uncertainty in a strategic context, the compression of

magnitude of domestic demand, are assumed to be deterministic and common knowledge between the firms. Domestic production and domestic sales are, consequently, done under full certainty. [9]

Since exchange rate uncertainty offers strategic opportunities to each of the domestic duopolists, optimal corporate behavior depends crucially upon the *timing* of production location and volume decisions. A firm can either precommit itself, through incurring the fixed investment cost G, to a desired production volume abroad before exchange rate uncertainty is resolved or, alternatively, it can remain flexible, making its production location and volume decisions after the uncertainty relevant for current production costs is resolved. Precommitment is, as a result, credible only when a foreign production level is chosen under uncertainty.

Each alternative strategy, precommitment or the retention of flexibility, has benefits and costs. By irreversibly precommitting in the first period to a foreign location for production, a firm suffers cost uncertainty but, because precommitment involves choosing both a location and a volume of production, the firm may obtain the advantage of potentially more profitable Stackelberg leadership in the domestic market if the rival firm delays its production decisions until the second period, after the relevant value of the exchange rate is realized and its implications for the marginal costs of foreign production, denominated in do-

---

infinite planning horizons and continuous price or cost uncertainty into an essentially static structure is a liability of such models. The exogenous resolution of exchange rate randomness, for the purposes of the production decision in our model, requires us to interpret the production decision of our firms as a short-run decision, or alternatively, if we view the fixed cost G of foreign production as an irreversible long-run investment, requires us to interpret the uncertainty in the exchange rate as being relative to some expected long- run average, since the ex ante periods of investment in real plants can be of a year or more in duration.

[9] While we assume that only foreign production is subject to random cost, when measured in domestic units, in order to emphasize the strategic opportunity afforded firms by exchange rate uncertainty, the essence of our results will remain robust to the inclusion of uncertainty in domestic demand or cost as long as the variance from these sources of randomness are small relative to that provided by the real exchange rate.

mestic units, are observed by both firms. By remaining flexible and delaying its production decisions until period 2, a firm does not have to face exchange rate uncertainty but will necessarily acquiesce to being a potentially less profitable Stackelberg follower in the domestic product market if the rival firm has, in the first period, precommited itself to foreign production. After the revelation of the value of the exchange rate in period 2, a firm that has not previously precommitted itself to foreign production will, of course, simply choose to produce where it is cheaper.

The firms in this duopoly, as a consequence of the benefits and costs associated with precommitment and with flexibility, can be regarded as playing a noncooperative game of timing in which each firm has to decide "location timings" as well as the optimal associated volumes of production. Firms that make their decisions about where to locate at the same time, whether this occurs under exchange rate uncertainty in the first period or after the resolution of this uncertainty in the second period, realize that the simultaneity of their decisions will create a Cournot equilibrium in sales in the second period. Alternatively, if one firm decides to commit to foreign production in the first period but the rival firm chooses to delay its location decision, then the precommited firm will act as a Stackelberg leader, producing and selling the volume of output corresponding to this status, while the flexible firm will, believing its rival's commitment to leadership status to be credible, necessarily wish to act as a Stackelberg follower in regard to the volume of its production and sales. [10]

While the expenditure G required to activate a foreign plant must be incurred in the first period in order for a firm to credibly

[10] The role of uncertainty in creating this tradeoff between precommitment and flexibility between ex ante symmetric firms can be clarified by considering what each such firm would wish to do if no exchange rate uncertainty existed. Since firms are identical, neither firm would wish to be a Stackelberg follower. Stackelberg leadership, however, is also precluded as a Nash equilibrium, since neither firm could credibly convince its rival of a commitment to produce a quantity sufficient to establish industry leadership. Under these conditions precommitment cannot occur between symmetric firms and such firms would knowingly participate in a Cournot equilibrium in production and domestic sales.

precommit, it should be noted that actual production and sales occur only during the second period. Precommitment to foreign production through foreign plant activation in the first period, therefore, is analogous to entry decisions in industrial organization models of stochastic oligopolies. Firms failing to exercise their option to activate a foreign plant in the first period will produce abroad or domestically, whichever is cheapest, in the second period. Three possible structures for the domestic industry could, consequently, endogenously emerge as a result of the influence of exchange rate uncertainty on each firm's strategic behavior. If neither of the firms precommits in the first period to foreign production, then both firms participate in a Cournot equilibrium in the domestic market in the second period, and make production location and volume decisions based on the realized value of the exchange rate. If one firm precommits in the first period to foreign production while the other firm remains flexible and waits for the exchange rate to be revealed, then the precommitted firm will be a Stackelberg leader in the output game and the other firm will be a follower. The follower firm may or may not produce abroad, depending on the realization of the exchange rate, and we can have foreign and domestic production coexisting, among initially symmetric firms, in the industry equilibrium. Finally, if both firms choose to precommit in the first period to foreign production, the industry is again in a Cournot equilibrium.

One of the primary implications of our analysis, then, will be that multinational firms and foreign production in equilibrium do not only arise because of *exogenously assumed* asymmetries among firms, such as the incumbent–entrant relationship between an established domestic firm and a potential foreign rival analyzed by Markusen (1984), Helpman (1984), Horstmann and Markusen (1987), Kogut and Kulatilka (1989) and others; nor does their existence necessarily rely on risk aversion and a desire to hedge against the nondiversifiable risk posed by a random real exchange rate, as discussed in Hodder and Jucker (1985) and in Shapiro (1987). Multinational firms and the foreign sourcing of production can ***endogenously*** arise among initially ***identical*** firms, owing only to the pure leadership advantage of precommitment under uncertainty. This is a unique explanation of the relationship between exchange rate volatility and multinational production, and serves to both link market structure to multinational production through the strategic opportunities offered by a fluctuating exchange rate, and to establish a robust correlation between multinational production and industry leadership. [11]

Assumptions about technology and consumer preferences in our model of duopoly are chosen for expositional simplicity. [12] Each of the two domestic duopolists enjoys common, deterministic and constant marginal costs C when production occurs at a domestic plant. The aggregate preferences of domestic consumers are assumed to be described by a linear inverse demand surface with a price intercept of A and a slope of -1. Such preferences are also assumed to satisfy the inequality $A - C > 0$ since, otherwise, neither firm will engage in any production. Production costs for each firm are the same domestically and are the same abroad, in the common location of (potential) foreign production, in the sense that identical factor prices obtain for each firm and each firm shares the same technology as its rival at home and abroad. While relaxing this assumption of symmetry

---

[11] While our explanation of the influence of exchange rate uncertainty is unique in its demonstration of multinational production among symmetric firms, it can be viewed as being complementary to the traditional explanations of multinational production among asymmetric firms described above. It also establishes a direct linkage between anticipated real exchange rate volatility and the volume of direct foreign investment which does not depend, as do the explanations of this phenomenon advanced by Shapiro (1987), Hodder and Jucker (1985), and others, on implicit assumptions about capital market imperfections which must be invoked to justify risk-averse corporate behavior.

[12] Selection of linear demand and constant marginal costs is made strictly for expositional convenience. While it is straightforward but mathematically tedious to prove propositions analogous to those appearing in the text in a more general context of cost and demand, assuming only continuous differentiability and compactness where required, no new insights are obtained by so doing and potential advantages of this generality for empirical implementation are, in our opinion, modest. The interested reader can refer to Nickerson and Sadanand (1989) for a discussion of these analogous propositions in a more general model.

does not alter the qualitative nature of the results, such symmetry makes our results more interesting because now firms may choose different production locations for ***purely strategic reasons.***

Due to the real rate of exchange e between foreign and domestic units of measurement, the marginal cost of foreign production is denoted by θ in domestic units and the exchange rate is defined by $e = \theta/C$. Since C is deterministic and is common knowledge between the firms, θ is regarded by the firms as stochastic and the magnitude of the difference between marginal costs of production at a domestic plant and at a foreign plant, measured in domestic units, is the unique common source of uncertainty faced by each firm. θ could, if desired, be measured as inclusive of constant and deterministic unit transportation costs or tariffs, incurred in shipping the commodity to the domestic market.

Domestic costs and demand are common knowledge, and the firms are also assumed to have identical beliefs about the distribution of θ. Again, while differences in initial beliefs about the distribution of θ do not change the nature of the results, our results are made more striking by the assumption that the firms have identical beliefs about exchange rate uncertainty. Firm are also assumed to behave as if they were risk- neutral and, consequently, do not engage in direct foreign investment or production for the purposes of hedging real exchange rate risk.

The strategy of each firm i consists, in period 1, of a probability, denoted by ν_i, that firm i will incur the fixed cost G of foreign plant activation in that period, and the corresponding quantity, denoted by x_{i1}, that firm i will announce in period 1 that it has credibly precommited to produce abroad in period 2, conditional on its expenditure of G. If firm i wishes to remain flexible and defer, with probability one, its decision on a production location until exchange rate uncertainty is resolved, ν_i and x_{i1} will each be zero, and, in this case, x_{i2}^r will denote the production volume of firm i in period 2, where $r = d$ corresponds to production at the domestic plant and $r = f$ corresponds to production at a foreign plant. Φ denotes the expectation operator over the distribution of θ and G denotes the fixed cost to each firm of activating a foreign plant to produce for the domestic market. Market equilibria are derived using the concept of sequential equilibrium. [13]

III. Equilibria in an Asymmetric Duopoly

As a useful benchmark against which to compare our later equilibrium among symmetric firms, we will first illustrate an obvious but important point: if strategic interaction in the domestic product market is *not* allowed to affect the choice of production location by firms, then the location selected by each firm has no strategic value and depends solely on the realized value of the exchange rate e and the fixed cost G of activating the foreign plant. We can obtain coexistence of foreign and domestic production in this artificial case only by a specification of the sales game in the domestic product market in which differential production locations are driven by the exogenous presence of some ad hoc form of asymmetry between firms. We will then show, in Section IV below, that in our general game, different production locations emerge endogenously as a result of the interaction between the timing of the choice of production location by each firm and its strategic behavior in the domestic product market, even though our firms are strategically and informationally symmetric.

Suppose first that firms are exogenously specified to play a Cournot game in outputs. Output and production timing decisions are made separately. Since the firms have no strategic advantage to precommitment in period 1, it is a dominant strategy for both firms to defer production decision until period 2. Since the firms are symmetric, in the symmetric Cournot equi-

[13] See Kreps and Wilson (1982) for the original discussion of this equilibrium concept for dynamic games.

librium their outputs will be identical. This implies that the decision to produce will also be identical. It is easy to see that if the firms choose foreign production, then each firm's output will be $(A - \theta)/3$, and if they produce domestically, each firm's output will be $(A - C)/3$. Production takes place abroad in period 2 whenever the profits from doing so are at least as large as the profits from domestic production. A sufficient condition for this to occur, taking into account the non-negativity of profits under either production location, is

$$2\theta\left(\frac{A-\theta}{3}\right) - 2C\left(\frac{A-C}{3}\right) > 2A\theta - 2AC + C^2 - \theta^2 + G.$$

Consequently, both firms will produce abroad whenever the realization of θ is less than the positive zero of the quadratic $\theta^2 - 4A\theta + (4AC - C^2 - 3G)$, and both firms will produce domestically otherwise. Regardless of the realization of θ, however, the symmetry between firms and the exogenously imposed separation of any strategic interaction between the timing of the choice of production location and firm behavior in the product market guarantee that precommitment to a foreign production location under exchange rate uncertainty has no value and that rival firms will not endogenously select different production locations. On the other hand, we can induce rival firms to select different production locations in equilibrium, but only if we introduce an ad hoc asymmetry between the rival firms, while keeping production volume and location timing decisions separate, by exogenously specifying a a Stackelberg game in the domestic product market. Allow one firm to produce abroad first with probability one and require the second firm to remain flexible and delay its choice of production location until period 2, when exchange rate uncertainty is resolved. It is clear that once θ is revealed, the firm that has delayed will decide whether or not to produce abroad by comparing the relative magnitudes of the fixed cost G and the relative change in marginal costs, $\theta - C$. This behavior will, in turn, affect the ex ante behavior of the first firm in period 1.

Optimal behavior for the follower firm in this case, which is similar to the Cournot behavior it exhibits in the equilibrium above, is described by the following proposition:

Proposition 1. *Given that one firm has decided to produce abroad in period 1, the decision rule for the follower firm is as follows: For sufficiently small G and for some $0 \leq \delta \leq C$ foreign production will occur if and only if $\theta < \delta$.*

Proof. Let x_1 denote, in this example, the output of the firm that has decided to produce abroad first, i.e., the exogenously specified Stackelberg leader. Then, if he were to produce abroad, the follower would choose an output

$$x_{22}^{f} = \frac{A - x_1 - \theta}{2}. \tag{1}$$

But if the follower firm were to produce domestically, then its reaction function is

$$x_{22}^{d} = \frac{A - x_1 - C}{2}. \tag{2}$$

The leader firm's output x_1 will depend upon whether the follower firm has reaction function (1) or reaction function (2). Let γ be the probability perceived by the leader that the follower produces abroad under this Stackelberg specification. [14] The leader's optimal behavior is described as the solution to:

$$\max_{x_1} \Phi\left\{\left((A - x_1 - \frac{A - x_1 - \theta}{2} - \theta)x_1 - G\right)\gamma + (1-\gamma)\left((A - x_1 - \frac{A - x_1 - C}{2} - \theta)x_1 - G\right)\right\}.$$

[14] Since these are subjective probabilities, and since the follower will never adopt a mixed strategy in this situation, we assume zero covariance between the leader's subjective forecast of γ and the random exchange rate e.

Consequently,

$$x_1 = \frac{\gamma \cdot \Phi(\theta) - \gamma \cdot C + C + A}{2} - \Phi(\theta) \tag{3}$$

Now, the follower's profit when it produces abroad is

$$\pi_f^f = \frac{(A - x_1 - \theta)^2}{4} - G \tag{4}$$

and its profit when it produces domestically is

$$\pi_f^d = \frac{(A - x_1 - C)^2}{4}, \tag{5}$$

so, the follower firm produces abroad whenever

$$\pi_f^f > \pi_f^d.$$

A sufficient condition for this inequality to hold is

$$2x_1\theta - 2x_1C > 2A \cdot \theta - 2A \cdot C + C^2 - \theta^2 + 4G. \tag{6}$$

Substituting for x_1 from (3) above, and since for values of θ which imply foreign production $\gamma = 1$, from condition (6) we see that all production takes place abroad if and only if θ is less than the positive zero of the quadratic $\theta^2 + \theta(A + \Phi(\theta)) - (3AC - C^2 - C\Phi(\theta) - 4G)$.

□

As long as the foreign marginal costs in domestic currency and the fixed cost of foreign plant activation are sufficiently low, the follower firm will produce abroad. Multinational production is cost driven, rather than being strategy driven, in this case, and the possibility of differential production locations arises here only as a result of the exogenous imposition of an asymmetric Stackelberg equilibrium in the domestic product market.

IV. Equilibrium in the Symmetric Duopoly

The endogenous emergence of multinational firms and foreign sourcing of production, as a direct response to the opportunity that exchange rate uncertainty creates for risk-neutral symmetric firms, will exist only when interaction between strategic behavior in the product market and the timing of each firm's production decisions is allowed to occur. Allowing this interaction to appear in an oligopolistic model of investment and production seems highly realistic, since most real business firms appear to be fully aware of their desired production and sales volumes prior to undertaking fixed investments, such as the creation or activation of a foreign plant.

We show below, as argued in Section II, that when symmetric, risk- neutral firms are allowed to make decisions concerning the volume and location of production *simultaneously*, and can choose to make these decisions either before or after the resolution of exchange rate uncertainty, a multinational firm will endogenously emerge and act as the Stackelberg leader in its industry. The strategy pursued by each firm i in the first period consists of announcing *both* ν_i and x_{i1}.

This is illustrated by an example of the extensive form of this game, as described in Section II, which appears in Figure 1. This example represents a case in which the support of the distributions of e and, consequently, θ, consist of two points. During the first stage of the game, which is illustrated in Figure 1, firms have the option, under uncertainty about the exchange rate, to either precommit (P) to foreign production, or remain flexible (F) to decide on a production location after the resolution of exchange rate uncertainty. Selection of the option to precommit in this first stage will also simultaneously involve a first-stage announcement of a volume of production to be undertaken in the second stage. Figure 1 depicts, for each firm, two such actions, each involving both a precommitment (P) to foreign production and an implicit quantity which will be produced in the second period. [15] Contingent on the first-stage choices described in Figure 1, second-stage Cournot or Stackelberg behavior by the firms in the domestic product market is then determined.

A unique symmetric sequential equilibrium in mixed strategies of the timing of the production decision, ν_i, and in pure strategies for the volume of production to be announced in the first period, x_{i1}, exists for this game. Firms in this symmetric equilibrium play a completely mixed strategy in production timing and pure strategies in output levels x_{i1}. Precommitment to foreign production occurs with a certain probability strictly between zero and one, while the volume of production, to which firms may precommit in the first period with this probability, is deterministic.

This symmetric sequential equilibrium in mixed strategies also exists under more general assumptions regarding the distributions of e and θ, as shown by the following proposition:

Proposition 2. *A unique symmetric sequential Nash equilibrium in mixed strategies, describing the timing of each firm's production decisions, will exist for the strategic model of production under exchange rate uncertainty for any distribution of the real exchange rate* e.

Proof. The method of proof involves derivation of the optimal volume of production to which a firm would optimally precommit under exchange rate uncertainty. If this volume of production is positive, substitution of this quantity into a condition expressing an equivalence between the expected value of becoming a Stackelberg leader in the product market, through precommitment to foreign production, and the expected value of remaining flexi-

[15] Since the volume of production is a continuous variable, there are implicitly a continuum of such branches in Figure 1.

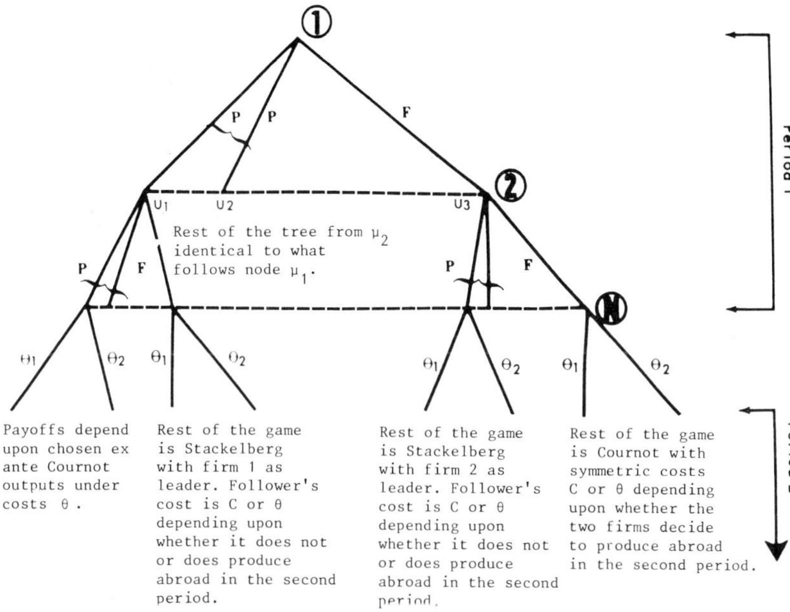

Notes:

1. This is a sample extensive form game with two realizations of the random exchange rate θ/C. Similar looking paths have not all been drawn. Dashed lines denote information sets.
2. "P" denotes "Precommit to foreign production" and "F" denotes "Remain flexible to decide production after resolution of uncertainty."
3. If a firm chooses to produce abroad then it has to choose its output level depicted by any one line under the heading "P". One line or branch will exist for each of the possible levels of production to which a firm could credibly precommit under exchange rate uncertainty, although we depict only two such lines for each firm.
4. The players are ①, ② and Ⓝ = nature.

FIGURE 1

ble and delaying decisions concerning production until period 2, generates the mixed strategy equilibrium. This equilibrium is expressed in terms of a value of ν_i for each firm i which lies in the strictly open unit interval.

In a symmetric sequential equilibrium, the optimal volume of production to which each firm i would optimally precommit in period 1, x_{i1}, solves the problem:

$$\max_{x_{i1}} \Phi\Big[\nu_j\Big\{(A - x_{i1} - x_{j1} - \theta)x_{i1} - G\Big\} + (1-\nu_j)\Big\{\epsilon\Big((A - x_{i1} - x^f_{j2} - \theta)x_{i1} - G\Big) + (1-\epsilon)\Big((A - x_{i1} - x^d_{j2} - \theta)x_{i1} - G\Big)\Big\}\Big] \tag{7}$$

where ν_j is the probability that the rival firm j will also precommit to foreign production in period 1 and where ϵ is the probability that the rival firm, should it remain flexible, decides, in period 2, to produce abroad. [16] Equation (7) is the ex ante expected profit of precommitted foreign production, conditional on the perceived belief by firm i that the rival firm j will simultaneously precommit to foreign production in period 1 with probability ν_j, while in period 2 the rival firm, should it not so precommit, may choose either domestic or foreign production after the revelation of the value of the exchange rate. Equation (7) exactly reflects the imperfect information embedded in the game and also makes the firms strategically and informationally symmetric.

If firms i and j are in fact identical, then the generalized mixed strategy symmetric equilibrium reflected in equation (7) must also satisfy the following symmetry conditions:

(a) $\nu_1 = \nu_2 = \nu$

[16] Note that this latter probability, ϵ, is, in general, different from the analogous probability γ appearing in equation (3) because the firms are in a different equilibrium.

(b) $x_{11} = x_{21} = x$

(c) $x^f_{12} = x^f_{22} = x^f_2$

(d) $x^d_{12} = x^d_{22} = x^d_2$

(e) The ex ante expected profit of precommiting to foreign production in period 1 is equal to the ex ante expected profit of remaining flexible and deferring the production location and volume decisions until period 2.

The above conditions imply that, in the symmetric mixed strategy equilibrium, the optimal volume of production under a precommitment to a foreign location for production in period 1 must satisfy:

$$\Phi\Big[\nu[(A - x - x - \theta)x - G] + (1-\nu)[\epsilon\big((A - x - x^f_2 - \theta)x - G\big) + (1-\epsilon)\big((A - x - x^d_2 - \theta)x - G\big)]\Big]$$
$$= \Phi\Big[\nu[\epsilon\big((A - x - x^f_2 - \theta)x^f_2 - G\big) + (1-\epsilon)\big((A - x - x^d_2 - C)x^d_2\big)] + (1-\nu)[\epsilon\big((A - x^f_2 - x^f_2 - \theta)x^f_2 - G\big) + (1-\epsilon)\big((A - x^d_2 - x^d_2 - C)x^d_2\big)]\Big] \quad (8)$$

Solving for the symmetric volume of production x under first period precommitment in the maximization problem (7), using conditions (a) and (b) above, we obtain:

$$x = \frac{(1-\epsilon)(1-\nu)(C - \Phi(\theta)) + (1+\nu)(A - \Phi(\theta))}{3(1+\nu)} \quad (9)$$

Substituting for x from equation (9) into condition (8) above we obtain a third degree polynomial in ν, the symmetric probability of first period precommitment to foreign production, with a constant term, which is a function of C, A, ϵ and $\Phi(\theta)$. The real–valued zero of this polynomial gives us a generalized mixed strategy symmetric equilibrium.

□

Proposition 2 demonstrates that multinational firms may arise because randomness in the exchange rate offers symmetric firms the strategic opportunity to emerge as industry leaders. Geographical dispersion in production is a mixed strategy symmetric equilibrium whenever the fixed costs of foreign production are sufficiently small and there is a potential leadership advantage to precommitted foreign production. Most importantly, this dispersion is, in our model, truly *endogenous*, with strategically symmetric firms facing identical costs and holding identical ex ante beliefs about the distribution of exchange rate fluctuations.

The intuition underlying the symmetric mixed strategy equilibrium described in Proposition 2 involves the timing of the production location decision undertaken by each firm, as well as the recognition that each firm rationally perceives that exchange rate uncertainty offers a unique but costly chance to credibly precommit to that volume of production which would enable it to emerge as a potentially profitable Stackelberg leader. First, note that the randomization in the strategy of each firm i is in the *timing* of the decisions concerning the location of its production and not in the volume x_{i1} of production itself. Decisions concerning the optimal volume of production reflect the outcome of accurately anticipated Cournot or Stackelberg equilibria in the domestic product market, resulting in the adoption by each firm of a pure strategy in the desired quantity of production. The probability ν_i adopted by each firm i as part of its mixed strategy in the timing of the production location decision, however, changes the expected gain of being a Stackelberg leader in the product market. Since firms make production location and volume decisions simultaneously, a symmetric mixed strategy equilibrium will ensue if each risk-neutral firm rationally perceives an equality to obtain between the expected value of precommitting to foreign production under exchange rate uncertainty and the value of retaining flexibility by delaying its location and volume decision until after the resolution of such uncertainty. This equality is expressed by equation (8).

Four specific implications for the relations between exchange rate volatility, the existence of multinational firms and the endogenous emergence of industry leadership through a strategic commitment to the foreign sourcing of production are immediate from equations (8) and (9). First, in the above polynomial, because of the constant term, $\nu = 0$ is not a solution, for sufficiently small G. [17] This means that a situation in which both firms choose to remain flexible and defer their production decisions until period 2, with probability one, cannot be an equilibrium. Consequently, even though there is a chance that the exchange rate may make foreign production unprofitable ex post, there is a positive probability that one firm may choose to become a multinational and invest in the activation of a foreign plant in period 1. This occurs, not because of an asymmetry between firms or because of some implicit imperfection in capital markets which drives risk-averse firms to hedge against real exchange risk through diversification of production locations, but precisely because there is a leadership advantage to precommitment, even if firms are entirely risk-neutral, and this advantage should clearly not be offset by G, the fixed cost of investing in a foreign plant. [18] Even approaching the limit, when θ is known almost surely to be equal to C, and when therefore ϵ will approach zero for any positive value of G, $\nu = 0$ cannot be a solution to the polynomial

[17] $G < \frac{(A^2-2AC-3C^2+8C\Phi(\theta)-4\Phi^2(\theta))}{4}$

[18] Although we concentrate our analysis solely on the *symmetric* equilibrium in mixed strategies, Nickerson and Sadanand (1989) show that, in a related model and under certain parametric assumptions on costs and the distribution of θ, an asymmetric market equilibrium may exist in pure strategies, with one of the duopolists committing with probability one to foreign production, and the rival firm acquieing to its status as a follower in the domestic market with probability one.

generated by equations (8) and (9). [19]

Second, as long as there is some uncertainty that foreign production, under the realized value of foreign marginal production cost θ, may not be profitable, $\nu = 1$ is not a zero of the polynomial. Consequently, both firms choosing foreign production in period 1 with probability one is also *not* an equilibrium. Precommited multinational production with probability one by both firms will result, as both firms rationally anticipate, in a Cournot equilibrium in the domestic product market. This, of course, cannot be a Nash equilibrium with timing as strategies, since given that one firm is producing a Cournot quantity in period 1 with probability one, the other firm knows that it is better off choosing Cournot outputs in the second period after the random value of the exchange rate e is revealed, as long as there is some chance that θ may not be profitable.

Third, the quantity of production in period 2 to which either firm would optimally precommit in period 1, x, may, from equation (9), be seen to be a linearly increasing function of the optimal expected quantity the firm would produce in a simple Cournot equilibrium, $(A - \Phi(\theta))/3$. The quantity x, which corresponds to the expected value of the quantity which would be produced by a Stackelberg leader in the domestic product market, may also be seen to be increasing in the known value of domestic marginal unit cost, C, decreasing in ν, the probability of the rival firm also precommitting to foreign production in period 1, and decreasing in $\Phi(\theta)$, the expected value of marginal unit production costs at a foreign plant. These results all accord well with our intuition of the firm's optimal strategy in the domestic market: having decided to precommit to foreign production, the firm wishes to produce more as the expected difference between foreign and domestic marginal costs increases and as the probability that the rival firm will also precommit in the first period decreases.

[19] In fact, under those circumstances, the outcome of a mixed strategy symmetric equilibrium will be a simple Stackelberg equilibrium.

Finally, the decision to engage in multinational production, even with risk-neutral firms, will in general depend, as illustrated by the dependence of the quantity x on the probability ν of precommitment in equation (9), on higher-order moments of the distribution of the exchange rate, as well as on its mean. Equations (8) and (9) imply, for example, that, in a symmetric equilibrium, both firms will randomize their production between domestic and foreign locations for finite values of the variance of the exchange rate, but that the probability of precommitment to multinational production can decline to zero for the limiting values, zero and infinity, of the variance of the exchange rate. [20] This implies that, for a sufficiently large variance in the exchange rate, the potential benefits of precommitment are dominated by the advantages of flexibility and both firms will choose domestic production. Alternatively, when exchange rate variance is zero, the value of precommitment disappears and both firms engage in a Cournot behavior under certainty, choosing to produce in the cheapest location.

V. Concluding Remarks

Conventional wisdom in both the academic literature and the business press explains corporate decisions to become multinational and to engage in foreign production sourcing for domestic sales as being motivated by one of two reasons. The first reason depends largely, if not entirely, on asymmetries which are assumed to exogenously distinguish firms. These asymmetries are especially assumed to exist in regard to intangible, firm-specific assets, such as management and marketing skills and the returns to previous expenditures on research and development, and also on such factors as expectations concerning firm-specific opportunities for lower foreign production costs, due to differential beliefs about the permanency of exchange rate movements or impend-

[20] Derivation of this relationship in (8) and (9) is straightforward but tedious, and is left for the interested reader.

ing changes in trade barriers, or access by some firms to foreign subsidies for investment abroad, or differential access by firms to domestic and foreign capital markets. The second reason rationalizes the diversification of production locations among nations as a means that risk-averse firms might use to hedge against real exchange rate risk. This explanation would be plausible if, for example, domestic equityholders cannot fully diversify their individual portfolios, so that corporations provide some intermediation services, international capital markets cannot be used to sufficiently hedge against exchange rate risk, and the return to hedging through foreign sourcing of production exceeds the potentially substantial fixed costs of investment in foreign plants.

This paper offers a new explanation of the endogenous emergence of multinational production, one that relies neither on assumptions about exogenous asymmetries between firms nor on assumptions about corporate risk aversion and imperfections in capital markets. The model of multinational production in this paper treats the decisions about *where* to produce and *how much* to produce as an inextricably linked equilibrium outcome of a purely strategic situation where *identical risk-neutral* firms evaluate the costs and benefits of the trade-off between precommitted foreign production under exchange rate uncertainty with market leadership on one hand, and the flexibility generated by temporarily deferring production decisions in order to obtain better information about the exchange rate and cost conditions relevant for current production, but possibly at the cost of being an industry follower, on the other.

The primary result of our paper is that multinational firms may arise for the purely strategic reasons of potentially profitable industry leadership which are created by random fluctuations in the exchange rate. Specifically, in a duopoly with identical firms and first-period uncertainty about the real exchange rate, there is a unique mixed strategy equilibrium which may result in a geographical dispersion of production. Under this equilibrium, foreign production may endogenously be undertaken by some firms and not others, solely due to the leadership advantages associated with precommitment to foreign production under exchange rate uncertainty. The nature of this equilibrium implies that the probability of precommitment to foreign production is strictly bounded between zero and one, for positive finite values of exchange rate variance, with the simultaneous selection of either domestic or foreign production by both firms being precluded as equilibrium outcomes. These results provide an explicit link between real exchange rate volatility, market structure and multinational production, and imply that, for purely strategic reasons, dominant or leading firms in an industry may be naturally multinational.

These results must, however, be interpreted in the context of our model, which was designed to exposit the intuition of strategic production opportunities under exchange rate uncertainty but is necessarily focused solely on the behavior of domestic duopolists. Desirable refinements to our model include the following extensions. First, in the current model, precommitment is tantamount to foreign production. We can relax this assumption by allowing firms to make simultaneously three decisions: quantity of output, timing of output and production location. Assuming both foreign and domestic plants require fixed investment expenditures in this case, this extension will not alter our results, since a mixed strategy equilibrium in the timing of production location decisions will still occur. It would, however, more fully depict the strategic options available to many domestic firms. Second, we have followed the traditional literature on multinational firms by implicitly assuming the presence of firm-specific, as well as plant-specific, fixed costs. These firm-specific costs can preclude foreign firms from simultaneoulsy entering the domestic market, as discussed in Nickerson and Sadanand (1989), as well as the possibility of domestic and foreign firms producing and selling in both domestic and foreign markets. The inclusion of these features would enhance the realism of our model, as well its complexity. Third, we can allow domestic firms to confront multiple sources of uncertainty, each of which would offer them a strategic opportunity for precommitment. Finally, we need not have a complete resolution of exchange rate uncertainty, but rather we can model periods of decreasing and increasing uncertainty in this rate.

The primary point we wish to emphasize in this paper is that exchange rate volatility offers a purely strategic explanation for the endogenous emergence of industry leadership and multinational production among initially symmetric risk-neutral firms. Our model provides an interesting and important example of this.

REFERENCES

Buckley, P. and M. Casson, "The Optimal Timing of Foreign Direct Investment," *Economic Journal*, 91 (1981), 75–82.

Butler, A., "A Generalized Approach to Product Cycle Models in International Trade," unpublished Ph.D. dissertation, Economics Department, University of Oregon (1989).

Calvet, A., "A Synthesis of Foreign Direct Investment Theories and Theories of the Multinational Firm," *Journal of International Business Studies*, 12 (1981), 43–59.

Caves, R., "International Corporations: The Industrial Economics of Foreign Investment," *Economica*, 38 (1971), 1–27.

Caves, R., *Multinational Enterprises and Economic Analysis*. Cambridge: Cambridge University Press, 1982.

Coughlin, C. and K. Koedijk, "What Do We Know About the Long-Run Real Exchange Rate?" *Federal Reserve Bank of St. Louis Review*, 72 (1990), 36–48.

Dixit, A., "The Role of Investment in Entry Deterrence," *Economic Journal*, 90 (1980), 95–106.

Dixit, A., "Hysteresis, Import Penetration and Exchange Rate Passthrough," Economics Department Working Paper, Princeton University (1988).

Dunning, J., "The Determinants of International Production," *Oxford Economic Papers*, 33 (1973), 289–336.

Dunning, J., "Trade, Location of Economic Activity and the MNE: A Search for an Eclectic Approach," in Ohlin, Hesselborn, and Wijkman (eds.), *The International Allocation of Economic Activity.* New York: Holmes and Meier Publishers, 1977.

Eaton, B. C. and R. Lipsey, "The Theory of Market Preemption: The Persistence of Excess Capacity and Monopoly in Growing Spatial Markets," *Economica*, 46 (1979), 149–158.

Eaton, B. C. and R. Lipsey, "The Durability of Capital as a Barrier to Entry," *Bell Journal of Economics*, 11 (1980), 721–729.

Gal-Or, E., "First Mover Disadvantages with Private Information," *Review of Economic Studies* 20 (1987), 279–292.

Green, E. and V. Sadanand, "Firm Scale and the Timing of Entry: A Choice between Commitment and Flexibility," Economics Department Working Paper, University of Pittsburgh (1987).

Grosse, R., "An Imperfect Competition Theory of the MNE," *Journal of International Business Studies*, 16 (1985), 57–80.

Grossman, G. and E. Helpman, "Product Development and International Trade," N.B.E.R. Working Paper 2540 (1988).

Helpman, E., "A Simple Theory of International Trade with Multinational Corporations," *Journal of Political Economy*, 92 (1984), 451–471.

Hodder, J. and J. Jucker, "International Plant Location under Price and Exchange Rate Uncertainty," *Engineering Costs and Production Economics*, 21 (1985), 39–46.

Horstmann, I. and J. Markusen, "Strategic Investments and the Development of Multinationals," *International Economic*

Review, 28 (1987), 109–121.

Hymer, S., *The International Operations of National Firms: A Study of Direct Foreign Investment*. Cambridge: M.I.T. Press, 1976.

Khoury, S., *Dynamics of International Banking*. New York: Praeger Publishers, 1980.

Khoury, S. and D. Nickerson, "Exchange Rates, Production and Prices in a Homogeneous Commodity Oligopoly," Faculty of Commerce Working Paper, University of British Columbia (1989).

Kogut, B. and N. Kulatilaka, "Foreign Direct Investment and Exchange Rate Volatility," Wharton School Working Paper, University of Pennsylvania (1989).

Kreps, D. and R. Wilson, "Sequential Equilibria," *Econometrica* 50 (1982), 863–894.

Markusen, J., "Multinationals, Multi-Plant Economies and the Gains from Trade," *Journal of International Economics*, 16 (1984), 205–226.

Meese, R. and K. Rogoff, "Was It Real? The Exchange Rate–Interest Rate Differential Relation over the Modern Floating–Rate Period," *Journal of Finance*, 43 (1988), 933–948.

Nickerson, D. and V. Sadanand, "Strategic Production under Exchange Rate Uncertainty," Faculty of Commerce Working Paper, University of British Columbia (1989).

Nickerson, D. and V. Sadanand, "Precommitment and Flexibility in Games of Endogenous Timing," Economics Department Working Paper, University of Guelph (1990).

Pindyck, R., "Irreversible Investment, Capacity Choice and the Value of the Firm," N.B.E.R. Working Paper 1980 (1987).

Robson, A., "Duopoly with Endogenous Strategic Timing: Stackelberg Regained," *International Economic Review*, 31 (1990), 263–274.

Rugman, A., "Internalization as a General Theory of Foreign Direct Investment: A Reappraisal of the Literature," *Weltwitschaftliches Archiv*, (1980), 365–379.

Rugman, A., *Inside the Multinationals: The Economics of Internal Markets*. London: Croon Helm, 1981.

Rugman, A., "New Theories of the Multinational Enterprise: An Assessment of Internalization Theory," *Bulletin of Economic Research*, 38 (1986), 101–118.

Shapiro, A., *Multinational Financial Management*. Boston: Allyn and Bacon, 1987.

Treece, J. and A. Borrus, "How Ford and Mazda Shared the Driver's Seat," *Business Week*, March 26 (1990), 94–95.

Recent Developments in International Banking
and Finance, S.J. Khoury (editor)

CHAPTER XV

Debt Over Hang and the Efficiency of International Rescheduling

Ronald M. Giammarino

Ed Nosal*

*The Faculty of Commerce, University of British Columbia and Department of Economics, University of Waterloo. Helpful comments were received from Arnoud Boot, Jonathan Eaton, and workshop participants at the Bank of Canada, UBC, Wilfrid Laurier University, the 1988 meetings of the Canadian Economic Association , the Western Finance Association, and the American Finance Association. The financial support of the Institute of International Relations and the Center of International Business Studies is gratefully acknowledged.

1 Introduction

The rash of countries that have experienced difficulties in meeting their scheduled payments to private lenders has fostered great interest in the issue of default on sovereign debt. Surprisingly, while it has been the large number of reschedulings that has precipitated this widespread interest, academic research has had little to say about rescheduling. Instead, the literature has largely focused on the repudiation decision of a sovereign borrower.[1] In particular, since bankruptcy law allows for the seizure of property in settlement of the debt claim, the absence of such laws raises the question of how debt markets could exist in the face of such strong incentives to repudiate debt.

Starting with Eaton and Gertsovitz (1981) many studies that address this question assume that a country borrows solely to smooth its intertemporal consumption in a way which maximizes expected utility. If a country fails to meet a scheduled payment for *whatever reason*, then it is considered to have repudiated its debt and is thereby excluded from participation in private capital markets forever. The repudiation decision therefore rests on a comparison of the benefit of continued access to capital markets with optimal future repudiation with the cost of making the scheduled payment (i.e.,

[1]See, for example, Eaton and Gertsovitz (1980,1981), Kletzer (1984), Grossman and Van Huyck (1985), Eaton, Gertsovitz and Stiglitz (1985) and Kulatilaka and Marcus (1986).

the cost of maintaining a reputation for repayment).[2]

The model adopted by Eaton and Gertsovitz is subject to the criticism that in practice there is no reason for the country and lenders not to renegotiate their debt after repudiation has occurred. However, Chowdhry (1987) employs a reputational argument to identify conditions under which a syndicate of lenders would not have the incentive to renegotiate following repudiation. In contrast to earlier work, in Chowdhry's model a country repudiates only when it is not able to meet required debt payments and, despite being aware of this, lenders refuse to ever lend again.

While outright repudiation is an interesting and important theoretical concept it is an empirically rare event,[3] and it is not clear that reputation for repayment can explain why it is not more commonly observed. For instance, Bulow and Rogoff (1988), argue that "... reputation for repayment in no way enhances a (country's) ability to borrow" and as an alternative suggest that "... loans to (countries) will not be made or repaid unless foreign creditors have legal or other direct sanctions they can exercise ...". Consistent with their conclusion is the fact that most countries which have defaulted on debt during the past decade have, in some periods subsequent to default,

[2]Other studies include Kletzer (1984) who characterizes the optimal contracts when lenders have varying information about the borrower, and Grossman and Van Huyck (1985) who characterize the debt arrangement as an implicit insurance scheme and use this framework to explain excusable default. Unfortunately, their model predicts that repudiation (i.e., a non-excusable default) is mostly likely to occur when the country's income is highest.

[3]The only country which has repudiated its debt in the recent past has been Iran in 1979.

made net payments on their debt obligations while in other periods they have received a net injection of funds. This 'business as usual' atmosphere supports the notion that, despite the absence of bankruptcy law, an enforcement mechanism exists which does not require expulsion of the delinquent debtor from capital markets.

The 'business as usual' behavior is even more interesting in light of the fact that the absence of bankruptcy law also means that debtors are unable to obtain a 'fresh start' by having unpaid obligations discharged by a court. As a result, new lending must take place in the presence of an existing contract. In particular, while the fresh start aspect of bankruptcy law has several implications, the one which we focus on is the fact that it clearly establishes property rights to investment opportunities that emerge; those that exist at the time of discharge are the property of the creditor, while those that emerge subsequent to bankruptcy are the property of the debtor. In both cases opportunities can be financed as new ventures which are not encumbered by previous obligations. In contrast, sovereign borrowing can only be discharged through repayment, repudiation, or forgiveness. In most cases, then, rescheduling debt involves the problem of financing projects to which both debtors and creditors have a claim.

The corporate finance literature starting with Myers (1977) has identified inefficiencies that can result when a firm with existing debt discovers a valuable investment option. The problem has only recently been recognized in the context of sovereign borrowing and has been labelled the 'debt over hang' problem. Our purpose is to add to this emerging literature by examining a particular aspect of the problem. Specifically, in this paper we focus on rescheduling by assuming that that there exists a repayment mechanism which allows the lender to collect a certain amount in each period in which debtor is in default. We further assume that the amount collected is based on some observable measure of the country's output. The repayment mechanism might be based on the ability of the lender to seize assets in foreign countries or the lender's ability to interfere with the borrower's trade.

The stylized situation we deal with is the following. In some previous period a country has borrowed to finance the development of a particular industry. Subsequent to the investment, the industry experiences a significant decline in value which essentially implies that the loan will not be repaid. Despite the 'economic insolvency' of the country, however, valuable investment opportunities emerge which require external financing.[4] An example is Mexico's development of the oil industry. Due to dramatic changes in the industry's outlook the country found that it could not (or would not) make currently scheduled debt payments and that meeting future scheduled payments was not feasible. Despite these severe economic set backs, how-

[4] Of course, it is usually the case that the ability to repay through taxation exists but would require, for instance, that severe hardships be imposed on the population at large. These hardships could generate political and macroeconomic problems which would then make future repayments even less likely. This would not be in either the borrower's *or lender's* best interest.

ever, the country continues to have valuable development opportunities in education, agriculture, construction, etc.. It seems reasonable to presume that lenders, especially those who are owed money, would have the incentive to cooperate in developing these opportunities.

Our goal is to characterize optimal rescheduling and examine its efficiency with respect to investment opportunities that emerge subsequent to a major default on existing debt. We assume that some of the rescheduling difficulties are eliminated by requiring that the current security holders (i.e., the original lenders) provide the resources for new developments. However, the rescheduling problem remains interesting due to the assumed existence of asymmetric information which results in adverse selection and moral hazard problems. The adverse selection relates to the value of the development opportunity which is better known to the country than to the lender. Moral hazard enters through the assumption that the actual investment behavior of the country is not observed so that it is possible for the country to consume the proceeds from any new loans. We are able to characterize the rescheduling process and identify conditions under which it will be inefficient in that mutually beneficial developments will not be undertaken.

In the following section we develop our model. This is followed by a presentation of the equilibria which exist. Concluding remarks are found in the final section of the paper.

2 The Model

We consider a situation where a country that has borrowed in the past currently finds that it has no resources with which to make a required debt payment of F. For simplicity we assume that the country will produce output only in the next period. We take as given a collection mechanism that allows lenders to collect the lesser of the amount specified in the debt contract or an alternative amount that is related to a commonly observable indicator of economic output, denoted Y. Specifically, the lender is assumed to be able to collect a particular fraction α of the country's net output, $Y - C^*$, where C^* represents a minimum level for domestic consumption. In this situation the payoff to the lender is equal to $max\{0, \alpha(Y - C^*)\}$. That is, because of the size of the existing debt contract, lenders effectively become equity claimants to the country.[5]

The principal economic problem that we focus on stems from the fact that, although the country has defaulted, valuable investment opportunities continue to arise which enhance economic activity. What makes this problem particularly interesting in an international context is the combination of the facts that

1. the borrower cannot achieve a 'fresh start' by having its debts dismissed by a court and

[5]In fact, recent reschedulings have explicitly recognized this by converting debt to equity.

2. the value of the outstanding debt is increased by the investment project.

These factors imply that the value of the outstanding debt and the exploitation of new investment opportunities are inseparable so that new investment becomes a part of the rescheduling process. Under symmetric information, the rescheduling process would, despite these factors, be efficient. The problem that we examine is complicated, however, by the fact that agents reschedule in the presence of asymmetric information.

Specifically, we assume that the country faces an investment opportunity which requires an outlay of m_t^*, where t represents the state of nature which is observable only to the country. For convenience we assume that there are only two possible states of nature, a 'strong' state s and a 'weak' state w. We will refer to the state of nature as the country's type and assume that the lender is only aware that a country is strong with probability P_s and weak with probability P_w.

The investment project affects the country's output according to $\text{Prob}(Y_t \leq y|m < m_t^*) > \text{Prob}(Y_t \leq y|m = m_t^*) = \text{Prob}(Y_t \leq y|m > m_t^*))$, where m represent the actual amount of resources invested. That is, the distribution of output with investment (first order) stochastically dominates the distribution generated without investment. Given the assumed collection mechanism, this implies that the value of the existing debt to the lender is enhanced if the country exploits the development opportunity.

The rescheduling proceeds as follows. We assume that the debt contract specifies that the unpaid portion of the current loan plus interest, $F(1+\ell)$, is the amount due next period.[6] The focus of rescheduling is in facilitating the new investment given that the country has no resources available for this purpose. In the rescheduling game the country requests new resources of an amount m and the lender either accepts or rejects. Rejection implies that the investment project cannot be undertaken.

All agents are risk neutral and face a common discount rate of r. Denote the value to the lender of any particular reorganization by $L(t,m)$ which is a function of the country's type $t \in \{s,w\}$, as well as the amount invested m and let $\theta_t(Y_t|m)$ represent the *pdf* for future output of a type t country that has invested m. Then

$$L(t,m) = \frac{1}{(1+r)}(\int_{Y_t=C^*}^{F(1+l)} \alpha(Y_t - C^*)\theta_t(Y_t|m)dY_t) \quad (1)$$

For simplicity we will assume that $r = 0$.

Moral hazard is introduced with the assumption that $m_s^* > m_w^*$ and that the investment behaviour of the country cannot be monitored by the lender. As a result both the borrower and the lender recognize that a country may find it optimal to consume all or some of the proceeds of the loan with no increase in future economic activity and no increase in loan value.[7]

---

[6]In practice ℓ is a typically a floating rate that is linked to LIBOR.

[7]The assumption that the optimal investment level is known to the country but not the lender has been criticized as unrealistic since it is typically the case that the technical expertise of developing countries is insufficient to evaluate many investment opportunities. It is then argued that it is lenders from developed counties that have superior information. However, technical information is typically provided by a third party (for example the IMF) and is available to both borrower and lender. This implies that the lender does

The borrower wishes to maximize the value of the reorganized loan which is a function of the country's type $t \in \{s, w\}$ and the amount requested m. We denote this value by $V(t, m)$ and assume that:

$$V(t,m) = \begin{cases} V(t,0) + m & \text{if } 0 \leq m < m_t^* \\ V(t,m_t^*) > V(t,0) + m & \text{if } m = m_t^* \\ V(t,m_t^*) + (m - m_t^*) & \text{if } m > m_t^* \end{cases}$$

According to this valuation function, a country will invest the optimal amount m_t^* and consume the rest of the loan if the loan is sufficiently large. If the loan is insufficient, then the entire proceeds will be consumed.

Given the behavior of the borrower, the value to the bank of the loan to a country of type $t \in \{w, s\}$ is

$$L(t,m) = \begin{cases} L(t,0) & \text{if } 0 \leq m < m_t^* \\ L(t,m_t^*) > L(t,0) & \text{if } m \geq m_t^* \end{cases}$$

The problem is only economically interesting if

$$L(t, m_t^*) - L(t,0) > m_t^*,$$

and

$$L(w, m_s^*) - L(w,0) < m_s^*.$$

The first expression states that, if the bank was aware of the country's type, it would grant a request for m_t^*. The second expression ensures that it is costly for the bank to grant a request for m_t^* when it believes that the country is type $t' \neq t$, $t, t' \in \{w, s\}$.

not have any obvious informational advantage over the borrower. But the borrower is better informed of the many other complex political, social, and economic factors that will determine the ultimate total impact of the development.

We take the values of P_s, m_t^*, and C^* as being exogenously specified and examine the interaction of the lender and the country within the context of a game of incomplete information. Our task is to identify strategies and beliefs for this game that form sequential equilibria and satisfy some restrictions, to be discussed below, for off-equilibrium-path beliefs, and to examine the implications of these strategies. The formal requirements of a sequential equilibrium are discussed in Kreps and Wilson (1982). Basically, a sequential equilibrium requires that all players select strategies that specify decision rules such that at each point at which an action must be taken, where the specified strategies maximize the player's expected utility for the remainder of the game. Since the game is one of incomplete information, it is clear that the selection of strategies depends upon beliefs held by the lender about the type of country involved. We require that beliefs at every information set be chosen in a consistent manner. If the player is called upon to make a move at an information set that has a positive probability of being reached in equilibrium, then the player, knowing the equilibrium strategies for all other players, can use Bayes' rule to update beliefs. However, if the player is called upon to make a move at an information set that has zero probability of being reached in equilibrium, he must then (re)construct a possible sequence of strategies that got him there and, given this set of strategies, use Bayes' rule to update his beliefs. We refine the set of equilibria further by requiring that off-equilibrium-path beliefs satisfy the requirements of a Perfect Sequential

Equilibrium (PSE) due to Grossman and Perry (1986). Unless otherwise specified, when we refer to an 'equilibrium' we mean a PSE.

Therefore, an equilibrium for the game is a specification of: (i) the set of strategies for all players at each information set of the game; and (ii) the set of beliefs for all players at each information set (including those reached with zero probability in equilibrium).

The structure of the game is as follows. A type t country selects an $m \in \mathcal{M}$ where $\mathcal{M}$ is the set of feasible offers. The probability that a type t country selects m is denoted by $\sigma(m|t)$. The lender must either agree to the new contract or reject it, in which case the amount lent is zero and the value of the rescheduling is $L(s,0)$ or $L(w,0)$. The probability with which offer m is accepted is denoted $\pi(m)$. We will let $\beta(s|m)$ denote the probability that the lender attaches to the possibility that the country is strong given that an offer of m has been presented, while $\beta(w|m)$ has a similar interpretation for the weak country.

An equilibrium for our model requires that we find three strategy sets – $\pi(m)$, $\sigma(m|s)$ and $\sigma(m|w)$ – and a set of consistent beliefs which satisfy the condition that a player can not increase his expected payoff by (unilaterally) defecting from the strategy being considered, given that all other players play and hold the prescribed strategies and beliefs, respectively.

The lender's expected payoff from offer m is given by

$$\pi(m)\Big(\beta(s|m)(L(s,m)-m)+\beta(w|m)(L(w,m)-m)\Big)+$$

$$(1-\pi(m))\Big(\beta(s|m)L(s,0)+\beta(w|m)L(w,0)\Big).$$

The borrower's expected payoff is given by

$$\sum_{m\in\mathcal{M}}\sigma(m|t)[\pi(m)V(t,m)+(1-\pi(m))V(t,0)]$$

where $\sum_{m\in\mathcal{M}}\sigma(m|t)=1$.

3 Characterization of Equilibria

We will examine three strategy configurations. A **separating strategy** is one in which each country type makes a distinct loan request. A separating strategy is fully revealing in that the borrower's type is known once an request is made. In a **pooling** strategy both country types make the identical request. The lender learns nothing about the borrower's type from the request and, therefore, treats the request as coming from the 'average' country type. Finally, a **semi-pooling** strategy is characterized by having one type of country make a particular request with probability one, which we refer to as the pooled request, and the other country type randomize over the pooled request and a separating request. In this case observing the separating request reveals the country's type whereas observing the pooled request provides a noisy signal of the country's type.

We will make the assumption that the country's loan request is selected from the discrete set $\mathcal{M}$ of values drawn from the interval $[m_w^*, m_{max}]$, where m_w^* represents the minimum level of funds required for any investment project and $m_{max}\geq m_s^*$ is the value of m which satisfies $L(s,m_{max})-$

$L(s,0) - m_{max} = 0$. m_{max} represents the maximum loan size that a bank could extend to a (strong) country without expecting to lose money. The intuition behind the assumption that $m \in \mathcal{M}$ is that the lender would not extend loans that are less than m_w^* since, given our assumption pertaining to the country's investment opportunities, both country types will consume the loan. On the other hand, the bank would not grant loans which exceed m_{max} because such loans, independent of country type, have a negative expected value to the bank.

3.1 Separating Strategies

Separating strategies are characterized by the fact that each country makes a distinct loan request which perfectly reveals the country's type to the bank. The following strategies capture this idea.

1. With probability one, the strong country requests a loan of m_s.
2. With probability one, the weak country requests a loan of $m_w \neq m_s$.
3. With probability one, the bank will grant a loan request for either m_w or m_s, and reject all other requests.

Proposition 1: *Separating strategies do not form an equilibrium.*[8]

To see this consider two values of m, $\{m_w, m_s\}$, such that $\pi(m) = 1$, i.e., those values of m where $L(t,m_t) - L(t,0) \geq m_t$. Suppose, contrary to

[8] In fact, separating strategies do not even form a Nash equilibrium so that our conclusion can be drawn independently of beliefs.

the proposition, that these loan requests represent a separating equilibrium. Then it must be the case that $\sigma(m_t|t) = 1$ for $t \in \{s, w\}$. However, the weak country would clearly defect from its strategy since it can demand $m_s > m_w$ and receive it with probability one (when the bank is playing its 'equilibrium' strategy). Therefore, the proposed equilibrium is destroyed.

A separating equilibrium does not exist because there is no cost incurred by the weak country in requesting loans in excess of m_w^*. Specifically, the country's future output, Y_w, will be the same for any (accepted) $m_w \in (m_w^*, m_{max})$ and it will pay the lender $\alpha(Y_w - C^*)$ regardless of the size of the loan. In addition, the benefit of obtaining a loan in excess of m_w^*, which is consuming the difference between the loan and m_w^* in the first period, is strictly positive. The fact that separating strategies do not form an equilibrium is an important result because it implies that the allocation of investment funds need not be optimal and that mutually beneficial developments may not be undertaken.

3.2 Pooling Strategies

Since in a pooling strategy both country types make the identical loan request, say m_p, the lender is unable to distinguish one country type from the other and treats all countries as if they were 'average'. If a pooling equilibrium exists and if a country requests the equilibrium pooled request m_p, it must be the case that $\beta(s|m_p) = P_s$ and $\beta(w|m_p) = P_w$. Therefore, a lender's expected profit, Π^p, from the equilibrium request m_p is

$$\Pi^p(m_p) = P_s(L(s,m_p) - L(s,0) - m_p) + P_w(L(w,m_p) - L(w,0) - m_p)$$

Intuitively, if a pooling equilibrium exists it must be the case for either one or both of the countries that the investment project has a 'large' effect on future output. Since (i) the lender will only extend a loan if the average expected payoff is non-negative and (ii) for any pooling loan at least one country type will always consume some portion of the loan, the expected return from one of the countries' loan must be sufficiently large to offset the 'loss' that occurs when the loan is granted to the other country. If a pooling equilibrium exists, then the set of possible equilibrium requests will be contained in

(a) interval $\mathbf{M_w} = (m_w^*, m_w^* + \delta_w)$ if $\Pi^p(m_w^*) > 0$, $\Pi^p(m_w^* + \delta_w) = 0$, where $\delta_w > 0$,

(b) interval $\mathbf{M_s} = (m_s^*, m_s^* + \delta_s)$ if $\Pi^p(m_s^*) > 0$, $\Pi^p(m_s^* + \delta_s) = 0$, where $\delta_s > 0$, or

(c) both intervals $\mathbf{M_w}$ and $\mathbf{M_s}$ if $\Pi^p(m_w^*) > 0$ and $\Pi^p(m_s^*) > 0$.

Note that $(\mathbf{M_w} \cup \mathbf{M_s}) \subset \mathcal{M}$ and that for $\mathbf{M_s}, \mathbf{M_w} \neq \emptyset$ $\partial \Pi^p(m_p)/\partial m_p < 0$ for $m_p \in \mathbf{M_w}, \mathbf{M_s}$. The set of pooling strategies and beliefs are given by

1. Both the strong and the weak country request a loan m_p;

2. The lender believes that any country that requests m_p is strong with probability P_s, i.e., $\beta(s|m_p) = P_s$ and $\beta(w|m_p) = P_w$;

3. The lender will grant a request for m_p with probability 1 and deny all other requests, and

4. The bank believes that any country that requests an amount $m \neq m_p$ is strong with probability P_s.

Proposition 2: *A unique pooling strategy equilibrium exists if and only if*

$$\frac{P_s}{P_w} \geq -\frac{L(w,m_p) - L(w,0) - m_p}{L(s,m_p) - L(s,0) - m_p}$$

This condition insures that $\mathbf{M_S} \cup \mathbf{M_W} \neq \emptyset$ and, therefore, there exists pooled loan requests such that $\Pi^p(m_p) \geq 0$. The lender will accept such a loan request with probability one.

The actual amount requested is unique and depends $\mathbf{M_W}$ and $\mathbf{M_S}$. The unique pooling equilibrium is sup $(\mathbf{M_W} \cup \mathbf{M_s})$, i.e., $m_p = m_w^* + \delta_w$ if $\mathbf{M_W} \neq \emptyset$ and $\mathbf{M_S} = \emptyset$ and $m_p = m_s^* + \delta_s$ if $M_s \neq \emptyset$. The bank will grant the loan with probability one since $\Pi^p(m_p) = 0$.

Given the assumed off equilibrium path beliefs, the country, independent of its type, will have no incentive to deviate from sup $(\mathbf{M_W} \cup \mathbf{M_S})$. To see this, consider the alternatives that are available to the country:

(a) If $m < m_p$, then regardless of whether or not the bank grants such a loan, both country types will be made worse off, relative to the equilibrium request m_p. A country, therefore, has no incentive to make a loan request of $m < m_p$.

(b) If $m > m_p$, the bank will not, with probability one, grant the loan request since $\Pi^p(m) < 0$. A country, therefore, does not have an incentive to request $m > m_p$ since such a request will be turned down with probability one, it will be worse off relative to the equilibrium loan request m_p.

The stated off-equilibrium-path beliefs, point 4. above, satisfy the requirements of a perfect sequential equilibrium. If $m > m_p$ and is granted with probability one, then both types will have an incentive to request m. Similarly, if $m < m_p$ and is granted with positive probability, then neither country type will have an incentive to request m. In both cases, then, off–equilibrium–path beliefs should reflect prior beliefs.

We now demonstrate that if the conditions in Proposition 2 hold, then the equilibrium is unique. Assume, for example, that $\mathbf{M_s} \neq \emptyset$ and that the proposed pooling equilibrium is m_p where $m_p < \sup \mathbf{M_s}$. If the country requests an (out-of-equilibrium) amount $m > m_p$ where $m \in \mathbf{M_s}$, since, given the lender's off-equilibrium-path beliefs, $\Pi^p(m) \geq 0$, the lender will grant a loan in the amount of m. Thus the proposed equilibrium is destroyed. In this case, given the stated behaviour of lenders, countries will always find it advantageous to defect from the proposed equilibrium, m_p, whenever $m_p < \sup \mathbf{M_s}$. Therefore, in general, if the proposed equilibrium is less than sup $(\mathbf{M_w} \cup \mathbf{M_s})$, given the behaviour of lenders, countries will defect from the proposed equilibrium and will request sup $(\mathbf{M_w} \cup \mathbf{M_s})$.

The economic implications of a pooling equilibrium are as follows. If $\mathbf{M_s} \neq \emptyset$, then all mutually beneficial projects will be undertaken. In this situation one might view the lender as taking a 'loss' in that a portion of each loan will be consumed and, therefore, will not generate any additional cash flow to the bank. However, while this involves a transference of wealth, it does not imply a social misallocation of funds. However, if $m_p =$ sup $\mathbf{M_w}$, i.e., $\mathbf{M_s} = \emptyset$, then some mutually beneficial projects may not be undertaken, i.e., there might be a social misallocation of funds. This will be the case if the loan is made to a strong country since it will consume the entire loan.

3.3 Semi-Pooling Equilibrium

We now consider the case where one country type requests a particular loan size with probability one – which will be referred to as the 'pooled request' – while the other type randomizes over the pooled request and another loan size – which will be referred to as the 'separating request'. When the lender receives a pooled request it is not certain which country type made the request whereas the separating request does perfectly reveal the country's type. It should be noted that the country that is randomizing must be indifferent between requesting the larger loan and the smaller loan.

There exist four possible semi-pooling strategy configurations; the pooled request can either be higher or lower than the separating request and either the strong country or the weak country can randomize. As it turns out, however, only one strategy configuration can form an equilibrium: Before we present and examine the sequential equilibrium we will first identify the three strategy sets that can not be equilibria and explain why this is so.

The strategy sets that have the separating request greater than the pooling request can not be equilibria (and this is independent of which country randomizes). Since the separating request is fully revealing the notion of subgame perfection requires that this request be either accepted or rejected with probability one,[9] i.e., the acceptance probability can not lie in the interval $(0, 1)$. If the separating request is accepted (rejected) with probability one, then the randomizing country would have no incentive to request the smaller (larger) loan, since the expected payoff associated with the smaller (larger) loan is less than that associated with the larger (smaller) loan, i.e., randomizing will not take place.

The two remaining candidates for a semi-pooling equilibrium are characterized by (i) the weak country randomizes and the separating request is less than the pooling request and (ii) the strong country randomizes and the separating request is less than the pooling request.

Consider the second case first and denote the separating request by m_l and the pooling request by m_h, $m_l < m_h$. Since the strong country random-

[9]This is in general due to the fact that the request represents either a positive or negative payoff to the bank. An exception occurs when the offer is one at which, with the type known, the amount requested has zero value to the bank so that acceptance, rejection, or a randomization are all possible.

izes and the separating loan request is less than the pooling request, both requests must exceed m_s^*. If, contrary to this, $m_l < m_s^*$, then a request for m_l would be rejected with probability one since $L(s, m_l) - L(s, 0) < m_l$. Thus, the separating and, therefore, the pooling requests must be greater than m_s^*. If there exists a semi-pooling equilibrium where the strong country randomizes, then the lower loan request, m_l, is accepted with probability one and m_h is accepted with probability $\pi(m_h) < 1$. Since the weak country requests m_h with probability one and the strong country randomizes, it must be the case that

1. $\pi(m_h)V(w, m_h) + (1 - \pi)V(w, 0) > V(w, m_l)$ and
2. $\pi(m_h)V(s, m_h) + (1 - \pi)V(s, 0) = V(s, m_l)$.

These strategies would form a sequential equilibrium as long as one specified that off equilibrium–path requests were, with sufficiently large probability, believed to be presented by the weak country. However, these strategies cannot form a PSE since a PSE would require that banks believe that off–equilibrium–path requests are made only by strong countries. To see this, consider an off–equilibrium–path request $m_l + \epsilon$ where ϵ is positive and 'small'. If this request is granted with probability one, then the strong country has an incentive to make such a request since $V(s, m_l + \epsilon) > V(s, m_l)$. However, for a small enough ϵ the weak country has no incentive to make such a request. This can easily been seen by noting that point 1. above implies that the weak country *strictly* prefers to request m_h when $\epsilon = 0$; therefore, by continuity of the country's value function around m_l, there exists an $\epsilon > 0$ such that the weak country still prefers to request m_h. Since the weak country is worse off relative to the equilibrium regardless of the response, and the strong country may be made better off, a PSE requires that off–equilibrium–path beliefs put a weight of one on the strong country. Hence, although the strategies form a sequential equilibrium, they do not form a PSE.

The only strategy configuration that can form an equilibrium is one where the weak country randomizes and the separating request is less than the pooled request. For this case the set of semi-pooling strategies and beliefs are given by:

1. The strong country requests m_h with probability one.

2. The weak country requests m_h with probability

$$\sigma(m_h|w) = -\frac{P_s(L(s,m_h) - L(s,0) - m_h)}{P_w(L(w,m_l) - L(w,0) - \hat{m}_h)},$$

   and requests $m_w^{**} < m_h$ with the complimentary probability, where m_w^{**} solves $L(w, m_w^{**}) - L(w,0) = m_w^{**}$.

3. The lender believes with probability one that m_w^{**} is requested by a weak country, and that the weak country requests m_h with probability

$$\frac{P_w\sigma(m_h|w)}{P_w\sigma(m_h|w) + P_s}$$

4. The lender grants m_l with probability one where $L(w,m_l) - L(w,0) \geq m_l$ and grants m_h with probability

$$\frac{V(w,m_l) - V(w,0)}{V(w,m_h) - V(w,0)}.$$

5. The lender holds the following off-equilibrium path beliefs. If an off equilibrium path offer m is presented, $m \neq \{m_w^{**}, m_h\}$, then if $V(s,m) < \pi(m_h)V(s,m_h)$, the lender believes that the request came from a weak country with probability one, i.e., $\beta(w|m) = 1$; otherwise the lender believes that the request came from a strong country with probability P_s.

Proposition 3: *Semi-pooling strategies with form an equilibrium if and only if*

$$(i) \quad \frac{V(w,m_w^{**}) - V(w,0)}{V(w,m_h) - V(w,0)} > \frac{V(s,m_w^{**}) - V(s,0)}{V(s,m_h) - V(s,0)},$$

$$(ii) \quad 0 < -\frac{P_s(L(s,m_h) - L(s,0) - m_h)}{P_w(L(w,m_h) - L(w,0) - m_h)} < 1,$$

and

$$(iii) \quad \frac{P_s}{P_w} < -\frac{L(w,\overline{m}) - L(w,0) - \overline{m}}{L(s,\overline{m}) - L(s,0) - \overline{m}}$$

where $\overline{m}$ solves $V(s,\overline{m}) = \pi(m_h)V(s,m_h)$ and $m_h > m_s^*$.

Condition (i) ensures that each country type will not wish to defect along the equilibrium path. In order for the weak country to randomize as indicated by the strategy, it must be the case that

$$\pi(m_h)(V(w,m_h) - V(w,0)) = (V(w,m_w^{**}) - V(w,0)). \tag{2}$$

The strong country requests m_h with probability one, i.e., $\sigma(m_h|s) = 1$, implying that

$$\pi(m_h)(V(s,m_h) - V(s,0)) > (V(s,m_w^{**}) - V(s,0)). \tag{3}$$

Thus, condition (i) ensures that equations (2) and (3) hold.

The lender grants loan requests in the amount of m_w^{**} with probability 1. Since the lender grants m_h with probability less than one, it must, therefore, be indifferent between granting the loan and not granting it, i.e.,

$$\frac{P_s}{P_s + \sigma(m_h|w)P_w}(L(s,m_h) - m_h)) + \frac{\sigma(m_h|w)P_w}{P_s + \sigma(m_h|w)P_w}(L(w,m_h) - m_h) =$$

$$\frac{P_s}{P_s + \sigma(m_h|w)P_w}L(s,0) + \frac{\sigma(m_h|w)P_w}{P_s + \sigma(m_h|w)P_w}L(w,0). \tag{4}$$

If equation (4) is rearranged to solve for $\sigma(m_h|w)$, we arrive at the ratio in condition (ii) which must be contained in the unit interval to have the interpretation of a strategy.

Condition (iii) relates to off-equilibrium-path beliefs and has the following interpretation. The strong country prefers to request the equilibrium amount compared to an amounts less than $\overline{m}$, even if these latter amounts are granted with probability one. Therefore, a PSE requires that off-equilibrium-path requests for less than $\overline{m}$ generate beliefs which place probability one on the weak country. On the other hand, both types have an incentive to request any amount at least equal to $\overline{m}$ if they expected these requests to be accepted. As a result any request for $m \geq \overline{m}$ will generate revised beliefs equal to prior beliefs. Condition 3 is required to ensure that, given these beliefs, off–equilibrium–path requests are denied.

We show in the appendix that the requirements of a PSE allow us to eliminate many sequential equilibria from consideration and leave us with the particular set of equilibria set out above. The implications of the equilibria that remain are as follows. Banks lend to some countries (weak ones) knowing that some of the proceeds of the loan will simply be consumed. They are willing to do so because the overall impact on the old and new loan does not make the bank worse off. In other cases, however, the weak country demands an even higher amount (i.e. m_h). The bank is not able to determine whether or not this demand is being made by the weak or strong country and, in equilibrium, will deny the request with positive probability. This is clearly inefficient in that both the strong and weak country are denied credit even though it is known that both types have valuable investment opportunities.

4 CONCLUSIONS

In this study we have analysed the rescheduling process under the assumption that a collection mechanism exists which renders outright repudiation by borrowers and permanent exclusion from capital markets by lenders sub-optimal. The problem which remains is that of exploiting valuable investment opportunities given that previously issued debt cannot be discharged through bankruptcy. The inability to have debt discharged implies that the rescheduling problem includes the financing of these opportunities. Because of the moral hazard problem that is assumed, we find that the process will be inefficient in that valuable investment opportunities may not be exploited.

There are two crucial aspects of our model which are somewhat controversial. The first is the assumption that a repayment mechanism exists which is not based on the reputation for repayment versus repudiation decision. Instead, we assume more of a business as usual approach, one which clearly requires a more rigorous foundation. The second important assumption is that investment opportunities arise that cannot be monitored by the lender. While this assumption may seem to be unreasonable at first glance, our feeling is that it captures an important element of lending to a sovereign nation. The value of a claim against the aggregate output of a country is influenced by investments in education, infrastructure and social programs. Hence, even if lending is for a specific project, to the extent that this affects the amount available for investment in social projects, it will affect the value of the existing loan.

5 REFERENCES

Bulow, Jeremy, and Kenneth Rogoff, "Sovereign Debt: Is to Forgive to Forget?" 1988, NBER working paper No.2623.

Cho, I. and D. M. Kreps,, "Signalling Games and Stable Equilibria," *Quarterly Journal of Economics*, 1987, 179–221.

Chowdhry, Bhagwan, "What is Different About International Lending", (1988), UCLA working paper.

Eaton, Jonathon, and Mark Gersovitz, "Poor Country Borrowing in Private Financial Markets and the Repudiation Issue", mimeo, Princeton University (1980).

———, "Debt With Potential Repudiation: Theoretical and Empirical Analysis," *Review of Economic Studies*, **48** (1981): 289–309.

———, and Joseph E. Stiglitz, "The Pure Theory of Country Risk", Woodrow Wilson School, Princeton University, Discussion Paper #124 (1985).

Grossman, Herschel and John B. VanHuyck, "Sovereign Debt as a Contingent Claim: Excusable Default, Repudiation, and Reputation", **NBER** Working Paper No.1673, July 1985.

Grossman, Sanford J. and Motty Perry, "Perfect Sequential Equilibria", it Journal of Economic Theory **39** (1986), 97–119

Kreps, David M., "Signalling Games and Stable Equilibria", Unpublished Paper, Stanford University (1984).

———, and Robert Wilson. "Sequential Equilibria" *Econometrica* **50** (1982):

863–894.

Kletzer, Kenneth I., "Asymmetries of Information and LDC Borrowing with Sovereign Risk," *Economic Journal*, **94** (1984): 287–307.

Kulatilaka, Nalin, and Alan J. Marcus, "A Model of Strategic Default of Sovereign Debt" Working Paper, Boston University School of Management (1986).

McLennan, Andrew, "Justifiable Beliefs in Sequential Equilibrium", *Econometrica* **53** (1985): 889–904.

Pearce, David G., "Rationalizable Strategic Behavior and the Problem of Perfection", *Econometrica* **52** (1984): 1029–1050.

A Refinement of Semi–pooling Equilibria

In this appendix we provide a rationale for the restrictions imposed on the form of the semi–pooling equilibria in which the weak country randomizes while the strong country follows a pure strategy. In doing so we consider candidate strategies which involve a separating demand m_l and a pooling demand m_h where $m_l < m_h$

First note that a configuration where both m_h and m_l are greater than or equal to m_s^* can not be an equilibrium. The lender will reject this request with probability one since only the weak country requests m_l where $m_l \geq m_s^*$, implying that $L(w, m_l) - L(w, 0) < m_l$. A request configuration where both m_l and m_h are less than m_s^* also can not be an equilibrium. In this situation, consider the out-of-equilibrium request $m_l + \epsilon$. If this request is accepted with probability one, then, clearly, the weak has an incentive to make such a request for any $\epsilon > 0$. However, for a small enough ϵ the strong country would not have an incentive to make such a request. Therefore, the lender will accept $m_l + \epsilon$ and, hence, the equilibrium is broken. The only possible equilibrium configuration has $m_l \leq m_w^{**}$ and $m_h \geq m_s^*$.

Consider the situation where $m_l = m_w^{**}$ and $m_h > m_s^*$. We can define a particular offer $\hat{m}$ as the value of m which satisfies $V(s, \hat{m}) = \pi(m_h)V(s, m_h)$, i.e., $\hat{m}$ is the loan size for which the strong country is indifferent between playing the equilibrium strategy or receiving $\hat{m}$ for certain. If the lender receives an out-of-equilibrium loan request of m, where $m_w^{**} < m < \hat{m}$, the lender will reject it with probability one since only a weak country would have an incentive to make such a request and $L(w, \hat{m}) - L(w, 0) < \hat{m}$. If $m_s^* < \hat{m} < m < m_h$, then both country types would have an incentive to make such a request, if it is accepted with probability one. The lender believes that such a request comes from a strong country with probability P_s. Given these beliefs, and the implied acceptance probabilities, both country types will be made worse off, relative to the proposed equilibrium. Finally, if $\hat{m} < m < m_s^*$, then given the stated off-equilibrium- path beliefs, the lender will reject such requests with probability one.

We now demonstrate that m_l has a unique value and is equal to m_w^{**}. Consider the situation where the proposed lower loan request, m_l, is strictly less than m_w^{**} and $L(w, m_l) - m_l > 0$. Using the same reasoning as above, an out-of-equilibrium request of $m_l + \epsilon$ will be granted by the lender, thus breaking all the proposed equilibria where $m_l < m_w^{**}$. When $m_l = m_w^{**}$, it is still true that only a weak country would make a request of $m_w^{**} + \epsilon$ if it was accepted with probability one. However, $L(w, w_w^{**} + \epsilon) - w_w^{**} + \epsilon < 0$ and such a loan request would be rejected with probability one.